I0893076

The Pattern

The 33rd Regiment and the British Infantry Experience During the American Revolution, 1770–1783

Robbie MacNiven

Helion & Company

This book is dedicated to my dad, Don. Once a soldier, always a soldier. With all my love.

Helion & Company Limited
Unit 8 Amherst Business Centre
Budbrooke Road
Warwick
CV34 5WE
England
Tel. 01926 499619
Email: info@helion.co.uk
Website: www.helion.co.uk
Twitter: @helionbooks
Visit our blog at http://blog.helion.co.uk/

Published by Helion & Company 2023
Designed and typeset by Mach 3 Solutions Ltd (www.mach3solutions.co.uk)
Cover designed by Paul Hewitt, Battlefield Design (www.battlefield-design.co.uk)

Text © Robbie MacNiven 2023
Cover: Soldier of the 33rd Foot, by Alexandr Chernushkin © Helion and Company 2023. A sketch of the battle near Camden in South Carolina, 16 Augst. 1780. (Library of Congress)
Maps by George Anderson © Helion & Co. 2023

Every reasonable effort has been made to trace copyright holders and to obtain their permission for the use of copyright material. The author and publisher apologise for any errors or omissions in this work, and would be grateful if notified of any corrections that should be incorporated in future reprints or editions of this book.

ISBN 978-1- 804511-89-3

British Library Cataloguing-in-Publication Data.
A catalogue record for this book is available from the British Library.

All rights reserved. No part of this publication may be reproduced, stored in a retrieval system, or transmitted, in any form, or by any means, electronic, mechanical, photocopying, recording or otherwise, without the express written consent of Helion & Company Limited.

For details of other military history titles published by Helion & Company Limited, contact the above address, or visit our website: http://www.helion.co.uk

We always welcome receiving book proposals from prospective authors.

Contents

Acknowledgements

This book would not have been possible without the time, effort, patience and kindness shown by a great many people, many of them experts in their field.

My foremost thanks goes out to Don Hagist, a master of the subject, who provided assistance in all matters, hunting down everything from archival sources to typos. His generosity does him great credit, and without him this book quite simply could not have been written. Also of great assistance was Thomas Whitfield, another man of great expertise in the subject, who supplied all of the newspaper sources which appear in this work and also provided invaluable help applying his knowledge to early drafts.

My thanks also to the Duke of Wellington's Regiment Museum at Bankfield House in Halifax for providing digital copies of the letters of Captain William Dansey. David Harrap, Scott Flaving, Peter Cole and Richard Harvey all deserve great credit. Likewise do Jennifer Potts, Edward Richi and Leigh Rifenburg of the Delaware Historical Society, the current owners of the Dansey letters.

Mark Lodge, Deputy Regimental Secretary of the Yorkshire Regiment and retired colonel of the Duke of Wellington's Regiment, wrote a thesis that forms the basis for much of the first section of this book that deals with the regiment from 1770 to 1775, and his research as well as the encouragement he provided have greatly enhanced my own attempts to chart the 33rd's pre-war years. Hopefully the final product is worthy of the regiment as it still exists today.

I owe a debt of gratitude to Radford Polinski, who has long represented the 33rd in America with a smartness and attention to detail that would surely make Cornwallis proud. He provided not only encouragement, but also an expert eye when it came to the early drafts. Another talented US-based researcher of the regiment, Colton Falletti, likewise was of great assistance when it came to the 33rd's officer corps.

The members of the modern 'Pattern,' the re-enactment group who recreate, as faithfully as possible, the 33rd during the Revolutionary War in the UK, deserve special mention. They are a wonderful group of enthusiasts and experts, and I am privileged to be a member. In particular, Gary Ashby, James Graves, Keith Bartlett, Rikki Williams, James Baugh, Michael-Shorty-Williams and Tom Conyard were of great assistance, especially when braving a freezing and snowy December morning to take the photos that appear in this book. It is not often that a writer can call upon a whole re-enactment group for assistance, and I am eternally grateful to them. Speaking of photos, the images would not exist without the expert work of English Heritage photographer Henry Gage who, like those mentioned above, gave his time freely to help make this possible.

Thanks are due also to Mark Urban, whose book *Fusiliers* I consumed as a teenager. His history of the 23rd Regiment during the Revolution helped me realise that history was not dry and intangible, but alive and engrossing, and I am very proud that he has read this work and offered it his commendation.

Mention must of course be made of my editors at Helion, Andrew Bamford and Rob Griffith, who have had to patiently endure as I attempt to craft my first full-length work of historical non-fiction. Any faults contained herein are, of course, my own.

Lastly, but never least, I must thank my beloved parents, Donald and Jessica McNiven, whose love and support has been unwavering these past three decades, and without whom I would be neither a historian nor a writer. To them, I owe it all.

Introduction

On 16 June 1773 a London newspaper, the *Morning Chronicle*, printed an account of a British militia battalion's review from the week before;

> Wednesday last the First Battalion of our Militia were reviewed on Wooldridge, and went through their manual exercise and different evolutions in a manner that both pleased and astonished the spectators. They were formed on the plan of Lord Cornwallis' Corps, the pattern regiment of the army, and were allowed to approach very near their precedent in the smartness and steadiness of their Manoeuvres, the salutes, the ambuscade formed by the light infantry and grenadiers, the march of the battalion into the wood in Indian files, where they were attacked by the light troops, afforded great amusement to the numerous company assembled on the hill.[1]

A pattern is a model or design used as a guide, typically in the making of clothing and fabrics. In eighteenth-century parlance, to be described as a pattern was to be attributed as the ideal standard, the original from which other works were produced. The writer was therefore stating that the militia battalion being reviewed were closely modelled – in the best way possible – on what he called Lord Cornwallis' Corps. That corps in question was the 33rd Regiment of Foot, of which Lord Charles Cornwallis was the colonel. Under his leadership, the 33rd – an ostensibly standard line regiment – acquired a reputation in the years immediately preceding the American Revolution as the best infantry regiment in the British Army.

That reputation would be tested in what the officers and men called the 'American War.' The 33rd were deployed to North America in 1776, arriving just over a year after the outbreak of hostilities. For the next eight years the regiment was one of the most heavily engaged of any unit in the British Army, playing a role in the battles of Long Island, Brandywine and Germantown, Camden, Guildford Courthouse and Yorktown, and even having a company involved in the debacle at Saratoga. At its core, this book seeks to follow the regiment on its American Odyssey, giving as complete a picture as possible of the officers and enlisted men and their experiences. The initial chapters

1 *Morning Chronicle*, 16 June 1773, p.8.

deal with the pre-war period, looking at recruitment, training, equipment and organisation, as well as the service of the 33rd in Britain and Ireland, and addressing how they attained such a high peacetime reputation. Following that, each chapter will cover one year, from 1776 to 1783, seeking to document the trials and tribulations of the service. It hopes to act as a modern regimental history, comprehensive and analytic, and addressing more than just the battles and troop movements. Disease and diet, discipline and desertion, the role of women, the nature of camp life, the experiences of transatlantic voyages – all of these topics and more are covered.

It is worth briefly addressing the nomenclatures that will be used throughout the book. The name 'redcoat,' while not unknown at the time, had nowhere near the popular usage it enjoys today, and so use of it here is minimal – terms like regulars, British soldiers or king's soldiers are more period-correct. The book also follows the example of Matthew H. Spring in his seminal work *With Zeal and With Bayonets Only* insomuch as it does away with the tired phrase 'Patriot' as the term for those fighting for American independence. Like Spring's book, this work is written from the perspective of the British Army, and so the period term 'rebels' is often used – more formally, the pro-independence soldiery are called revolutionary forces, Congressional forces or, where relevant, the Continental Army. Not all 'Hessians' actually came from the states of Hesse-Kassel (indeed, a majority did not), therefore unless the units being described were specifically from Hesse-Kassel or Hesse-Hanau, 'Hessian' forces will be called Germans. Germany, of course, did not exist as a unified state until almost a century after the American Revolution, but the general concept of Germany and Germans was well enough understood during the period. Where possible, 'Crown forces' is a better collective name for those troops attempting to stymie American independence, giving that they included not only British soldiers but also the aforementioned Germans, Loyalist Americans and Native Americans, but I cannot claim to have been absolute in its application – 'British' is still sometimes used for the collective.

It should be noted that due to how heavily involved the 33rd were, this book covers almost all of the major theatres of operation during the war, but it is still intended as a history only of the regiment itself, and not of the Revolution as a whole. This applies even to the numerous battles, which are seen largely from the 33rd's perspective. Every engagement dealt with has numerous more general works that cover any given battle in its entirety – for example, Thomas J. McGuire's two books on the 1777 Philadelphia campaign are an excellent account of the battles of Brandywine and Germantown in their entirety. The same is true for the sprawling political, social and economic histories of the war. The bibliography should be consulted for this wider reading.

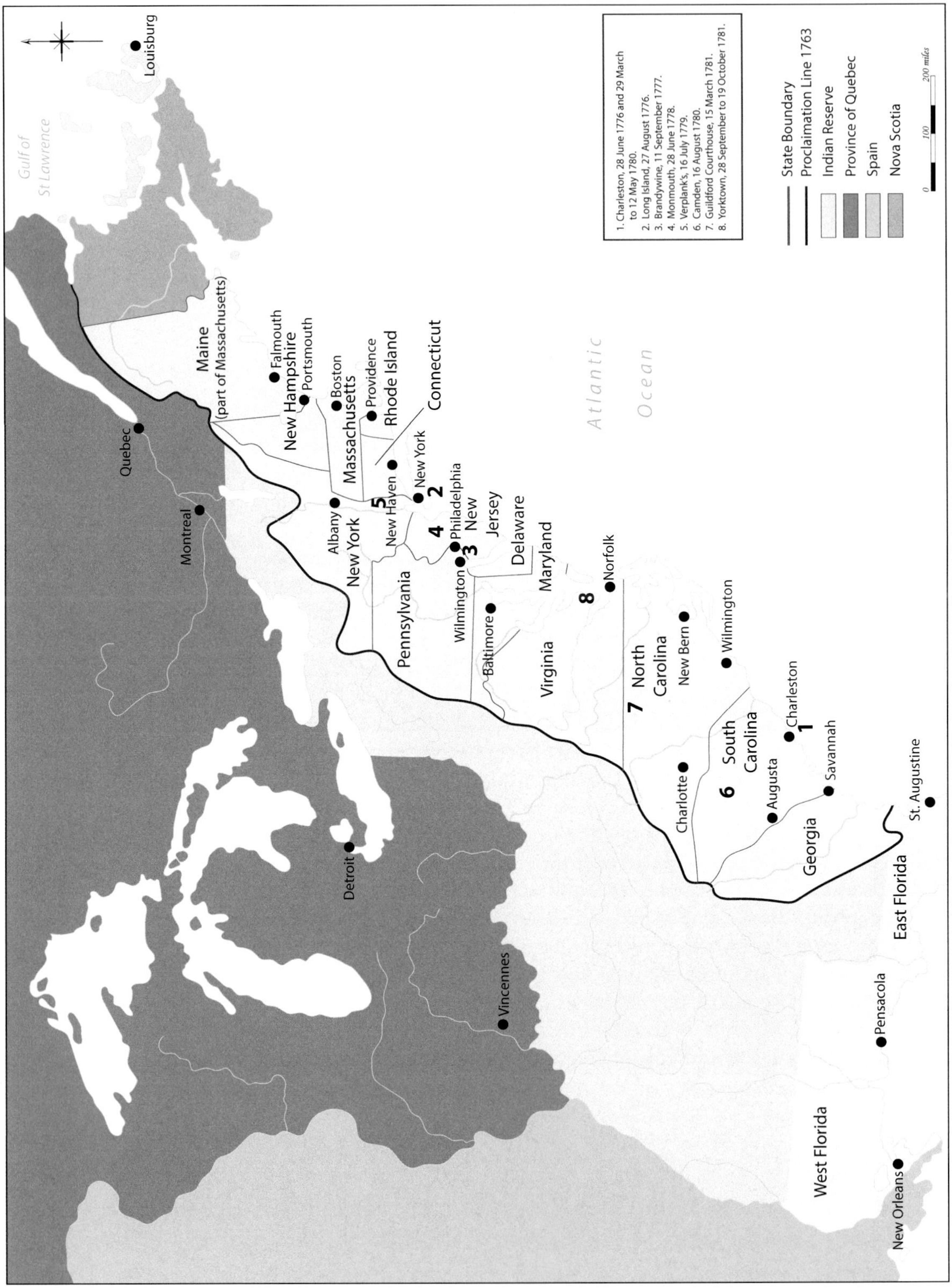

Major engagements involving the 33rd Regiment of Foot during the American Revolution, 1776–1781.

Chapter 1

The Place Where the Streets are Paved with Pancakes

Recruiting

John Robert Shaw was about to make a decision that would forever alter the course of his life. The 16-year-old was going to run away from home. He later attributed his choice to the ill treatment of his stepmother, though there was a more immediate spur – his father, a weaver by trade, had departed to the mill one Monday morning having told his son that, if he did not complete his previous week's work by the time he had returned, he would give him a beating. In response, after his father had left, Shaw put on his 'best apparel' and set out for Leeds.[1]

He did so with a measure of uncertainty. The Yorkshire lad's route took him through the town of Shipley and then, at a place called Windal, he paused to have his fortune told by a magician. Whatever the nature of the auguries, they do not appear to have wholly dissuaded him. He carried on to Coverly, where he paused upon the moor, vacillating. 'I seriously deliberated with myself what was best to be done,' he later wrote. 'At first I thought of returning home again; but the dread of paternal chastisement, and the ridicule of my acquaintances, to which I must be exposed… banished all thoughts of domestic concern.' Shaw's mind became fixed. He carried on to Leeds with one intention – 'enlisting as a king's soldier.'[2]

This was not, in fact, the first time Shaw had fled his native Baildon with such an intention. Two years earlier he had fallen into the company of some bad friends, including one Thomas Field, who convinced the naive young Shaw to borrow money from one of his father's acquaintances under the pretence that he was doing so in his father's name. The ruse was soon discovered and, as Shaw later put it, 'broke the way to my total overthrow.' More teenage misdemeanours followed, included breaking the sabbath, a

1 John Robert Shaw, *A Narrative of the Life & Travels of John Robert Shaw, the Well-Digger, Now Resident in Lexington, Kentucky* (Lexington: Daniel Bradford, 1807), p.7.

2 Shaw, *A Narrative*, pp.7–8.

grievous sin as far as his religiously attentive father was concerned. After one indiscretion too many, Shaw asked Tom and his other accomplices what might be done 'to avoid the effects of my father's displeasure.' Tom and another wayward friend, Jack, 'immediately proposed that we should all go and enlist for soldiers, get clear of work, and be gentlemen at once.' Consequently, Shaw embarked for Leeds, where he appears to have singularly failed to find a recruiting party, instead ending up living in the house of his uncle, John Hall. Missing the comforts of home, he meekly returned to his father, and there stayed until he 'grew weary of labour,' his stepmother and his chores.[3]

His second excursion met with better fortune than his first. He swiftly encountered a recruit of the 33rd Regiment of Foot who, after discovering Shaw's intention, inveigled him with the sort of fantastical verbosity that seems to have been common of the period;

> Come, my fine lad, the king wants soldiers: come on, my fine boy, I'll shew you the place where the streets are paved with pancakes; and where the hogs are going through the streets carrying knives and forks on their backs, and crying *who will come and eat*?[4]

The impressionable weaver's son was brought post-haste 'to the recruiting party's place of rendezvous, at the sign of the Leopard, behind the Shambles, in Bridge street,' where he was introduced to the recruiting sergeant, one James Shackleton, and his corporal, Samuel Coggill. Shackleton briefly interrogated him about his name and where he came from, and asked him whether he was willing to serve the king. On Shaw's affirmation, he stated 'well, here is a shilling to serve king George the III, in the honourable 33d regiment of foot, commanded by the honourable lord Cornwallis, knight and baronet of the star and garter.' Shackleton then promptly whisked Shaw away to his captain, a man named John Kerr (misremembered by Shaw as Carr) who, on discovering the boy was neither old enough nor tall enough, offered him a shilling and told him to 'go home and be a good boy, and go to school, and come to me two or three years hence, and I will enlist you.'[5]

Having already determined his course of action and been further lured on by the promises of the recruiting party, Shaw had little time for the captain's suggestion. He told him bluntly that if he would not take him on, he would go to the 59th Regiment, who were also recruiting in the area, and enlist with them as a drummer. Shaw's determination seemingly impressed Captain Kerr, for he agreed to take him on, initially to supplement the recruiting party as his waiter.[6]

By enlisting in the British Army, Shaw trod a path undertaken by tens of thousands in the 1770s and 1780s. In the centuries since these foot-soldiers of empire campaigned to stymie the American Revolution, popular histories have stereotyped them as the scum of the earth. One historian, in a book first

---

3 Shaw, *A Narrative*, pp.6–7.
4 Shaw, *A Narrative*, p.8.
5 Shaw, *A Narrative*, pp.8–9.
6 Shaw, *A Narrative*, p.9.

published in 1982 but rereleased in a new edition as recently as 2015, claimed that 'a soldier's existence was an alternative to filching in the streets, rotting in prison, or starving or freezing to death for want of food and clothing.' British soldiers in the eighteenth century were the dregs of society, while the military itself was 'a means of helping the British care for their poor population.' It was a quasi-slave institution where destitute peasantry and vagabonds languished under the lash of uncaring, elitist officers, locked into a draconian system of discipline designed as much to keep the rank-and-file from rebelling as it was to produce an effective fighting force. Ordinary British soldiers were, ultimately, 'cannon fodder' for Britain's imperial establishment.[7]

All of these views are false. At a basic level, barring short periods in 1778 and 1779, the army was a wholly voluntary organisation, and was not in the habit of enlisting the poorest elements of Britain's eighteenth-century society.[8] Far from it, officers charged with leading recruiting parties were instructed about the sort of men they should take on, and furnished with lists of undesirables to be avoided. One contemporary military manual by Captain Bennett Cuthbertson offered specific advice on who to avoid recruiting – convicts, sailors and colliers, those who were 'in-kneed, or splay-footed' or 'those with round shoulders, or past thirty years of age' or those with 'ruptures, seald heads, convulsion-fits, or other extraordinary complaints,' all of whom were to be kept from the service. He also stressed that during peacetime recruiters should be on the lookout for men who had already served in other regiments and to avoid taking such in case 'ill behaviour was the cause of his being discharged.' Were there any doubt about a man having previously served, a recruiting officer or sergeant was advised to inspect 'his naked back, on which may perhaps be found some certain marks, to make that matter very clear' – the tell-tale signs of a past flogging.[9]

Ideal recruits were 'young, active Men, from 17 to 25 years of age … nor should they be desired taller than six feet, nor lower than five feet, six inches and a half … Great attention must be paid to the faces, legs and shoulders of Recruits, and that the Lads under eighteen have stout, thick joints, and not too much the look of being set: fine hair is also particularly desired, it being so great an ornament and addition to the appearance of a soldier.'[10] An even more popular military author and officer, Thomas Simes, gave similar advice in his 1768 book, *The Military Medley*. Recruits were to be ideally between 17 and 25, to not include any man 'who has been whipped or drummed out of any regiment,' to not be under the size of five feet without shoes, and should

7 James Kirby Martin and Mark Edward Lender, *A Respectable Army: The Military Origins of the Republic, 1763–1789* (Chichester: John Wiley & Sons, 2015), pp.12–13.

8 The Recruiting Acts of 1778 and 1779 briefly allowed the impressment of certain petty criminals. The scope of the Acts was limited however, and the number of men taken was small. Those who did supplement the army were rarely deployed to active combat theatres.

9 Bennett Cuthbertson, *Cuthbertson's System for the Complete Interior Management and Œconomy of a Battalion of Infantry* (Bristol: Rouths and Nelson, 1776), pp.55–56.

10 Cuthbertson, *Cuthbertson's System*, pp.56–57.

possess 'straight limbs, broad shoulders, a good face, and is every way well made.'[11]

The sort of man who consequently filled the ranks was usually either born or had been living in a town or city, came from lower or middle-class background, and had a pre-existing professional skill.[12] He was physically capable, almost always recently in work or, occasionally, as in the case of Shaw, was too young to have had a serious past profession, but rarely, if ever, was he without a skill, trade or some other means of alternative employment. Such were the findings of Sylvia Frey's ground-breaking 1981 study *The British Soldier in America*. Frey sought to dispel the tired notion that ordinary eighteenth-century British soldiers were criminals and wastrels kept in line only by the threat of brutal punishment.[13] In this she succeeded, applying a statistical and analytic focus to the subject in order to establish that a range of factors, including population surplus, high levels of migration, static wages, the seasonal nature of many popular professions (especially in building and agriculture), and the first tremors of the industrial revolution, all helped contribute to ordinary, working men choosing to enlist in the king's service in the 1760s and 1770s.

The British Army only occasionally recorded the past professions of its enlistees, though its pension service, based at the Royal Hospital Chelsea in London, required old soldiers to list their former mode of employment as part of their application. From one such record roll come the listings of 67 men who served at various times in the regiment John Robert Shaw joined – the 33rd Foot – over the course of the American Revolution. All 67 give some form of past employment (albeit one illegibly written). There are 20 different trades listed, speaking to the breadth of society that the army drew from. Among the ranks of the 33rd were tailors, butchers, hatters and shoemakers, a chairmaker, a fuller, a chandler, a miner, a potter, a stonecutter and a linen printer.[14] The presence of artisans or craftsmen was not unusual – they likely represented a clear majority of regular enlisted men, with individual company records sometimes showing as many as 76 percent of recruits being listed as skilled craftsmen.[15]

The two most common occupations undertaken by the sample of the 33rd were those of labourer and weaver, with 21 listed among the former and 12 the latter.[16] This appears to be in line with the recruits furnishing regiments throughout the British Isles during the period. Of the many and varied trades that soldiers followed before their enlistment, it was the textile industry which saw some of the earliest industrialisation, as the use of machine yarns

11 Thomas Simes, *The Military Medley: Containing the Most Necessary Rules and Directions for Attaining a Competent Knowledge of the Art* (London: published by the author, 1768), p.34.

12 Sylvia R. Frey, *The British Soldier in America: A Social History of Military Life in the Revolutionary Period* (Austin: University of Texas Press, 1981), p.6.

13 Frey, *The British Soldier in America*, p.xi.

14 The National Archives (TNA): WO 116/4–8: Royal Hospital, Chelsea: Disability and Royal Artillery Out-Pensions, Admission Books.

15 Stephen Conway, *The British Army, 1714–1783: An Institutional History* (Croydon: Pen & Sword Military, 2021), p.49.

16 TNA: WO 116/4–8.

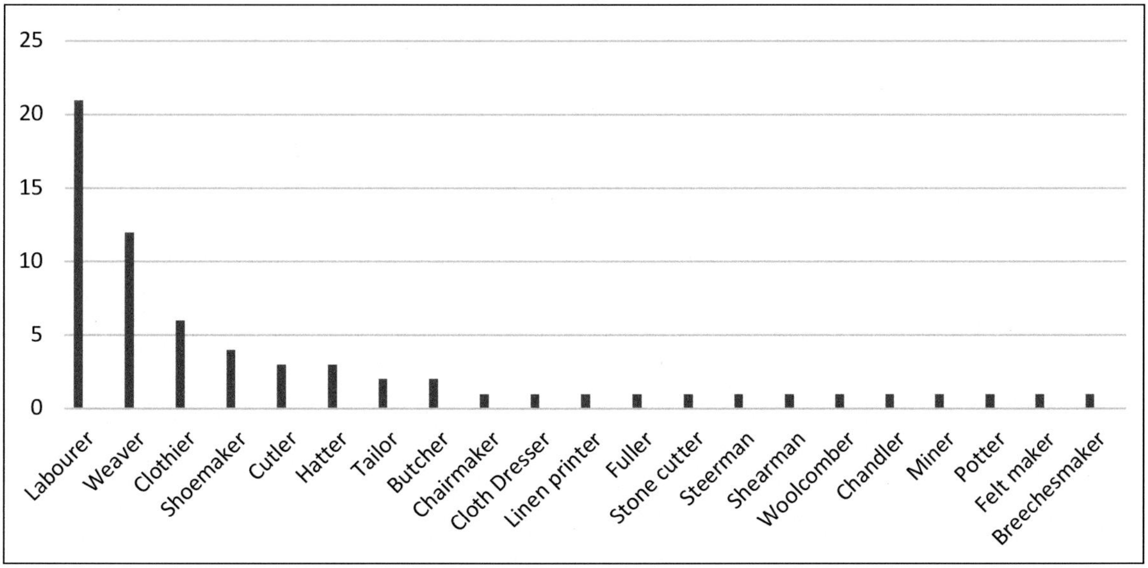

Previous occupation by soldiers of the 33rd from a sample of 66 men.

boosted production and created an excess of labour. The subsequent drop in wages played into the hands of military recruiters, with estimates putting 20 percent of the army's recruits as having worked previously in jobs relating to the textile industry.[17]

The other largest employer in the group, labourer, is more difficult to define. Typically, it has been taken to indicate those on the bottom rung of society who performed manual labour in exchange for basic wages.[18] In reality though, the listing of labourer can also simply be shorthand for someone who did not pursue a single, specified trade, and did not necessarily guarantee the kind of destitution which such a description sometimes seems to imply. The fact that the term can encompass a relatively broad socio-economic range also points to the limits of the other occupations listed. The hatters, shoemakers and tailors recorded as having joined the 33rd did not have their level of proficiency graded in the Chelsea records. Indeed, there were different degrees of skill and expertise within many eighteenth century trades, which in turn marked out different social and economic statuses.[19] A novice stonecutter would certainly have received different wages and, to a degree, have a different social standing to a master of the same trade, yet such nuance is not recognized in the Chelsea registers. The true depth of the past work undertaken by the army's recruits therefore remains hidden.

What is clear is that, despite the evidence of socio-economic pressures, the concept of British soldiers being men driven into the ranks by financial hardship is largely unfounded. Though surviving written accounts from

17 Frey, *The British Soldier in America*, p.12.
18 Frey, *The British Soldier in America*, p.14.
19 Frey, *The British Soldier in America*, p.11.

Reenactors portraying the 33rd Foot at the 'present arms' position, typically used as a form of salute. (Photo by Henry Gage)

regular soldiers are few, and the literacy of those authors may have pointed to them being more employable, no regular soldier who left behind a record of why he enlisted gave unemployment or destitution as the reason he became a soldier between the years 1765 and 1775.[20] This is a stark contrast to the picture often painted of regular soldiers as a collection of paupers and out-of-luck tradesmen, and speaks to the realities of attempting to define just why any one individual chose to join the army. It should not be imagined that there was a single aspect or even a set of circumstances that commonly led men and, in the case of Shaw, boys to join the military, and nor should we feel bound to seek one in an effort to satisfy a desire for retrospectively unambiguous and analytic reasoning.

Shaw himself gives three reasons for enlisting – being bored with his work, being disaffected towards his stepmother, and desirous to throw off the yolk of chores and punishment doled out by his father. A fourth reason can be inferred from the bad company of his erstwhile friends, who seem to have first put the idea of going for a soldier into his head. No single, hard factor can therefore be identified, and nor does Shaw try to.

The Chelsea rolls provide important data when it comes to the past occupations of recruits, but they also contain further information, namely the birthplaces of the applicants. The fact that it was a recruit of the 33rd Foot that Shaw happened upon when he eloped to Leeds was no coincidence. While the regiments of the British Army had yet to assume formal ties with specific parts of the country, some were associated with particular localities. By the 1770s the 33rd had developed links to West Riding, one of the three areas (along with East and North Ridings) that constituted the county of Yorkshire. This connection was spelled out by the 33rd's recruits. Of the 67 mentioned in the specific Chelsea roll, 61 gave identifiable birthplaces – 13 were from Ireland, one was from Hollywell in Wales and the remaining 47 were English. Of that latter portion, 32 hailed from Yorkshire, including locations such as Halifax, Hallam, Waddington, Bradford, and Leeds itself. The neighbouring county of Lancashire was also represented by four men.[21] The strength of the Yorkshire presence within the regiment is further corroborated by the returns of a number of prisoners subsequently captured during the fighting in America. Of the 69 English, 38 were from Yorkshire. The origins of the remaining 33 soldiers were divided between Ireland (26), Scotland (four) and abroad (two Americans and a Gibraltarian).[22] One newspaper reported in 1776 that the 33rd were 'chiefly composed of recruits from the above places [Wakefield and Leeds, in Yorkshire], and are usually called "The Have a Cake, Lads." The Serjeants who recruit in those places always carrying a large oat cake on the top of their halberds and frequently in

20 Don N. Hagist, *Noble Volunteers: The British Soldiers Who Fought the American Revolution* (Yardley: Westholme Publishing, 2020), p.14.

21 TNA: WO 116/4–8.

22 Don N. Hagist, *British Soldiers American War: Voices of the American Revolution* (Yardley: Westholme Publishing, 2012), p.290.

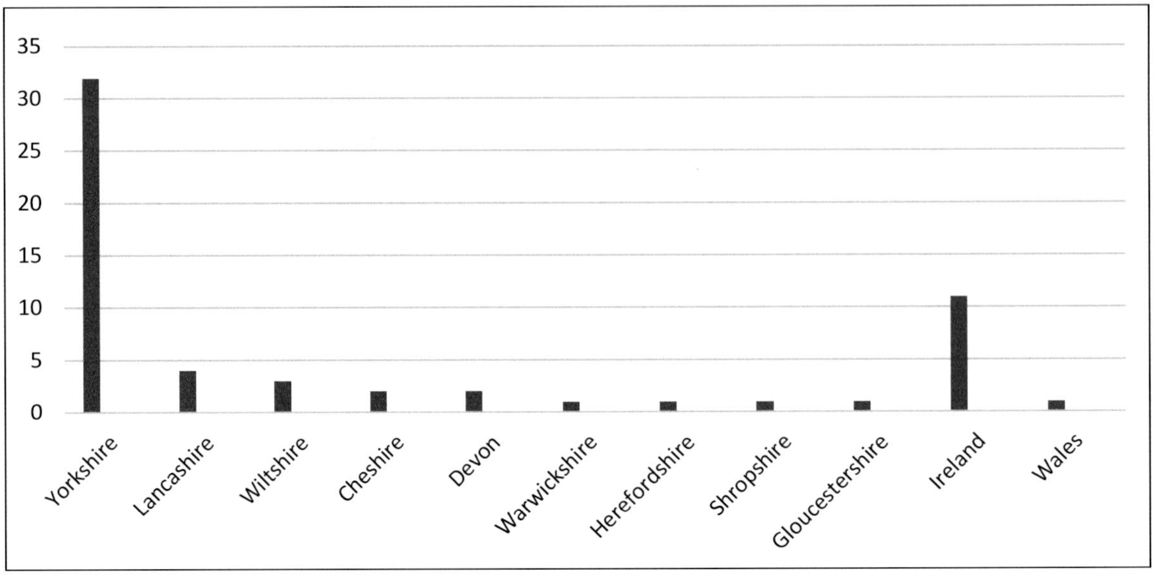

Place of birth for the soldiers of the 33rd from a sample of 61 men.

the course of their recruiting orations, address their auditory with the kind invitation "Have a Cake, Lads."'[23]

While the size of the Yorkshire contingent among the 33rd is significant, it is important to also note that a majority of soldiers still were not from that specific county. Among the ranks were men born in Cheshire, Warwickshire, Wiltshire and Devon. The Irish contingent was also diverse, with men hailing from the likes of Dublin, Enniskillen, County Londonderry and Killkenny.[24] Nor should it be assumed that a soldier's listed birthplace was necessarily where they had grown up and spent their life prior to enlisting. While these factors prove that the 33rd was not yet truly a county regiment in the 1770s, it was well on the way to becoming one, and would have been familiar to Shaw and many of his fellow recruits.

The teenage weaver's son seems to have enjoyed his first taste of military life. Now ensconced with the 33rd's recruiting party at the sign of the Leopard in Leeds, a crown bowl of punch was called for and used to toast the king. 'So we spent the night merrily,' he later recalled, 'and all retired to bed at 12 o'clock.'[25] When discussing army recruitment, much is often made of the role of alcohol, of tall tales, and of financial incentives, all combined to entice young men to take the king's shilling. While all of those elements regularly did play a role, their nature is often distorted by secondary narratives. Recruiting parties offered a bounty on enlistment, typically 21 shillings, though sometimes more.[26] Shaw reported that recruits received

23 *Gazetteer and New Daily Advertiser*, 26 October 1776, p.4.
24 TNA: WO 116/4–8.
25 Shaw, *A Narrative*, p.9.
26 Hagist, *Noble Volunteers*, pp.15–16.

seven guineas and a crown.[27] Part of this was immediately spent by the army to cover the cost of basic clothing, but this was no different from any other profession.[28] The bounty was therefore rarely seen as the devious form of entrapment it is sometimes described as today.

Recruits were also not routinely plied with drink and tricked into swearing on with the army. The concept, as well as the actual act, of taking a shilling was not what legally bound a man to the military. Rather, it was their attestation before a magistrate that they were enlisting voluntarily, an act typically performed within four days of agreeing to join, rather than immediately. This time interval was at least partly designed to give men the chance to reconsider.[29]

Even if a recruit did fully enlist, it was still possible to be 'bought off' out of the ranks following an attestation, essentially offering a sum of money that would see the recruit released from his service. This was the fate that almost befell Shaw. On discovering that his son had joined the 33rd, Shaw's father, accompanied by his uncle, tracked him down and attempted to negotiate with the recruiting party and, more saliently, with Shaw. 'He proposed to me to be bought off, and return home; but I obstinately refused it, and replied "if you buy me off to day, I will enlist to-morrow for a drummer" … My father finding me inflexibly determined to continue in the army, gave over all entreaties, and departed in tears.'[30]

Shaw's military education soon began. He was required to 'march round with the recruiting party; and exercise myself in running, jumping and learning to walk straight.'[31] These, along with other basic lessons, formed the basis of a new recruit's training, undertaken while he was still with the group that had enlisted him. Said recruit was learned matters like hygine standards and military deportment under the instruction of the recruiting officer while assisting him with his duties.[32] So it continued until the party in question joined their regiment to undertake the main body of their training or, after the outbreak of the Revolutionary War, the Additional Companies at the various training depots in Great Britain and Ireland.

Even as he learned his first lessons, the opportunities for Shaw to recant the military life did not end. After injuring himself attempting to jump a fence, he spent some time recuperating in Leeds, and was then given an eight-week furlough to return to Baildon and visit his father. While at home he weathered 'frequent visits from several of my relations and neighbours; all endeavouring to persuade me to be bought off, and abandon the army.'[33] Such entreaties were mixed with threats from his grandfather, 'who was in tolerable circumstances,' and who claimed that he would receive no future financial support from him if he followed through with his desire to remain

27 Shaw, *A Narrative*, p.12.
28 Hagist, *Noble Volunteers*, p.37.
29 Hagist, *Noble Volunteers*, p.22.
30 Shaw, *A Narrative*, pp.10–11.
31 Shaw, *A Narrative*, p.11.
32 Hagist, *British Soldiers American War*, pp.10–11.
33 Shaw, *A Narrative*, p.12.

in the army.[34] All of this Shaw withstood, seemingly to the surprise of the likes of Captain Kerr, Sergeant Shackleton and Corporal Coggill, for when he re-joined the recruiting party in Leeds after his furlough he 'was received with expression of great applause for my constancy.'[35]

The Officers

The officer who enlisted John Robert Shaw, John Kerr, was a Scotsman who had himself first joined the army at the age of 16, in 1760. He did so as an ensign, the most junior rank of commissioned officer. Raised to lieutenant in 1768, he then became captain of one of the 33rd's Additional Companies and led it between 1776 and 1778. These units were in excess to a battalion's 10 fighting companies, and were formed to act as a locus for new recruits prior to being shipped to join the regiment in whichever theatre it was operating.

Much as the regular soldiers of the Revolutionary-era British Army have been inaccurately stereotyped by later histories, so too have their officers. Enlisted men and commissioned officers were, according to one writer, 'from the least productive elements at the two ends of the social scale.'[36] For their own part, British officers of the period have been characterised as foppish dandies, dilettantes, martinets and oafish brutes – sometimes all at once. Again, such a view is inaccurate.

Becoming an officer required the purchase of a commission ratified by the king, usually bought for a set sum from an existing officer who was himself taking on promotion or leaving the service. The officer in question recouped this sum upon retirement, but stood to lose it if cashiered for poor service, and it thus served as a surety towards his good performance. Funds were also frequently provided not in full by the officer himself, but often by a wealthy patron. Subsequent ranks required greater payments. In 1766 prices were fixed for the line regiments at £400 for an ensigncy, £550 for a lieutenancy, £1,500 for a captaincy, £2,600 for a majority and £3,500 for a lieutenant colonelcy, though in reality these figures tended to fluctuate (usually upward) quite significantly.[37] This ensured that on the face of it, command of the British Army was based on wealth rather than merit, a system that followed in line with the practices of wider period society.[38] Eighteenth-century Britain was indeed hierarchical in nature, as was its army. Despite this, the characterisation of officers as 'inexperienced and often indifferent amateurs' is incorrect, as is the idea that the purchase system ensured the officer corps remained the preserve of only the wealthy.[39]

34 Shaw, *A Narrative*, p.9.

35 Shaw, *A Narrative*, p.12.

36 Walter Mills, *Arms and Men: A Study in American Military History* (New Brunswick: New Jersey, 1981), p.17.

37 Conway, *The British Army*, p.39.

38 Anthony Clayton, *The British Officer: Leading the Army from 1660 to the Present* (Oxford: Routledge, 2006), p.36.

39 J.A. Houlding, *Fit for Service: The Training of the British Army, 1715-1795* (Oxford: Clarendon Press, 1981), p.151.

A reenactor portraying Captain James Campbell, the regiment's most senior company-level officer during the Revolutionary War. (Photo by Henry Gage)

Deaths, especially during wartime, ensured that a third of vacancies were taken up without purchase.[40] It was not unusual for senior NCOs to receive ensigncies or lieutenancies – three NCOs in the 33rd, for example, received commissions in 1756.[41] Indeed the Secretary of War, Lord Barrington, commented after the heavy losses at the Battle of Bunker Hill in 1775 that the officers who had replaced those fallen were practically penniless.[42] It was also not impossible for enlisted men to be promoted up from the ranks for particularly long or meritorious service. While such instances were rare, neither could most officers be considered among the wealthy elite. The majority hailed from minor gentry or the emerging professional middle classes.[43]

If few of the army's officers could be considered notably wealthy, an even smaller number of them could be considered as such courtesy of their military employment. Standard army pay was often thought of as meagre.[44] They often had to rely on family funds, loans and the patronage of wealthy allies, and even then, progress in such a competitive system of preferment was not guaranteed. Most officers spent a considerable amount of time in junior roles. At the outbreak of the Revolution in 1775, 15 years after joining the army, John Kerr was still a lieutenant. It had taken him eight years to purchase his way from ensign to that next rung of promotion. That was longer than any of his 10 fellow-lieutenants parading with the 33rd in July 1775. The next nearest was Thomas Greening, who had served as an ensign for a little over five years, while the fastest climber was James Bailey, who spent just shy of one year and nine months as an ensign before he was able to purchase his lieutenancy.[45]

Bailey was not the most meteoric climber in the regiment. John Dyke Acland purchased his ensign's commission with the 33rd on 26 March 1774. The son of Sir Thomas Dyke Acland, 7th Baronet of Killerton, John Dyke Acland personified the privileged and influential stereotype of the British officer class, a stereotype that in reality was confined to only a lucky few. The eldest son of the Devonshire Aclands, in 1774 he was elected Member of Parliament for the rotten borough of Callington in Cornwell, a small town with only a few dozen eligible voters that never-the-less secured him a seat at Westminster. Acland was a committed Tory and a vehement opponent of American independence. He agitated to be given command of a new regiment, and only joined the 33rd as an ensign on the understanding that he would be able to purchase his way to the command of a company post-haste. When such rapid advancement, in the face of officers many years his senior, was not immediately forthcoming, he brought pressure to bear. His chain of influence reached all the way to the king, via the powerful Earl of Rochford. On 13 March 1775, a letter was written by Rochford to the Lord Lieutenant

40 Alan J. Guy, 'The Army of the Georges 1714–1783' in David Chandler and Ian Beckett (eds), *The Oxford History of the British Army* (Oxford: Oxford University Press, 1994), p.105.

41 Hagist, *Noble Volunteers*, p.11.

42 Conway, *The British Army*, p.48.

43 Conway, *The British Army*, p.48.

44 Clayton, *The British Officer*, p.x.

45 TNA: WO 12/4802/1: Muster books 33rd Foot.

of Ireland, in whose jurisdiction the 33rd were currently operating, directing him to 'transmit such a proposal [Acland's promotion] when it shall be offered' by the 33rd's colonel.[46] Twelve days later, Acland had his captain's commission, not even a full year after joining the regular army.

Nor did Acland's ambitions end there. In August 1775 the Earl of Rochford received a request from Acland to the king, asking that he be permitted to raise, at his own expense, his own infantry regiment, of which he would be appointed lieutenant colonel, with the power to choose his own officers.[47] The king was largely unimpressed by Acland's zeal, and cautioned that things would go better for him if he tried to follow a more regular military career.

Those with less substantial reserves of cash and influence – the vast majority – took a more ponderous route up the chain of command. William Collins Dansey, born in 1745 into the country gentry of Herefordshire, was commissioned as an ensign the same year as Kerr, 1760, reached the rank of lieutenant in 1763, but did not receive his captaincy until early 1774, aged 29. Most of Dansey's fellow-officers could tell similar stories – Captain James Campbell had, like Dansey, served 15 years by 1775, though he received his captaincy a little earlier, in 1772. Captain George Burnett had been in the service for 15 years and had been a captain for the past four. On average it took the 11 lieutenants of the regiment in mid-1775 a little over four years to rise to their rank from ensign, and six of the seven captains (removing the outlier that is Captain Acland) just over nine and a half years to take the next step up from lieutenant. It therefore took over a decade of soldiering for most officers in the 33rd to attain the command of one of the regiment's 10 combat companies.

Military service, especially given the difficulties inherent in acquiring the funding necessary to pursue it, was not an easy pathway to wealth or authority. Young gentlemen who chose to purchase commissions, therefore, rarely seem to have done so out of veniality. They were not idle dabblers, but were required to put in years, sometimes decades, of service in order to achieve notable station.

Military traditions within certain families also often played a role in encouraging men to join the army as officers. Dansey's father was a captain in the 33rd when he bought his son an ensign's commission in the same regiment. Lieutenant Hildebrand Oakes's father, also named Hildebrand Oakes, was the 33rd's lieutenant colonel when he bought his son his ensign's commission in 1767, when Hildebrand junior was just 13. Such literal familial bonds helped foster the more abstract concept of the British Army's officer corps as an extended family, one which was full of quirks, cliques and occasional squabbles but which, ultimately, took its duties seriously. The 33rd's cadre of officers in particular seem to have been quite closely bonded. All of the captains commanding companies between 1769 and 1774 'joined the regiment as Ensigns and served with each other for an average of 15 years,'

46 TNA: SP 63/445: ff.256, 257.

47 TNA: SP 63/448: ff.48, 49, 50.

An epaulette was worn on the right shoulder only by officers below the rank of major, except in the flank companies. The exact style varied from regiment to regiment. (Photo by Henry Gage)

with many having experience of campaigning during the Seven Years War.[48] Major General William Howe wrote of the 33rd that 'the officers have a Sutler, eat together and live in friendship.'[49] Turnover among the regiment's officers was low, possibly in part because of just how stable the officer cadre of the 33rd was.[50] For example, nine of the 13 ensigns who joined the 33rd between 1770 and 1774 would serve with the regiment for six years or more, a higher number than the army average.[51]

Most officers were professionals. Even among the higher echelons of regimental command, where wealth and social standing grew ever more apparent as the numbers of potential competitors were whittled away, the 33rd's major and lieutenant colonel in 1775 were experienced, long-standing members of the military. Major Henry Creed had been in the king's service longer than any other officer in the regiment, for 23 of his 40 years, while the 34-year-old Lieutenant Colonel James Webster had first become an ensign in 1758, 17 years before. For every John Dyke Acland there were many more officers like Webster and Creed, Dansey and Oakes, men who had spent the better part of their lives in their chosen profession. The officer corps was therefore considerably experienced, and comprised of men who treated the army as a profession and rose through it by constant and competent service – in a word, careerists.[52]

Around the time when Shaw was undertaking his first, botched attempt at joining the army with his friends Tom and Jack, and as William Dansey, Hildebrand Oakes and their fellow officers readied the 33rd for impending foreign service, an advertisement for the regiment appeared in the *Hereford Journal*. It sought out 'any able-bodied Young Man, between the age of 17 and 22, and not under five feet six inches high, straight and well made, who is fired with ambition, has a roving disposition, and whose spirit soars above the dull sameness of staying at home, having courage, inclination and freedom.' Such a likely lad was instructed to report either to 'Capt. William Dansey, of Brinsop near Hereford, or Capt. Thomas Gorges, of Eye near Leominster,' and would thereafter 'enter into present pay and good quarters, and also immediately receive new cloathing.' The advertisement noted furthermore

48 Mark Andrew Lodge, *To What Extent Can the 33rd Foot be Considered a Model of a Late Eighteenth-Century Infantry Regiment During the Period 1769–1781* (The University of Leeds, School of History, 2005), p.14.
49 TNA: WO 27/30–31: Inspection returns 1774, in Lodge, *To What Extent*, p.25.
50 Lodge, *To What Extent*, p.26.
51 Lodge, *To What Extent*, p.26.
52 Houlding, *Fit for Service*, p.151.

Along with the sash, epaulette, sword or spontoon the gorget was a symbol denoting an officer. Symbolic relics from the era of armoured soldiers, they were sometimes, though not always, discarded when on campaign. Their style varied from regiment to regiment. (Photo by Henry Gage)

that 'it is desired that none will apply who cannot have an honest character, as those men only will be taken who promise to be a credit to their officers, and an honor to their country.'[53]

This then was the sort of recruit hoped for by the 33rd Foot, and the wider army as a whole. It was reflected in Shaw's narrative where, despite the entreaties of his family and neighbours, he remained 'determined to be a *gentleman soldier*.'[54] Throughout the 1760s and 1770s men joined up for adventure, for stability, or simply because of an abstract desire to serve in the military.[55] Shaw's wish was set to come true. After spending 'considerable time in recruiting at the country villages, and with a great deal of success,' his party set out for London, and then Chatham Barracks.[56]

53 *British Chronicle or Pugh's Hereford Journal*, 31 August 1775.
54 Shaw, *A Narrative*, p.12.
55 Hagist, *Noble Volunteers*, p.31.
56 Shaw, *A Narrative*, p.12.

Chapter 2

The Most Disagreeable Days of a Soldier

Training, Organisation and Equipment

John Robert Shaw and the rest of the 'Have a Cake Lads' marched from Sheffield to Nottingham and Northampton, then on to London. On reaching the city they partook of what seems to have been a regimental tradition. Shaw related how 'there was a Yorkshire man in London, who made it a constant rule to treat all the Yorkshire recruits enlisted for the 33d regiment; having himself been an old soldier, and served the king in that regiment formerly in Flanders. So we all ate and drank heartily, and parted with our generous host in high spirits.' Shaw was particularly in awe of the Royal Hospital at Greenwich, built in the seventeenth century as a retirement home for select Royal Navy sailors. 'Upwards of 2000 old disabled seamen are maintained in this hospital,' he recalled. 'They are vulgarly called the *king's beef eaters*. The buildings are undoubtedly the finest in the world.'[1] Onwards the volunteers went, until they reached 'the finest garrison in old England' – Chatham barracks, in Kent.

Built in the 1750s, the army's barracks at Chatham – close to the naval dockyard – had the largest training facilities in the England by the 1780s.[2] While the exact numbers of those in residence fluctuated, during Shaw's stay it was home to 30 Additional Companies as well as a battalion of the 1st Foot, the Royal Scots. Here many of the army's recruits were put through their paces prior to being sent to join their parent regiments on active service.

At first glance a reader familiar with the training of modern armies might view the eighteenth-century British equivalent as incredibly decentralised and inefficient. There were no boot camps or universal training schedules, as well as very little in the way of formal manuals.[3] Despite this, the Army of the 1760s and 1770s went about training new recruits using tried and tested

1 Shaw, *A Narrative*, p.12.
2 Houlding, *Fit for Service*, p.40.
3 Hagist, *British Soldiers American War*, p.10.

Soldiers of the 33rd in the process of returning their rammers, one of the ostensibly large number of individual motions involved in the loading and firing of a musket. (Photo by Henry Gage)

methods based on roughly a century of experience. The army's preparation of its new soldiers was founded on knowledge gained through studying the large amount of literature available that covered everything from military theory to history, as well as common sense and the effectiveness of past practice.[4] What Don Hagist called 'corporate retention,'[5] and J.A. Houlding the 'fulsome expertise in the living, accumulated custom of the service,'[6] ensured that a great deal of knowledge was passed on via experienced officers and soldiers giving training and advice to new ones.[7] The reality was that the system in place, while imperfect, did succeed in producing an army that was fit for service, and continued to do so despite the pressures of the Revolutionary War.

In his manual, Cuthbertson stressed first of all that a recruit was to be taught soldierly bearing, 'to hold up his head; to stand quite straight and motionless; to cast his eyes to the right, without the least appearance of a formal stiffness.'[8] With this often done while they were still part of the roving recruiting party, on reaching a barracks or depot they were to be issued further items of clothing and were instructed 'to march in Ranks and Files; to be taught the different orders of March and Steps, and to be informed

4 Houlding, *Fit for Service*, p.166.
5 Hagist, *British Soldiers American War*, p.10.
6 Houlding, *Fit for Service*, p.165.
7 Hagist, *British Soldiers American War*, p.10.
8 Cuthbertson, *Cuthbertson's System*, p.161.

of all the proper differences of Ranks; when these matters are thoroughly grounded, they may then (and not before) be taught the Manual and Platoon Exercise.'[9]

The writings of Cuthbertson and other period authors such as George Hanger and Roger Lamb describe then learning the 'evolutions,' which provided a soldier with the ability to perform simple movements such as left or right turns and the opening and closing of ranks and files. After this *The Manual Exercise, As Ordered by his Majesty, in 1764* covered standard weapons handling. It formed a basis for drill, that was then expanded with the platoon exercise, which taught a soldier how to fire in volleys. Upon these building blocks were added the two final stages of training; the firings and the manoeuvres. The former covered firing, how it was given and controlled, with sections divided into fire-divisions and groups of fire-divisions.[10] The final section of the training, manoeuvres, taught recruits how to operate in concert together, at a company or battalion level.

One British officer who served in the Revolutionary War, George Hanger, described part of the general training process of 'a raw countryman, or a mechanic from Birmingham';

> He is first taught to walk, next to march, and hold himself tolerably erect; then a firelock is placed in his hands, which he handles at first as awkwardly as a bear would a plumb-cake. When he is taught the manual exercise, and fit to do regimental duty, they then take him to fire powder; whilst the drill sergeant is teaching him to fire either by files or by platoons, the sergeant says to him, laying his cane along the barrels of the firelocks, Lower the muzzles of your pieces, my lads, otherwise, when you come to action, you will fire over the enemy. After this, the recruit is taken to fire ball at a target; how is he taught? Thus he is spoken to: Take steady aim, my lad, at the bull's eye of the target; hold your piece fast to the shoulder, that it may not hurt you in the recoil; when you get your sight, pull smartly.[11]

Popular history holds that smoothbore flintlock muskets were hopelessly inaccurate and British regulars received no instruction in marksmanship. Smoothbores were indeed outclassed in accuracy by the rifles of the period, and Hangar's other much-repeated, pithy line about a man having as much hope of hitting the moon as hitting a man with one at two hundreds yards is not wholly without merit, but the reality was that many firefights during the Revolutionary War occurred at ranges beyond the supposed 'optimal' distance of 100 yards, and British soldiers were indeed trained to aim and did so with great effect.

The fact that during peacetime British troops were rarely issued with live ammunition for training purposes is sometimes used to demonstrate the

9 Cuthbertson, *Cuthbertson's System*, p.162.
10 Houlding, *Fit for Service*, p.160.
11 George Hanger, *Reflections on the Menaced Invasion and the Means of Protecting the Capital by Preventing the Enemy from Landing in any Part Contiguous to it* (London: John Stockdale, 1804), pp.152–153.

army's aversion to target practice. As war in the colonies loomed however, preparations were ramped up considerably, with troops practicing on a weekly basis. Lieutenant General Thomas Gage, in command of Crown forces in North America in 1775, stressed on several occasions the importance of careful aiming. A Scots-born Virginian doctor, Robert Honyman, visiting Boston that same year, recorded British soldiers firing at targets on two occasions. A British officer, Lieutenant Frederick Mackenzie, described setting up targets out in Boston harbour, using the motion of the waves to make the exercise more challenging, and stating that a number of men became effective marksmen due to the training and spurred on by financial bonuses for those who struck their marks consistently. Soldiers were even advised to chisel small channels in the bases of their musket barrels to better facilitate aiming with the forward sight.[12]

Cuthbertson's advice bears out the importance placed in loading and accuracy during the period of a soldier's training. He states that new recruits were to use live ammunition 'as soon as possible be done ... they are to be taught to load and fire singly, that each man may be distinctly instructed in the proper methods of using a Cartridge ... they should be taught to fire at marks, at different distances.'[13] Simes similarly stressed that 'great attention must be had in the instruction of recruits how to take aim,'[14] and that 'soldiers should be exhorted to take their aim well, to adjust their shot, and not fire too high.'[15] Lieutenant General George Townshend even believed that action with the enemy might be decided by a single well-placed bullet, writing that the men should be 'taught to fire at Marks ... Existence may depend upon a Single Shot's taking place.'[16] Certainly – and unsurprisingly for any professional army armed with missile weaponry – accuracy was not neglected either during training or in the field.

Shaw soon fell into the rhythm of military life at Chatham. He was placed in barrack quarters, '16 or 20 privates in a room, with a sergeant to keep good order, and purchase provisions, and see it divided, when cooked and prepared according to the place.'[17] Four pence a day for each private were 'laid out for provisions at market' which were purchased and collected by NCOs who were allowed to venture out of the barracks with a few select men.[18]

This was Shaw's first taste of how the army functioned at a basic level. Soldiers within each of the 10 companies that formed a battalion were subdivided into two types of smaller group, the mess and the squad of inspection. Both of these were for administrative rather than tactical,

---

12 Matthew H. Spring, *With Zeal and With Bayonets Only: The British Army on Campaign in North America, 1775–1783* (Norman: University of Oklahoma Press, 2008), pp.207–208.

13 Cuthbertson, *Cuthbertson's System*, pp.162–163.

14 Simes, *The Military Medley*, p.23.

15 Simes, *The Military Medley*, p.119.

16 George Townshend, 'Rules and Orders for the Discipline of the Light Infantry Companies in His Majesty's Army in Ireland' in Raymond Henry Raymond Smythies, *Historical Records of the 40th (2nd Somersetshire) Regiment* (Devonport: Swiss, 1894), p.551.

17 Shaw, *A Narrative*, p.14.

18 Shaw, *A Narrative*, p.14.

battlefield purposes. The mess generally consisted of five men who were responsible for procuring food, cooking and eating together. Unconnected to this grouping, the squad of inspection usually consisted of between seven and 12 private soldiers overseen by a sergeant or corporal. The NCO was responsible for 'the clothing, equipment, and behaviour' of their squad and that their clothing was clean and worn correctly, that all leathers and brass had been fully polished, that hair was clean, cut and combed, that weapons were in good working order, among other things.[19] Shaw recalled how 'a review of clothing was then and probably is yet in practice every Monday morning: each soldier marching on the parade, with his knap sack on his back, and his firelock and accoutrements in complete order: – drums beating and colour flying.'[20] Recruits also often slept naked, which Shaw related as 'common custom with soldiers in order to save their linens, as it is the policy of soldiers to preserve their clothing; for we had to appear three times a day dressed and powdered.'[21] A soldier of the 68th gives a similar account, with clothing not being worn when sleeping in quarters while on home service to avoid it being worn out by straw and to stop the men from catching what he described as distempers.[22]

While at Chatham the recruits 'were constantly exercising and learning the military evolutions under corporal Coggell [Coggill]; whose experience and skill in such matters were equalled by few in the army. There were nineteen in number of the 33d regiment, who after only six months practice, challenged the whole garrison to contend with them in military discipline.'[23] Shaw does indeed seem to have been fortunate to have Coggill as one of his overseers. Originally a labourer from Leeds, Samuel Coggill, described as five foot eight inches, with grey eyes and a fair complexion, enlisted in the 33rd at the age of 19, four years prior to Shaw. He went on to serve a total of 40 years in the regiment, not mustering out and receiving his pension until 1812.[24] The 33rd in particular was noted for its discipline and steadiness, elements that will be examined later. Upon men such as Coggill were the foundations of the regiment's reputation for excellence built.

Shaw spent a year at Chatham, learning how to soldier. This length of time was typical of the period, even under the pressure of war. Shaw's other experiences of army training match the accounts of other enlisted men. Roger Lamb of the 9th (and later the 23rd) Foot recalled how upon joining up he was placed into the

> … hands of a drill sergeant, and taught to walk and step out like a soldier. This at first glance was a disagreeable task to me. During twenty-one days I was thus drilled four hours each day. However, having at last rectified the most prominent appearance of my awkwardness, I received a set of accoutrements, a firelock, and

19 Hagist, *Noble Volunteers*, pp.40–41.
20 Shaw, *A Narrative*, pp.14–15.
21 Shaw, *A Narrative*, p.9.
22 Hagist, *British Soldiers American War*, p.291.
23 Shaw, *A Narrative*, p.14.
24 TNA: WO 116/19: Royal Hospital, Chelsea: Disability and Royal Artillery Out-Pensions, Admission Books.

Sergeants and corporals were the ones largely responsible for the training of new recruits. Even during wartime, the Army understood that these efforts could not be overly-rushed. Most recruits spent about a year learning military basics before joining their regiments in the field. (Photo by Henry Gage)

> was marched every morning from the barrack to the bowling green, near the water-side, to be instructed in the manual exercise.[25]

In Lamb's opinion, 'the most disagreeable days of a soldier, are these in which he begins to learn his exercise … I must own that some of the old drill-serjeants were unnecessarily, if not wantonly severe.'[26]

Officer Training

One group of new recruits less vulnerable to the drill sergeant's wrath (at least nominally), were the ensigns. Junior officers did not tend to experience the rigours of the training depots. An ensign's role was widely understood to be akin to what we might today think of as an internship. A new officer learned on the job, initially with relatively minimal responsibilities. They were, however, expected to be fully conversant in every aspect taught to the enlisted men, including dexterous handling of the firelock. One period text summed up an ensign's training and initial roles; 'When a young officer first joins his corps he is immediately to attend the drill, till he is perfect master of the exercise, both of the firelock and spontoon. He must remain at the headquarters of the regiment, and be present at all parades and courts-martial, until he is acquainted with every particular of his duty.'[27]

Most young officers took their position seriously, and there was a good deal of aid on hand to see them through the first few months of service. The works of Cuthbertson and Simes, and many others besides, marketed themselves as comprehensive guides for junior officers who were in the process of learning the military art, and were heavily subscribed to. Cuthberston, for example, had a listed readership of 939 officers in 1768, and Simes was even more popular.[28] The latter's treatises even included a helpful list of items a young officer should purchase, with objects ranging from the practical (two hats and two cockades, as well as one pair of leather gloves) to the borderline frivolous (six towels and six linen night-caps). Simes also opined that it was 'essential that he should have a Watch, that he may mark the Hour exactly when he sends any Report, or what he may have discovered that is of Consequence.'[29]

Along with items to buy, the manuals and handbooks tried to give examples of the duties an officer was expected to carry out. A lieutenant's role, besides assuming command of the company in his captain's absence, included paying 'particular attention to the arms, accoutrements, ammunition, cloaths, necessaries and dress of the soldiers, and to every circumstance which may contribute to their health,' as well as to receive a 'return every market-day,

---

25 Roger Lamb, *Memoir of His Own Life* (Dublin: J. Jones, 1811), p.62

26 Lamb, *Memoir*, p.62.

27 John Williamson, *The Elements of Military Arrangement; Comprehending, the Tactick, Exercise, Manoevres, and Discipline of the British Infantry* (London: published by the author, 1781), p.16

28 Houlding, *Fit for Service*, p.170.

29 Simes, *The Military Medley*, p.151.

Officers were expected to study military matters attentively, and were often conversant in the latest theories. The spontoon seen here, another symbol of rank, was not carried in combat during the Revolutionary War. (Photo by Henry Gage)

specifying what quantity of provisions, and of what kind they have laid in, and the amount thereof.'[30] He was to;

> Examine their messes, and see if the quantity answers to their returns; also visit the sick, and see that they are properly attended... attend roll-calling at least once a day, and make Non-commissioned Officers give an exact return every morning, wherein they are to insert all Occurrences that have happened during the preceding twenty-four hours, and redress all complaints from the soldiers with readiness and exactness.[31]

Along with these sorts of description came slightly more nebulous advice. A new ensign was warned that 'honour is the peculiar characteristick [*sic*] of an Officer; consequently, all your actions should be guided by it,' and that he should 'avoid the company of those who are given to slander, scandal, personal or national reflections, as the pests of society.'[32] An ensign should always 'be attentive that the Serjeants and Corporals support a proper authority; but let it be done with decency and good order.'[33] Such a description emphasises the fact that the NCOs bore up the weight of the army's running on their shoulders – sergeants trained recruits, saw rations distributed and inspected billets, as well as overseeing the work of the corporals. They in turn were responsible for getting the men up, dressed and equipped each day and marched them to their drills or duties.[34] A wise junior officer knew to heed the opinion of these men, but on the whole they were also able to fall back on the advice of private publications that 'served as an all-important vehicle for preserving and passing on the accumulated custom of the service.'[35]

Besides book-learning, officers could count on the assistance of the fraternity to which they now belonged. Lieutenants and captains acted as a source of knowledge and support for their ensigns, and taught them indirectly by way of example. There was also the fact that many junior officers already had ties to the army. Besides friends already commissioned, familial bonds gave many an intimate understanding of the military from an early age. As already mentioned, Captain William Dansey's father was a captain, and the father and brother of Hildebrand Oakes were both in the service. This sort of support network, coupled with the corporate knowledge of the army, passed on from one officer and regiment to another, helped junior officers learn their duties. With the ensigns of the 33rd taking an average of around four years to attain their lieutenant's commissions, there was plenty of time to establish a basis of competency.

30 Simes, *The Military Medley*, p.194.
31 Simes, *The Military Medley*, p.195.
32 Simes, *The Military Medley*, p.198.
33 Simes, *The Military Medley*, p.198.
34 Lodge, *To What Extent*, p.29.
35 Houlding, *Fit for Service*, p.171.

The Clothing and Equipment

While Shaw was at Chatham he described being issued with '1 hat, 1 vest, 1 pair of breeches, 1 shirt, 1 pair of shoes, 1 pair of stocking and 1 stock and stock buckle.'[36] From when they first joined the recruiting party, enlistees were given their military clothing in a staggered fashion. Commonly they were first provided with their shoes and stockings as well as shirts, neck stocks, a black cockade and items for dressing their hair, such as combs.[37] This was then added to once they reached barracks, or their parent regiment.

The clothing worn by a regiment was divided into two main categories, necessary and regimental. Necessary clothing was provided by the regiment on an as-needed basis. There were soft foraging caps for headwear and neck stocks often made from horsehair and strengthened by a leather band, to which was fixed brass clasps. A linen or wool flannel shirt acted as undergarments, usually with a deep front slit and a collar closed by two or three thread buttons, with long bodies running to mid-thigh. Woollen or linen stockings accounted for the lower half of the legs, secured just below the knee by black leather garter straps with small brass buckles. Over the stockings were worn gaiters or half-gaiters. Initially these were made from linen which was blackened with shoe blacking in order to render it more weatherproof. Evidently these were found to be insufficient for service in America as, in 1776, thousands of pairs of black woollen cloth half gaiters were sent out for the use of the army. Linen gaiters however continued to appear in inspection returns for regiments outside of America. Leather shoes were also supplied, along with spare soles, each secured with a single brass buckle.

Breeches, stockings secured by garter belts, and half-gaiters comprised the legwear of most British soldiers for the first few years of the Revolutionary War. (Photo by Henry Gage)

The regimental clothing was provided by the king via each regiment's colonel and paid for by the men annually or on a multiannual basis. It included cloth waistcoats or vests, military hats usually made of felt with white tape, black military cockades often made from horsehair, and cloth breeches, as well as the most iconic piece of clothing, the red regimental coat. Made from heavy wool, for enlisted men it was dyed a somewhat dark shade of red and was usually replaced each year. It was functional, with skirts that could be let down and breast turnbacks that could be folded over in cold weather. Its trim also differentiated one regiment from another. The army used a combination of facing colours, lace design and button spacing to ensure that no

36 Shaw, *A Narrative*, p.14.

37 Hagist, *British Soldiers American War*, p.21.

two regiment's coats were identical. The 33rd was one of only two regiments during the period that had red facings (cuffs, turnbacks and collars) that matched the shade of the rest of the coat, though other regiments had yellow, blue, white, or even purple, orange or black. The 33rd's buttons were spaced evenly and surrounded by white lace designed to strengthen the buttonholes. The lace's design was what is now called 'bastion-shaped' – curving to a point – and had a single slender stripe of red running centrally through it. The buttons, made of pewter, bore the numeral 33 surrounded by a rope relief border that encompassed the entirety of the button's edge.

Clothing was shipped ready-made to the regiments, and then disassembled and fitted to each individual by the regimental tailors, usually enlisted men who were already skilled in the trade and who would adjust each item to fit each man. On average about three to five percent of soldiers in the army possessed past experience as tailors.[38] A snugly-fitted set of clothing was considered becoming of a soldier and was also functional, helping to keep out everything from wind to dirt and debris. Reviewing officers commented on the quality and exactness of the 33rd's tailoring. The muster books in 1772, 1774 and 1775 – unfortunately the 33rd's 1773 issue has been lost – all noted that the regiment's clothing was 'good and well fitted.'[39] With cobblers, leatherworkers and gunsmiths also within its ranks, a regiment was almost wholly self-sufficient when it came to maintaining the clothing and equipment shipped to it.

In terms of the distinctions of rank, a corporal's uniform was only differentiated from that of a private's by the strip of tasselled white silk or cloth he wore over his right shoulder-strap. It replaced the knot of white cord worn there in the pre-1768 uniform regulations. Sergeants wore jackets of a brighter red, and their lace was always white, with no red thread running through it. Their hats were banded with silver tape rather than white, and their buttons were silver-plated. Most recognisably, they wore a sash tied round the waist, crimson worsted shot through with whichever facing colour the regiment wore. As the 33rd's facings were also red, their sergeant's sashes had a white stripe through the middle, to avoid confusing a sergeant's sash with an officer's sash.

As for the officers themselves, uniform regulations allowed a greater degree of leeway regarding the style of clothing worn. Officer's coats were scarlet, a brighter red than those of the enlisted men. Sometimes they eschewed lace and tape, though where it was worn it was silver for the 33rd, and the buttons appear to have been spaced in twos. The two most symbolically important items of an officer's clothing were his gorget, a small metal plate, also silver for the 33rd, worn on a silken ribbon around the neck, and his crimson silk sash, worn around the waist above the waistcoat but underneath the coat. To this ensemble an officer would add their stockings, breeches and sometimes riding boots and gloves. Wigs were also still somewhat fashionable, though far from universal, and also not always worn on campaign. Dansey wrote about the financial difficulty involved in assembling all of this and maintaining the

38 Hagist, *Noble Volunteers*, p.32.

39 TNA: WO 12/4802/1, WO 12/4802/2: Muster books, 33rd Foot

33rd's high standards, complaining to his family that 'we have had new Hats and Silver Hilted Swords besides our Regimentals [coats] which we expect down from the Taylor every day, and when we are reviewed by the King we must have new Sashes and Gorgets … we are run over head in Debt. It is next to impossible to live on ones Pay here.'[40]

After they had been taught how to hold themselves in a soldier-like fashion and march properly, recruits were issued with their firelocks and accoutrements. Like their clothing, the equipment provided to British soldiers once they joined the ranks was divided into categories, in this case accoutrements, camp equipage and arms. The former two were usually supplied after the recruits joined their regiment proper, but the arms were issued while in depot.

The stand of arms, provided by the army, consisted of a musket, bayonet and cartridge box as well as a bayonet belt and frog, was usually the first set of equipment recruits were provided with. The boxes were different from cartridge pouches insomuch as they were simply drilled wooden blocks with a leather flap nailed to the side, rather than complete leather bags. Between 1769 and 1775 the regiment found themselves needing between 153 and 196 cartridge boxes, which seemingly had been lost in Germany.[41] It seems that, due to the fact that boxes were being phased out in favour of being equipped with just the pouches, these were never replaced. The regiment was also noted as still using the pre-1768, wider style of buff belting in 1770, and were admonished accordingly – they received new pattern buff belts and cartridge pouches that same year.

The accoutrements were, like the regimental clothing, provided by each regiment's colonel, and technically remained his property. They consisted of a leather cartridge pouch, containing a wooden box drilled with holes where ammunition cartridges could be slotted home, secured over the shoulder by a leather belt. These were buff leather which soldiers then whitened. A musket sling, made and treated the same way, was also added, as were the brush and picker tools used to clean the fouling from a musket's pan and touchhole. Ordinary camp necessaries belonged to the government, and included a tin, often kidney-shaped water canteen secured with a length of string, a haversack, a goatskin knapsack (changing to linen about midway through the war), and camp equipment shared between mess groups, such as a tin kettle with a cover and bag, a tent with its attendant ropes, pegs and mallets, and a hatchet.

The 33rd's arms consisted of 1769 pattern short land firelocks – smoothbore flintlock muskets. These were the latest type of arms issued to British forces. The older long land model was still in use by many regiments, with some even armed with a mixture, but, as we shall see, the 33rd were issued a full set of short land patterns just prior to sailing for America. With a total length of 58.5 inches, the short land was shorter than the long land's 62.5 inches, though there was little difference in weight, with both coming it at about 10.5 pounds, and they were both 0.75 inch calibre.

---

40 Delaware Historical Society (DHS): William Dansey Letters: 17 June 1769. With thanks to The Duke of Wellington's Regiment Museum, Halifax, UK.

41 Lodge, *To What Extent*, p.16.

A contemporary sketch of a Royal Artillery officer during the Revolutionary War. Due to the lack of colour, the uniform is not heavily dissimilar to the ones likely worn by most officers of the 33rd (Royal Artillery uniforms were dark blue rather than red). Note the lack of gorget – officers sometimes dispensed with these. (Anne S. K. Brown Military Collection)

Besides the muskets, each soldier had a 17-inch bayonet, kept in a black leather scabbard that hooked into a belt worn round the waist, but which the 33rd were wearing over their right shoulders by at least 1774; the year's review mentions soldiers having shoulder straps on their right as well as their left shoulders to keep the belts in place.[42] Bayonets of the period slotted over the muzzle of each firelock without restricting it, ensuring it could still be loaded and fired. The weapons were a triangular wedge shape, designed in such a way due to the limitations of eighteenth-century metalwork – a flat blade could not be made as strong as a triangular one, which was less likely to bend and break. Such a shape had nothing to do with the idea that triangular wounds are more difficult to stitch up. Similarly, most bayonets contained two fullers – popularly called blood channels – not to allow blood to run off or to break the suction with a stabbed body, but simply to reduce the weapon's weight without compromising its structural integrity.[43]

Sergeants were ostensibly issued with halberds, ideal for prodding and hassling soldiers into their proper ranks and files, and short swords, but these were left behind on campaign in America and usually replaced by carbines, which were shorter firelocks. Officers were armed with swords bought at their own expense and made to no standard pattern, though on campaign some also used fusils – more elegantly crafted muskets, again privately purchased except in the case of the flank companies, whose officers carried the army's 1770 pattern fusil.

Organisation

Broadly speaking, the British Army of the eighteenth century was divided into two Establishments, the British and the Irish. The differences were almost wholly administrative – the Irish Parliament footed the bill for those

42 Huw Strachan, *British Military Uniforms, 1768–1796: The Dress of the British Army from Official Sources* (London: Arms and Armour Press, 1975), p.223.

43 Athol Mayhew, 'British Bayonets' in *The Illustrated Naval and Military Magazine* (London: The Illustrated London News, 1884), vol.I, pp.58–59.

regiments stationed in Ireland, meaning it was a useful place to garrison units in order to ease both Parliamentary and public concerns about the army in Britain. Officially, regiments left the British Establishment for the Irish once they arrived on the island and returned to the British Establishment again as soon as they left, with units being rotated in and out on a regular basis. This created issues due to the fact that Irish Establishment regiments were smaller (and thus cheaper to pay for) than the British Establishment ones, but this problem of manpower inconsistency was largely solved in 1770 when the standing strength of the Irish Establishment was increased and the standing strength of the British Establishment was decreased, bringing regiments generally into line.

In terms of structure, most regiments in the British Army consisted of a single battalion. These in turn were divided into nine companies until 1771, when a light company was added to bring each battalion on the British Establishment up to 10 (light companies were added to Irish Establishment regiments a year later). In August 1775 all regiments to be deployed overseas were increased by half, rising from 360 privates to 540. Some of these men were drafted in from regiments not being sent abroad, while recruiting accounted for the other missing numbers.[44] Before this augmentation a regular company, at full strength, was comprised of one captain, one lieutenant, one ensign, two sergeants, three corporals, one drummer and 36 privates. After the late 1775 augmentation however a company consisted of one captain, one lieutenant, one ensign, three sergeants, three corporals, two drummers and 54 privates. From 1778 the standard regulation company size for regiments in America increased again to one captain, one lieutenant, one ensign, three sergeants, four corporals, two drummers and 70 privates.

Above the company structure were a battalion's command staff, chiefly a major and a lieutenant colonel. The regiment was commanded overall by a colonel, though they rarely served together in the field – the 33rd were fortunate in this regard to have Cornwallis close at hand during much of their campaigning in America. There were also various regimental ancillaries – a surgeon and surgeon's mate, a chaplain, an adjutant and a quartermaster, all of whom provided for the running of the unit in one capacity or another.

Once they joined their regiment, recruits were generally distributed evenly among the regiment's eight hat companies, so-called because their headgear differentiated them from the two remaining elite flank companies. These two more experienced companies were the grenadiers, who formed up on the right when the battalion was arrayed in line, and the light infantry, who formed up on the left. They had two lieutenants rather than an ensign and a lieutenant, and the grenadier company included two fife-players along with its drummers. The uniform details of the flank companies also differed – light infantry wore black belting, had small black leather caps, extra cartridge boxes, powder horns, shot pouches and hatchets, while the grenadiers had tall, distinctive bearskin caps and the vestigial kit for the grenades they no longer carried, such as the slow match case or a length of match cord.

44 Hagist, *Noble Volunteers*, p.103.

Much of this equipment seems not to have been carried on campaign. In general, the light companies ostensibly consisted of shorter men noted for their stamina, speed, marksmanship, and ability to operate independently, often in loose skirmish order fighting in broken terrain such as forests. Grenadier companies took the tallest, strongest and hardiest men, and were traditionally considered shock troops or heavy infantry. In practice, both companies represented the regiment's best, most experienced soldiers.

Chapter 3

Established upon the Truest Principles

Home Service, 1770–1775

At midnight, the cold air was rent by the crash of musketry. It was early November, and a sergeant of the 33rd had found himself in a desperate situation – he was surrounded by angry, armed vagabonds intent on killing him. He was not, however, anywhere near the American colonies.

It was 10 November 1770, and the fighting was happening in Happisburgh, a small village on the east coast of Norfolk, England. The sergeant had gotten caught up in service to the law. He had assisted a constable in apprehending a shipmaster and smuggler by the name of Captain Thomas Tanner. As they were directing him to The Swan alehouse to hold him for the night, 'they were overtaken by three smugglers, to whom the Captain addressing himself saying, "Now is your time, if you have a mind to be of service to me."' Encouraged by Tanner, one of the smugglers attacked and grappled with the constable while Tanner shoved the 33rd's sergeant into a ditch. The constable, however, was able to keep hold of Tanner, and the sergeant righted himself and demanded that the smugglers withdraw. Unarmed, the men fled, abandoning Tanner, who was left 'cursing them for cowards.'[1]

This was not to be the end of the exchange. The constable and the sergeant got the captain to The Swan without further incident, but that night the house 'was surrounded by twelve persons, armed with pistols, blunderbusses, axes, &c. who demanded the Captain.' The sergeant refused to surrender him, and the men opened fire. Bullets and buckshot peppered the alehouse's kitchen windows, with four balls lodging in the chimney and another grazing Tanner's shoulder. After running out of ammunition the smugglers 'began to chop down the window frame and the door.' One of them sought entry through a window, but the sergeant, bayonet fixed, thrust his weapon and 'stabbed him in the side.' As the struggle played out the constable kept Tanner

1 *London Evening Post*, 13 November 1770, p.3.

restrained with a drawn sword. Seemingly dissuaded by their comrade's bayonetting, the rest of the smugglers retrieved him and retreated, leaving Tanner in custody.[2]

Peacetime soldiering in eighteenth-century Britain was rarely peaceful. Cities were the scenes of riots and unrest, and the coastline was infested by smugglers.[3] When soldiers of the 29th Foot killed six rioters in Boston in 1770, they might have been forgiven for exhibiting surprise at the furore the incident generated in the colonies. Two years prior, in 1768, six or seven people were killed by soldiers at Saint George's Fields, London, during a riot triggered by the imprisonment of the radical MP John Wilkes. In 1769, soldiers deliberately fired into a crowd of weavers at Spitalfields agitating for more pay, killing two. At the height of the Revolutionary War in 1780, London was engulfed in turmoil as anti-Roman Catholic riots broke out in the wake of the Papists Act of 1778. The British Army engaged the rioters directly, resulting in hundreds of deaths. In short, the army preserved civil order, and imposed that order with violence.[4]

Britain was beset by civil and political unrest throughout the century, from the Sacheverell Riots of 1710 and the Coronation Riots of 1714 to the Priestly Riots of 1791 and Bristol Bridge Riot of 1793. Bread riots also flared in various parts of the country in the years 1709, 1740, 1756, 1757, 1766, 1767, 1773, 1782 and 1785. Indeed, in England between 1740 and 1775 there were 159 major riots recorded, not to mention the 1745 Jacobite rebellion and suppression, as well as minor uprisings in Ireland in 1771 and 1772.[5] With a civil policing force still in its early infancy, it was the army which was often called upon to restore order.

Nor were disgruntled rioters the only threat to be contended with at home. As the short but desperate siege of The Swan alehouse showed, smuggling was a dangerous and endemic practice. From Liverpool to Cornwall, Essex, Norfolk and Suffolk, a vast criminal network conducted a concealed, illicit trade designed to avoid customs duties and taxes. Tea smuggling in particular was rife during the period of the American Revolution, as it had been earlier in the century, when it had replaced the primacy of silk and linen on the black market. Around 1740, for example, it was estimated that smuggled tea accounted for no less than 75 precent of national consumption.[6] Without the means to deal with the trade in contraband goods directly, the civil powers were often forced to rely on the military, just as the unnamed constable relied upon the unnamed sergeant of the 33rd to ensure Captain Tanner's arrest. Nor was he the only smuggler seized by the regiment in the vicinity of Happisburgh. A month earlier one Thomas Dean was taken and charged 'with lurking and loitering at Happisburgh near the Sea in this County, and as he believes and suspects

---

2 *London Evening Post*, 13 November 1770, p.3.

3 Houlding, *Fit for Service*, p.36.

4 Houlding, *Fit for Service*, p.58.

5 David Hackett Fischer, *Paul Revere's Ride* (Oxford: Oxford University Press, 1994), p.77.

6 Jeff Horn, *Economic Development in Early Modern France: The Privilege of Liberty, 1650–1820* (Cambridge: Cambridge University Press, 2015), p.103.

While some were still children, the drummers during the period tended to be the same age as most of the other men, with the more senior providing tutelage to the younger. All soldiers were expected to understand the various different drum calls. (Photo by Henry Gage)

with Intent to be aiding and assisting in the running, landing and carrying away prohibited and uncustomed Good. He was escorted to Castle by a party of the 33d Regiment of Foot.' In 1773 the regiment were deployed to Cornwall and Devon, an area described by Houlding as one of the most restless in Britain, giving the 33rd ample opportunity to assist the overwhelmed civil authorities in combatting smugglers. Captain Dansey grimly described the local inhabitants 'which we were come to war against and being the thickest part of them Barbarians in Cornwall so remarkable for their cruelty in plundering wrecks.' He found his opinion misplaced however, noting that 'we got amongst them and finding their politeness far beyond our expectations although I had a red coat on … I think the Tinners [tin miners] the finest body of people I ever saw, and the civilest to strangers.'[7] Similarly, while stationed in Ireland in 1774 the 33rd helped an inspector of excise and two excise officers unearth 'two subteraneous vaults, constructed for the concentrating of contraband goods, in one of which was a small parcel of leaf tobacco, which they seized, and lodged in his Majesty's Stores … Also seized near Cloughnakilty, by Mr. James Cheney, Excise Officer, and a part of the 33d regiment of foot, twenty bags of leaf tobacco.'[8]

The army of the early 1770s, therefore, spent much of its time assisting civil authorities in suppressing riots and smuggling,[9] and the activities of many of the regiments that would go on to see service in America in the late 1760s and early 1770s show this. The Royal Welsh Fusiliers and the 4th Foot, for example, spent much time combatting smugglers along the south coast, while the 18th Foot put down riots against naval impressment in Whitehaven and the 43rd defeated an agrarian uprising.[10] Such duties occupied much of the time of regiments on so-called home service.

When the units of the British Army were not hunting smugglers or quashing minor unrest they were dispersed across billets in a rough locale, usually the 15 duty-areas that much of England was divided into, or in motion along main march-corridors. Generally, regiments rarely stayed in one place for more than a few months before they moved or were deployed overseas.'[11]

During their stay in the British Isles, there were a number of other jobs that tended to occupy the time of soldiers besides assisting the civil authorities. Barracks and fortifications in particular had to be maintained, and supplies transported.[12] Commonly, detachments of varying sizes were often put to work as labourers on roads or fortifications. Soldiers were paid for all of these activities in addition to their regular income. Soldiers were also often at liberty to seek employment outside the army, time permitting and with their officers' permission. Men were able to pursue trades they might have mastered before joining the military, or

7 DHS: Dansey Letters: Dansey to his father, 1 May1773, quoted in Lodge, *To What Extent*, p.6.
8 *Morning Chronicle*, 2 September 1774, p.4.
9 Houlding, *Fit for Service*, p.3.
10 Fischer, *Paul Revere's Ride*, pp.76–77.
11 Houlding, *Fit for Service*, pp.87, 29, 36.
12 Hagist, *Noble Volunteers*, p.31.

undertake local seasonal work, often agricultural in nature. There was even employment to be had for the regiment's musicians. The *London Evening Post* reported on 19 November 1771 that 'last night the New Assembly Room [at Gloucester] was opened to a very numerous and brilliant company … a most ravishing band of music struck up, composed of all the ablest musicians of the town, together with the bands of the marines and the 33d regiment.'[13]

In June 1771 the 33rd were employed, 'to go to work on the new Fortifications that are to enclose our Dock-yard,'[14] in Portsmouth, while in March 1773 the regiment were recorded as having arrived 'in order to carry on the Fortification Works on the Common of Portsea, which are in great Forwardness.'[15] It seems at least part of the regiment spent more than a year working on the defences of Portsmouth. On 2 July 1771 a newspaper reported that 'yesterday part of his Majesty's 33d regiment of foot arrived here from London; they are to be employed during the summer in digging ditches, &c. where the fortifications are to be made for the security of his Majesty's dock-yard at this port. The rest of the above regiment are expected here this morning.'[16] Three months later it was reported that 'they have done a great deal of Work since they have been here and the Whole of them have behaved remarkably well.'[17] The *London Evening Post* noted, with a hint of humour, that 'it is amazing to behold the quantity of earth dug and removed by the 33d regiment last summer: It must be acknowledged they were young, able men; and it must also be owned their strength was tried, and that when they left Portsmouth they were not so plump … as when they came there.'[18] On 1 August 1772 the regiment marched out of Portsmouth and were replaced by the 11th Foot, who were 'to be employed on the same work,' thus continuing the regular rotation of home service duties.[19]

If the army was dispersed and engaged in policing activities or acting as labourers, it stood to reason that training and drill was neglected.[20] This was certainly the case for some regiments, and prolonged periods in Britain or in garrison abroad could render whole battalions unfit for active military service. That was not, however, the fate of all British regiments in the years immediately preceding the American Revolution. A system of regular official reviews, training exercises and mock battles helped to keep units in a state of readiness. Some were more successful at this than others, but few achieved the preparedness of the 33rd Regiment.

---

13 *London Evening Post*, 19 November 1771, p.4. Somewhat horrifically, the *Public Advertiser* of 19 February 1772 related how one of the members of the 33rd's band perished after falling behind in a snowstorm on a journey from Gloucester to Cirencester, three months after the concert at the New Assembly Rooms. He was found frozen dead a week after disappearing, his body partially eaten by mice.

14 *Public Advertiser*, 25 June 1771, p.2.

15 *Daily Advertiser*, 2 April 1773, p.1.

16 *Craftsman or Say's Weekly Journal*, 6 July 1771, p.3.

17 *Public Advertiser*, 15 October 1771, p.2.

18 *London Evening Post*, 24 March 1772, p.4.

19 *Morning Chronicle*, 4 August 1772, p.2.

20 Houlding, *Fit for Service*, p.3.

History of the Regiment to 1770

First formed as the Earl of Huntingdon's Regiment of Foot in Gloucestershire in 1702, the 33rd was initially raised to fight in the War of the Spanish Succession. Their first overseas operations were a largely desultory series of campaigns in Spain and Portugal, including the siege of Barcelona, before their first major battle at Almansa, on 25 April 1707. They were in the thick of the fighting, and suffered heavy casualties as the alliance of British, Portuguese, Dutch and German troops were forced back by the Franco-Spanish army. Part of a detachment that was separated from the main army, they were forced to surrender the next day. After this inauspicious start, the regiment was reformed in Britain and active again by 1710. Besides minor raids against Spain in 1719, they spent the next three decades serving in Britain or Ireland.

With the outbreak of the War of the Austrian Succession in 1740 the regiment was ordered back to the continent. It participated at the Battle of Dettingen where, under the eye of King George II, the regiment were engaged by the massed charge of the French cavalry at the height of the battle, standing their ground and halting the onslaught.[21] More officers of the 33rd were killed than among any other regiment during the battle, but this time the allied forces were victorious.[22] Dettingen became the regiment's first battle honour. They went on to serve in major engagements at Fontenoy in 1745, Rocoux in 1746 and Lauffeld in 1747, and were involved in the suppression of the Jacobite rising in Scotland in 1745.

With the end of the war in 1748 they were posted to the Mediterranean island of Minorca. There they spent four years before returning to Britain, garrisoning Edinburgh for two years. At the onset of the Seven Years War the regiment were part of the seaborne expeditions against St Malo and Cherbourg, both of which saw little in the way of success. Like many other regiments, the 33rd were augmented to two battalions as the war reached its height. In 1760 they were deployed to Germany as part of the British contingent in the allied army commanded by Duke Ferdinand of Brunswick-Wolfenbüttel. They were engaged at Villinghausen and again at Zierenberg. The 33rd acted with the rearguard during Ferdinand's later retreat to the Rhine, enduring difficult conditions as the army fell back to Westphalia. Following the failed siege of Cassel, they were present at Ferdinand's victory at Wilhelmsthal and then participated in driving the French from Hesse. It was during these two years of hard campaigning, and indeed across the many other theatres of operation during the Seven Years War, that a large number of the older soldiers who served during the American Revolution received their first taste of combat. Captain William Dansey, for example, initially enlisted as a volunteer under his father, Captain Dansey Collins. William

21 Albert Lee, *History of the Thirty-third Foot, Duke of Wellington's (West Riding) Regiment* (Norwich: The Empire Press, 1922), pp.43–44.

22 Lee, *History of the Thirty-third*, p.45.

received his ensign's commission on 30 July 1760, and the pair served in the 33rd together during the German campaigns under Ferdinand.[23]

The 33rd returned to Britain in 1763, and their second battalion disbanded following the successful conclusion of the war. In 1764 they were assigned once more to the drudgery of garrison duties on Minorca. Dansey summed up the idleness of the post in a letter home, writing that;

> I spend the morning in my Quarter in dishabille sitting in a Banian [loose house coat] and Trousers, and read, write, draw or Net, just what happens to be my favourite at the time ... about 3 o'clock I take my Dinner ... I generally drink a Pint of Wine which costs about a Penny. After Dinner I put on a clean shirt, dress and powder my hair and walk up into town ... I seldom find my way back to my Fort again till between 11 and 12 o'clock.[24]

It is notable that none of Dansey's letters from Minorca mention any references at all to military activities.[25] The 33rd thus remained at their dull posting until 1769, when they were rotated back to Britain. It was during their time in the Mediterranean that an appointment was made that likely changed the fate of the regiment.

Charles Cornwallis

On 21 March 1766, the 33rd received a new colonel, Charles Cornwallis. At the age of 27, he was relatively young for such a rank, having acquired it (but not, initially, a regiment to go with it) in August the year before, but his pedigree was prestigious. He was the oldest son of Charles, the first Earl Cornwallis, and could trace his aristocratic lineage back to the fourteenth century. Despite his age, he was militarily experienced. After an education at Eton and a brief spell at Cambridge University he had been commissioned into the 1st Foot Guards on 8 December 1757, venturing to the continent to study the art of war and enrolling in the military academy at Turin. He served as a staff officer during the Seven Years War in Europe and was present at the celebrated victory at Minden. He fought in the same campaigns as the 33rd in Germany, becoming a captain in the 85th Foot and then a lieutenant colonel in the 12th, leading them at Wilhelmsthal, Lutterberg and Vellinghausen, where the regiment suffered heavy casualties.

Cornwallis's political career progressed in parallel – and with similar rapidity – to his military one. He became a Member of Parliament in 1760 and was raised to the House of Lords after inheriting his father's title in 1762. A supporter of the Whigs, he showed solidarity with Britain's American colonists by voting against the Stamp Act of 1765, though this likely stemmed from the desire to help his friend Lord Shelburne more than from

---

23 Paul Dansey (ed.), *Captured Rebel Flag: The Letters of Captain William Dansey, 33rd Regiment of Foot, 1776–1777* (Godmanchester: Ken Trotman Publishing, 2010), p.4.

24 DHS: Dansey Letters: Dansey to his father, 1 May1773, quoted in Lodge, *To What Extent*, p.4.

25 Lodge, *To What Extent*, p.4.

Charles Cornwallis, British general, politician, and colonel of the 33rd Regiment of Foot for almost four decades. (Public Domain)

any particular belief in colonial liberties.[26] He climbed swiftly through both military and social ranks, and was noted as a man of authority, though not of haughtiness. A little corpulent, with a wall eye (resulting from a hockey injury at Eton), he did not partake in the many vices that a man of wealth could be tempted by, but preferred restraint and moderation. He was, in short, someone with a strong sense of determination, who strived for success in everything he attempted.[27] In the late 1760s and early 1770s, the 33rd were one of the targets of his ambitions.

It would not be unduly harsh to say that before Cornwallis's arrival – and, indeed, during the last few years of their garrison duties in Minorca – the 33rd were an unexceptional regiment. The 1769 inspection returns indicate an indifferent nature. The inspecting officer recorded that the non-commissioned officers had 'in general a pretty good appearance,' that the regiment as a whole marched 'exceedingly well,' performed manoeuvres 'with

26 Richard Middleton, *Cornwallis: Soldiers and Statesman in a Revolutionary World* (New Haven: Yale University Press, 2022), p.14.

27 O'Shaughnessey, *The Men Who Lost America*, pp.249–250; David McCullough, *1776: Britain and America at War* (St Ives: Penguin Books, 2006), p.253.

great exactness,' and that the soldiers were 'clean under arms, and attentive.' However, the officers were 'very young, and had been lately appointed' while the men were 'many old, and short.' They 'performed the Manual to music in too slow time; they deviated from the practice of the army in doubling their files to make intervals for the officers to go thro, to take their post of exercise in the rear.' The firings 'were not all equally good, occasioned by the inexperience of the young officers.' Their accoutrements were 'very good and clean, except some waistbelts' and their clothing was 'old, but in very good repair.'[28] In short, they were an acceptable regiment, but not exceptional, a regular unit of the line unlikely to excel itself on operations.

This was the force that Cornwallis spent the years immediately preceding the American Revolution moulding into The Pattern. Success was not immediate, indeed it seems as though Cornwallis decided against undertaking the task while the regiment was still garrisoning Minorca, where lack of space and the general indolence of Mediterranean, peace-time garrison life would have worked against his efforts. He visited the regiment in the summer of 1766, five months after his appointment as its colonel, but appears to have departed after only a few months on the island.[29] However, once the regiment was back in Britain, improvements were rapid. General observations of the inspecting officer in 1770 noted that 'the attention of the Officers is admirable, great pains must have been taken to give the Men that Soldierlike air for which they are remarkable.'[30] This time the Manual Exercise was 'very well performed, and in proper and equal time' while the firings were 'well performed in every respect.' There remained points to work upon – the manoeuvres were 'too slow' and the accoutrements were 'not according to the regulation,' but the change was clear, and the improvements continued.[31] In 1772, for example, the manoeuvres were listed as 'very well performed' and the accoutrements were 'good and according to Regulations.'[32] Cornwallis himself was continuing to acquire a growing reputation as an officer – he was appointed constable of the Tower of London in January 1771 and, due to the fact that the position was typically awarded to serving soldiers, Middleton claims the award of the post 'probably reflected his growing reputation as a soldier.'[33]

Peacetime Training and Duties

Improving the training and general discipline of a regiment in Britain or Ireland during the period was no easy task. As mentioned, units often found themselves assisting the local authorities in maintaining the peace or were assigned to the construction of roads and fortifications. Due to the lack of

28 TNA: WO 12/4802/1: Muster books, 33rd Foot.
29 Middleton, *Cornwallis*, pp.14–15.
30 TNA: WO 12/4802/1: Muster books, 33rd Foot.
31 TNA: WO 12/4802/1: Muster books, 33rd Foot.
32 TNA: WO 12/4802/1: Muster books, 33rd Foot.
33 Middleton, *Cornwallis*, p.16.

dedicated barracks, regiments were also often divided into detachments rather than kept as a cohesive whole, and even marched to new locations by different roads. All of this meant that it was difficult to keep a regiment together and assign time for training and drill. This problem beset the 33rd as much as it did any other unit, indeed perhaps more so.

The 33rd arrived back in Britain from Minorca in May 1769. The regiment was at Salisbury in its entirety until June that year, when there was a general inspection. From July it was split into two halves for almost a year – five companies marched to Derby and four to Leicester. The regiment remained split until May 1770 and was then moved 'around England from Derby to Norwich and then to Chatham, Portsmouth, Gloucester and finally to Devon and Cornwall in 1773,' where detachments of one or two companies were deployed to Falmouth, Penryn, Truro, Helstone, Padstow and Wardbridge to help combat smugglers.[34] As indicated in the location data and marching orders in the Appendix, the regiment rarely stayed as a coherent unit together in one place for long, but between 1769 and embarking for Ireland in 1774 were moved rather haphazardly around England.

This should have created problems regarding overall drill and competency. Between September 1772 and April 1774, for example, the 33rd was dispersed into detachments 41 percent of the time, a higher figure than the 31.5 percent average for other regiments in England over the same period. Where matters improved for the 33rd came down to the fact that when they were detached, or when they received new marching orders, it was generally to move and billet in only two groupings (called grand divisions), often of five companies each. This was a greater level of coherence than that enjoyed by most regiments, who were often divided into three or four divisions of a few companies each. The 33rd spent 41 percent of its time with the regiment split into two halves rather than smaller portions, compared to an average of just 7.5 percent for most regiments.[35] The fact that the 33rd seems to have been happy performing maneuverers at the level of grand division during reviews probably speaks to the fact that it was able to maintain its strength at this level for a good amount of its home service.

The 33rd were also able to concentrate before inspections for longer periods than most. Prior to the annual inspections in 1770, 1771, 1772, 1774 and 1775 the regiment averaged around eight weeks of preparation time where they could drill as a single body. In 1773 they managed only seven to 10 days, though the inspection comments imply this did not negatively impact them.[36] Dansey had to march his company 48 miles in three days from Truro to Plymouth in order to arrive in time for the 1773 inspection, which he seems to have achieved with some aplomb;

> I came to the Barracks fresh and easy for the men to settle themselves, and as clean and well powdered as if going to a Ball for which I got Lord Cornwallis's Approbation; altho' I had two such long Day's Marches in a very hilly Country I

34 Lodge, *To What Extent*, p.14.
35 Lodge, *To What Extent*, p.14.
36 Lodge, *To What Extent*, p.14.

> did not leave a Man behind: in the afternoon the Regiment was under Arms and Exercise and the Company I have the honour to command was order'd to join the Battalion which I thought very hard after so long a march and two Months absence; but we received the highest Satisfaction by Lord Cornwallis declaring at the Head of the Regiment that it was impossible to tell from their cleanness of Dress and good Exercising that they had been absent at all, and expressed to me his highest Approbation.[37]

As a further aid to drill and preparation, the regiment had access to training areas at all of its major postings between 1772 and 1774, which it took advantage of.[38] All told, the regiment was able to maintain a tolerable level of coherence while moving around the country, found time to concentrate as a unit to rehearse prior to reviews, and made good use of training areas, all of which contributed to the high regard the regiment was held in prior to the outbreak of fighting in America.

Reviews and Light Infantry Training

In 1771 the 33rd were reviewed by the King at Blackheath. George III was;

> … so pleased with the fine Appearance of the Men, and the Dexterity, as well as Readiness, with which they performed some new Evolutions and Manoeuvres, lately introduced by their Colonel, that he expressed a Desire to see them go through their Exercise again, and accordingly did them the singular Honour to review them a second Time yesterday Morning in Hyde Park.[39]

Unfortunately, the newspapers reporting the review did not mention exactly what the new evolutions and manoeuvres that Cornwallis had introduced were, but the subsequent Hyde Park review showed that they involved the progressive light infantry style tactics that were rising in popularity within the military establishment. The *General Evening Post* reported that;

> Yesterday the 33d regiment, commanded by the Earl of Cornwallis, who had been reviewed last week by his Majesty upon Blackheath, were again, at his particular request, assembled in Hyde-park on their march to Portsmouth; where they again exhibited all their new manoeuvres as light Infantry: their quickness of motion and marching, and various order of firing, is really astonishing; and their whole exercise and discipline, beyond parallel and example in any troops in the army. They passed the pales, ditches and defiles quite up to Kensington Gardens, and then back again through the Grove by the powder magazine, with as much agility and alertness, as if they had been unincumbered [*sic*] with arms, upon a regular march, in open campaign country; here they formed in an instant, the Indian

37 DHS: Dansey Letters: Dansey to his mother, 16 May 1773, quoted in Lodge, *To What Extent*, p.15.

38 Lodge, *To What Extent*, p.15.

39 *Virginia Gazette*, 12 September 1771, p.1.

> file, and fired in ambuscade. Upon the whole, the performance was excellent and highly merited the just applause of his Majesty, the Duke of Gloucester, General Harvey, Count de Guignes, and many other General Officers.[40]

The Blackheath and Hyde Park reviews seem to have caused quite a stir and were still being mentioned by commentators four years later. Captain Dansey also wrote to his father speaking about 'all our Glory on Blackheath and Hyde Park.'[41] A year later the regiment was demonstrating its abilities again. In May 1772, it fought a mock battle before observers at Gloucester, with the reviewing officer describing them as 'in every Respect one of the finest Regiments in His Majesty's Service.' During one part of the exercise the regiment;

> Wheeled to the left by Companies, & Crossed a Deep & Rugged Valley, the Light Company forming a flanking party on the Right, among some Bushes, & thick Hedges. When the Battalion Gained the Brow of the opposite Hill, the Light Company was Drove in, the Battalion Companies then wheeled to the Right, & rushed down the Hill, to Line a Strong Hedge in the Bottom where they kept up a brisk & Irregular Fire. On the Retreat beating, the Men run back Independently, to the Brow of the Hill, where they Instantly formed, & fired by Companies.[42]

These activities, with even the battalion companies moving at haste, taking advantage of cover and shooting irregularly (that is, firing individually, as fast as each man was able to load) indicate that the 33rd had embraced the sort of fighting usually reserved for the recently re-formed light companies. Following the end of the Seven Years War, the light companies that had so impressed had been disbanded, but light infantry doctrine remained in vogue, especially with a number of officers who would come to particular prominence during the Revolutionary War. Thomas Gage and William Howe, for example, had both led light infantry during the Seven Years War, and their positive attitude to light infantry tactics was becoming fashionable within military circles. The light companies were reintroduced into the regular battalions in 1771 and 1772. Cornwallis had also spent time during the Seven Years War in a light infantry unit, specifically as a captain in the 85th Foot, which was raised in 1759 with the intention of being a light infantry regiment. He did not see action with it however before his promotion to lieutenant colonel of the 12th Foot. Nor were the 33rd being drilled in light tactics with an eye to a possible conflict in America – besides a few notable incidents, the early 1770s seemed less fraught than the preceding decade had been in the American colonies, and there has never been evidence that Cornwallis expected war there.[43] Regardless, it seems clear that Cornwallis was part of the avant-garde of military thinkers who saw value in light infantry tactics,

40 *General Evening Post*, 27 June 1771, p.1.

41 DHS: Dansey Letters: Dansey to his father, 23 October 1771, quoted in Lodge, *To What Extent*, p.12.

42 TNA: WO 27/24 in Houlding, *Fit for Service*, p.306.

43 Middleton, *Cornwallis*, p.17.

and the colonel drilled his entire regiment in them. The fact that the battalion companies were able to withdraw, reform and resume a more regular fire by companies during the 1772 Gloucester display would have indicated to observers that they retained their discipline and their reliability as a body of steady, formed line infantry. They were, in short, proving an impressive tactical flexibility.

While light infantry doctrine was all the rage among a section of the officer corps, it was viewed with distrust or outright distaste by others. At least one anonymous writer in particular seems to have taken a strong dislike to Cornwallis's efforts to introduce light infantry tactics into the 33rd Foot. His scathing commentary appeared in the *Morning Post* on 2 May 1775 (not long before news of fighting in America reached Britain). The author styled themselves as 'Phalanx,' recalling the ancient Greek fighting formation involving close-packed, heavily armoured warriors. His complaint was about British regiments going into battle in loose, open files rather than in tight, close order, and he believed that the 33rd and their reviews had played a large part in what they saw as an unwise innovation;

> The thirty-third regiment had open files, and looked very pretty in Hyde Park [the 33rd were reviewed at Hyde Park in 1771]: so, right or wrong, all the army must have them. Why don't you order the army to follow the system entirely of that regiment, and not partially all their absurdities? Why suffer that regiment to run counter in every part of their exercise and appointments to that paltry half regulation given out sometime ago? I think they have great merit, but you cannot find it out, by having adopted almost the only foolish part of their system.[44]

It is possible Phalanx was a disgruntled officer, possibly even a former member of the 33rd who had found themselves out of favour with Cornwallis and the style of fighting he was attempting to inculcate. Certainly, the anonymous writer's complaints appear to have fallen on deaf ears, for the open order of fighting would become the standard for British forces operating in North America.

In June 1773 the militia reviewed at Woolridge went through their exercises in emulation of the 33rd, with notable use of light infantry and grenadiers in ambush and the manoeuvring of the whole battalion in what was termed Indian files, the rapid movement of a loose column in one or two files, perfect for woodland combat. The exercises, as well as the general reviews, continued for the 33rd as the threat of war in the colonies grew. In May 1773, at Plymouth, the regiment had been 'divided into two opposing forces, fought a realistic manoeuvre action over the possession of an eminence.' The next year 'they went through a more involved simulation for the possession of a hill … this time including the effects of cannon-fire.'[45] The 33rd were reviewed at Plymouth on 31 March 1774 by Major General

44 *Morning Post*, 2 May 1775, p.4.
45 Houlding, *Fit for Service*, p.305.

William Howe showed praised the light company in particular, who 'acted with great spirit.'[46] In April 1774 the *Morning Chronicle* described how;

> The 33d, or Lord Cornwallis's, was reviewed; the satisfaction this regiment gave both in the field and in quarters deserves notice. The General [Howe] expressed his entire approbation of their performances, and the spectators, who, as the weather was very fine were almost without number, seemed astonished at the quickness and regularity of their motions and manoeuvres. In private few regiments ever behaved like them, none exceeded them, punishments are never known in the corps, and yet there is not a man in the regiment above forty.[47]

The light infantry drills in early 1774 were significant as later that year at Salisbury Howe held a series of exercises with companies from different regiments specifically designed to inculcate new light infantry drills. Middleton states that 33rd's 'inspection seems to have inspired Howe to organise a wider demonstration of light infantry tactics at Salisbury Plain,' though the 33rd were not present, having by that time been deployed to Ireland.[48]

In May 1774 the 33rd conducted perhaps their most complex exercise of the pre-war period, at Charles Fort, overlooking the Cove of Kinsale in Ireland. John Robert Shaw later described how Kinsale was 'defended by a strong fort called *Charles's Fort*; and on the opposite shore there are two villages, called *Cove* and *Scilly*: the inhabitants of which are generally native Irish, and live in low built houses made of mud, on a beautiful eminence, ranging with the barracks, and facing the inlet of the harbour.'[49] It was in this setting that the 33rd was ranged against the 20th Foot in a complex mock battle. The 33rd were tasked with capturing Charles Fort. Under Cornwallis's direct command they began with an amphibious operation. The whole regiment made a beach landing, and were confronted by the 20th Foot who advance from Fort Kinsale and took up a strong position. The 33rd attacked them, collapsed both flanks and pushed them back towards the fort. Covered by the fort's artillery, the 33rd declined to push the attack further.[50]

Here we see not only the 33rd besting a fellow regiment of the line, driving in their flanks despite the 20th holding the superior ground, but we also see the 33rd displaying competence in combined arms operations. More so than any other major power, Britain's army was frequently asked to operate alongside its navy, and the ability of regiments to conduct landings and likewise withdraw in good order to naval assets was almost as important as the displays of both formed and irregular fighting at previous reviews.

The regiment had certainly come a long way from the somewhat indifferent figure it presented in 1769. The reviews of the early 1770s made

46 Brian E. Hubner, *The Formation of the British Light Infantry Companies and their Employment in the Saratoga Campaign of 1777* (Saskatoon: unpublished dissertation, 1986), p.73.
47 *Morning Chronicle*, 5 April 1774, p.2.
48 Middleton, *Cornwallis*, p.18.
49 Shaw, *A Narrative*, p.17.
50 Houlding, *Fit for Service*, p.308.

it clear that the 33rd had improved considerably in their uniforms, bearing, and their capacity to fire and manoeuvre, while the officer and NCO cadres also drew praise, to such an extent that of the 21 regiments of foot in Ireland in 1775, the 33rd's review is a prime example.[51] Indeed, while in Ireland the regiment found themselves tasked with training other units on that Establishment.

While serving with the 9th in Ireland shortly before the Revolutionary War, Roger Lamb related that 'after I had acquired a knowledge of the new discipline from the non-commissioned officers of the 33d regiment, I was appointed to take charge of a squad of our regiment, and executed that important and laborious task to the best of my ability.'[52] This 'new discipline' was undoubtedly related to light infantry tactics, for the 33rd 'held a camp of instruction' at Dublin in the spring of 1775 to teach drills being practiced by the likes of Major General Sir William Howe at Salisbury in 1774.[53] Though 33rd were not present at Howe's light infantry drills, such a method of dissemination, with one regiment passing on new drills to another, and that regiment doing likewise with others, was a common means for spreading developments in tactics during the period. In Dublin the 33rd helped train the garrison force of the 9th, 15th, 34th, 37th and 46th Regiments their new exercises, with Lamb recounting how he was 'sent among several other non-commissioned officers to be instructed in the new exercise which shortly before had been introduced by General Sir William Howe. It consisted of a set of manoeuvres for light infantry, and was ordered by his Majesty to be practiced in the different regiments ... our regiment was instructed in them by the 33d, at that time quartered in Dublin, and commanded by Lord Cornwallis.'[54] The 33rd had already taught the 20th Foot the drill in March, April and May of 1774, before leaving Plymouth for Ireland with them.[55] Lamb recorded that 'the

Unfortunately, there are no known contemporary images of regular soldiers of the 33rd Foot during the American Revolution. This sketch, by Philip James de Loutherbourg and dating from around 1778, shows a soldier (possibly a corporal, due to the tassel on the right shoulder) from another regiment, however the uniform would be similar to that of the 33rd in the early years of the war, with the only major differences being the shape of the coat's lace and the belt plate on the chest. (Anne S. K. Brown Military Collection)

51 Lodge, *To What Extent*, p.7.
52 Lamb, *Memoir*, p.94.
53 Hubner, *The Formation of the British Light Infantry Companies*, p.72.
54 Lamb, *Memoir*, pp.89–90.
55 Hubner, *The Formation of the British Light Infantry Companies*, p.73.

manoeuvres were chiefly intended for the woody and intricate districts, with which North America abounds, where an army cannot act in line.'[56] It is noteworthy that Lamb was not an NCO in a light company, but was from a standard battalion company. As we have already seen, it appears the whole of the 33rd was conversant with light tactics, and it is likely the intention was to drill the line regiments so they could act as full battalions of light infantry.

Nor is it necessarily the case that it was just Howe's ideas being put into practice – as we have already seen, Cornwallis himself was using the 33rd as innovators for new tactics. Indeed, in 1771 a London newspaper reported that 'on Wednesday his Majesty's first regiment of guards began to learn the new exercise which Lord Cornwallis has introduced into the 33d regiment which is esteemed the best disciplined in the army.'[57] The fact that the Foot Guards, traditionally the army's elite, were being drilled by the 33rd in 1771 speaks volumes. It is also interesting that at the time the Guards did not have a dedicated light infantry company, and that it can therefore be assumed the whole regiment were being taught light infantry drill, much as the 33rd themselves had learned light infantry doctrine in their entirety.

All of this resulted in what Houlding has called an 'excellent state of advanced training.'[58] In the three years prior to the outbreak of fighting in America, the 33rd proved themselves capable as regular infantry, as light infantry, and in amphibious operations. Nor does their participation in reviews and mock battles alone qualify them as an exceptional regiment. The commentary of both military peers and civilians lends credence to the formidable corps that Cornwallis had been steadily forming. Lamb in particular was fulsome regarding the regiment. He wrote that;

> The 33d was in a high state of appointment, and exceedingly well disciplined, by that able disciplinarian [Lieutenant] Colonel Webster… I never witnessed any regiment that excelled it in discipline and military appearance. The men mounted guard in a superior style. Each sentinel, during the two hours he remained on his post, continued always in motion, and could not walk less than seven miles in that time. The soldier was ever alert and alive in attention; when on duty – all eye – all ear. Even in the sentry box, which the sentinel never entered unless when it rained, he was not allowed to keep the palm of his hand carelessly on the muzzle of his firelock, which, if the piece were loaded, was considered dangerous and always an awkward attitude for the soldier. This soldierly character they always maintained while they served in North America.[59]

Lamb's recollections may well have been biased – the book containing his account was dedicated to the then-colonel of the 33rd. But they do not stand alone. The 33rd's reputation even spread beyond the army and into society life. In a letter to his son written in 1781, Henry Herbert, 10th Earl of Pembroke, mentioned the abilities of the 25th Foot, commenting 'what

56 Lamb, *Memoir*, pp.89–90.
57 *Crafstman, or Say's Weekly Journal*, 29 June 1771, p.2.
58 Houlding, *Fit for Service*, p.305.
59 Lamb, *Memoir*, p.90.

Hats were supposed to be uniformly worn cocked to one side, to achieve what was considered at the time to be a military appearance and to avoid the edges of the hat interfering with the musket barrel when shouldered. (Author's photo)

ye say of Ld. G. Lenox's Regt., the 25th, surprises me, for it had hitherto been the best we have, since Cornwallis's [33rd] went to America.'[60] In 1779 a reviewer of a regiment of Devon militia stated that they 'appear by much the steadiest and best regiment I have seen; they seem to copy the 33d, a corps deservedly admired by all ranks of the military."'[61]

Houlding describes the 33rd as 'unquestionably the best-trained regiment in the British Army' from the 1770s to 1800. [62] In 1772 it was noted as 'one of the finest Regiments in His Majesty's Service' while in 1774 Major General William Howe declared the 33rd 'Established upon the truest principles, far Superior to any other Corps within my Observation.'[63] There seems no doubt that at the commencement of hostilities in the American colonies, the 33rd stood as exemplars of British military ability.

That ability would be tested beyond breaking point over the next eight years.

60 Lord George Herbert from his Father, 1781, quoted in Mark Frederick Odintz, *The British Officer Corps, 1754–1783* (Ann Arbor: University of Michigan Dissertation Services, 1988), p.21.

61 *Morning Post*, 28 June 1779, p.3.

62 Houlding, *Fit for Service*, p.316.

63 TNA: WO 27/15, WO 27/24: Inspection returns 1769 and 1772.

Chapter 4

In Perfect Good Order

On the Eve of Revolution

On 17 July 1775, the 33rd assembled in Dublin. Exactly one month earlier, the British army in Boston had thrown itself again and again into a series of bloody, desperate assaults on rebel positions on Bunker Hill and a neighbouring promontory later known as Breed's Hill. The casualties sustained – over a thousand killed or wounded, including no less than 81 officers – shook the military. All of that, however, was unknown to the 33rd that day. News of the battle reached Britain on 25 July. The latest information available to the regiment was that the King's American subjects had risen in rebellion and confined the main British force in the colonies to Boston. The senior officers also likely knew that their colonel, Charles Cornwallis, was seeking active service, and that meant the regiment was probably only months away from being deployed to a major theatre of operations.

The 33rd had spent the last 15 months in Ireland, having been rotated onto the Irish Establishment in April 1774 to replace a regiment sent to America. The 33rd had spent time in Dublin, where it had helped other units on the Establishment learn light infantry drill, but was quartered for the most part in Cork and the surrounding areas – Inchigeelagh, Clonakilty and Youghal. Service in Ireland was rarely to the taste of British soldiers or their officers. Danger was far more present than in Britain, with the threat of agrarian risings and sectarian clashes overlaying simmering, gang-like scuffles between soldiers – often off-duty – and local Irishmen, usually representing trades that the soldiers were seen to be infringing upon in their spare time. It was not uncommon for soldiers to be assaulted, even in Dublin. Some were subjected to a particular practice known as hocking, which involved permanently maiming a man by cutting his Achilles tendon.[1] In the midst of all this, the 33rd spent their time in Ireland hunting smugglers and conducting drills.

---

1 Hagist, *Noble Volunteers*, p.7.

The regiment were reviewed on 17 July at Dublin by Lieutenant General John Irwin. Fully uniformed and equipped, they performed the standard series of drills, manoeuvres and firings that tested the serviceability of every regiment on the Establishments. Irwin remarked that the Manual Exercise was 'exceedingly well performed' and the vital evolutions, firings and manoeuvres were likewise 'exceedingly well performed.' The only black mark was against their weaponry – the arms were described as 'clean but unserviceable.'[2] This observation has interesting connotations. The arms being clean indicated that the regiment had not grown slack in its discipline, but the use of the word unserviceable implies that a replacement would have to be found before being sent overseas. Given that these same weapons had been marked good in the previous year's review, this may well have been a case of Cornwallis using his influence to have Irvine declare the regiment's arms as unfit for use in combat, opening the door to a full refit before deployment. This was forthcoming. On 11 August 1775, less than a month after the review, the 33rd were issued with a 'complete set' of muskets and bayonets from the Dublin Castle armoury. In mid-November they were issued a further batch of muskets and bayonets as they continued to augment their strength, and again in January the next year, including two sergeant's fusils with bayonets.[3] The regiment thus found themselves fully rearmed prior to embarking on campaign.

British muskets were stamped with their armoury of origin, either 'Tower' for the Tower of London, or Dublin Castle. The 33rd shipped to America armed mostly with weapons from the Dublin storage. (Photo by Henry Gage)

Irvine summarised the 33rd's general state and readiness for action; 'the regiment is in perfect good order, and [is] in every respected fit for service.'[4] It would have seemed, therefore, that bar augmenting their strength with more enlisted men, the regiment was ready for action. Much like the passing comment on their firearms, however, the review fails to capture the full situation faced by the 33rd in 1775. Cornwallis, seeking active service abroad, and knowing his regiment would likely accompany him, was busy pursuing changes that he believed would see them properly prepared for combat.

The regiment assembled on 17 July 1775 consisted of their colonel, six captains, 10 lieutenants, seven ensigns, 13 sergeants, 21 corporals, eight drummers and 268 privates, as well as an ancillary staff of one chaplain, one adjutant, one quartermaster, one surgeon and his mate. Absent due to being on duty at the time was one captain, one lieutenant, one ensign, five

2 TNA: WO 12/4802/1: Muster books 33rd Foot.
3 De Witt Bailey, *Small Arms of the British Forces, 1664–1815* (Woonsocket: Andrew Mowbray Publishers, 2009), pp.308–309.
4 TNA: WO 12/4803: Muster books 33rd Foot.

sergeants, five corporals, two drummers and 25 privates. The regiment's lieutenant colonel, one sergeant, four corporals, one drummer and 17 privates were also absent, in quarters. One sergeant, one drummer and six privates were confined to hospital, while the regiment's major, one captain and two privates were absent by leave. The 33rd's full strength in July 1775, including the absentees, was therefore one colonel, one lieutenant colonel, one major, eight captains, 11 lieutenants, eight ensigns, one chaplain, one adjutant, one quartermaster, one surgeon, one surgeon's mate, 20 sergeants, 30 corporals, 12 drummers, and 318 privates. Excluding the ancillary staff – and bearing in mind corporals were counted among the rank-and-file during the period – the regimental strength thus stood at 30 officers, 20 sergeants, 12 drummers and 348 rank-and-file.

These numbers would increase as the year progressed and the 33rd conducted frenetic recruiting activity in an effort to reach the full establishment strength. A total of 89 men joined the regiment between June and September 1775, an average of eight or nine men per company. Of these recruits, 66 were Irishmen, showing that the regiment was recruiting locally and at a fearsome pace. On the whole this intake of new men would have diluted the age and experience of the regiment, but it is not clear that all the men had no prior military service, so it is difficult to quantify. This sudden increase came on top of the fact that the regiment as a whole had a relatively large number of new or recent inductees. In 1772 the regiment carried out a spate of particularly vigorous recruiting, bringing the number of soldiers aged between 18 and 25 from approximately 32 percent of the regiment's total strength to 60 percent.[5] In 1775, of the 380 privates, drummers and NCOs, 260 were aged 25 or under. Despite the regiment's youthfulness, in mid-1775 59 percent, a total of 227 men, had still served in the army for at least five years. The most experienced soldier in the regiment, a sergeant in Captain Dansey's company, had spent 25 years in the military. At the opposite end of the spectrum, there were 44 men (11 percent) spread across the regiment who had served for only a year or less. The regiment's rank-and-file were therefore generally young by period standards – in their early-to-mid-twenties – and without lengthy service, but nor were they wholly without experience. It is also noteworthy that in 1769 14 percent of the regiment's total had served 15 years or more, and that figure remained largely consistent at 16 percent in 1775. This implies that there was a cadre of long-serving men which remained consistent over the seven periods surveyed, and which likely provided the core from which sergeants and corporals were drawn. [6] These NCOs ultimately went and served with their men during the opening campaigns in America, with 75 percent of sergeants from seven of the regiment's companies in 1774 still serving in July of 1776, providing a core of battlefield leadership to the younger recruits.[7]

Regarding the officers, the cadre established by 1775 also remained consistent upon deployment to America – approximately 85 percent of

5 Lodge, *To What Extent*, p.29.
6 Lodge, *To What Extent*, p.18.
7 Lodge, *To What Extent*, p.35.

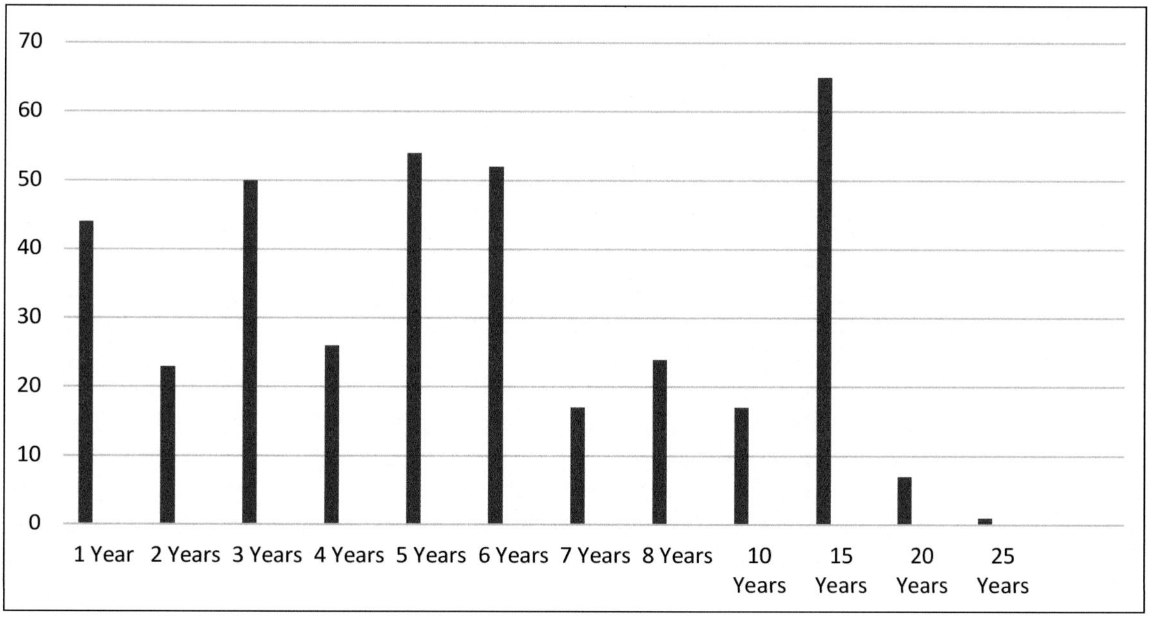

Years of service in the 33rd by number of men, 1775.

those serving in Ireland were still with the regiment on its first campaigns.[8] Cornwallis appears to have implemented minor changes within the regiment's command structure prior to embarking in 1776. Of the company commanders on parade in July 1775, seven out of 10 would still be leading their companies (albeit nominally in the case of Colonel Cornwallis himself) by the time of the New York campaign of 1776. Major Creed left the service in 1776, his role in the regiment taken on by Captain John Yorke of the grenadier company, while Captain Burnett of the light company was replaced, as we shall see, by Captain Dansey. The only other change in the company command structure of the loss of Captain Acland. The wealthy young officer transferred to the 20th Foot not long before the 33rd sailed for America. No reason was given, though it might be inferred that the well-connected gentleman, with his uncommonly rapid rise through the regiment and his history of agitating for even higher commands, did not fit well with the 33rd's officer culture or the cadre Cornwallis was looking to build and maintain within his regiment.

Certainly, Cornwallis took a close, active interest in the structure of his regiment at every level. In a letter written in 1771 to Captain Sackville Turner, the colonel specified that he was 'very anxious' to make a sergeant, George Ward, 'Qr Master [Quartermaster], Fielding will succeed him, I shall then have rewarded my three best serj:s. [*sic*]'[9] He also informed Turner that 'you shall certainly have Celler's company, Burnett will be glad of the Light Infantry.'[10] Ward did indeed become the regiment's quartermaster,

8 Lodge, *To What Extent*, p.33.

9 Charles Cornwallis to Sackville Turner, 15 March 1771, from a letter sold at auction on 27 June 2015 by Goldberg Coins & Collectibles (Lot 276).

10 Charles Cornwallis to Sackville Turner, 15 March 1771.

receiving his ensigncy in 1776 and a lieutenancy in 1778, while Turner and Burnett did get the companies that Cornwallis specified, prior to Burnett's later dismissal from the light company. In this way we see the colonel managing his subordinates, not only fellow-officers but also the regiment's non-commissioned officers – he was aware, and mindful, of who the best sergeants here.

An even more potent example of Cornwallis's desire to closely handle his regiment's officer corps came in 1774. In what seems to have been a fairly extraordinary exchange during a visit to the War Office, Cornwallis went head-to-head with the Secretary at War over the appointment of the 33rd's new lieutenant colonel;

> His Lordship [Cornwallis] applied that Major [James] Webster might have leave to purchase the Lieutenant Colonelcy. After the usual polite compliments of a courtier, Lord Barrington the Secretary at War, insinuated that Major Norton,[11] was the first on the list for preferment, and being an older Major, and an officer of distinguished merit and interest, could not be passed by. To this Lord Cornwallis replied, that he had no doubt of Major Norton's merit, but that he had a value for Major Webster, whose merit he had long been witness to; that the regiment was going to Ireland, where he could not attend it himself, on account of his duty in Parliament; and that he chose it should be under the direction of an officer whom the regiment knew and esteemed. The Secretary expressed his regret, that it could not be as his Lordship wished. When the Earl found what he had urged did not make the proper impression, he told the Secretary with a firmness that staggered him, that if Major Webster was not appointed Lieut. Colonel, he might also look out for another Colonel. This settled the business, and Major Webster was Lieutenant Colonel of the 33d April the 9th, 1774.[12]

The second son of the Reverend Dr Webster of Edinburgh, James Webster had initially intended to study law, but his friends helped him to purchase a commission in the 33rd. Much like William Dansey and his father, he served in Germany with the regiment during the Seven Years War and became the 33rd's major in March 1771. We have already seen that Dansey had a low opinion of Webster, at least prior to his service in America, but Cornwallis was impressed with Webster's competency and character, and his decision to back him was well rewarded. Webster was remembered as a man 'of a serious and religious turn of mind; and in general had great command over himself.'[13] An account written in 1781 recalled an incident between the 33rd's lieutenant colonel and an unnamed officer who had committed some form of offence. Webster;

---

11 Major Chapel Norton was indeed 'reckoned an excellent officer' – he went on to command a company in the Coldstream Guards and served in America during the Revolution.

12 Anon., 'For the Political Magazine', *The Political Magazine and Parliamentary, Naval, Military, and Literary Journal*, 1781, vol.II, pp.341–343.

13 Anon., 'For the Political Magazine', p.342.

> Ordered him [the offender] to be sent for, but feeling his passion rising, he said to a gentleman present, 'I will endeavour to be quite calm.' However the sight of so odious a delinquent overcame all his resolves, and even made him, for some minutes, forget his religious habits, for he swore very heartily at the offender, and immediately had him turned out of the regiment.[14]

It is notable that after sailing for America, only two of the 17 captains who served over the next six years had purchased commissions into the 33rd from other regiments (Charles Eustace in 1777 and Allan Malcolm in 1780), the rest were all promoted or purchased their commissions from within. Thanks in large part to Cornwallis the 33rd was therefore able to maintain a coherent and familiar management team that seems to have functioned well throughout the entirety of the conflict.

The regimental inspection return of 1775 offers a further wealth of data when it comes to painting a picture of the 33rd in the middle of that year. Their rank-and-file consisted of 316 Englishmen, five Scots, 58 Irish and one listed as a 'foreigner.' It is interesting to note that, despite having spent a year in Ireland, the number of Irish recruits was not especially high until the post-inspection recruiting drive added another 66 Irish recruits, and the unit seems to have maintained its close links with Yorkshire. The total percentage of Irishmen in the regiment following the final recruiting spree before embarkation was 26 percent. The height of the men varied between one who was 6'1, and the 49 who were listed as 'under 5'6.' A majority of the men stood between 5'6 and 5'8 tall, with a rough average of slightly above 5'6. This was a little shorter than the period average, so the 33rd as a whole appeared slightly on the short side, a fact noted by Lieutenant General Irvine. The light and grenadier companies lived up to their stereotypes, with the lights having the joint-most men under 5'6 (eight), and the shortest company average of about 5'6 and no man over 5'7, while the grenadiers had the tallest company with an average height of slightly over 5'10, including the first, second and third tallest enlisted men in the regiment.[15]

During the review Irwin described the officers as 'remarkably steady and attentive,' as well as 'properly armed' and making 'a very good appearance.' The sergeants were 'clean and well dressed and very attentive.' The drummers and fifers likewise, and were said to 'beat and play very well.' The enlisted men were noted to be 'not of a great size, but of good countenances, young and well made.' They were 'extremely well dressed and clean, silent, steady, and very attentive.' Their hats were 'well put on, and agreeable to the King's Regulations, black gaiters according to orders.' The clothing in general was 'good and well fitted,' the accoutrements 'good.'[16] All things being told, once the 33rd received their new shipment of short land pattern muskets they were fit for service.

In late November news began to break about the regiment's fate. Orders were published instructing 'all officers belonging to his Majesty's 33d

14 Anon., 'For the Political Magazine', p.342.
15 TNA: WO 12/4803/1: Muster books 33rd Foot.
16 TNA: WO 12/4803/1: Muster books 33rd Foot.

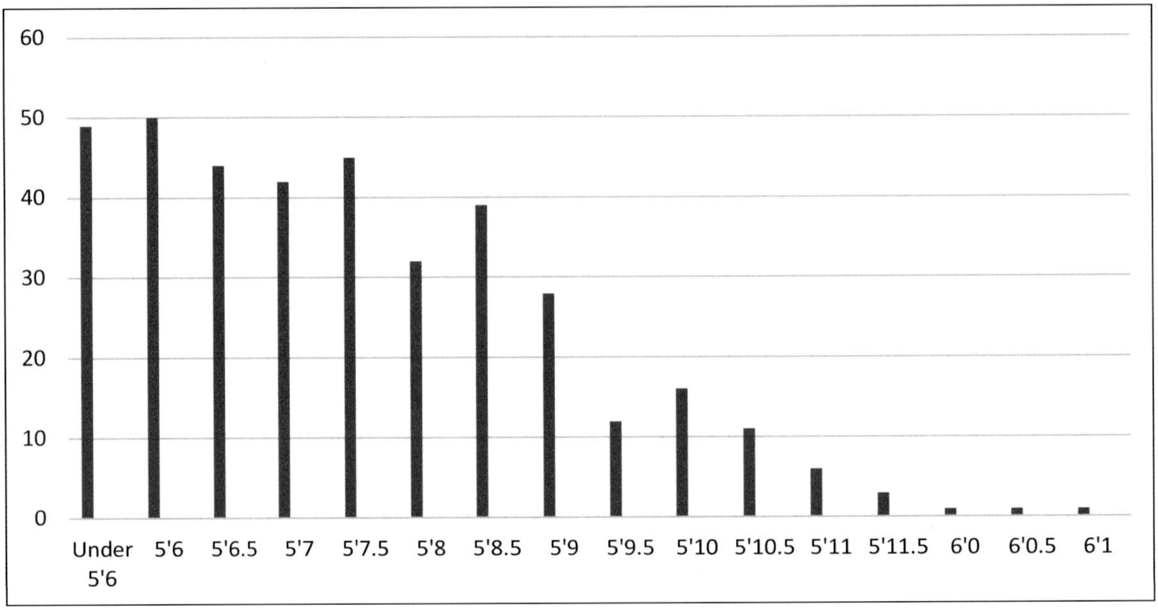

Height of the 33rd by number of men, 1775.

regiment of foot, now serving in Ireland, to immediately repair to their corps in the kingdom, except such as belong to the additional [recruiting] companies of that regiment, or may be employed in Ireland on the recruiting service.'[17] The *London Post* recorded that 'the 33d regiment of foot, of which Lord Cornwallis is Colonel, is ordered for America.'[18] The movement came somewhat abruptly, and may have related to the desire to keep the 33rd with Cornwallis, who was to head a British reinforcement set to sail from Cork. The 33rd displaced the 53rd Regiment on the expedition, even going so far as to sail with the 53rd's camp equipage, though the officers had their own tents. An invoice, provided by one John Trotter and dated to the same day that notice of the 33rd's deployment was printed in the newspapers, shows that 18 tents plus the necessary ropes, painted poles and valises were provided to the captains and subalterns of the regiment for a total sum of a little over £310.[19]

Ahead of overseas service, Cornwallis further enhanced his regiment by having cloaks made for each man, even the rank-and-file. Treasury out letters from Ireland on 1 June 1775 record '1,924 yards of coarse twilled kerseys to make cloaks for the Regiment, provided by Earl Cornwallis.'[20] On 5 December 1775 a further letter was written 'To the Right Honble, The Ld & Commr of his Majesty's Treasury, Memorial of earl Cornwallis, Col of the 33d Regt of Foot, Sheweth that he has caused 600 yards of coarse twilled kersey to be sent from Scotland to Dublin for furnishing cloaks for the soldiers of

17 *London Chronicle*, 30 November 1775, p.9
18 *London Evening Post*, 30 November 1775, p.9.
19 Clements Library, University of Michigan (CL): Henry Clinton Papers: Volume 12, f.18. Courtesy of Jason R. Wickersty.
20 Strachan, *British Military Uniforms*, p.223.

Sometimes described as 'Portuguese cloaks,' the fact that even enlisted men in the 33rd were so equipped indicates the amount of effort Cornwallis was willing to put into his regiment. (Photo by Henry Gage)

the regt under his command.'[21] Such extra clothing can only have further enhanced the regiment's standing, and goes some way to explaining why, as we shall see, the 33rd were considered an exceptionally well equipped corps.

Prior to departure two dragoons from the 5th Dragoons and another two from the 13th Light Dragoons were drafted into the 33rd to help with bringing them up to strength, a far lower number of drafts than the other regiments embarking, who each required an average of 82 men to boost their numbers. The 33rd took none from other infantry regiments.[22] The force that embarked totalled 29 officers and staff, 20 sergeants, 18 drummers, 390 rank-and-file and 42 recruits, the only regiment among those set to embark to have any of the latter listed. There were also 60 women and 12 children.[23]

The 33rd were divided between four transports, which they boarded on 30 December 1775. Three companies were assigned to the *Nancy of London*, three to the *Michel and Mary*, two to the *Golden Rule,* and two to the *Jenny*.[24] Between receiving the orders to make for Cork and embarkation at the end of December, only 10 members of the regiment were listed as deserting, a much lower number than any of the other regiments on the expedition. By way of contrast, the 57th Foot reported that 42 men had deserted, and the 15th Foot 48. Among those who abandoned the 33rd before they sailed for

21 TNA: T14/15: 5 December 1775, p.368.
22 TNA: SP 63/451: ff.128.
23 TNA: SP 63/451: ff.131, 132, 133, 134, 135.
24 TNA: SP: 63/451: ff.140, 141, 142.

war, none were older than the age of 30. Notably, two were only 16, and were acquaintances of one another – Robert Clarke and Roger Shepard. Both were from Middleton, and had enlisted together just three months earlier, in September 1775. Doubtless regretting their choice, they deserted together on 19 December.[25]

On 13 December five companies led by Cornwallis passed through Kilkenny from Dublin, on their way to the port of Cork. The regiment's five other companies followed the next day, the regiment manoeuvring in its familiar fashion, by two grand divisions. An anonymous 'constant Reader, and Admirer of Real Merit' in the Public Advertiser wrote that the regiment's deployment was 'at the request of the Right Hon. Colonel who commands it … they now go out of their Turn, from an *honourable Zeal* to support the Dignity and Rights of this Country over her ungrateful colonies.'[26]

25 TNA: SP 63/451: ff.140, 141, 142. It is unclear if this is Middleton, near Manchester in England, or more likely perhaps Middleton, near Cork in Ireland – if it was the latter they likely simply went home on their way to embarkation.

26 *Public Advertiser*, 11 December 1775, p.3.

Chapter 5

Going to the Devil

The Voyage

The 33rd Regiment suffered its first casualty of the American War while still in Ireland, at the beginning of 1776. Captain George Burnett, commander of the regiment's light company, was informed that he would not be leading his men in America. As part of Cornwallis's ongoing minor adjustments of the regiment's command staff in preparation for overseas service, Burnett, who had been with the army for 15 years, was judged unsuitable for what was considered to be one of the most active combat roles. He was transferred to one of the Additional Companies and would remain behind in Britain overseeing regimental recruitment.

After writing a letter to a friend and leaving it in his lodgings, George Burnett committed suicide by jumping from the quay into the sea. The incident was described by Captain William Dansey, the man Burnett had been ousted in favour of, in letters to his mother and fiancé: 'I have succeeded at last to my long wish'd for Post the Company of Light Infantry but upon a most melancholy Occasion,' he wrote.[1]

As was so often the case for officers, Burnett's last concerns and Dansey's first were related to finances. 'A Hardship upon me in Money Matters I have now two Companys upon Hand and each £100 in Debt and I can't clear the Debt of my Battalion Company,' wrote Dansey.[2] He contacted his mother, Martha Dansey Dansey, asking for her 'to sell two or three hundred pounds Stock,'[3] to be delivered to a Mr. Meyrick, the 33rd's regimental agent, a financier who 'dealt with post, supplies to the Regiment and individuals, banking, prize money.'[4]

Time was pressing. The 33rd was preparing to sail for America, and certain action, with a powerful convoy assembling in Cork harbour. Lord Cornwallis and the commodore in command of the accompanying fleet, Sir

1 Dansey (ed.), *Captured Rebel Flag*, p.7.
2 Dansey (ed.), *Captured Rebel Flag*, p.8.
3 Dansey (ed.), *Captured Rebel Flag*, p.9.
4 Dansey (ed.), *Captured Rebel Flag*, p.45.

Peter Parker, overcame 'adverse winds and tempestuous weather' to arrive on the night of 5 January, amidst the ongoing preparations.[5] Dansey visited Cornwallis the next morning to enquire about the fleet's hospital ship, *Pigot*. Six days later he boarded another ship, the *Golden Rule*, where the 33rd's light company were ensconced, and introduced himself to his new command, 'the most flattering Post I cou'd have in the whole Armament.'[6] That same day the unfortunate Captain Burnett's effects were sold. 'I don't know when I shall cease being in a hurry,' Dansey wrote to his fiancé, Catherine Malet, 'but you shall have one long letter before we sail.'[7]

Besides having to try and balance the books of both his new company and his old, Dansey had two new officers, Lieutenant Richard Cotton and Ensign Thomas Gorges, to meet with. In this particular case, it seems to have been more of a reunion. Dansey was already friends with both men, and their progress through their commissions gives a good example of how the process worked throughout the army as a whole. Dansey had purchased his captain's commission in the 33rd from Thomas Duke in 1774. This left behind a lieutenant's vacancy, which Richard Cotton purchased, rising from his existing rank of ensign, which he had held since the age of just 14. This in turn left an ensign role in the 33rd vacant, which allowed Thomas Gorges to buy into the regiment. It seems that all three men were known to each other outside the military. Gorges appears to have owned a property at Eye in Dansey's native Herefordshire (not to be confused with Cornwallis's parliamentary constituency of Eye in Suffolk), and the name appears alongside Dansey's in a declaration of loyalty sent to the King in 1775, backing his stance over the rebellion in the colonies. Cotton, meanwhile, was from the nearby county of Cheshire, and was the younger brother to Sir Robert Salusbury Cotton, 5th Baronet. 'I am now on board with Mr. Cotton I expect soon to have Mr. Gorges in the Light Company,' Dansey wrote, hinting at Cornwallis's ongoing reshuffle of the officer cadre, 'and then we three Welshmen shall have the Honor to ourselves.'[8]

With peers from the Herefordshire and Cheshire gentry, Dansey had a close support network while leading the 33rd's light company, but he also had the direct assistance of his servant. It was not uncommon for officers on all sides during the American Revolution to take on soldiers in such a role. The British Army permitted up to two servants per captain and one per lieutenant or ensign. Due to the fact that soldiers were often at liberty to pursue other trades in their spare time, such a job was not unusual. In exchange for the additional work of assisting their officer they received roughly a shilling a week on top of their regular pay, meaning that each was earning at least a

5 Anon., 'Precis Prepared for the King of the Events Leading up to the Expedition against the Southern Colonies', in Bell Clark (ed.), *Naval Documents of the American Revolution* (Washington DC: U.S. Government Printing Office, 1969) vol.4, p.944.

6 Dansey (ed.), *Captured Rebel Flag*, p.9.

7 Dansey (ed.), *Captured Rebel Flag*, p.8.

8 Dansey (ed.), *Captured Rebel Flag*, p.10. While Herefordshire and Cheshire are in England, they share their borders with Wales, and many of their inhabitants appear to have identified themselves as Welsh during the eighteenth century.

third more than their base pay.[9] Dansey's servant, however, does not appear to have been a soldier, but the son of a family known to the Danseys back in Herefordshire, quite probably one working in some capacity for Martha, William's mother. Referred to only as Ben, he was described during the preparations in Cork as 'a very good Boy and cou'd he but write he wou'd be a very valuable Servant.'[10] Ben likely 'received food, lodging and probably clothes at his employer's expense,' and made about two guineas annually.[11]

Dansey confided in his letters home that 'we expect to sail the Beginning of next week but where nobody can guess.'[12] The truth was that it was not only the captain of the 33rd's light company who felt as though he was beset by troubles. The expedition amassing at Cork had been plagued by logistical issues and delays caused by bad weather. The transport ships in question, vital for the ferrying of men and supplies to the theatres of operations in the colonies, were privately owned vessels of all shapes and sizes, contracted for by the Royal Navy. Most were able to carry two or three companies. Military planners had anticipated that the fleet would be underway in December, yet even by early February the ships were still sheltering from winter squalls in the Cove of Cork. This particular port, on the south-east coast of Ireland, had long been a hub for British forces enroute to the American colonies. It was described by John Robert Shaw as 'perhaps the most spacious and commodious haven in the world. The entrance is safe, and the whole navy of England might ride in it, secure from every wind that blows.'[13]

At the opposite end of the spectrum from Dansey, Shaw recalled his first experiences of a long voyage by sea with the 33rd. Although he enlisted after the regiment had sailed from Cork, his detachment of recruits were marched to Portsmouth once they had completed their training at Chatham, two years after the 33rd had first sailed for America, in 1778. 'The cries and lamentations of the poor raw country soldiers were sufficient to have excited compassion in the breast of the rudest barbarian,' Shaw recalled. 'As for myself, I thought I was going to the Devil, when they rolled us down the hatchways, like so much lumber. Having each received some bedding, and an allowance of provisions, we lay promiscuously, crowded together in the utmost confusion.'[14]

Shaw's transport sailed first from Portsmouth to the Isle of Wight and remained there for four weeks, likely awaiting favourable conditions. They then carried on bound for Cork, but had not gone 12 hours 'before we were surprised with a thunder storm and contrary wind.' In the darkness 'a man on the forecastle espied a rock,' and the ship was brought about. 'And so,' wrote Shaw, 'by the skill and dexterity of the mariners and the mercy of Providence, we were preserved from being wrecked on the rocks of Scilly.'[15] Unfortunately this did not apply to all the ships in the convoy – one ship, the

---

9 Hagist, *Noble Volunteers*, pp.32–33.
10 Dansey (ed.), *Captured Rebel Flag*, p.9.
11 Dansey (ed.), *Captured Rebel Flag*, p.53.
12 Dansey (ed.), *Captured Rebel Flag*, p.10.
13 Shaw, *A Narrative*, p.16.
14 Shaw, *A Narrative*, p.15.
15 Shaw, *A Narrative*, pp.15–16. The Scilly Isles lie off the south-west tip of Cornwall, England.

Rockingham, was wrecked with the loss of all hands as it later tried to enter the Cove of Cork.

On 29 September 1775 Cornwallis was promoted major general, ensuring he would be among the most senior British officers in North America. On 12 February 1776, the expedition including Dansey and the main body of the 33rd finally set sail. A totally of 44 ships, including frigates, troop transports, victuallers loaded with supplies, ordnance vessels and a hospital ship, set out into the Atlantic carrying in their midst seven regiments of infantry. Their objective, initially known only to the senior officers, was to rendezvous with another, smaller British force sent from Boston off the largest natural harbour in North Carolina, Cape Fear, and trigger a Loyalist uprising in the southern colonies.

War Office orders for the voyage were brusque and practical. No smoking was permitted below decks, and gambling and the distribution of spirits and liquors was forbidden. When putting into harbour, soldiers were only allowed on shore with the permission of an officer, and even then only when accompanied by an non-commissioned officer 'who is to be answerable for their Conduct whilst on shore.' To help check disease 'every Morning all the Men be brought upon Deck, the Births cleaned, and the Bedding brought up to air, if the Weather will permit ... as many Men as possible be kept on Deck during the day-time.'[16]

The strain of a long, arduous Atlantic crossing undoubtedly told on those required to undertake it. During a separate voyage with the 9th Foot, Roger Lamb recorded in his journal how 'a soldier whose name was Brooks, leaped off the forecastle into the ocean; the vessel in a moment made her way over him, and he arose at her stern. He immediately with all his might, swam from the ship.' Incredibly, Brooks was successfully recovered and placed under arrest. 'The fear of punishment was the cause of this desperate action,' Lamb wrote. 'The day before he had stolen a shirt from one of his messmates knapsacks.' Similarly, 10 days later, 'a sergeant had an altercation with his wife while they were sitting at breakfast, in consequence of which he got up in a rage, leaped overboard and was seen no more.' Another three days later 'one of the recruits, standing on the forecastle was so provoked by his comrades, that in a fit of rage he jumped over board, uttering at the same time dreadful curses upon them. He was swallowed up by the great deep in a moment!'[17]

The fate of the fleet carrying the 33rd was even more arduous than Lamb's passage. A few days after setting sail 'they met with a violent gale of wind at South West, which dispersed the whole fleet & forced back, into different ports several of the Transports and Storeships, disabled & distressed.'[18] On 7 March Cornwallis wrote a letter to the Secretary of State for America, George Germain, from onboard the flagship *Bristol*, reporting 'that our Voyage

16 TNA: WO 26/29: pp.156–157, 'Orders and Instructions for His Majesty's 33d Regiment of Foot, commanded by Major General Earl Cornwallis, on their embarking for North America.'

17 Roger Lamb, *An Original and Authentic Journal of Occurrences During the Late American War From Its Commencement to the Year 1783* (Dublin: Wilkinson and Courtney, 1809), pp.66–67.

18 Anon., 'Precis Prepared for the King of the Events Leading up to the Expedition against the Southern Colonies', p.944.

hitherto has been very unsuccessfull [*sic*], the wind has been almost always contrary & 'till the first of this month constant & most violent gales of Wind, we now have but fourteen sail in Company with us ... of the fourteen there are but six or seven transports with troops ... Your Lordship will make allowances for the motion of the Ship when you are decyphering this scrawl.'[19] The vessels of the fleet found themselves driven back variously to Portsmouth, Plymouth, Falmouth, Kingroad and Cork, or scattered upon the high seas. Those that could, pressed on to the rendezvous point off Cape Fear.

One of the transports carrying part of the 33rd, accompanied by the frigate *Acteon*, stopped at the small Atlantic island of Madeira, where they were able to send word that they would be able to make the rendezvous, and that 'The Men & Officers on board [are] all well.'[20] During his later voyage, Shaw and the 33rd's newly trained recruits likewise found their fleet stopping off at Madeira, where they 'got in exchange for such necessaries as we could spare, oranges, cocoa-nuts and pine-apples.'[21]

The smaller expedition sent from Boston, commanded by Major General Sir Henry Clinton, arrived off Cape Fear on 12 March to two pieces of unwelcome news. Firstly, it was reported that the hoped-for Loyalist uprising in the south had begun prematurely, and had already met with disaster at the battle of Moore's Creek Bridge on 27 February. Secondly, and perhaps even more ominously, there was no sign of the fleet expected from Cork.

Clinton spent a fretful month in the mouth of the Fear River, 'casting an anxious Eye every day towards the cape, in expectation of a signal for the Fleet.'[22] Eventually, on 18 April, the first bedraggled ships from the Cork convoy arrived. They continued to trail in for the next two weeks, the 33rd among them. The captain of the sloop *Cruizer*, Francis Parry, recorded in his ship's journal that at midday on 20 April there 'came in a transport with part of the 33d Regiment.'[23] Cornwallis himself arrived on 3 May.

It was as the fleet continued to collect itself that the 33rd experienced their first combat – and won their first action – of the war. At daybreak on 24 April the *Golden Rule*, transporting Captain Dansey, his light company, and another company of the regiment, sighted a sail on the horizon off Cape Romain, South Carolina. She was the *Defiance*, a rebel-owned sloop that had set sail from Providence, Rhode Island on 30 March, bound for Charleston. In her hold were 700 gallons of rum, 50 casks of cider, six barrels of oil, 30 boxes of candles, 237 bunches of onions, 1,000 pounds of chocolate and 1,000 pounds of coffee.[24]

---

19 Charles Cornwallis, 'On board the Bristol March 7th 1776', in Bell Clark (ed.), *Naval Documents*, vol.4, p.952.

20 John Boddington, 'John Boddington to John Pownall', in Bell Clark (ed.), *Naval Documents*, vol.4, p.1076.

21 Shaw, *A Narrative*, p.15.

22 Henry Clinton, 'Narrative of Sir Henry Clinton' in Bell Clark (ed.), *Naval Documents*, vol.4, p.876.

23 Francis Parry, 'Journal of H.M. Sloop *Cruizer*' in Bell Clark (ed.), *Naval Documents*, vol.4, p.1348.

24 Anon., 'Account of Permissions Granted by His Honor the Governor' in Bell Clark (ed.), *Naval Documents*, vol.4, 1969), p.1480.

The *Golden Rule* gave chase. After several cannon shots and a pursuit of half an hour, the *Defiance* was overhauled. Likely not wanting to face almost a hundred British regulars acting as marines, the master of the rebel ship, Captain John Chace, struck his colours and surrendered. The prize was 'carried into Cape Fear River to General Clinton.'[25] The goods seized by the 33rd, amounting to 500 pounds sterling, left Clinton in something of a quandary. The general wrote to his superior, General William Howe, that 'as the Gentlemen of the Navy seem to express a doubt whether she can be condemned to the Military I have thought it my duty to lay it before Your Excellency and the Commander in Chief at Sea; till such time as I receive your Commands; The Money arising from the Sale will remain in the hands of the Agent appointed by the Captors.'[26] For his own part, Dansey almost neglected to mention the excitement of the sloop's capture. He alerted his mother that 'the Newspapers will inform you of having taken a Prize at Sea.' More pressing, it seemed, was his report that he had almost 'lost poor Ben on the Passage but he is now got pretty well and is a good Boy.'[27]

The regiment was largely assembled by early May, and donned their new, annual clothing, presenting perhaps the smartest and most uniform appearance they would throughout the entire conflict.[28] Operations now began in earnest along the Cape Fear region. Clinton had been landing and drilling troops on the coast, out of range of the rebel marksmen who haunted the interior. The 33rd, having spent the better part of four months in the stinking, swaying, claustrophobic confines of their transport ships, were likely thankful to be able to return to dry land, if only for brief spells. It was not long before they experienced their first military actions on American soil.

On 11 May Clinton authorised a raid upriver to be conducted by the 33rd and 37th Foot and the light company of the 44th. Muffling their oars to disguise their movements on the water, they came ashore at 2:00 or 3:00 a.m. at Kendal Plantation, the home of Continental Army officer Robert Howe, a senior North Carolina revolutionary. During the seizure of the plantation rebel forces skirmished with the raiding party, resulting in two men killed and several wounded. In the darkness and confusion, a sergeant of the 33rd was also taken prisoner. In response, several women staying at the plantation were wounded, and the plantation itself was torched, with Howe's freed slaves assisting in its destruction. The expedition then carried on to the nearby Orton mill, where 90 men of the 1st North Carolina Regiment were stationed. Alerted to the British approach, the Continentals withdrew.[29] The mill, like the plantation, was burned, and the regulars returned to their boats

25 *Edinburgh Advertiser*, 30 July 1776.

26 Henry Clinton, 'Cape Fear River April 29th 1776' in Bell Clark (ed.), *Naval Documents*, vol.4, p.1321; *Edinburgh Advertiser*, 30 July 1776.

27 Dansey (ed.), *Captured Rebel Flag*, p.11.

28 DHS: Dansey Letters: 'The 33d. Regiment was paid for their Clothing of 74.'

29 Robert M. Dunkerly, *Redcoats on the Cape Fear: The Revolutionary War in Southeastern North Carolina* (Jefferson: McFarland, 2012), p.79.

with five prisoners and, according to Howe, his plantation's 'chairs, tables, glasses, china and plate … suppos'd to amount to £1500.'[30]

After this first taste of action, the regiment disembarked again near the mouth of the Fear River on 15 May and 'encamped near a demolished post opposite our shipping.'[31] This post was Fort Johnston, which overlooked Bald Head Island and the entrance to the Fear River. Burned by the rebels in 1775, its remains had been used by revolutionary riflemen to target Clinton's shipping anchored nearby. The marksmen and a detachment of the 1st North Carolina Continentals withdrew from the fort prior to the massed British landing.

On 17 May the 33rd combined with the 27th Foot in another expedition upriver. Penetrating 15 miles into what few would have denied was hostile territory, they 'dispossessed the rebels of a post they had at that place called Brunswick. They took a few prisoners, and had one man killed; after executing this business, they returned to the ships a reasonable supply of 20 bullocks.'[32] The man killed, seemingly, was not a member of the 33rd. Brunswick, which had already been torched by a British landing party in February, was burned for a second time. The regiment continued to conduct minor foraging operations while remaining alert for the enemy's presence. An officer in the 15th Foot, encamped with the 33rd, reported that 'part of the rebels are within two or three miles of us, but their strongest post, or chief dependence, is at Wilmington, about 20 miles from hence.'[33]

It was during this period that the 33rd suffered its first injury due to enemy action in America. Rebel forces attacked British sentries under cover of darkness, and it fell to Dansey's company to be the first of the 33rd to be hit in such a manner. James Wilcox of the light company was on sentry duty at 11:00 p.m. when a trio of rebels approached his post secretly, on their hands and knees. Wilcox, alert to his duty, spotted the ambushers and fired on them, but as he hurried to reload they closed the distance and returned fire. Wilcox was hit in the wrist, his assailants fleeing. The injury initially seemed bad enough to require amputation, but such a drastic measure proved unnecessary. Dansey described the event and its aftermath in a letter to his mother, reporting that;

> I believe his [Wilcox's] Father lives near you, at first we were afraid he wou'd loose his Hand but I hope he is now near well and will be able to do his Duty again and have his Revenge, he is a fine spirited lad and vows it, I went on board the Hospital Ship several times to see him 'till he was out of Danger, he is the first Man wounded in our Regiment, and in my Company, I wish I had some more of my Countrymen I wou'd see what Blood old Cider makes.[34]

30 'The Lee Papers, Volume 1, 1754–1776' in Anon. (ed.), *Collections of New York Historical Society for the Year 1871* (New York: New York Historical Society, 1872), p.402. The Lee Family Papers are now held by Stanford University: Special Collections M0220.

31 *London Evening Post*, 6 August 1776, p.4.

32 *Lloyd's Evening Post and British Chronicle,* August 5 to August 7, 1776, p.3.

33 *London Evening Post*, 6 August 1776, p.4.

34 Dansey (ed.), *Captured Rebel Flag*, p.12. Dansey is referring to the cider-making, and drinking, that Herefordshire was, and is, known for.

Though Wilcox avoided amputation, the injury was bad enough to see him discharged and going before the Chelsea pension board in 1777.

As their men probed the interior for supplies and resistance, the British expedition's senior commanders debated the next course of action. The capture of the sloop *Defiance* by Dansey had not only resulted in a haul of chocolate, coffee and onions. It had also brought vital, if chilling, intelligence. The seized crewmen reported that the British Army had abandoned Boston. After almost a year of siege, the city was evacuated on 17 March 1776. There was now no major British military presence in America north of Florida and south of Quebec.

Clinton's superiors had told him that if he deemed that success was unlikely or would be incurred with too great a loss he was to give up on the southern expedition and 'proceed immediately to join Major General Howe.'[35] That was reckoning without the input of the British royal governors of the who had been recently dispossessed of their holdings and had since joined the expedition seeking redress. The governor of Virginia, the Earl of Dunmore, pleaded with Clinton to take his forces to drive the rebels from that oldest colony, while the governor of South Carolina, William Campbell, demanded that intervention should occur in his colony.[36] In Campbell's favour was the fact that Charleston was one of the most vital ports in North America, and its defences were unfinished. Campbell's arguments won out. At the end of May the regulars reboarded their transports and the now-reassembled fleet set sail once more. On 1 June they arrived off Charleston.

The 33rd's first campaign in America was underway.

35 Anon., 'Precis Prepared for the King of the Events Leading up to the Expedition against the Southern Colonies', p.944.

36 Christopher Ward, *The War of the Revolution* (New York: The MacMillan Company, 1952), vol.2, p.670.

Chapter 6

These Feats of War

1776

Almost since ousting their royal governor, the people of Charleston had been struggling to prepare their city for the inevitable riposte. While the defences were still far from complete, they were not wholly negligible. As the British expedition was to find out, the coast of South Carolina itself presented something of an obstacle to seaborne invasion. The area around Charleston was fringed by sandy islands cut up by creeks and swamps, often shielded too by stands of palmetto trees and thickets of myrtle.[1] This febrile landscape bordered onto Charleston harbour, which was flanked to the north by Sullivan's Island and the south by James Island. Nor were these the only points that had to be navigated, for a ship approaching the inner harbour first had to pass the submerged sandbanks of Charleston Bar. An anchorage called Five Fathom Hole stood between the bar and Morris Island – shipping was required to head north then turn west through a narrow channel. A shoal named Middle Ground projected out from James Island, forcing shipping to pass by the southern end of Sullivan's Island.[2]

It was this southern tip of the island overlooking the outer entrance to Charleston harbour that the city's defenders decided to utilise. In February construction was started on what would go on to become Fort Moultrie, named after its commander, Continental Army officer William Moultrie. Built from sand and palmetto logs, it was well-placed to protect Charleston from a seaborne invasion. A vessel was forced to approach bow-first, then turn to port, leaving her stern exposed to the fort as she passed by.[3]

By late June the palmetto walls were 16 feet wide, filled with sand, and rose 10 feet high. A timber palisade protected a rudimentary powder magazine, while an eclectic mix of 9 and 12-pounder cannon, and larger English

1 Ward, *The War*, vol.2, p.671.

2 Jim Stokeley, *Fort Moultrie: Constant Defender* (Washington DC: US Department of the Interior, 1985), p.14.

3 Stokeley, *Fort Moultrie*, p.15.

18-pounders and French 26-pounders provided the fort with its firepower.[4] While William Moultrie was confident in his ability to defend it, the overall commander of the rebel forces in Charleston, Major General Charles Lee, doubted the fort could provide much resistance.

The defences would soon be put to the test. The British fleet arrived off the coast, crossing Charleston Bar and anchoring at Five Fathom Hole. On 9 June Clinton began landing men on Long Island, just north of Sullivan Island. By 10 June the fleet's flagship and the last of the deep-draft transports had crossed the bar.[5] The 33rd were among the forces that disembarked on Long Island. They soon found just how inimical the place was. An officer of another regiment sharing the island wrote;

> We have been encamped on this island for this month past, and have lived upon nothing else but salt pork and pease. We sleep upon the sea shore, nothing to shelter us from the violent rains, but our coats or miserable paltry blankets. There is nothing that grows upon this island, it being a mere sand bank, and a few bushes which harbour millions of musketoes, a greater plague than there can be in hell itself … The oldest of the officers do not remember of ever undergoing such hardships as we have done since our arrival here.[6]

The 33rd endured these miserable conditions as the British continued their slow build-up. On 20 June Cornwallis took the 33rd and the rest of the brigade under his command on his first independent expedition of the Revolutionary War, marching them to the southern end of Long Island. Here it was separated from the northern end of Sullivan's Island by a narrow stretch of water known as the Breach. It was believed that the channel was fordable, with Clinton convinced that at ebb tide the water did not reach higher than half a yard. To defend Sullivan Island's northern end from a possible British crossing a rebel advance guard commanded by one William Thompson, consisting of around 300 rangers and an 18-pounder cannon, were securely placed amidst the myrtle and the dunes.[7]

The 33rd and other units of the expedition pitched camp within sight of the Breach.[8] Several days were spent hunting in vain for a crossing point, with Clinton finally having to accept that even at low tide the channel was not actually fordable on foot. The infantry on Long Island were unable to reach Sullivan's Island.[9] As an alternative plan, Clinton hoped to use boats to land troops inside the harbour close to Haddrell Point or at the southern end of Sullivan's Island, with Commodore Parker leaving the specifics up to him. By the end of June therefore 'the British had settled on a vague, uncoordinated strategy.'[10]

---

4 Stokeley, *Fort Moultrie*, p.19.

5 Stokeley, *Fort Moultrie*, p.16.

6 William Falconer, 'Camp, Long Island, July 13, 1776,', in Anon. (ed.) *Collections of the New-York Historical Society for the Year 1872* (New York: The New-York Historical Society, 1873), p.194.

7 Stokeley, *Fort Moultrie*, p.20.

8 Stokeley, *Fort Moultrie*, p.21.

9 Dan L. Morrill, *Southern Campaigns of the American Revolution* (Mount Pleasant: The Nautical & Aviation Publishing Company of America, 1993), p.22.

10 Stokeley, *Fort Moultrie*, p.21.

In the meantime, the two sides skirmished at distance over the Breach. Captain Dansey reported that he and his men 'lay a Week within Reach of Canon, Grape and small Arms' but without suffering any harm.[11] The Royal Highland Emigrants, who counted among their ranks some Loyalists local to the Charleston area, proved particularly effective. For a week Clinton skirmished at range and manoeuvred his troops across Long Island in defiance of ineffective rebel rifle fire. They even forced the enemy's 18-pounder cannon to be withdrawn a quarter mile to the rear, removing its threat towards any future amphibious landing.[12] The 33rd appear to have played little part in the sniping, but continued to endure life on the sparse island, the monotony interspersed by the cannon fire of the Royal Artillery detachment embedded overlooking the Breach.

The long-awaited British attack finally began on 28 June. A little before 6:00 a.m. British forces were roused from their camp, with some boarding 15 flat-bottomed boats. At 9:00 a.m. Commodore Parker ordered the firing of a signal gun that indicated his ships were moving into position. At 11.30 a.m., the Royal Navy began its bombardment. The engagement between the fleet and Fort Moultrie lasted throughout the day, with a fearsome barrage unleashed by both sides. One vessel, for example, burned through 160 barrels of gunpowder over the course of the nine-hour engagement.[13] Despite the weight of firepower, however, little impression was made on the sturdy palmetto defences.

Originally the army would have coordinated with the naval assault against Sullivan's Island, just the sort of combined arms undertaking the 33rd trained for at Charles Fort in Ireland, but the depth of the Breach and a lack of sufficient boats to ferry his men over convinced Clinton not to attempt a contested landing. Instead, he paraded his brigades on the southern end of Long Island and in their flat-bottomed boats as a feint, convincing the rebels his forces planned on crossing over under the cover of the Royal Artillery and an armed sloop and schooner.[14] Some popular accounts claim the British set out across the Breach and were repulsed with great loss by a furious barrage from Thompson's riflemen. In reality the boats never left the shore – Clinton did not intend to make a crossing but hoped only to distract and divert forces from Fort Moultrie. The manoeuvring and loaded boats damaged rebel moral and caused Lee and his staff to panic, sending off requests for reinforcements.[15]

The 33rd and the other regiments paraded in the late June heat and provided the rebels with a view of the level of their training, firing off volleys by platoon, company, battalion, and brigade. Once it became clear that the Royal Navy had failed to force Fort Moultrie's surrender, Clinton ceased the firing. He briefly considered ordering a night-time attack across the Breach,

11 Dansey (ed.), *Captured Rebel Flag*, p.12.

12 Kim R. Stacy, 'The Land Battle for Sullivan's Island, Charles Town, South Carolina, June–July 1776', *Journal of the Society for Army Historical Research*, vol.92, no.371. Autumn 2014, p.202.

13 Morrill, *Southern Campaigns*, p.23.

14 Stacy, 'The Land Battle for Sullivan's Island', p.203.

15 Stacy, 'The Land Battle for Sullivan's Island', p.204.

but his officers considered that the risk was too great when so many of the soldiers were new recruits, and so young.[16] Here we see a hint at the fact that, while the 33rd were trained and equipped to the highest standard, the vast majority had not yet been tested in serious, sustained combat.

Instead of a night crossing Clinton repeated his distraction techniques the next day while the fleet salvaged or destroyed a number of ships that had been grounded during the attack. The expedition had been a total failure, but casualties were light – at least among the army if not the navy – and morale remained high. On 6 July, not long before British forces evacuated Long Island, Captain Dansey wrote to his mother describing 'Our Army in good Health and rare Spirits full of anxiety to get away to the Northward in the hopes of better Success.'[17] The campaigning – the first Dansey had done since he had been a young subaltern serving with his father in the German states during the Seven Years war – had surprised him. He recalled that 'Campaigns in Germany were Campaigns of Pleasure to what we have undergone here … but thank God and the Prudence of our Generals our little Army is safe and well as I have said before after encountering such Dangers and Difficulties Germany never afforded.'[18] He was pleased to report however that 'All my Herefordshire Recruits are well and behave very well' and that 'Ben is wonderfully recover'd and bears Fatigue very well, I wou'd not be without him for any Money and I hope theres no danger but of his making me an excellent Servant, he begs you will let his Father and Mother know that he is very well contented.'[19]

It seems safe to assume that the 33rd, along with the rest of the expedition, were glad to be sailing north and leaving Charleston behind, at least for the time being. In fact, the 33rd's destination was to have been further north than most. Initially Cornwallis and the regiment were to have carried on past New York and made for Canada, where British forces were assembling under Major General Guy Carleton for a riposte following the repulse of the rebel invasion launched in late 1775. George Germain wrote to Carleton stating that Major General John Burgoyne, along 'with Major General Lord Cornwallis, is appointed by the King to serve under you on the side of Canada; but it will possibly be sometime before you can have the assistance of Lord Cornwallis, as he is at present appointed to serve under Major General Clinton … but he will proceed to Quebec with his regiment as soon as that service is over.'[20] Similarly, on 28 March Germain's letter to General William Howe noted that 'you will observe that in Speaking of the Force to be employed in Canada, I have mentioned only 9 British Battalions, in which I have not included Lord Cornwallis's Regiment, which I acquainted You in my letter of the 1st

16 Edwin C. Bearss, *The Battle of Sullivan's Island and the Capture of Fort Moultrie* (Washington DC: National Park Service Division of History, 1968), p.91.
17 Dansey (ed.), *Captured Rebel Flag*, p.11.
18 Dansey (ed.), *Captured Rebel Flag*, pp.11–12.
19 Dansey (ed.), *Captured Rebel Flag*, p.12.
20 Germain to Carleton, 17 February 1776, in James M. Hadden (ed.), *Hadden's Journal and Orderly Books: A Journal Kept in Canada and upon Burgoyne's Campaign in 1776 and 1777* (Albany: Joel Munsell's Sons, 1884), p.lxix.

of February was to be sent to Quebec as soon as it returned from the Expedition to the Southward.'[21]

Ultimately, however, it was decided that Cornwallis and the 33rd should remain with Clinton's force and join the main British army assembling under Howe outside New York, an order that was to have unfortunate consequences for the 33rd's future recruits, as we shall see. It also caused some supply issues. Captain Dansey complained that 'I have an unfortunate drawback in some things I sent for to upwards a hundred pound value miscarrying and [are] going to Quebec – shoud I get them before Summer I shall do, as they are mostly Necessaries for my Company.'[22]

Ammunition cartridges were made up regularly by the soldiers themselves, combining a measured portion of gunpowder with a lead musket ball wrapped up in 'cartridge' paper. (Photo by Henry Gage)

New York had been chosen as the objective for the great British counter-offensive of 1776. The main British army in North America, commanded by General William Howe, had sailed from where it had been training and reorganising in Halifax, Nova Scotia, on 9 June. The first British ships began to arrive outside New York on 29 June, prompting panic in the city and consternation among the ranks of George Washington's Continental Army. Over the next few weeks, the British landed on Staten Island and used it as a base to begin the build-up of what would be the largest concentration of British soldiers and ships of the entire war. On 1 August the southern expeditionary fleet, including Cornwallis and the 33rd, arrived. The 33rd joined the vast encampment springing up on Staten Island, as more than 30,000 troops – supported by over 400 ships offshore – prepared to attack rebel positions on Long Island or Manhattan.

As part of these preparations, it is quite likely the 33rd took the unusual expedient of cutting their hair short, probably to about an inch in length. Generally British soldiers, like almost all European militaries, wore their hair long, and conformed to one of three styles, that of plait, club or queue, all of which required long hair in the back. British light infantry during the Seven Years War had on occasion cropped their hair, as they deemed it more practical for campaigning, and it seems that Howe (himself once a light infantry officer) may have repeated the style in 1776. A letter in late September 1776 from Doctor Benjamin Rush to a friend in the Continental Army mentioned a prisoner from the 23rd Regiment who had his hair cut short all over on Howe's orders. Other descriptions of deserters or of later orders about the tying back of hair imply that this was an army-wide practice, though it only seems to have been conducted in 1776 and was repudiated by

21 George Germain, 'Whitehall, 28th March 1776' in Bell Clark (ed.), *Naval Documents*, vol.4, p.1003–1004.

22 Dansey (ed.), *Captured Rebel Flag*, p.21.

the king.[23] In general British soldiers wore their hair short on the front, top and sides, occasionally with a small curl above the ear. The long hair at the back was kept tied and dressed up in the style of a plait, queue or club.[24]

Hair cutting would have been done by the men within the regiment with barbering experience, while in camp. The actual nature of British encampments themselves throughout the war tended to vary quite considerably depending on numbers, location and resources. Camp equipage was supplied from Britain at the start of each year's campaigning season. Each five-man mess grouping would receive a tent, six feet wide and seven feet high, staked at the sides and secured over the frame of a ridge pole to create an A-frame. They were also given two vertical wooden and one horizontal pole, a tin-platted kettle plus a lid to transport it, a pair of hatches, straw, and fresh bedding every two or so weeks.[25]

The most standard camp arrangement, when tents were available and the weather was clement enough, involved the creation of streets. The 33rd would have arrived at a set location on Staten Island, the area to be occupied demarcated by the quartermaster with lengths of rope or string. The seven or eight tents in a company, usually made from linen or hemp canvas and marked with the relevant regiment and company numbers, would be pitched in a row, with a second row facing it to create a street. Each street therefore housed two companies, with a regiment consisting of five streets laid out in parallel. Sergeants' tents were placed side-on at the end of each street, while conical bell tents with caps were used for storing the company's firelocks, which could be easily reached when the regiment formed on parade across the width of the camp's frontage.[26] Officers' tents were laid out on the opposite ends of the streets from the sergeants' tents and the bell tents. Captain Dansey actually attempted to design his own tent, which he hoped would prove lighter and more commodious than most. He wrote that;

> I had one of the sort last Campaign which I have improved to such perfection that I am copied by all that can get my Instructions for the making of it, and if we have another Campaign the great Utility of them will so much appear that they will be made use of in stead of the old Tents and if I can get my Invention patronized by some Great Man, I shall immortalize my Name by the simplicity and Use of it, for they are call'd Danseys now, not Tents. I was bold enough to be singular in the whole Army last year and now I have the pleasure of my Invention being generally approved and was I at home I would get a Patent for it.[27]

Set back from the tents were the camp kitchens, consisting of 'circular ditches with fire boxes for each mess dug into the interior perimeter, the earth

23 Stephen Gilbert, 'The Long and the Short of It: Military Hairstyles during the American Revolution Part 1 (of 3): British Army Hairstyles', *The Brigade Dispatch*, vol.XXXV, No. 1 Spring 2005, p.15.

24 Gilbert, 'The Long and the Short of It', p.18.

25 Hagist, *Noble Volunteers*, p.125.

26 Hagist, *Noble Volunteers*, pp.58–59.

27 DHS: William Dansey Letters: 7 June 1778.

heaped into the centre of the circle.'[28] At the front a quarter guard was housed in five or six wedge tents, set out in a U shape, sometimes with a bell tent of arms, while a smaller rear guard served a similar purpose, for protection and for holding those charged with minor infractions. While camp layout naturally varied depending on 'terrain, vegetation, and hostile threats,' and tended to avoid low, wet ground for reasons of health and sanitation, in this general way the 33rd would have made themselves at home on Staten Island throughout most of the month of August.[29]

Issues of discipline began to rear their head as the regulars waited for the build-up to be completed. Local inhabitants were at times threatened, outright robbed, or worse. One British officer, Lord Francis Rawdon, wrote mockingly of rapes being regularly committed by British soldiers and what he considered the amusing courts-martial which followed. His letter is regularly used as evidence of British brutality, but the courts martial are evidence that there was a sustained effort to curb such criminal activity, and show due process with both soldiers and civilians.[30]

In fact Rawdon had only been on Staten Island for five days when he penned the infamous letter, and the orderly books that recorded the general courts martial held during the period showed only six trials on Staten Island between the army's arrival and Rawdon's letter, none of which dealt with the rape of local women.[31] Rawdon may have been exaggerating for effect. Despite this, even during what would become the first major British campaign of the war, the strain between the desire of British commanders to maintain good relations with the American colonists and the general disdain that many regular soldiers held for them was evident.

The New York Campaign

On 21 August a massive storm broke over New York. Lightning struck ferociously, igniting houses and striking men down indiscriminately. One Continental Army soldier in the city was badly injured by one strike, while 10 soldiers encamped by East River were killed, and three officers likewise killed by a single bolt, their skin blackened and swords and coins melted.[32] These grim deaths were held by some as portents for the bloodshed to come. Their prophesies would soon be realised.

On Staten Island the British, Loyalist and German forces were completing their final preparations. The 33rd were subjected to the wider restructuring of his army that Howe had been undertaking almost since the evacuation of Boston. Most notably, the light infantry and grenadier companies of each of the regular regiments had been detached from their parent units and

28 Hagist, *Noble Volunteers*, p.59.

29 Hagist, *Noble Volunteers*, p.127.

30 David Hackett Fischer, *Washington's Crossing* (Oxford: Oxford University Press, 2004), p.46.

31 Don N. Hagist, *These Distinguished Corps: British Grenadier and Light Infantry Battalions in the American Revolution* (Warwick: Helion, 2021), pp.53–54.

32 McCullough, *1776*, p.155–156.

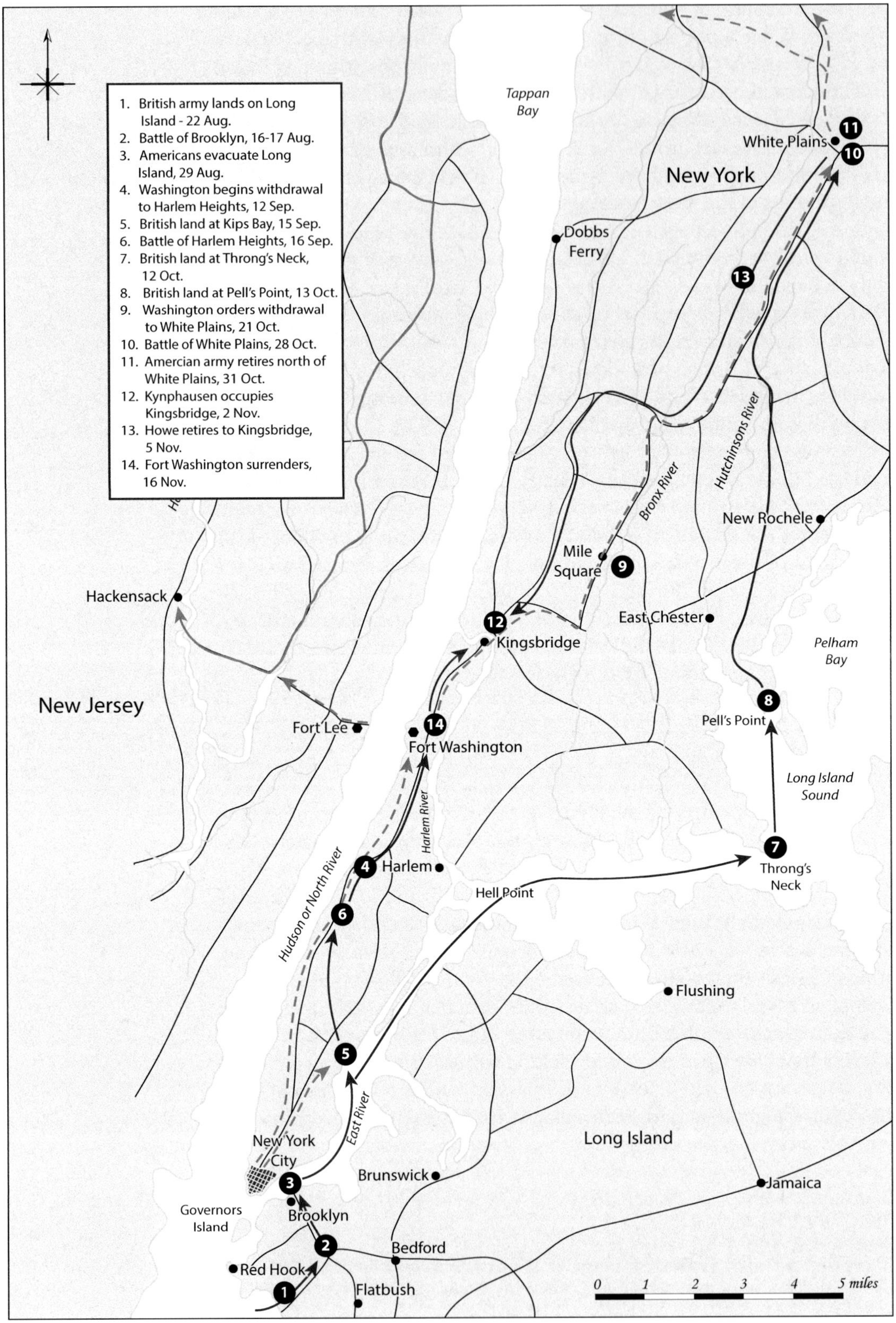

The campaign for New York, August–November, 1776.

reorganised into composite flank battalions. Two battalions of light infantry and two of grenadiers were thus created, and when the southern expedition arrived at the start of August their flank companies were likewise organised into their own composite battalions, with a fourth grenadier battalion formed from the larger companies of the highland regiments. The grenadiers of the 33rd Foot, commanded by Captain Hildebrand Oakes, therefore found themselves detached from the main body of the regiment and placed into the 3rd grenadier battalion, while the 33rd's light company, commanded by Captain Dansey, were assigned to the 3rd light infantry battalion. Howe had learned this method of organisation from his experiences during the Seven Years War – amalgamating the disparate light and grenadier companies gave him a cadre of elite battalions, at the cost of removing the best men from the regular regiments.

Tactical doctrine was also officially modified, and the loose style of fighting displayed by the likes of the 33rd at demonstrations and reviews now became the standard battlefield formation for British soldiers in America. Howe had spent much of his time at Halifax drilling his regiments in these loose formations, specifying a line that was two ranks deep, with 18 inches between files.[33] This provided the flexibility needed to operate over rugged American battlefields, and widened the frontage of oft-outnumbered British battalions so they could avoid being outflanked. Such a loose formation was susceptible to the sudden shock of a bayonet or cavalry charge, but for much of the war the ability of the Continental Army to mount either on British regulars was minimal.

The 33rd were also assigned a place within Howe's forces, one that befitted their reputation as an excellent regiment. Howe's three light battalions formed the army's advanced corps, but backing them up would be a reserve consisting of the grenadier battalions, the 33rd and the 42nd Foot – the Royal Highland Regiment, later known as the Black Watch. This force would not act in reserve to the army as a whole, but to the light infantry corps specifically, providing weight of reinforcement as soon as the light troops engaged the enemy. The light and grenadier battalions and the 33rd and 42nd were therefore envisaged as the army's elite, who were expected to carry the greatest burden of combat. In 1781 it was declared that 'the 33d was looked upon as the pattern regiment in America. In conjunction with the Grenadiers, Light Infantry and 42d, it formed the reserve of the Army which is always composed of the flower of the troops.'[34] This reserve corps was put under Cornwallis's direct command.

On 22 August, the day after the thunderstorm had lashed at New York, the British began to cross from Staten Island via Denyse's Ferry to neighbouring Long Island. Here a large portion of Washington's Continental Army were encamped along the Heights of Guana and, beyond them, the Brooklyn Heights. With the Royal Navy in complete control of the waterways around the islands, the initial landing went completely uncontested.

33 Spring, *With Zeal*, pp.141–142.
34 Anon., 'For the Political Magazine', p.342.

The 33rd, along with the 42nd and the elite light infantry and grenadier battalions and some Germans, were ordered to press inland. They advanced a short distance to the settlement of Flatbush, just below the Heights of Guana. Here an officer recorded 'the Enemy made it prudent to halt. The Rebels had Command of the Heights and the Woods were strongly lined by them. A constant popping Fire, with little Loss on either Side, was kept up without gaining much Ground.'[35] This remained the state of affairs as Howe settled into a routine that would become familiar in its ponderousness, continuing to ferry troops and material across from Staten to Long Island for the next few days.

Finally, on 26 August it became apparent that something was afoot. Orders filtered down for the regiment to stand to, though even for senior officers the specifics remained painfully vague. Oakes and Dansey did likewise with their new comrades in the grenadier and light battalions. Tents that had been shifted from Staten to Long Island remained up and campfires remained smouldering, lulling rebel observers into believing that the British were still encamped. The 33rd fell in with a growing column of men, Cornwallis's force assuming the vanguard with a small troop of dragoons and the light infantry battalions acting as the tip of the spear. At 9:00 p.m., with darkness having fallen, the formation stepped off, led by two mounted officers and three local Loyalist guides.

The going was torturously slow. It would have become apparent as the hours crawled by that the British forces were heading not directly north into the enemy lines on the Heights of Guana, but north-east. Such a movement was fraught with danger and difficulty. The rough, narrow tracks were entirely unfit for the detachment of 10,000 men the 33rd were now a part of, with their attendant horses and artillery. The column itself stretched for more than two miles. Everything 'was conducted in the most silent manner possible, and the movements were performed with such caution against surprise.'[36] With painful, exhausting slowness, the column felt its way forward through the darkness. The 33rd endured with the rest, halting with unwelcome regularity, some men snatching a few moments sleep before they were roused again and carried on a short way before another unexplained halt was called.[37]

Dansey, with the 33rd's detached light company, would have had a slightly better understanding of what was occurring than the column stacked up behind him. The light battalions were called upon to move with greater alacrity, following up on the dragoons and Loyalist guides to secure potential points of ambush or resistance on the path before the regular regiments reached them.[38] The few locals living along the army's route were seized and taken with the column so they could not ride ahead and warn the enemy of their approach – a tactic learned the hard way following the debacle of

35 *Public Advertiser*, 17 October 1776, p.1.

36 William Howard Jr., 'The Rising Sun Tavern and the Rockaway Pass', in Anon. (ed.), *Manual of the Common Council of the City of Brooklyn* (New York: Arthur Brown, 1868), p.475.

37 McCullough, *1776*, p.168–169.

38 Interestingly, multiple rebel sources claim the British light infantry battalions wore colonial-style hunting shirts at Long Island, perhaps as a means of disguise, though this seems to appear nowhere in any British account.

the supposedly secret night march to reach Lexington and Concord the year before.

Eventually the vanguard reached the entrance to Jamaica Pass, the crucial junction of the expedition. Lying east of the rebel lines, it marked a passage through the Heights of Guana to Bedford Pass, which lay in the rear of the enemy's defences, between Guana and the secondary rebel fortifications on the Brooklyn Heights, directly opposite Manhattan Island. If the army could make it through Jamaica Pass, they could strike between the rebel forces like a dagger between ribs. Alternatively, if the pass had even a small holding force or, even worse, if the revolutionaries were aware of the plan and had laid an ambush, the unwieldy column would be decimated.[39]

At the foot of Jamaica Pass lay Howard's Tavern. It seemed like an ideal post for a rebel picket. It was 2:00 a.m. light infantry and dragoons surrounded the building and burst inside. Within they found no sentries, only a few guests with the tavern owner and his son. The latter, William Howard Jr, recalled the event; 'I was awakened by seeing a soldier at the side of my bed. I got up and dressed, and went down into the bar-room, where I saw my father standing in one corner, with three British soldiers before him with muskets and bayonets fixed… General Howe and another officer were standing in the bar room.'[40]

After ordering a drink, Howe interrogated the pair and demanded that they assist his guides. The two protested that they were loyal to Congress but were coerced. At every step the British expected to be discovered. They anticipated:

> A serious resistance in crossing the bridge over Goose Creek, half a mile south of the Jamaica road, and had made preparations for an assault upon the defences supposed to be thrown up there. The woods which their spies and guides informed them lined the route, it was believed, were occupied by the American riflemen, and as these various strong positions were passed without resistance, the British officers were apprehensive that the American forces had been withdrawn only to be concentrated upon some other point.[41]

Into Jamaica Pass the British went. It was an even less ideal place to take an army than the tracks used so far, a twisting and stony path through a gorge overlooked by woodland.[42] Pioneers 'sawed down the trees which came in the way of the cannon, as the noise made by felling them with axes, it was expected, would alarm the American guard.'[43] Each delay could only have been torturous for the thousands of men waiting in the darkness behind, surrounded by unknown, forested slopes, aware they were on some secret and deadly endeavour but oblivious to the detail.

---

39 McCullough, *1776*, p.169.
40 Howard Jr, 'The Rising Sun Tavern and the Rockaway Pass', p.473.
41 Howard Jr, 'The Rising Sun Tavern and the Rockaway Pass', pp.475–476.
42 McCullough, *1776*, p.169.
43 Howard Jr, 'The Rising Sun Tavern and the Rockaway Pass', p.474.

Not long after leaving the tavern with the Howards, the vanguard finally encountered the enemy. A patrol of five revolutionaries were surprised and seized without a shot being fired. They admitted that they were the only guards monitoring the pass. Scarcely believing their good fortune, the British pressed on. It took two hours for the whole column to traverse the winding pass, and by then the sun was beginning to rise. Finally, after a total of nine hours marching, they reached the Bedford road. The whole manoeuvre had gone completely undetected by the main rebel army.

The Howards were released and returned to their tavern, where a small force of light infantry had been left behind to keep the other occupants inside and unable to warn the enemy. Howard Jr remembered that the guards 'were apparently without the slightest feeling of hatred, or embittered feeling in their position as enemies, and we experienced nothing disagreeable from them during their stay. In fact most of the plundering during the war was perpetrated by thc inhabitants upon each other.'[44]

The Howards made it home in time to avoid what was coming. Back in the pass, the British paused to collect themselves. The men, the 33rd among them, were ordered to lie and rest in the tall grass by the roadside.[45] It was now daylight.

At 9:00 a.m., not daring to wait any longer, Howe ordered the discharge of two artillery pieces into the morning air, signalling to other British forces back at Flatbush and further west and giving the rebels the first indication that the enemy was where they least expected – behind them. The Battle of Long Island had begun.

The Battle of Long Island

In truth the battle had already started while the main column was still traversing up to Jamaica Pass. The force intended to pin the revolutionaries on Guana heights had started to engage early, beginning their attack at 1:00 a.m. This, however, did not give away the wide flanking manoeuvre.

Dansey and the 33rd's light company, as part of the light battalions, were the first part of the main column to meet the enemy. As they pushed through a pleasant landscape of small fields and forests, the light infantry encountered their enemy properly for the first time. Dansey, with Cotton, Gorges and the rest of his light bobs, found that, for all their surprise, the Congressional forces had responded to the sudden attack with alacrity. Dansey's company passed over a wall and crossed a field, which reminded the captain of a similar clearing back home near his manor house at Brinsop, in Herefordshire. Beyond it lay bushes and a forest, which the light company entered, led by Dansey and five or six other men. It was here that the rebels struck.

Dansey realised too late that he had walked his company of around 40 men into the midst of 300 enemy riflemen. Whether they intended to ambush

44 Howard Jr, 'The Rising Sun Tavern and the Rockaway Pass', p.474.
45 McCullough, *1776*, p.170.

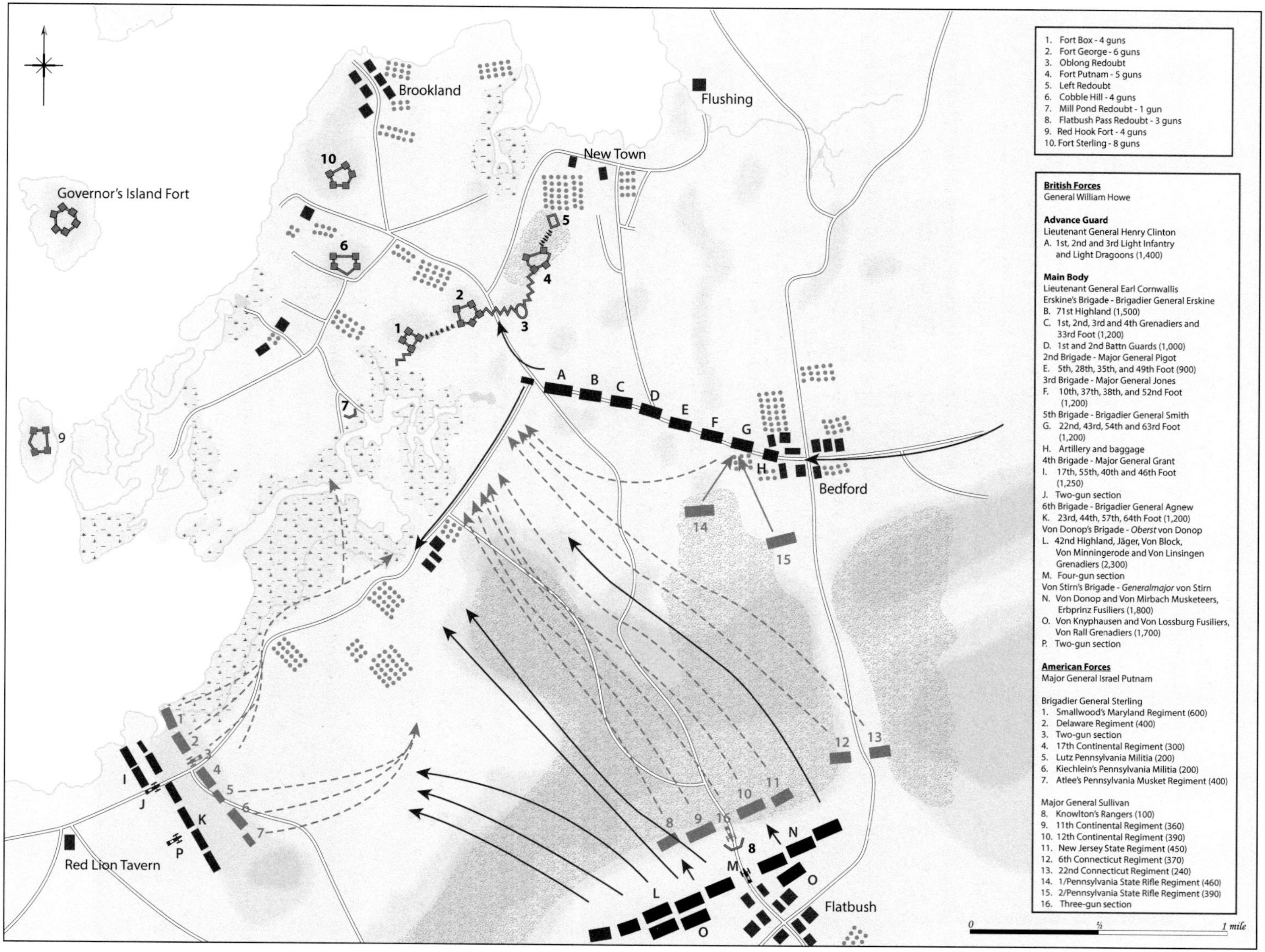

The Battle of Long Island, 27 August 1776.

him, or were simply caught unawares by the British advance, is unclear. The first Dansey knew of their presence was when some leapt up just 10 yards away and fired. Miraculously, no harm was done, at least initially. The captain 'ordered my Men to get behind the Trees and return it.'[46] The light infantry's fire was more telling – one rebel officer 20 yards away was killed by the burst of shots.

The advantage was short lived. Riflemen swarmed in and gave a second fire from multiple angles. Both the men immediately to the left and the right of Dansey were hit and dropped dead. Realising that he was heavily outnumbered and almost surrounded, Dansey shouted at his men to fall back. Some took cover in amongst some bushes while the rest streamed back across the field towards the wall they had passed over.

Dansey made the dash with one other man at his side, the rebel's shouts for him to surrender ringing in his ears. He stopped twice to see riflemen flooding the woodland's edge. Running for the wall 'as hard as I cou'd drive,' he found his thoughts filled with one specific, terrible idea – that he would be hit in the legs and would be unable to continue to run. The rebels fired at him, 'peppering at me seeing very plain I was the Officer… the Balls flew about me.' Afterwards he did his best to relate the experience of being shot at by dozens of men; 'Suppose yourself under a large Apple Tree full of ripe Fruit and a person is in the Tree Shaking as hard as they can, how thick the Apples will drop about you and perhaps not one hit you.'[47]

Doubtless with his heart racing and short of breath, Dansey somehow reached the wall. He vaulted it with such haste that his leg struck one of the wooden rails, and he thought for a moment that he had been hit.

The whole incident, Dansey estimated, had taken about three minutes. On the other side of the wall the remnants of his company were gathering. Lieutenant Cotton had been hit, a grazing wound to his shoulder. The sheer weight of the enemy fire would certainly have overwhelmed the 33rd's lights in a matter of minutes had support not arrived just when it was most needed. Three more companies from the light battalion, as well as elements of a grenadier battalion, swung into action, relieving Dansey's men and falling upon the rebels, who Dansey claimed 'were all either kill'd or taken.'[48]

The rest of the 33rd were not far off. While rebel forces further west continued to fight furiously, in the east the Congressional army had collapsed and was streaming back to the Brooklyn Heights. Along with the grenadier battalions, the 33rd's hat companies pressed on, crossing over the Flatbush road in the centre-rear of the enemy's first line, driving scattered and confused rebel forces before them. They pushed ahead of the rest of the army until they were beginning to threaten the second line of enemy defences on the Heights. Dansey told how the regiment was 'so near the Rebel Lines where they very effectually revenged my Cause.'[49]

46 Dansey (ed.), *Captured Rebel Flag*, p.15.
47 Dansey (ed.), *Captured Rebel Flag*, p.16.
48 Dansey (ed.), *Captured Rebel Flag*, p.14.
49 Dansey (ed.), *Captured Rebel Flag*, p.15.

The rebels on the promontory above them had manned their positions and began to fire down into the British as they pursued their comrades towards their breastworks, which were described by British Major General James Robertson as 'semicircular and the parapets lined with spears and lances.'[50] However the rebel artillery brought to bear was poorly handled, and most of the roundshot whipped harmlessly overhead. The 33rd and the grenadiers were ordered to halt beneath the barrage. Major General John Vaughan, in immediate command, wanted to attack the nearest redoubt on the Heights straight away, convinced that with the rebels on the run the defenders would not stand. Howe was against it, despite the fact that 'Vaughan stormed with rage at being stopped.'[51] Howe repeated his orders that they were to go no further. The British commander in chief later recalled;

> The grenadiers and 33d Regiment being in Front of the Column, soon approached within Musquet Shot of the Enemies Lines at Brooklyn, from whence these Battalions without regarding their Fire of Cannon and Small Arms upon them, pursued Numbers of the Rebels that were retiring from the Heights so close to their principal Redoubt and with such Eagerness to attack it by storm, that it required repeated Orders to prevail upon them to desist from the Attempt. Had they been permitted to do on, it is my opinion that they would have carried the Redoubt; but as it was apparent the Lines must have been ours at a very cheap Rate by regular Approaches, I would not risk the Loss that might have been sustained in the Assault, and ordered them back to a hollow Way, in the Front of the Works out of the reach of Musquetry.[52]

While their ardour was beyond reproach, it is likely that the men of the 33rd welcomed the battle's end as they sank down in the cover of the hollow path at the bottom of the Heights. It was almost mid-afternoon, and 17 hours had passed since they had stepped off the night before. Aside from snatches of sleep during pauses on the march or for an hour or two after negotiating Jamaica Pass, the men had been awake for over 30 hours, had marched nine miles and had fought a running battle over woods and fields. The main body of the regiment had suffered just four rank and file wounded. The same, however, could not be said of Dansey's company.

Dansey's letters show the potent mixture of emotions following the battle. He was thankful for 'a most miraculous Escape… I have to thank God for my safety under the heaviest fire of Musquetry ever people escaped from.' His first experience of American riflemen left him less fearful than he had been before, relating that 'they are not so dreadfull as I expected or they must have destroyed me and my whole Company before we were supported by anybody else.' Nevertheless, the state of his company as he rallied them behind the wall after the initial clash 'was too affecting to be described with the clear

50 James Robertson, in Henry Onderdonk Jr. (ed.), *Documents and Letters Intended to Illustrate the Revolutionary Incidents of Queens County* (New York: Leavitt, Trow and Company, 1846), p.138.

51 *London Chronicle* report, in Onderdonk (ed.), *Documents and Letters*, p.138.

52 *London Gazette Extraordinary*, 10 October 1776, p.1.

fullness of the foregoing lines.'[53] At the end of the day three of Dansey's men had been killed – Elias Broadbent, Edward Ogden and James Wilson – and six wounded, a casualty rate of around 30 percent. It had been a hard day's work.[54]

Washington Withdraws

The defeat was a shock to the rebels, and a delight to the British. Howe, Clinton and Cornwallis safely assumed that they had the rest of Washington's army trapped on the Brooklyn Heights, and could force their surrender with a conventional siege. It is at this point that hindsight is at its most damning, for the night after the battle Washington conducted a daring escape across the East River, successfully evacuating his army from right under the noses of the Crown forces.

It is common to question Howe's generalship for allowing this to happen or, at the very least, cast aspersion on the Royal Navy, who should have patrolled the river and thus made escape impossible. Such views, however, ignore the realities of the moment. Since the bloodshed of Bunker Hill, British forces had wisely relied on flanking efforts rather than direct assaults on rebel strongholds, hence the very basis for the strategy on Long Island. With the rebels cornered on the Brooklyn Heights, a frontal assault would likely have incurred heavy losses for no certain gain, quite probably turning victory into defeat. British troops were exhausted and low on supplies in the immediate aftermath of the battle, and there were still over 7,000 Congressional troops holding the Heights. Lastly, it was a contrary north wind that kept the Royal Navy from East River rather than laziness and arrogance, though even if they had sought to block it off, their ships would have been raked from both sides by dozens of cannon and hundreds if not thousands of riflemen – Washington still had 20,000 troops occupying Manhattan Island.

Even after Washington's surprise escape, the British believed the victory was won and the war almost done, and their enemies had scarcely a better view of their own prospects. From Bedford on Long Island Dansey wrote to his mother that 'the Glorious Victory obtain'd over the Rebels on the 27th has made them abandon all their strong Works on this Island and has struck such a damp among them that we hope we have now nothing to do but pursue them.'[55] Back in Britain, news of the victory stirred the populace. The efforts of the 33rd in particular were noted. The *Gazetteer and New Daily Advertiser* reported; 'We hear from Wakefield and Leeds, in Yorkshire, that the common people there express themselves with great rapture on the intrepid, glorious behaviour of the thirty-third regiment, in their engagement on Long-Island; that regiment being chiefly composed of recruits from the above places, and are usually called "The Have a Cake, Lads."'[56]

---

53 Dansey (ed.), *Captured Rebel Flag*, pp.14–16.
54 Hagist, *These Distinguished Corps*, p.57.
55 Dansey (ed.), *Captured Rebel Flag*, p.13.
56 *Gazetteer and New Daily Advertiser*, 26 October 1776, p.4.

John Robert Shaw, who at that time had just enlisted and was still assisting the recruiting party in their duties, remembered 'we had an account of the battle of Long-Island, and of the gallant and soldier like behaviour of the 33d regiment, commanded by lieutenant colonel Webster, for which as a mark of distinction an additional ribband of the orange colour was bestowed: the whole consisting of the red, blue, white and yellow. These colours compose our cockade.'[57]

Three weeks passed, with most of the army shifting a little further north on Long Island, to Newtown. There was a brief set of peace talks between Howe and three members of congress, but as neither side had permission from their superiors to act with any discretion it came to nothing. British commanders were largely occupied with planning how to extricate Washington from Manhattan Island, while Washington was occupied with planning how to extricate himself. The Continental Army, not wishing to be trapped as it so nearly had been on Long Island, began preparations to withdraw further north. Not knowing this, the British prepared to land at Kip's Bay, on the eastern side of Manhattan.

The choice of Kip's Bay was, as was so often the case, disputed between Howe and Clinton, with the latter favouring landing further north at King's Bridge, an act that would have cut the Continentals off from their only avenue of escape. As with patrolling East River prior to the escape from Long Island however, this was easier said than done. The navy – and, even more so, local Loyalist pilots – did not want to risk the treacherous currents of Hell's Gate, at the confluence of the East River and the Harlem. Furthermore, a rebel battery of artillery remained unsilenced at Horn's Hook, which would have further jeopardised the operation. Kip's Bay was far more navigable and would still allow New York city to be cut off from the north.

Consequently, the 33rd, along with its light and grenadier companies in their respective composite battalions, were reembarked. The light infantry, as ever, were in the forefront, facing the threat of a contested landing. Howe issued general orders to the army on 13 September, exhorting them and reminded them to rely upon cold steel in the coming assault;

> An attack upon the enemy being shortly intended, the soldiers are reminded of their evident superiority on the 27th of August by charging the Rebels with Bayonets even in the woods where they had thought themselves invincible: they now place their security in slight breastworks of the weakest Construction, and which are to be carried with little loss by the same high spirited mode of attack. The Gen'l therefore recommends to the troops an entire dependence on their Bayonets with which they will always command that success which their bravery so well deserves.[58]

The day chosen for the landing was 15 September. Howe had initially hoped it could be performed on 13 September, the anniversary of Wolfe's celebrated

57 Shaw, *A Narrative*, p.12.

58 Howe's Orders, 13 September, in Henry P. Johnston, *The Battle of Harlem Heights, September 16, 1776* (New York: The Columbia University Press, 1897), p.35.

landing outside Quebec in 1759, an attack that Howe, as a young officer, had spearheaded. The 15th proved to be a warm day. The light infantry and grenadiers initially embarked at Newtown Cove, on broad, flat-bottomed rowing boats, while the rest of the army marched to the point of land opposite Kip's Bay to do the same. The navy opened up a truly thunderous barrage. It lasted 'without stop for a full hour, a total of nearly eighty guns pounding point-blank at the shore and shrouding the river with acrid smoke.'[59] The British and German soldiers crammed into the boats doubtless experienced the fearful thoughts of assault troops since time immemorial, wondering if anything could possibly survive the display of ear-aching firepower. Eventually the barrage ended and the flatboats glided forward, the British venting their nerves with their usual, prodigious cursing, the Germans by singing hymns.[60]

For once, the preliminary bombardment really had done its job. The light infantry and grenadiers landed amidst the rebel positions to find them wrecked by the navy's cannonade, their defenders almost all killed or fled. All that remained was to mop up. The 33rd's main body came ashore, joining the grenadiers and the 42nd Foot in a push inland to the promontory known as Inclenberg Hill. As they ascended it, the grenadiers 'met with a party of the Rebels and exchanged a few shot.'[61] Major General Vaughan was slightly wounded. The British continued pushing inland just as the last of Washington's army were able to escape from New York and march north past the potential bottleneck.

New York had fallen or, in the opinions of its large Loyalist population, had been liberated. Rebel forces consolidated at Harlem Heights, still on Manhattan Island, north of the city. The British bedded in opposite them, straddling the island's length. In the centre were the 33rd and the rest of the Reserve, encamped alongside the Black Horse Tavern. The grenadier battalions lay to the 33rd's right (east), the 42nd to their left (west), and the whole screened by the 1st Light Infantry battalion in front. Dansey, in the 3rd Light Infantry battalion, lay further north-west. The account of a captain of the 5th Foot, serving in one of the grenadier battalions bivouacked just to the 33rd's right, gives an indication of the sort of night spent by the British regiments;

> We took post opposite to them [the rebels], placed our picquets, borrowed a sheep, killed, cooked, and ate some of it and then went up to sleep on a gate, which we took the liberty of throwing off its hinges, covering our feet with an American tent, for which we should have cut poles and pitched, had it not been so dark.[62]

The next morning the 33rd and the rest of the Reserve went about their encampment duties with the ominous sound of musketry crackling away just

59 McCullough, *1776*, p.211.
60 McCullough, *1776*, p.211.
61 Stephen Kemble, *Journals of Lieut. Col. Stephen Kemble, 1773-1789: And British Army Orders* (Boston: Gregg Press, 1972), p.88.
62 George Harris, in Johnston, *The Battle of Harlem Heights*, p.207.

to the north-west. As the day wore on the noise rose in intensity, accompanied by the notes of the hunting horns used by the British light infantry. Unease would have grown as staff officers arrived to relay orders to Lieutenant Colonel Webster. At around 11:00 a.m. the regiment were ordered to stand to their arms and prepare for action.

Part of the regiment was already in the fight. Dansey and the light bobs received an earlier summons to provide reinforcements to the light infantry of another battalion, beset in the western portion of Harlem Heights, close to the Hudson River. Fearing a British attack that morning, Washington had sent forward a force of rebel rangers to reconnoitre the British lines. They had made contact with pickets of the 2nd Light Infantry battalion and had given as good as they had received. Both sides advanced and retreated in turn as Washington began to feed reinforcements from the rebel-held Heights into the meeting engagement. The local British commander, Major General Alexander Leslie, likewise sent for aid.

The 3rd Light Infantry battalion, of which Dansey was a part, mobilised to assist the 2nd battalion, as did the Reserve.[63] Cornwallis seems to have fed his regiments into the engagement in a somewhat piecemeal fashion, with the 42nd, bivouacked just west of the 33rd, and some supporting artillery and Germans arriving around the same time as the light battalions.

The fighting flared in a buckwheat field, as the Crown and Continental troops traded blows for an hour or more. As often seemed to be the case, Dansey was in the midst of it. He described the engagement as 'a long and heavy fire.'[64] During it one private was killed and Lieutenant Cotton was injured for a second time, as was a sergeant and a private. Outnumbered and with their ammunition exhausted, the highlanders, Germans and light infantry gave ground, retreating back through an orchard.

By this point the 33rd and the rest of the Reserve had come up. The 5th Foot's grenadier captain described how they had 'trotted about three miles (without a halt to draw breath).'[65] As the 33rd covered the withdrawal, they took fire from the enemy. One round hit the instrument of one of the regiment's drummers, and he abandoned it before the regiment retreated. The drum was claimed by a Continental, as later recounted by one of his comrade;

> … there was a drum of the 33d regiment brought off the field which had a hole in the side of it made by a musketball. The drummer of our company bought this drum and used it in our camp, as he said it was much superior to the drum he was using. He was a deserter from the British while our army lay before Boston.[66]

---

63 On p.62 of *These Distinguished Corps*, Hagist speculates that the 33rd's light company was one of the two picket companies engaged at the start of the day. Sadly, the regiments to which the two companies belonged have never been fully identified.

64 Dansey (ed.), *Captured Rebel Flag*, p.17.

65 George Harris, in Johnstone, *The Battle of Harlem Heights*, p.207.

66 Howard Henry Peckham (ed.), *Memoirs of the Life of John Adlum in the Revolutionary War* (Chicago: The Caxton Club, 1968), p.22.

Having initially driven the British back to their lines, the rebels decided it prudent to return to their own, marching off in good order following a triumphant huzzah. British sources dismissed the day's skirmish as an affair of posts, but Congressional troops were buoyed by the fact that they had finally fought British regulars face-to-face in the open field and seen the backs of their enemies. The propaganda benefit of the engagement was not lost on Dansey, who urged his mother in his next letter home to 'be sure never to believe the infamous Lies told on the Rebel's part in the Newspapers.'[67]

The 5th Foot's captain had a kingly feast to look forward to once the engagement was over, describing how the Reserve returned to the centre of the line after the Harlem Heights fracas had died down;

> Before we started in the morning, our dinner, consisting of a goose and piece of mutton, had been put on the fire. The moment we marched, our domestic deposited the above named delicacies on a chaise, and followed us with it to our ground. When the fight was over, he again hung the goose to the fire, but the poor bird had been scarce half done, when we were ordered to return to our station. There again we commenced cooking, and though without dish, plate, or knife did ample justice to our fare, which we washed down with bad rum and water, and then composed ourselves to rest on our friendly gate. Our baggage joined us the next day.[68]

Dansey did not relate whether he ate as well as the 5th's grenadiers, though with the Kip's Bay landing the day before followed by the morning's sharp engagement, he admitted that he was 'not in Spirits to write so much as my Inclination leads me to.'[69]

Fort Washington

Dansey would have time to recover from at least some of his fatigue for, while both armies remained primed for battle, there was no notable fighting over the next month. Washington stayed entrenched on his heights and Howe, strategically ponderous, had no intention of committing the mistake of a costly frontal assault. While the two sides watched one another Dansey wrote home, including the happy news that his servant Ben was 'very well and bears the Fatigues of War with good humour, indeed he fares as well as I.'[70] After the battle on Long Island he had praised the boy in his usual glowing terms, noting that 'Ben now follows me he is very well and not afraid tho' he has been often in Danger of Canon & Musquetry.' Dansey hoped in his letters home to his family that 'you will hear me personally describing these Feats of War to our Good Neighbours over a clear Glass of the best Cid'r by this time twelve month,' and apologised for running out of writing paper.[71]

67 Dansey (ed.), *Captured Rebel Flag*, p.17.
68 George Harris, in Johnstone, *The Battle of Harlem Heights*, p.208.
69 Dansey (ed.), *Captured Rebel Flag*, p.17.
70 Dansey (ed.), *Captured Rebel Flag*, p.17.
71 Dansey (ed.), *Captured Rebel Flag*, pp.15–16.

Eventually, Howe decided to repeat his preferred strategy, using his naval superiority to outflank the Congressional positions. On 12 October the 33rd were among troops embarked aboard a fleet that finally negotiated Hell's Gate and sailed up the East River to a marshy spit of land called Throg's Neck. A bridge and a ford connected it to the mainland and offered a road that would lead around the rear of the rebel defences at Harlem. The British troops landed under the cover of a fog but discovered that the revolutionaries were guarding both the bridge, which they had dismantled, and the ford in strength.

Dansey's light company, along with another, encountered the rebels holding the Neck. Advancing through an area of sparse trees and rocks, they came upon a mill with a wall which, initially unbeknownst to them, was sheltering around 150 riflemen. The enemy struck first, but the sudden salvo failed to find a target. Dansey ordered his men to take cover behind the trees and rocks and called upon volunteers to work their way forward and keep up a return fire. A company of Hessian jäger – rifle-armed German light infantry – arrived as reinforcements, adding their rifles to the firefight, though Dansey reported they 'did not stay above an Hour.'[72]

The two sides 'continued the popping fire' for seven hours 'at their [the riflemen's] favourite Distance about 200 yards.' The rebels enjoying better cover than Dansey's men, but their fire was ineffective, while the light infantrymen brought down several of the enemy. This skirmishing continued for several days as both sides fired at each other over the water separating the Neck from the mainland, 'till we had kil'd an Officer of theirs besides several Men and not one of ours wounded, and they at last fairly gave up firing finding themselves beat in their own way.' The encounters further convinced Dansey that despite the belief early in the war that 'we were all to be kill'd with Rifles' the rebel's sharpshooters were indifferent combatants. 'There's no people in the World can shoot Black Ducks better than they can, but the Ducks carry no Firelocks and Bayonets,' he wrote;

> It's astonishing to think how the Leaders of this Rebellion have made the poor ignorant People believe, because they are brought up to Gunning, as they call it that they must be at everything, but now they are convinced that being a good Marksman is only a trifling requisite for a Soldier … a cool Soldier with a good Firelock was beyond a Rifleman with all his Skill.[73]

While the British might have done well at 'popping fire,' the strategic situation was less fruitful. With strong rebel forces covering Throg's Neck, Howe decided against forcing the issue. After spending six days there, and realising that no headway would be made, he reembarked his army on 18 October and tried a second landing further north, at Pell's Point. On 16 October the 33rd struck their tents at 3:00 a.m. and were conducted by a deputy quartermaster general to the embarkation point. The men were admonished 'not to throw

72 Dansey (ed.), *Captured Rebel Flag*, p.19.
73 Dansey (ed.), *Captured Rebel Flag*, pp.19–20.

away or waste any Part of their Provisions, as they may be Liable, by so doing, to the greatest Distress.'[74]

The move to Pell's Point was more successful, but stiff resistance by outnumbered Continentals slowed the British drive inland to East Chester and New Rochelle, with the light infantry, grenadiers and Germans taking the brunt of the fighting. As on 16 September, the Continentals acquitted themselves well. Regardless, Washington had yet again been outflanked, and his defences on Harlem Heights were no longer tenable. He withdrew from Manhattan, concentrating on the road hub at White Plains, to the north-east.

Howe pursued as slowly as ever. Washington placed his army on the hills above White Plains and there waited for an attack. Howe obliged on 28 October, outflanking and overrunning the rebel positions in relatively short order. The 33rd were involved in a flanking manoeuvre that did not make contact with the enemy before they withdrew. The regiment spent the night encamped behind an amalgamated battalion of German grenadiers. Heavy rains over the following days prevented Howe from mounting another attack, and the rebels conducted yet another ordered retreat, this time to North Castle.

After a week spent attempting to lure Washington back out into the open, Howe resolved to deal with unfinished business further south. A substantial rebel garrison still occupied Fort Washington, on Manhattan Island. On 2 November, a senior Continental officer deserted to the British and supplied Howe with intelligence regarding the fort's weaknesses. On 6 November the army encamped at Dobbs Ferry, where they met with several supply ships that had made it past the fire of forts Lee and Washington, then progressed to the Heights of Fordham just north of Manhattan, which they reached on 13 November. On the way there the light battalion Dansey was attached to 'took several Boats belonging to the Rebels, about 2 Miles above our Advanced Posts – no resistance; some Stores found; propose to bring them off.'[75]

The army's passage was marked by instances of ill-discipline and pillaging, in spite of increasingly stringent orders from Howe to avoid irregularities. Lieutenant Colonel Stephen Kemble noted in his diary that 'the March of our Baggage [was] marked by the Licentionness [*sic*] of the Troops, who committed every species of Rapine and plunder.' The next day Kemble recorded his dissatisfaction with the army's current state; 'Scandalous behavior for British Troops; and the Hessians Outrageously Licentious, and Cruel to such a degree as to threaten with death all such as dare obstruct them in their depredations. Violence to Officers frequently used, and every Degree of Insolence offered. Shudder for Jersey, the Army being thought to move there Shortly.'[76]

Kemble, a Loyalist and native of Brunswick, in New Jersey, was correct to be concerned. British designs did indeed lie with that colony, but first New York had to be finally subdued.

---

74 Stephen Kemble, 'The Kemble Papers, Volume 1', in Anon. (ed.), *Collections of the New-York Historical Society for the Year 1883* (New York: New-York Historical Society, 1884), p.391.

75 Kemble, *Journals of Lieut. Col. Stephen Kemble*, p.98.

76 Kemble, *Journals of Lieut. Col. Stephen Kemble*, pp.97–98.

Fort Washington stood upon the highest point of Manhattan Island, north of Harlem Heights, on a length of tough schist that was so rocky the Continentals who constructed it had to haul soil for the redoubts up from further down the slope. The fort was pentagonal, with five bastions jutting from its core and abattis surrounding it. It was in turn surrounded by further defences, most notably a triple line of entrenchments to the south that covered the width of Manhattan, and a number of other outworks to the north and on Laurel Hill, which lay directly to the east.

By 16 November the fort was surrounded. Washington had unwisely acceded to the suggestions of his subordinates, reinforcing rather than evacuating it. The defenders amounted to 3,000 men, which were too many for Fort Washington to contain, but too few to properly garrison all of the entrenchments and outworks beyond the fort's bastions. Nevertheless, the fort's commander, Colonel Robert Magaw, was confident, believing that he could hold out until December if need be, thus maintaining a Congressional toehold on Manhattan and stymieing British intentions towards New Jersey.

It was to be a costly mistake, because for once Howe was prepared to overcome his aversion to attacking rebel strongpoints head-on. In the cold, pre-dawn darkness the 33rd conducted what by that point must have been a familiar procedure – marching to the shores of the Harlem River and shaking out into their platoons in preparation for a crossing by boat. On this occasion, however, there was no sign of the transports.

The 33rd were once again under the command of their colonel, as were the 1st and 2nd grenadier battalions. Beside them were the 1st and 2nd Light Infantry battalions and the 1st and 2nd battalions of Guards, led by Major General Edward Mathew. The task of the grenadiers and the 33rd was to support the light infantry and Guards as they crossed the Harlem and mounted an attack up the dauntingly steep slopes of Laurel Hill, beyond which lay Fort Washington.

It would be only one of four assaults intended to crash against the fort and its outer defences that day. To the north, Germans under *Generallieutenant* Wilhelm von Knyphausen would attack the steepest, rockiest slope leading to the defences, while to the south more Germans and British regulars commanded by Lieutenant General Hugh Percy would be charged with breaking through the three lines of entrenchments set before the fort's promontory. A fourth attack by the 42nd Foot, intended only as a diversion, would go in just to the south of the 33rd, crossing the Harlem at the same time.

Or so it was hoped. Hours passed and the dawn began to show itself. It emerged that, after ferrying von Knyphausen's Germans across at King's Bridge, the flatboats had been bedevilled by the tide, and could not reach the east bank of the Harlem to link up with Cornwallis's and Mathew's brigades.

At 7:00 a.m. artillery began bombarding the rebel positions – German gunners from the north, the Royal Artillery from the south and from the small redoubts that had been built on the slope above the 33rd to cover their advance across the river. From the far side of the fort a British frigate in the Hudson, the *Pearl*, also added its cannon to the barrage.

The tide had delayed the entire operation, and the other prongs of the assault were forced to halt and wait for the crossings over the Harlem. For five hours the cannon thumped, until finally, at midday, the eastern flank of the attack was able to get underway.

The attack on Fort Washington had the potential to be a bloody one. Laurel Hill was steep, rocky and forested, and the invading troops would be completely exposed in their flatboats before having to scale the brutal incline. To the north the Germans soon found themselves struggling to gain ground – rebel riflemen extracted a toll on them, effectively pinning them down amidst the boulders and straggling trees. To the east, however, the extended nature of the fort's outer defences told. The Harlem landing sites were sparsely defended. A grenadier captain, part of the second wave alongside the 33rd, watched as the light infantry and Guards successfully landed and began to scramble, almost unopposed, to the hill's summit. He wrote that 'the Light Infantry and Guards were landed at the foot of the high ground and dashed up the hill with great alacrity, driving the enemy before them.'[77] The flatboats immediately returned for the grenadiers and 33rd, but their presence was largely unnecessary – Laurel Hill was in British hands.

The battle quickly began to turn elsewhere as well. To the south the 42nd's own ascent was likewise only lightly resisted, while Percy's two assault columns were able to gain the first line of entrenchments. In the north the rebel defence began to falter as rifles became befouled and jammed from repeated use. The Germans, led by the 60-year-old von Knyphausen, in places hauling themselves hand-over-hand using the undergrowth for purchase, stormed the slope.

The rebel lines collapsed. Thousands of soldiers streamed back into Fort Washington as Crown forces closed in from the north, east and south. By the time the 33rd gained Laurel Hill in the wake of the light bobs and Guards, it was almost all over. Despite facing the hardest fighting of the day, the Germans had taken the fort from the north. Four hours after the start of the joint assault, 2,837 Congressional soldiers, including some of Washington's finest infantry, marched out of Fort Washington and surrendered.[78] It was the last major action of the New York campaign, and the worst defeat yet suffered by Congress. Washington despaired.

For the 33rd, however, the work was not yet done. Fort Washington (rechristened Fort Knyphausen) may have fallen, but it still had a twin sister in revolutionary hands – Fort Lee, which lay almost directly opposite across the Hudson, guarding the New Jersey shore. Aware that the momentum was still with him, Howe resolved to take the fort, and assigned Cornwallis to lead the operation.

The Race Through New Jersey

Besides the short excursion on Long Island outside Charleston, it was to be Cornwallis's first independent command. Again the 33rd were brigaded with the army's elite, joining two battalions of light infantry, two battalions

77 Ira D. Gruber (ed.), *John Peebles' American War: The Diary of a Scottish Grenadier, 1776–1782* (Stroud: Sutton Publishing, 1997), p.63.

78 McCullough, *1776*, p.243.

of British grenadiers and another two of German grenadiers, the two Guards battalions and the 42nd Foot. This strong force crossed the Hudson from Dobb's Ferry on Manhattan Island to the Jersey shore, landing at Closter, north of Fort Lee on 18 November. The flatboats once again ferried the men across in darkness, this time with the added, unwelcome addition of a heavy rain, soaking through the men's red coats and swilling in the bottoms of the boats. This stretch of the Hudson was dominated by the Palisades, a towering length of cliffs than dropped almost directly down into the river. Rising to 540 feet at their highest point, they would have loomed like monoliths in the dark as the British expedition landed on the narrow strip of ground between the base of the cliffs and the water's edge. From there, still beset by darkness and rain, they clambered up the exceedingly steep path leading to the crest of the Palisades.[79] Even a small guard would have seen the pathway cut off and the crossing defeated but, as had so often been the case, there were no enemies to oppose the regulars. The expedition gained the heights and pressed on, first to a redoubt designed to protect the fort from the north, and then to fort itself.

They found it almost abandoned. Washington, learning of the crossing and not wanting a repeat of what had happened on Manhattan, had ordered it evacuated just hours before. The British discovered a dozen men in the fort, drunk, and rounded up about 150 stragglers in the immediate vicinity. The rebels had left in such haste that they had abandoned 50 cannons, 1,000 barrels of flour, ammunition and other sundries, including almost all their entrenching tools. Cornwallis ordered no immediate pursuit that night, though Howe tasked him with hunting Washington through New Jersey. After a period of heavy rain Cornwallis's force, swollen to 10,000 men, set off.

A week of marching on filthy roads, with little to no enemy contact, followed. The British movement was ponderous and, as it had been in New York, hampered by indiscipline. New Jersey was one of the wealthier and more prosperous colonies, with large and fertile farms full of livestock and produce.[80] The regulars set about thoroughly looting the area, acts which did nothing to endear them to American colonists of either persuasion.[81] Responding to the concerns of one Loyalist woman about 'the depredations of our Troops' William Howe was noted to be 'very sorry, but, in the present situation of affairs, cannot prevent it; think, from his probity the next Campaign will be more regular, and prevent every Irregularity of this nature.'[82] It is worth pointing out that during their plundering, the British blamed the Hessians and the Hessians blamed the British, while the locals blamed both, along with the Loyalists, who themselves had been subject to plundering by the forces of Congress.[83]

---

79 McCullough, *1776*, p.246.
80 McCullough, *1776*, p.260.
81 Gregory J.W. Urwin, '"To bring the American Army under strict Discipline": British Army Foraging Policy in the South, 1780–81', *War in History*, 2019, vol.26 (1), p.7.
82 Kemble, *Journals of Lieut. Col. Stephen Kemble*, p.99.
83 McCullough, *1776*, pp.260–261.

There was a general expectation that Washington might make a stand at Newark, west of the Great Cedar Swamp and the ferry at Paulus Hook, but the British arrived to find the Continentals gone, carrying on south-west towards Pennsylvania. On the rebels marched, through Elizabethtown, Rahway, and then Brunswick, over the Raritan River. By then there were less than two brigades-worth of soldiers left, their period of enlistment over and their military obligations finished.[84] Washington now had only a skeleton force, bedraggled and ill-equipped. Panic gripped congress, based in Philadelphia just 60 miles away.

Cornwallis paused at Brunswick, allowing Howe and the rest of the army to catch up. On 7 December they pressed on, but the Continentals continued their withdrawal, into Pennsylvania. On 13 December, with the weather starting to turn, Howe brought the campaigning season to a close. In order to protect their gains and continue the reinstitution of Crown authority, British, Loyalist and German forces were dispersed through a chain of townships across the breadth of New Jersey. From Trenton in the south-west to New York itself, via Princeton, Brunswick, Elizabethtown and Newbridge, Howe's army went into their billets, confident that the campaigning season was over.

The 33rd were assigned to Amboy, a settlement near the centre of the chain of towns along the route from New York to Trenton, at the mouth of the Raritan River. It lay four miles south of the nearest other outpost at Woodbridge, where the 46th Foot were initially stationed, and 10 miles north-east of Brunswick, which housed the Guards, grenadiers and three troops of the 16th Light Dragoons. Amboy was an important site both strategically and politically. Founded in 1683 by Scottish Quakers, it sat upon a bluff overlooking Raritan Bay and the southern end of Staten Island. The capital of New Jersey, it included the mansion of the royal governor as well as the grand houses of the colony's administrators and gentry.

The 33rd were put into winter quarters there and enjoyed the good fortune of garrisoning a town that included one of the few purpose-built barracks buildings in North America. Disputes over the quartering of soldiers in private property during the Seven Years War had led to the local Provincial Assembly building a set of barracks fit for 300 men. Completed in 1759, the buildings consisted of a central three-story block for the officers, and flanking L-shaped wings for the enlisted men. The rooms of such purpose-built barracks 'held twelve to sixteen men' who slept on 'bunks built of boards,' sometimes occupied by two men who topped-and-tailed. The army provided the means necessary for barrack living, including bedding and furniture, sheets, blankets and all manner of necessities such as pots, fire shovels and grates, candlesticks, tables, bowls, spoons, ladles, and whatever was required for daily living.[85] Arms and accoutrements were kept in easy reach in case of sudden alarms, hung from pegs in the walls along with other clothing and equipment. Rooms were also furnished with fireplaces that provided both a place for cooking and a source of heat in the bitterly cold New Jersey winter – the Amboy barracks had a total of 26 hearths. Soldiers

84 McCullough, *1776*, p.256.
85 Hagist, *Noble Volunteers*, p.120.

were expected to regularly shake out or wash their bedding, sweep floors, and not misuse furniture or blankets. In all, it was possibly some of the best accommodation the 33rd enjoyed while in North America. Detachments, pickets and patrols, however, had to make do with the warehouses, barns and empty or abandoned properties on the edge of the town and in the smaller neighbourhoods to the west, Bonhamtown and Metuchen.

The 33rd remained Amboy's most constant companions, though other units were stationed with them at various points through to the spring of 1777. For a while they shared quarters with the 57th Foot, and then with the 71st, a detachment of dragoons, a German regiment from Waldeck and the remnants of the 7th and 26th, recently returned to the army as part of a prisoner exchange in December.[86] Amboy's harbour also played host to the Royal Navy, and the town was a hub of military life and activity throughout the winter. The regiment's light and grenadier companies only experienced it late on, however – the composite battalions to which they were attached sailed north for a time in an effort to occupy Rhode Island in late 1776 but, with little in the way of opposition, returned to New Jersey in early 1777.

In the days of mid-December 1776, it seemed as though the 33rd's fighting in America was all but done. The New York campaign had been a success. The Continental Army had been driven from one post to the next, consistently outflanked, outmanoeuvred, and defeated. Only Howe's strategic ponderousness – and some said, leniency – had permitted Washington to escape with the scraps of his force. The 33rd had played its part, performing admirably in a tough campaign that, besides the short debacle outside Charleston, had been its first overseas military service in 13 years. The prevailing belief was that the rebellion would collapse in the coming months or, if it did not, that in the spring Howe would strike its death-blow. Besides that final act, all that remained was to see out the dull monotony of winter quarters. Cornwallis received leave to return to England to visit his dying wife.

On Christmas Day at Newport, five of the officers from the 33rd's grenadier and light companies enjoyed dinner together. The festive period was celebrated, and likely so too was the good news that Dansey's friend and subaltern, Lieutenant Richard Cotton, had that day achieved his promotion to the command of one of his own companies in the 33rd, replacing Captain Jeremiah Tinker, who was at last taking his retirement. Tinker had also served as aide-de-camp to Cornwallis, and this role was taken by the 33rd's Lieutenant Henry Broderick. Ensign William Raymond was promoted to lieutenant and transferred to the light company to replace Cotton. The regiment appeared to have a quiet winter ahead.

Such a belief was mistaken, for in reality the Continental Army was far from beaten, and the war had barely begun. Before even the next Christmas was reached, two of the 33rd's flank company officers enjoying their dinner that day would be dead, and the other three would have suffered wounds.

86 *Westminster Journal and London Political Miscellany*, 8 March 1777, p.2.

Chapter 7

The Glory of this War Over

1777

On 26 December 1776 Washington's army fell upon the Hessian garrison at Trenton, the most advanced of the outposts in New Jersey. The attack was a complete success, taking the Germans by surprise and capturing the majority. The British response to this unexpected setback was immediate. From New York, Howe cancelled Cornwallis's leave and ordered him to assemble a force to strike south-west after the victorious rebels. Consequently, the 33rd found themselves turned out of their quarters in Amboy and once again marching the frost-hardened roads of New Jersey.

The army reached Princeton on New Year's Day, 1777. Leaving behind a rearguard, Cornwallis continued, through Maidenhead and on towards rebel-occupied Trenton. The weather turned unexpectedly mild, melting the frost and once more turning the roads to mud, quickly churned up by feet, hooves, and the wheels of wagons and artillery. Tramping through the muck, the British vanguard engaged rebel riflemen on 2 January, driving them back through Trenton itself.

The rebels retreated across the Assunpink creek bridge to where Washington's main body lay, south-east of Trenton and on the east bank of the Delaware, the same side as the British. After an artillery duel, Crown forces tried three times to storm the bridge, but to no avail. Darkness fell, with Cornwallis waiting to see if Washington remained to fight the next day, or whether he withdrew via the small fleet of boats he had assembled back across the Delaware and into Pennsylvania. The 33rd, like the rest of the army, spent a miserable night as the January weather closed in again, sleeping on the frozen ground without campfires.[1]

The fact that the winter sun rose to reveal that those same fires had been left burning while the enemy marched out under cover of darkness was not, perhaps, a great surprise. What was surprising was the sound of artillery fire coming from the north-east, in the direction the British had approached

1 McCullough, *1776*, p.288.

from. Washington, it seemed, had not retreated across the Delaware after all. Instead, he had struck boldly into enemy territory, leaving behind Cornwallis's army at Trenton and attacking his rearguard at Princeton. The 33rd and the rest of the force countermarched after the revolutionaries but failed to catch up as they withdrew south-east following their successful strike on Princeton. While the numbers involved were not great, Washington had won his second victory in a little over a week, routing three regiments of British regulars and taking several hundred prisoners in the process.

The 33rd returned to Amboy as the decision was made to withdraw from the more far-flung outposts in New Jersey. Brunswick and Amboy were to be the main focus of the new concentration, and the latter became so full that troops had to remain onboard their transport ships in Raritan Bay.

On 28 January men of the 33rd were turned out of their billets in the town to the clanging of alarm bells. A fire had broken out at the home of Loyalist Stephen Skinner, completely consuming it and spreading to neighbouring warehouses. These 'were filled with military stores, which were saved from destruction by the activity of the 33rd regiment quartered there, and of the sailors belonging to the ships in the harbour.'[2]

By the start of April, it also became apparent that the new clothing required by the 33rd – in line with the refit the entire army had during each winter season – had been waylaid. The transport, the *Nottingham*, had not arrived as expected in Quebec five months previously. Word arrived from Britain that new clothing would be packed for shipping by 10 March.

The British presence in New Jersey, while welcomed by some Loyalists, was fiercely opposed by New Jersey's Whigs. In the aftermath of the Continental Army's withdrawal and the brutalities of British pillaging there was a general rising of the local revolutionary militia, aided and abetted by Washington in January as he moved to reclaim the outposts given up by the British after Princeton. The 33rd subsequently found itself caught up in a low-level guerrilla war, where small bands of revolutionaries, or even individuals, would take opportunistic pot-shots around British posts, especially at sentries and pickets. One German officer declared that that;

> It is now very unsafe for us to travel in Jersey. The rascal peasants meet our men alone or in small, unarmed groups. They have their rifles hidden in the bushes or ditches and the like. When they believe they are sure of success and they see one or several men belonging to our army, they shoot them in the head, then quickly hide their rifles and pretend they know nothing.[3]

The withdrawal from their more extended lines meant Crown forces had less security over the forage required to feed the army in and around New York. Cattle, grain and fodder had to be rounded up by patrols sent out into the countryside. Naturally, these patrols made good targets for rebel forces

2 *Morning Chronicle*, 25 February 1777, p.1.

3 Friedrich Ernst Von Muenchhausen, *At General Howe's Side, 1776-1778: The Diary of General William Howe's Aide de Camp, Captain Friedrich Von Muenchhausen* (Monmouth Beach: Philip Freneau Press, 1974), p.7.

Leather cartridge pouches had wooden blocks with holes drilled in them for storing the premade ammunition cartridges. Beneath the blocks was a compartment where musket cleaning tools and other small objects could be kept. (Photo by Henry Gage)

that knew the area. Washington had ordered the removal or destruction of potential supplies in an effort to exacerbate such difficulties. The winter and spring were therefore full of clashes between the Crown forces and the Whigs looking for food, precipitating a localised guerrilla war.

This petite guerre, as it was known in the period, took its toll on the 33rd, as it did all regiments stationed in New Jersey. 'Again and again marauders who caused them extreme annoyance, shot down the pickets. The 33rd lost many men by reason of this winter activity on the part of the enemy.'[4] It seems however that Lieutenant Colonel James Webster proved adept at this trying style of warfare. A 1781 account speaks of how his attention to detail spared the 33rd the level of losses suffered by other units;

> It was his constant practice to shift is picquet ground every night, by which means, the rebel parties, who constantly surrounded our quarters from January to June 1777, in feeling in the dark for the picquet, generally fell into the trap and suffered for their forwardness; so that in a short time his quarter was less molested than any part of the cantonment. This mode of shifting the picquet ground, was ridiculed by some, who had more presumption than judgement, they following their own plans, and paid for it; their picquets were attacked every night, and their whole quarter incessantly harassed.[5]

Between January and April both Amboy and neighbouring Bonhamtown were involved in around 10 skirmishes, with both sides playing cat and mouse.[6] On 12 April, for example, two battalions of light infantry and one of grenadiers marched out at 8:00 p.m. and surprised rebel forces the next day at Bound Brook, scattering them after a sharp skirmish and taking prisoners, horses, cattle, sheep and three brass cannon back to British lines. On 14 April the revolutionaries retaliated, specifically against the 33rd while they were posted at Bonhamtown. They 'brought down five hundred men in order to surprize a post of ours where the thirty-third, and one battalion of the seventy-first are quartered.'[7] According to one newspaper the raid was

4 Lee, *History of the Thirty-third*, p.101.

5 Anon., 'For the Political Magazine', p.342.

6 David C. Munn, *Battles and Skirmishes of the American Revolution in New Jersey* (Trenton: Department of Environmental Protection, Bureau of Geology and Topography, 1976), pp.6–16.

7 *Shrewsbury Chronicle*, 14 June 1777, p.3.

commanded by a former sergeant of the 33rd who had deserted, joined the revolutionaries, and been given an officer's commission. In a personal blow against his old regiment, the unnamed deserter and his men; 'Surrounded a picquet consisting of a serjeant and twelve men, which they took, but being a little frighted, mistook their own people for ours and began firing upon each other, which threw them into such confusion that they took to their heels leaving behind them two of their wounded, thirty-five stand of arms and a number of hats bloody.'[8]

It is important to note the newspapers of the period often printed incorrect information, and no sergeant of the 33rd is recorded as having deserted during this period, unless it was the sergeant captured at Cape Fear in May 1776. The rebels claimed a captain, and seven privates were killed and 16 men taken prisoner.[9] Dansey recorded it somewhat differently, generally corroborating the other British report in a letter home when he claimed that the attack 'miscarried they took 13 Men from one of the out Guards and in their hurry and Confusion fired upon one another, they left two of their own men wounded and upwards of 30 Stand of Arms so we suppose they must have a great many of them kill'd and wounded which they carried off.'[10] Regardless, prisoners were certainly taken, for records remain of one of the 33rd's men, Joseph Driver, being question by his captors two days later. Driver, born in Leeds in 1750, had been with the army since 1769 and with the 33rd since at least 1775.[11] He admitted that the men were subsisting on salt provisions rather than fresh ones, doubtless because of the difficulty in taking supplies from New Jersey, and that they had cut up old tents to make new trousers due to not having yet been sent new ones. There was 'plenty of Oats' and 'some fresh Hay' as fodder, and the horses were 'in tolerable order.' He repeated the usual rumours that percolated through the army, in this case that there was 'talk of the Army that Carlton [the British commander in Canada] is to join before the Campaign opens, and that 20,000 Foreigners [Hessians] are to come over.' This and his claim that Howe had 50,000 men fit for duty and Carlton 60,000 plus 30,000 allied Natives unsurprisingly caused his questioner to note that he was 'most extravagant in all his Accounts.'[12]

Joseph Driver had a relatively active time both in captivity and out of it. During the posting at Bonhamtown a different private soldier in the 33rd, William Walch, deserted his post, fleeing without his arms or necessaries. Walch was a veteran, having spent at least 16 years in the regiment, and the reasons for his flight are not recorded. After Joseph Driver was captured and interrogated, he was held with other British prisoners at the town of Lancaster. Driver had fallen ill, and during his convalescing he saw someone he recognised, a fellow former soldier of the 33rd, William Walch. However, Walch was not also a prisoner – he had swapped his uniform for that of

8 *Shrewsbury Chronicle*, 14 June 1777, p.3.

9 Munn, *Battles and Skirmishes*, p.15. There is no record of one of the 33rd's captains being taken prisoner, though it may have been an officer from a different regiment.

10 Dansey (ed.), *Captured Rebel Flag*, pp.26–27.

11 TNA: WO 121/10/48: Certificate of John Driver.

12 Library of Congress (LOC): George Washington Papers: Series 4, Reel 41, 6 April 1777–29 May 1777.

the Continental Army, having not only deserted, but then enlisted with the rebel forces. Recognizing Driver, Walch 'asked him how he did, and upon his answering that he was not well,' Walsh 'said to him "the Devil relieve you."'[13] After this insult, Driver observed Walsh 'parading a Guard of Rebels, and that he was acting as a Corporal.'[14] Another prisoner from the 33rd, John Collins, likewise recognised Walsh, noting that he was now serving in the Continental Army's 4th Georgia Regiment, an infamous unit made up of British deserters.

A year and a half later, fate saw fit to turn the tables. Joseph Driver not only survived his sickness but was part of a prisoner exchange in 1778, re-joining the 33rd. Later on, William Walch was in turn captured by the British while being transported aboard a schooner sailing from Sandbury to Charleston. A court martial was convened in New York and Walch was tried, with Driver, Collins, and other old comrades of the 33rd called forward as witnesses. Walch's only defence was that he had not been captured while bearing arms, and that he had immediately admitted his identity. It was not enough. The court sentenced him 'to Suffer Death.'[15] Walch was duly executed.

Six days after the raid that first captured Joseph Driver at Bonhamtown, another rebel party of 25 men attempted to surprise the pickets but were themselves killed or captured, with those taken prisoners marched to Amboy the next day.[16] On 23 April the rebels attempted to surprise another outpost at Amboy but found that the sentries had already been withdrawn from the position. The next day they tried again. On their third attempt on 25 April their attack was pre-empted and those involved were killed or captured.[17] So the back-and-forth affair of posts continued.

At the start of February Stephen Kemble recorded 'the Weather Milder, Rebels Lurking about Kings Bridge and infesting our Ports in Jersey, our Foraging Parties not exempt from Insult, but come off with Credit upon every occasion.'[18] The 33rd missed out on the largest of these skirmishes at Bound Brook, Millstone, Drake's Farm and Quibbletown, but they felt the effects – privation and frustration – as much as the rest of the army. It was a war of posts, exactly the Fabian strategy that Washington hoped to pursue, one which slowly wore down Crown forces while denying them a decisive pitched battle. And while the 33rd's battalion companies were not engaged in the larger New Jersey skirmishes their flank companies, unsurprisingly, were more active. Dansey and his lights were in action, striking back against Whig raiders and foragers following their return from Rhode Island.

On 23 February the 33rd's light company clashed with the rebels at Ash Swamp, about 11 miles north-west of Amboy. Dansey surprised himself with his marksmanship, recalling how;

13 TNA: WO 71/88: Courts Martial Proceedings, pp.418–420.
14 TNA: WO 71/88: Courts Martial Proceedings, pp.418–420.
15 TNA: WO 71/88: Courts Martial Proceedings, pp.418–420.
16 Munn, *Battles and Skirmishes*, pp.15–16.
17 Munn, *Battles and Skirmishes*, pp.6–7.
18 Kemble, *Journals of Lieut. Col. Stephen Kemble*, p.110.

> … you know I was never a famous Shot … a Fellow jum'd from behind a Bush very near me ran behind a Tree and presented at us, I up with my Fuzee and knock'd him as quick as a Cockshooter wou'd a Cock, so don't fear [for] me, who never was cool enough at home to kill a Woodcock, yet now am got cool enough to shoot a Man.[19]

During another skirmish Dansey noted how many of the injuries suffered by his men were in their arms, as they had become accustomed to taking cover behind trees during forest fighting in the same way the rebels did, leaving only their extremities occasionally exposed to fire.[20] Indeed, light infantry were encouraged to make use of trees as cover, and the very phrase 'to tree' entered into the army's lexicon as a word of command.[21]

During one such skirmish Dansey found himself and the rest of the 33rd's light company facing 200 revolutionaries in forested terrain. Hoping 'they would be bullied to surrender,' he called out to the enemy, who were only 20 yards away, 'by God my Lads we have you now' but 'they answer'd me with heavy fire.' Both sides exchanged shots as Dansey 'got my men to the trees round about me' and received another light company, who came up in support. Seeing the rebels 'snug behind the Trees and showing no disposition to run, and too many of them to charge,' Dansey resolved on a different ruse de guerre;

> I cried as loud as I cou'd hollow that they might be sure to hear me 'by God Soldiers they run, have at them my brave Boys' which had the desired effect, one thought the other run and they all set off as if the D–l drove them we clear'd the Wood of them and they never travelled themselves within Shot again that Day.[22]

When writing home Dansey alternated between expressing thankfulness at his continued survival and reassuring his loved ones that he was safe. 'I tell you this Story as it really happen'd that you may be less afraid of the Dangers I undergo,' he wrote about the above skirmish, 'as I now pretty well understand how to encounter them.'[23] In March he noted that 'as to War's Alarms they are now come so familiar that a Day's Yankie Hunting is no more minded than a Day's Fox Hunting, at both Diversions a Broken Bone may be got.'[24] In reality matters were more precarious than he sometimes admitted, for the light and grenadier companies were constantly exposed to the hardest fighting. Indeed, over the course of 1776 and throughout 1777, the 33rd's light company that had paraded with the rest of the regiment in Ireland in 1775 practically ceased to exist. Of the 36 privates, 13 were killed during that period, 20 wounded and four taken prisoner, while the drummers and NCOs also suffered near-total casualties. Indeed, as Dansey noted, between 1776

19 Dansey (ed.), *Captured Rebel Flag*, p.23.
20 Dansey (ed.), *Captured Rebel Flag*, p.27.
21 Spring, *With Zeal and With Bayonets Only*, pp.254–255.
22 Dansey (ed.), *Captured Rebel Flag*, p.27.
23 Dansey (ed.), *Captured Rebel Flag*, p.27.
24 Dansey (ed.), *Captured Rebel Flag*, p.23.

and the end of 1777 his company suffered more casualties than its original standing strength in Ireland and was only sustained 'by getting fresh Men for those kill'd and disabled.'[25] The light company of the 33rd had 119 men serve in it over the course of the war, while 120 men served in the 33rd's grenadier company. The attrition in the flank companies was brutal.

While the winter of 1776 to 1777 certainly was not a peaceful one, it was still a far cry from active campaigning. Dansey's letters at times speak to the monotony experienced by the whole regiment. With the light battalion, he remained onboard transport ships outside Amboy after returning from Rhode Island because the town was too full of billeted troops to find lodgings. 'Here we are likely to stay for some time as there is no Room for us on Shore till Sir William Howe thinks proper we should fight for it,' he wrote. 'For my part I had rather stay on board this time of Year than fight for bad Quarters.'[26] In his letters home he commented on his young cousin Richard, advising his mother to 'give him every Encouragement in your power to his Learning and let him have any Mathematical Books of mine he may want,' and stating that if he 'is likely to turn out clever I shall be proud when I come back again of paying him a great deal of Attention.' He did his best to save money, foregoing the luxuries sometimes associated with the officers, and wondered about life back in England, asking after the familiar figures of his home at Brinsop and pointing out that 'I dread more any dispute there than all the Rebels in America.' He relayed praise of his friend and fellow 33rd light company officer Ensign Gorges, whose mother was friends with his own, writing that he 'bears the best Character I ever knew a young Gentleman of his years.'[27] He passed on that his young servant Ben was very happy to have heard from his own parents via the Dansey family's correspondence.

He also wrote about the enlisted men in his company with whom he had a personal acquaintance, adding in one letter that his mother was to 'send word to Ludlow that Drumr. [Edward] Peach, Son to a Miller at Ludlow, one of my first Herefordshire Recruits, was missing in the Skirmish of the 23d. Feb. last and is supposed to be taken Prisoner.' Peach was eventually exchanged in 1780 but died in 1784. In another letter to his mother he told of how he had written to a certain Mrs Thomas 'to tell her that her husband is Prisoner with the Rebels, he is a fine Soldier you may remember him for he was a favorite of yours.'[28] The man in question, William Thomas, was listed as having deserted on 8 February 1778, either because he deserted after being exchanged, or never returned after his captivity.

Dansey's comments about his men, especially ones he had personally enlisted, were not uncommon in his writing, and shows a degree of concern that eighteenth-century British officers are rarely credited with. In reality 'a paternalistic relationship existed between at least some officers and their

25 DHS: William Dansey Letters: 19 January 1778.

26 Dansey (ed.), *Captured Rebel Flag*, p.21.

27 Dansey (ed.), *Captured Rebel Flag*, pp.21–23.

28 Dansey (ed.), *Captured Rebel Flag*, pp.25–26. Ludlow is actually in Shropshire rather than Herefordshire, though Edward Peach may have come from somewhere in Herefordshire originally.

men,' with soldiers aware that they had certain unwritten rights and privileges and would be cared for by a good officer. It was 'likely that the nature of this relationship differed from company to company and that the conditions of active service significantly altered its dynamics.'[29] As we have already seen, the 33rd's flank companies in particular suffered an extreme turnover in men during the course of just a few campaigns, and the sense of shared hardship and dutiful attachment between officers and men could not always be guaranteed. However, as Roger Lamb noted, 'the military man, like the civil individual, is won by generous treatment and humanity.'[30] A fact that many officers seem to have been aware of. British soldiers understood their rights, but also showed great loyalty and, at times, selfless sacrifice for commanders who had earned their respect and trust.[31] Ultimately, officers could not assume obedience or enforce it with brute discipline alone. They were forced to accept that their soldiers were thinking beings, and not automata. The best officers accepted this.[32] The good regard, and even empathy, felt between many officers and enlisted men was a notable reality of soldiering during the Revolution.

The Shift Towards Philadelphia

There had been high anticipation during the winter about finally defeating the rebellion in 1777, but the 33rd had to endure along with the rest of the army as their commanders delayed the beginning of that year's campaigning season. Howe had started to despair of ever drawing Washington's Continentals into a battle of annihilation. Instead, he fixed his hopes on capturing Philadelphia, seat of the rebel Congress, a blow that he believed would finally snuff out the revolution's spark. In late May the 33rd were still waiting, Cornwallis's movements delayed due to a lack of tents and field equipment from Britain.[33]

In fact, it was Washington who made the first notable move of the summer, marching his army from its winter quarters at Morristown to Middlebrook. From there he was capable of threatening Howe if the British made a strike towards Philadelphia but could still withdraw into the mountainous region further north if he decided to continue to avoid a pitched battle. In early June Howe finally responded, collecting the army from around New York, Amboy and Brunswick and marching to Somerset Courthouse, where he hoped to lure Washington into battle. Washington declined, and Howe returned to Amboy, abandoning Brunswick entirely.

Washington pursued cautiously. On 26 June Howe turned abruptly and struck at an extended part of Washington's army, an engagement which included the 33rd's flank companies in their composite battalions. Dansey

29 Spring, *With Zeal*, p.107.
30 Lamb, *Memoir*, p.63.
31 Conway, *The British Army*, p.99.
32 Conway, *The British Army*, p.107.
33 Lee, *History of the Thirty-third*, p.102.

reported it as 'a Brush or two with the Rebels lately in the Jerseys.'[34] The engagement was indecisive, the rebels retreating to safety. The British returned to Amboy, Howe's designs frustrated and, on 30 June, evacuated the town along with the last of their holdings in New Jersey. The ground that had been won in November the previous year and held onto with not inconsiderable loss had been given up.

The British commanders had decided upon a strategic redeployment. The first half of July was spent in and around New York preparing for a strike against Philadelphia. The army would not repeat its march across the breadth of New Jersey to get there, however. Utilising his seaborne superiority, Howe intended to embark on transports and sail south to the Chesapeake before marching north overland, striking at Philadelphia from the opposite side. As part of the preparations for the new campaign, the makeup of the composite flank battalions as well as the regular brigades underwent a reshuffle. The 33rd's light company and grenadier company were both assigned to the 1st of their respective flank battalions, while the remainder of the 33rd's eight companies joined the 37th, 46th and 64th Regiments of Foot in the 4th Brigade, commanded by Brigadier General James Agnew. It is notable that both the 33rd and 42nd were no longer part of the army's elite vanguard, which now consisted of the Queen's Rangers, the light and grenadier battalions, and the Brigade of Guards. Whether this was because the 33rd had not impressed sufficiently since the end of 1776, or whether it was simply down to the practicalities of reorganising the line battalions is unclear. It may also have been because the newly-formed Queen's Rangers were more suited to the role, and the 33rd who, as we shall see, had recently lost a large intake of recruits at Saratoga, was operating with smaller numbers than most other regiments in the army.

In May the 33rd received their waylaid clothing for the year while based in Bonhamtown. By 30 June the army had shifted to Staten Island, where they encamped until 8 July, when the embarkations began. On 20 July the fleet of over 260 ships set sail, bearing almost 17,000 men south. Contrary winds made the journey, in Dansey's words, 'long, tedious and dangerous.'[35] Eventually, on 25 August, the ships arrived at the Elk River, at the north-eastern extreme of Chesapeake Bay. While the Elk brought the army close to Philadelphia, it was a far from ideal location for a large-scale disembarkation. The river's neck was shallow and the banks muddy. The army was required to land in five separate waves. The 33rd were part of the fourth disembarkation. That night they built shelters and encamped parallel with the river.

News of the British approach seems to have resulted in a local exodus. As the army began to march towards Philadelphia one officer reported that they 'found the habitations in general deserted, but some cattle remaining in the fields.'[36] This did not, however, stop the profligate activities the regulars had become accustomed to in New York and New Jersey. The first day

34 Dansey (ed.), *Captured Rebel Flag*, p.28.

35 Dansey (ed.), *Captured Rebel Flag*, p.33.

36 John André, *André's Journal: An Authentic Record of the Movements and Engagements of the British Army in America* (Boston: Bibliophile Society, 1903), vol.1, p.71.

after disembarking it was reported that 'there was a good deal of plunder committed by the troops, notwithstanding the strictest prohibitions. No method was yet fixed upon for supplying the troops with fresh provisions in a regular manner. The soldiers slaughtered a great deal of cattle clandestinely.'[37] These actions may not have been quite so clandestine in the eyes of the junior officers, for it was generally accepted that occasional fresh food was something a soldier had a right to take if it could not be provided. Officers realised that if their men were not kept supplied with fresh produce as a supplement for their salt rations, there would be problems.[38] On Long Island in 1779, for example, a number of soldiers from the 43rd Foot went on trial after being accused of stealing and slaughtering an ox. Their defence was that their ration of small items such as butter, cheese and peas had not been supplied, and they had thus felt themselves within their rights to supplement their diet in another fashion.[39] It is unlikely that company-level officers were wholly unaware of these sorts of violations, indeed some seem to have actively encouraged the pillaging. Lieutenant Martin Hunter of the 52nd's light infantry company described with pride the abilities of the light battalions to plunder American homesteads.[40] If the price of keeping soldiers well-fed and contented was the despoiling of colonial property, then at least a few captains, lieutenants and ensigns seem to have been willing to allow it. Such complicity helps explain Howe's complaints following the pillaging in New York, that it simply could not be avoided. The general officers knew that even their authority had its limitations while on campaign. Far from being servile, British regulars possessed a streak of entitlement and confidence that contributed to their effectiveness as soldiers even as it harmed their standing in the American colonies.

Five days after landing, Dansey sat down beneath a tree in a wood near the Head of Elk and penned a roughly-written letter to his mother where he described the journey from Philadelphia and the beauty of the Chesapeake Bay. He also spoke of the anticipated privation of soldiering. With much of the camp equipage left behind, the 33rd had landed 'with no other Conveniences than what we cou'd carry on our Backs.' Dansey confided that 'I don't expect to have my Cloths off or see the inside of a House on this Side Christmas.'[41] Such realities were not uncommon during hard campaigning, especially for the light companies. Lieutenant Colin Campbell of the 74th Foot wrote, for example, that for 10 weeks 'I had neither my clothes or side-arms off, except while shifting, or never lay down to sleep without my fuzee stretched alongside of me, or within my arms, ready to start up with it to the first sound of the bugle horn.'[42] Captain Charles Cochrane of the 4th Foot complained during the New Jersey skirmishing that 'I don't believe a man of this army, ever since the affair of Tronton [*sic*]... have had their clothes off' – a period

37 André, *André's Journal*, vol.1, p.71.
38 Conway, *The British Army*, p.105.
39 Conway, *The British Army*, p.105.
40 Spring, *With Zeal*, p.115.
41 Dansey (ed.), *Captured Rebel Flag*, p.33.
42 Colin Campbell, 20 November 1780, in Anthony Sterling, *The Story of the Highland Brigade in the Crimea* (London: Remington and Company, 1895), pp.xv–xvi.

of over two months.[43] Nevertheless, Dansey and his men were 'in rare Spirits' and anticipated 'our being in the Possession of Philadelphia' presently.[44] The campaign for 1777 was finally underway.

The British pushed inland. As they did so they dispersed small groups of rebels, and foraged. On 28 August the lead elements of the army 'took a considerable quantity of tobacco, Indian corn, oats and other articles' whilst 'General Grey sent out a party from the 3rd Brigade for cattle; they brought in eighteen head; a distribution was made of it the next day.' On 30 August 'parties were sent out … to drive in cattle and gather roots,' following instructions issued the day before by Howe to 'have as many cattle and horses collected as possible, and driven with the Army.' On 31 August it was reported '350 sheep, 55 horned cattle and about 24 horses or mules were brought in. Several people assisted in bringing in their cattle and of their own accord drove it to camp next day. Some Germans belonging to a baggage guard demolished 'a whole flock of sheep which the owners were voluntarily driving to us.'[45] On 2 September 'detachments of 100 men each marched to the right and left of the Column, at about half a mile distance to collect cattle … 60 barrels of flour were taken. The inhabitants were in general fled and a great deal of cattle driven off.' These activities were typical of the British Army on the march in America, where supplies shipped from Britain were supplemented as much as possible by local produce, both bought and stolen. The local inhabitants made 'great complaints… of the plunder committed by the troops, chiefly the Hessians.'[46]

The 33rd saw little of this foraging. With the rest of the 4th Brigade, among others, they were detailed to remain in the army's rear, keeping open communications between the steadily-advancing columns and the shipping that remained at the Head of Elk. On 6 September orders arrived for them to join the main force, thus severing the army's connection with the sea as Howe struck inland, towards Philadelphia. Reports circulated that Washington was positioning his forces to defend the rebel capital, a belief corroborated by deserters who 'insisted that their General was in the intention to stand an action.'[47]

On 9 September the unglamorous realities of manoeuvring large bodies of soldiers, supplies and camp followers in unknown countryside became more apparent. Typically, the armies of both sides were divided into two or three columns of march that could best utilise the comparatively primitive road systems without clogging them. Mistakes, however, were sometimes made. On 9 September Howe issued orders for the army to march at 1:00 p.m. in two columns. There were unspecified delays that meant the troops did not set off until sunset. The 33rd, with the 4th Brigade in the right-hand column, found the road to be in a very bad condition and, 'were ordered, together

43 Charles Cochran, 8 March 1777, in James Paterson, *History of the County of Ayr, with a Genealogical Account of the Families of Ayrshire* (Edinburgh: Thomas George Stevenson, 1852) vol.II, p.28.

44 Dansey (ed.), *Captured Rebel Flag*, p.33.

45 André, *André's Journal*, pp.71–78.

46 André, *André's Journal*, pp.71–79.

47 André, *André's Journal*, p.78.

with a brigade of artillery and the baggage of that column, to turn back' and take the road already used by the other column. This 'was attended with a great deal of trouble and protracted the march of the Brigade in the rear till near 3 o'clock the next day.' The 33rd and the other regiments of the 4th Brigade were at the front of the column, and unwisely quickened their pace to catch the column ahead of them on the same road, which lead to a gap of two or three miles opening between them and the more ponderous supply wagons. Major John André, an officer of the 26th Foot who held a number of different staff roles, noted that 'it was fortunate we had not an enterprising well-informed enemy near us' to take advantage in the lapse of security.[48] To compound the problems further, there was a delay at a crossroads as the 4th Brigade struggled to ascertain just which road the column they were trying to catch up with had taken. Eventually the right road was found, and the arduous march completed.

Around this time Dansey and the 33rd's lights had a stroke of good fortune. While acting as a flanking party they fell in with a set of supplies belonging to the Delaware militia, capturing them seemingly without a fight. Among the effects taken were horses, weapons, drums and a flag, as well as the brother of a militia colonel, possibly Colonel Patterson of Christina. The silken flag, likely a grand divisional colour rather than a regimental one, was dark green with 13 red and white stripes in its upper canton and two passementerie tassels made from interlaced green, blue, and yellow silk that hung from green and gold silk cords. Dansey reported that the colonel's personal effects were returned to him, but 'the Horse, Arms & Colours came to my share, the later I hope to bring as a Trophy to Brinsop, I have not told Miss M. this but you must, and she has something to tell you.'[49] The captured rebel flag was indeed taken to Brinsop, and remained the property of the Dansey family until it was auctioned in 1927. It was purchased by the Historical Society of Delaware, who currently display it in their museum.

After days spent advancing with almost no enemy contact, it looked as though the rebels had finally decided to make a stand. Washington, torn between continuing his Fabian strategy of battle-denial and defending Philadelphia, decided on the latter. The site he chose to fight his battle was a strong one. South of the city ran the river Brandywine, which the British would have to cross if they were to reach the seat of congress. Washington planted the Continental Army at one of the passages over the river, Chadd's Ford. Attacking head-on over the crossing would doubtless incur fearful losses. Washington's flanks, meanwhile, seemed secure enough, for the terrain was a mixture of small farms and settlements interspersed among forests, hills and ravines, ground that would inevitably delay and break up any flanking manoeuvre. Or so Washington believed.

48 André, *André's Journal*, p.83.
49 Dansey (ed.), *Captured Rebel Flag*, p.36.

The first phase of the Battle of Brandywine, 11 September 1777.

The Battle of Brandywine

The dawn of 11 September was shrouded by a heavy fog. Howe intended to test Washington's generalship by repeating the same trick that had so decisively won the Battle of Long Island. While a portion of the army demonstrated in front of the rebels to keep their attention fixed at Chadd's Ford, the main part of the army would swing wide to the north-east, cross the Brandywine further upstream, and sweep down on Washington's forces in a grand flanking manoeuvre.

The 33rd, with the rest of the 4th Brigade, were to be part of that left hook, commanded by Cornwallis. Orders were circulated among the 33rd the night before that they were to be ready to march at daybreak and were to have their baggage loaded an hour before. The column moved out from Kennett Square, west of Chadd's Ford, at 5:00 a.m. The fog soon burned off as the sun rose. It promised to be a hot day, and dust from the tramping column soon befouled the soldiers. On they marched, first north via the Great Valley Road, crossing the western fork of the Brandywine at Trimble's Ford and the eastern at Jeffery's Ford. Finally, they turned south through the small settlement of Sconneltown, bearing down on Washington's flank from the north. As they went, they could hear the thunderclap of artillery from Chadd's Ford. Half an hour after they had stepped off, the ever-redoubtable von Knyphausen, who had been given command of the pinning force, had led his division against rebel advance guards west of the ford. The Continentals were driven back from their positions at Welch's Tavern, Kennett Meeting House – where a congregation of Quakers held a service in serene defiance of the fighting raging around them – and the house of James Brinton before falling back over the river, where Washington prepared his forces for what he believed would be a frontal assault.

Intelligence of the flanking march disabused him of this notion. He deployed forces north to cover his right, aided by the fact that Howe and Cornwallis had momentarily paused. The flanking force had marched over 12 miles in nine hours, including crossing two fords, and all on the back of several days hard marching. Exhaustion threatened to break the combat effectiveness of the regulars. One officer, Lieutenant Loftus Cliffe, wrote that 'the fatigues of this Day were excessive: some of our best men were obliged to yield, one of [the]33[rd Regiment] droped dead.'[50] One of the 33rd's own officers, 20-year-old Lieutenant George Duke, wrote after that Washington intended to make 'a Stand, but not long Marching above Sixteen Miles, which We was from Day break to three o Clock in the Afternoon a doing owing greatly to the badness of the Roads which did not allow the Cannon to get on faster, by that time you must imagine our men were pretty much fatigued.'[51] Knowing that his men had been pushed to their limit – and, in the case of the 33rd's one casualty, beyond it – Howe authorised a pause much as he had done before striking the fatal blow at Long Island. The British occupied

50 Loftus Cliffe, 24 October 1777, in Spring, *With Zeal*, p.277.

51 George Duke, 'German Town Camp Octr 13, 1777,' from a letter sold in May 2008 at a private auction. Transcript courtesy of Don Hagist.

Osborne Hill, facing Continental positions further south on Birmingham Hill, and were allowed to sit down, draw food from their haversacks, and eat. A number of locals, curious about the army marching through their land, mingled with the soldiers on their route and during the break. One, a Quaker named Joseph Townsend, left a detailed account;

> We walked on until we approached the flanking party, where a soldier under arms called out, 'Where are you going?' We replied that we wished to see the army, if there was no objection. He observed that there was their captain, we must speak to him; which being done, leave was readily obtained, and in a few minutes we found ourselves in the midst of military characters, rank and file ... My brother called to me ... to see Gen. Lord Cornwallis, who was passing by. He was on horseback, appeared very tall and sat very erect. His rich scarlet clothing, loaded with gold lace, epaulets, etc., occasioned him to make a brilliant and martial appearance. The advance portion of the army made a halt at this place, and refreshed their horses by hastily clearing off some of the corn patches.[52]

The locals talked with a number of officers, who variously lambasted Washington for taking up arms against his king and complimented the beauty of the local countryside. Meanwhile their men ate what food they had with them. General Howe, after observing rebel movements on Birmingham Hill, likewise sat down to eat, his calm countenance noted by one of his subordinates.[53]

After about an hour's pause, the British reformed and began to spread out into their battle lines. Townsend 'was met by several companies of soldiers who were ordered into the field to form and prepare for the approaching engagement' and was ordered by a German officer to assist in taking down rails from a fence to widen a gap and allow more soldiers through.[54] Howe deployed a front line consisting of, from his right to left, the brigade of Guards, the British 1st and 2nd Grenadier battalions, the 1st and 2nd Light Infantry battalions, and German jäger. Immediately behind them was a second line consisting of the German grenadiers and the regiments of the 4th Brigade, and behind them, in reserve, the 3rd Brigade and a force of light dragoons. The 33rd, on the far right of the 4th Brigade, were therefore in the centre of the second line of attack.

Prior to stepping off a light infantry officer, Lieutenant Martin Hunter of the 52nd Regiment, recalled that Lieutenant Colonel William Medows, made an often quoted speech to his 1st Battalion of Grenadiers: 'Grenadiers, put on your caps; for damned fighting and drinking I'll match you against the world.'[55] Captain Hildebrand Oakes and the rest of the 33rd's grenadiers were among the elite infantrymen who donned their famous bearskin caps – a

52 Joseph Townsend, in J. Smith Futhey and Gilbert Cope, *History of Chester County, Pennsylvania, with Genealogical and Biographical Sketches* (Philadelphia: Louis H. Everts, 1881), p.75.

53 Mark Urban, *Fusiliers: Eight Years with the Redcoats in America* (London: Faber and Faber, 2007), pp.117–118.

54 Joseph Townsend, in Futhey and Cope, *History of Chester County*, p.76.

55 Martin Hunter, in Spring, *With Zeal*, p.116.

rarity in combat – during their commander's fiery oration, moments before those fifes and drums that accompanied them struck up the familiar tune of The Grenadiers' March. Not to be outdone, the German grenadiers donned their brass-plated caps and advanced to their own march.[56] One British grenadier officer wrote that 'nothing could be more dreadfully pleasing than the line moving on to the attack … believe me I would not exchange those three minutes of rapture to avoid ten thousand times the danger.'[57] The 33rd's Lieutenant Duke similarly recalled 'when they formed at 3 o'Clock the enemy so close, the March and fatigue was all forgot, it's impossible for Men ever to go into the field, with more spirit and determined resolution then [*sic*] they did, to drive them out of the Field.'[58] Townsend, watching on, remembered 'a grand view of the British army, as they advanced over and down the side of Osborne's Hill and the lands of James Carter; scarcely a vacant space left.'[59] For once in America, the popular imagination of the pomp and splendour of eighteenth-century combat was fully realised.

The British and Germans marched down Osborne Hill, meeting as they went fences and stone walls amidst the small hills and steep valleys. The ragged terrain meant line of sight was restricted, and there was no clear view of the enemy ahead.[60] Intending to contest with them for Birmingham Hill was a force of 3,400 Continental Army regulars arraying for combat, the largest concentrated force of Congressional troops yet committed to a line-of-battle. Unfortunately for them, their dispositions were not yet complete as the British advanced, as the Maryland troops assigned to the left flank were not yet in position.

Artillery on both sides began to play. The effects of British cannon fire were vividly described by one Continental artillerist, Elisha Stevens, who wrote how 'the fire took such effect that it would cut a swath right through and sweep down whole companies as it were in an instant, upon which our men could close and fill up the vacancy and in an instant have the same fate.'[61] For their own part, Continental artillery on Birmingham Hill – including French-made pieces ironically bearing the inscription 'The Final Argument of Kings' – had a reasonable view of the British light battalions as they moved onto the lower slope of the hillside, but lost the British Guards and much of the grenadiers in the patchy woodland and a small ravine that lay between Birmingham Hill and Osborne Hill.[62]

First contact between the infantry of both armies came when soldiers of the 3rd Virginia, who were occupying an orchard ahead of Birmingham meetinghouse on the north side of the hill, engaged the British light infantry advancing towards them. The 1st light infantry battalion, including Dansey and the 33rd's company, advanced to within 70 or 80 yards of the orchard

56 Spring, *With Zeal*, p.308.
57 William Hale, in Spring, *With Zeal*, p.116.
58 George Duke, 'German Town Cap Octr 13, 1777.'
59 Joseph Townsend, in Futhey and Cope, *History of Chester County*, p.76.
60 Robert M. Dunkerly, *Decision at Brandywine: The Battle on Birmingham Hill* (Yardley: Westholme Publishing, 2021), p.27.
61 Elisha Stevens, in Dunkerly, *Brandywine*, p.61.
62 Dunkerly, *Brandywine*, p.34.

and engaged the 3rd Virginia in a small but potent firefight. The Virginians were overwhelmed and fell back about 1,000 yards uphill, rallying on the stone wall of the graveyard outside Birmingham meetinghouse, which lay between the main Continental line still attempting to order itself on Birmingham Hill and the regulars advancing below them. During the firefight the Continentals expended 30 rounds of ammunition each and suffered almost 50 percent casualties.[63]

The initial engagement showed how the light battalions operated as individual companies rather than a single, coherent unit, indicating flexibility and initiative as they worked with one another to deal with localised threats and the tactical challenges of difficult terrain. While some companies in the 1st battalion kept the Virginians pinned at the wall, others bypassed the graveyard and outflanked them, forcing the remnants of the 3rd to fall back to the main line on Birmingham Hill. The 33rd's lights were with this bypassing manoeuvre, taking them over a fence and along a hedgerow that was cut up by Continental artillery fire, the greenery twitching as it was shredded by grapeshot. The advance continued.

To the right of the light infantry, the British grenadiers, including the 33rd's company under Captain Oakes with the 1st battalion, continued their advance to the strains of The Grenadier's March – Lieutenant Ebenezer Elmer of the 3rd New Jersey recalled hearing it as the Continentals waited for the enemy to strike home.[64] Trees and a small ravine helped obscure the grenadiers from the rebel artillery on the hilltop until they approached the final portion of the slope, an open, ploughed field that began about 160 yards from the Continental line. A British engineer officer, Captain John Montresor, noted that the grenadiers were sweating and dusty as they began the final ascent.[65]

As the grenadiers continued to climb, crossing over a number of rail fences, the Continental infantry opened fire, perhaps from as close as 40 yards. The battalion volleys were described as the heaviest some of the British officers had experienced.[66] Lieutenant Colonel William Medows, who had given such fiery oration to his grenadiers prior to the start of the advance, was struck by a musket ball just above the elbow as he raised his sword to again encourage his men. The bullet passed through his arm and knocked him from his horse, the fall breaking his collarbone.[67]

Sources differ as to how prolonged the firefight was. Some claimed the British grenadiers and Continentals traded salvoes at close quarters for an extended period, others that the British quickly mounted a bayonet charge. German officer Friedrich von Muenchhausen wrote that the grenadiers 'fired a volley, and then ran furiously at the rebels with fixed bayonets.'[68] A rapid advance was also corroborated by Lieutenant William Hale of the

63 Dunkerly, *Brandywine*, p.40.
64 Dunkerly, *Brandywine*, pp.50–51.
65 Dunkerly, *Brandywine*, p.54.
66 Dunkerly, *Brandywine*, p.64.
67 Dunkerly, *Brandywine*, p.68.
68 Friedrich von Muenchhausen, in Dunkerly, *Brandywine*, p.64.

45th's grenadier company. The Continentals gave way following a stern engagement, retreating to even higher ground to their rear.

Further to the left of the grenadiers, the light infantry had also begun to engage the Continentals on the crest of the hill, though they did so in their own style. The 1st battalion's companies were still operating semi-independently – those initially present beneath the crest were the men of the 17th, 33rd and 38th's companies. An officer in the 17th's light company, wrote that they were 'compelled to throw ourselves on our knees and bellies, and keep up a fire from the slope of the hill.'[69] Fighting from a prone position was not unknown even for regular British troops during the Revolutionary War, and was a tactic happily employed by light infantry. During the engagement at Harlem Heights, for example, the captain of the 46th Regiment's light company was described as using a whistle to signal to his men to lie down when about to receive enemy fire. [70] In this way the light infantry traded fire with the Continentals on the crest of Birmingham hill, who seem to have attempted to advance against their prone foes several times but were driven back on each occasion.

It is likely around this time that Dansey was shot. The 33rd's captain received a musket ball in the joint of his right thumb. Despite the injury, he refused to quit the field but continued to lead his company through the heat of the engagement.[71] The commander of the Continentals, Major General John Sullivan, was observed by the light infantry to be desperately exhorting his men to drive the British back, but to no avail as both sides traded heavy musket fire. An officer of the 17th's light company recalled that 'the Inspiration & Courage of both Officers & Men including them to ascend the Heights, the whole Rebel Line presented itself to View & so close that those who compos'd this spirited Attack had nothing to Expect but Slaughter.'[72]

The three light companies were joined by the light bobs of the 4th and the 43rd Foot. Knowing that the closest supporting unit was the grenadier company of the 43rd Foot, who comprised the far left of the 1st Grenadier battalion to their right, the light infantry sent Major Charles Stuart of the 43rd to seek the assistance of the grenadiers. However, it seems the grenadiers had already pre-empted that their aid was required – Captain William Scott of the 17th related how he observed Captain 'Cochrane of the 4th company on my left throw up his cap and cry "Victory!"' and, looking round, saw the 43rd [Foot's grenadier] company hastening to our relief. We dashed forward, passed the five pieces of cannon which the enemy had abandoned, and made some few prisoners – the enemy running away from us with too much speed to be overtaken.'[73] Here then we see how not only a light infantry, but also a grenadier officer 'exercised near-total independence in conducting his men, which enabled the companies to pick their way forward according to terrain and the strength of the opposition to their front.'[74]

---

69 William Scott , in Dunkerly, *Brandywine*, p.63.

70 Spring, *With Zeal*, p.109.

71 Dansey (ed.), *Captured Rebel Flag*, p.34.

72 Augustus Wetherall, in Dunkerly, *Brandywine*, p.64.

73 William Scott, in Spring, *With Zeal*, pp.186–187.

74 Spring, *With Zeal*, p.187.

The engagement was now general across the hillside. Elisha Stevens of the Continental artillery recalled 'cannons roaring, muskets cracking, Drums Beating Bombs Flying all Round, men a dying & wounded Horred Grones.'[75] Lieutenant Richard St George of the 52nd's light company wrote of 'a most infernal Fire of cannon & musketry – halt! – charge! … the balls ploughing up the ground. The Trees cracking over ones head, The branches riven by the artillery – The leaves falling as in autumn by grapeshot.'[76] Much as the battle had opened with the majesty of eighteenth-century military spectacle, so it continued with the horror of eighteenth-century combat, fought with a close intensity rarely matched during the Revolutionary War.

On the far right of the British attack, the Guards had already routed the Continental left flank, catching the Maryland regiments there before they could finish deploying. On the far left, the Hessian and Anspach jäger had turned the right of the Continental line. Combined with the grenadier and light infantry driving in the heart of the rebel position, the defence of Birmingham Hill collapsed, with Continental units becoming fragmented as they were driven onto higher ground in their rear. Here some seem to have made a further stand before withdrawing.

Exhaustion prevented most of the Crown troops from closely pursuing. They paused to collect themselves, with the 33rd's light company and the others who had helped storm the centre of Birmingham Hill eventually finding the rest of their 1st battalion.[77] The 4th Brigade, and the main body of the 33rd, was ordered up as the front line sought to regain their order. Lieutenant George Duke of the 33rd recalled 'the 33d was orderd from the Brigade to Support them [the 2nd Light Infantry battalion]; in which to be sure we had a very heavy fire; but in a few Minutes we disperst them.'[78] An exception to the pause was the 2nd Grenadier battalion, who continued their furious pursuit of the rebels. Lieutenant William Hale of the 45th Regiment's grenadier company recalled that the men drove the enemy from six separate fences spanning three miles, conducting one bayonet charge after another. One German grenadier, following up on the British, fell down dead from exhaustion. While the 2nd Grenadier battalion's relentlessness helped keep the rebels on the run, it also left them dangerously over-exposed and isolated.

Not initially aware of the plight of the grenadiers, the 4th Brigade was ordered to take up the pursuit of the enemy. The small village of Dilworth lay to the south-east of the advancing British, and Congressional forces were pouring through it as they withdrew towards the town of Chester, further east. Lieutenant George Duke related that 'Genl How[e] came up, and beg the favor of the 33d to fall back, and form in the Rear of the Light Infantry, he then desired Coln Webster to take Possession of a Village calld Dillworth; which the Rebels had retreated to.'[79] The 33rd and 46th Regiments were ordered by

75 Elisha Stevens, in Dunkerly, *Brandywine*, p.61.

76 Richard St George Mansergh-St George, in Dunkerly, *Brandywine*, p.73.

77 Thomas J. McGuire, *The Philadelphia Campaign Volume I: Brandywine and the Fall of Philadelphia* (Mechanicsburg: Stackpole Books, 2006), p.254.

78 George Duke, 'German Town Cap Octr 13, 1777.'

79 George Duke, 'German Town Camp Octr 13, 1777.'

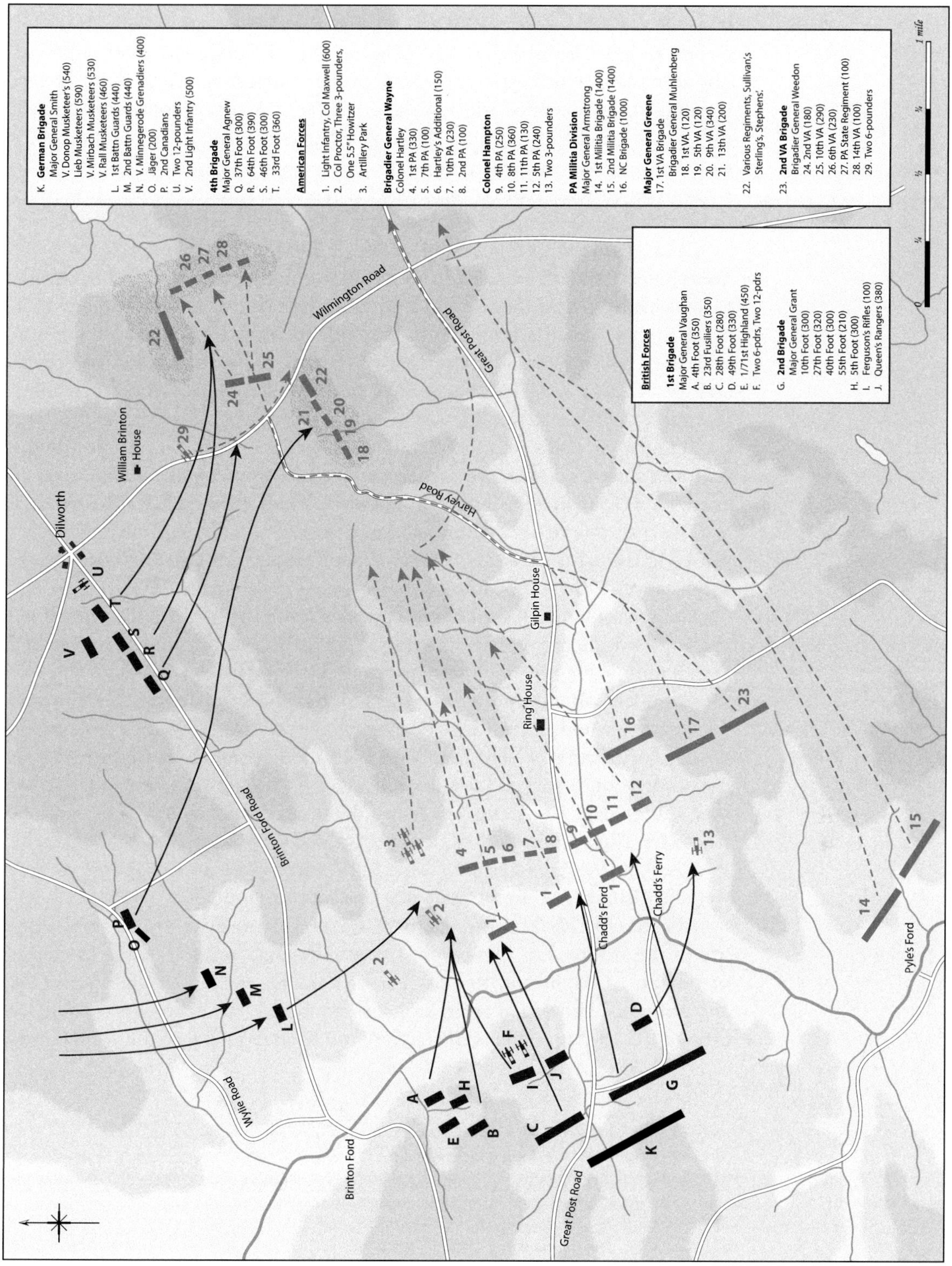

The second phase of the Battle of Brandywine, 11 September 1777.

General Howe to detach from the rest of the brigade and scour the village of the enemy.[80] As Lieutenant Colonel Webster prepared to move his men, however, a rider approached with concerning news – *Kapitän* Johann Ewald, a Hessian jäger commander, had fallen in with the 2nd Grenadier battalion. The grenadiers, who had kept up so vigorous a pursuit, now found themselves isolated to the south of Dilworth as fresh Continental troops were pushed forward to cover the withdrawal and other units rallied. The rebels had laid a trap for the grenadiers, using reverse slopes, some fences and woods to catch them in an enfilade from three sides.[81] Ewald had ridden to the commander of the 4th Brigade, Scotsman James Agnew, seeking assistance.[82]

Dusk was beginning to fall as the Continentals opened fire on the grenadiers, the flash of musketry lighting up the gathering gloom.[83] Agnew turned his brigade and pushed towards a small rise that, if captured, would shore up the grenadiers' left flank. The 46th and 64th Regiments led the way, with the 33rd and 38th following up. What none realised was that the reverse side of the slope was occupied by Continental infantry who were about to attack the grenadiers from their exposed side. So, it was the 46th, and particularly the 64th, who found themselves having fire poured into them. To make matters worse, the British troops initially mistook the blue-coated enemy for German allies. In just a matter of minutes the 64th was decimated, losing seven officers, six wounded and one, Captain Henry Nairn, who had served in the army for over 20 years, killed. Along with him fell four privates dead, as well as five sergeants and thirty-one privates injured.[84]

Lieutenant Duke described the casualties suffered by the 64th, and added that 'the Grandiers [*sic*] had at that time; a very heavy fire; and was rather at a Stand, upon which the Genl orderd the 33d Support them.'[85] Along with two six-pounder battalion guns assigned to assist the brigade, the 33rd poured fire into the woods enfilading the engagement to the left – their volleys and the artillery's canister-shot finally decided the encounter, causing the rebels to withdraw and marked the end of the day's fighting. Duke wrote that 'it was then quite Dark, it was the best Stand they [the rebels] ever Made, but their whole Army was then Routed, we only wanted a few More hours of Daylight, if we had, its the general opinion the Rebellion must have been over, for they were all dispersed some run one way and some another.'[86]

Another British officer wrote that 'The rebels were driven back by superior fire of the troops, but these were too much exhausted to be able to charge or pursue ... Night and the fatigue the soldiers had undergone prevented any pursuit.'[87] Howe had again won a fine pitched battle, but again could do little to follow it up – his infantry were too tired from a day's hard marching

80 McGuire, *The Philadelphia Campaign*, p.255.
81 McGuire, *The Philadelphia Campaign*, p.255.
82 British engineering officer Captain John Montresor was also dispatched by the grenadiers to seek Agnew's assistance, riding through the enemy's fire.
83 McGuire, *The Philadelphia Campaign*, p.258.
84 McGuire, *The Philadelphia Campaign*, p.259.
85 George Duke, 'German Town Camp Octr 13, 1777.'
86 George Duke, 'German Town Camp Octr 13, 1777.'
87 André, *André's Journal*, p.87.

and fighting, and he lacked the cavalry force that, in a large-scale European engagement, would have turned the enemy's retreat into a rout.

The 33rd had played their part in the engagement. Their after-action returns included one private killed, one sergeant and 14 rank-and-file wounded and one man missing. There were four officers wounded – Captain Dansey and Lieutenant Thomas Nicholl of the light company (Nicholl had replaced Lieutenant Richard Cotton, who was promoted to captain on Christmas Day 1776) and lieutenants John Hill Harris and Adam Drummond of the grenadier company.[88] Both Drummond and Harris died of their wounds, nine and 19 days later respectively. Drummond was replaced by Ensign Charles Darby and Harris by Ensign Anthony Salvin, both raised to lieutenant in the grenadiers, while their vacated ensigncies were filled by John Wheeler Collington and a suitable volunteer from the ranks, James Cummings.[89] It was notable that the officers of the flank companies were the ones who suffered the most, an unsurprising consequence of the heavy fighting endured by the grenadiers and light infantry. For his own part, though wounded in the hand, Dansey gave thanks that during the intensity of the fighting 'that's no worse for where I expected to have lost my head.'[90]

Philadelphia Captured

Over the next four days the two armies collected themselves and recuperated. Poor roads and a lack of wagons to carry the wounded hampered British manoeuvres. Cornwallis was given command of the light and grenadier battalions and pushed out to secure the local towns of Concord and Chester. Dilworth was converted into a hospital for the wounded, and after that nearby Wilmington, where surgeons from the rebel army arrived to attend their own captured casualties.

At midnight on 16 September Howe set off with the main body of the army in a second attempt to engage Washington, who had shifted to the north. While marching through the village of Turk's Head, five miles from Brandywine, an opportunistic attack by a small force of rebel militia resulted in one soldier of the 33rd being shot dead, and another wounded along with an officer. Washington deployed a delaying force as he attempted to form for battle, but they gave way before the British and German advanced corps. Around the same time a thunderstorm broke overhead. The weather had already been bad, and the deluge now further churned the roads into muck and soaked soldiers' firelocks and any cartridges left exposed. Washington, who had changed his mind about engaging the oncoming Crown forces, began to withdraw, and with the nature of the weather there was little chance of a pursuit. The 33rd spent a miserable night in whatever makeshift shelters they could construct, as the quagmire the roads had become meant the

88 *London Gazette Extraordinary*, 2 December 1777, p.4.
89 Kemble, 'The Kemble Papers, Volume 1', p.531.
90 Dansey (ed.), *Captured Rebel Flag*, pp.34–35.

baggage wagons carrying the tents were not able to catch up until the next day.

Following this abortive 'battle of the clouds,' both sides continued to manoeuvre. The British took various forage, including 4,000 barrels of flour, 'a great quantity of camp kettles, axes, horseshoes, nails' and 150 horses, as well as rebel deserters who had been coming in in large numbers since Brandywine.[91]

It was discovered that a section of Washington's army had been detached and lay in an exposed state dangerously close to British positions, near Paoli tavern. During a late-night assault the Continentals were surprised by the 2nd Light Infantry battalion, supported by 42nd and 44th Foot with the 40th and 55th in reserve. A total route ensued. Two days later, as Washington still attempted to contest Philadelphia, a British feint drew him out of position, allowing Howe's forces to counter-march through the night, cross the Schuylkill River and leave Washington thoroughly outmanoeuvred. On 26 September Cornwallis led the British and German grenadiers, two squadrons of light dragoons and 10 pieces of artillery into Philadelphia, marching through the rebel capital to the strains of God Save the King while the main army occupied the nearby village of Germantown. A British officer described how 'a good many people came in from Philadelphia; most of them represented that place as in the greatest confusion and expressed fears of its being burnt.'[92]

The city was to be spared, though rumours abounded that the rebels themselves had intended to burn it. Rumours also began to percolate, related by Congressional deserters, that the Crown forces commanded by Lieutenant General John Burgoyne, operating on the northern end of the Hudson River, had been defeated, though other deserters claimed the opposite 'and insisted that Burgoyne had had great success.'[93] As these tales were debated the 33rd remained with the main body of the army at Germantown.

Howe still hoped to engage Washington before the end of the campaign season. Little did he realise that in fact Washington had decided that he would be the one to directly attack and destroy his enemy, or that an even more dangerous situation was unfolding far to the north.

At least some of the rumours that had been going around Howe's army were true. On 17 October Lieutenant General John Burgoyne had surrendered, along with his entire force, to Continental General Horatio Gates. The defeat had come near Saratoga, on the Hudson River, north of New York. At a stroke the hard-earned British successes earlier in the year had been reversed and the rebellion had yet again been pulled back from the brink.

While the small, open settlement of Germantown or the busy streets of Philadelphia may have seemed a world away from the dense forests and deep ravines of the upper Hudson, the 33rd were actually more intimately involved in the disaster at Saratoga than almost any other regiment then in

91 André, *André's Journal*, p.92.

92 André, *André's Journal*, p.98.

93 André, *André's Journal*, p.101.

or near to the rebel capital. A quirk of fate had ensured that, while the main body of the 33rd had campaigned with Howe, one part of the regiment had actually found itself in Canada earlier in 1777. They had become embroiled in Burgoyne's expedition and were now set for captivity.

The Saratoga Campaign

By late 1776 Lieutenant George Anson Nutt had been with the army for five years. Born in 1750, his father had been a Royal Navy captain – Nutt was partly named after his father's superior, George Anson, who circumnavigated the world in 1740 as part of a campaign during the War of Jenkins' Ear. Nutt's father died in 1758, and the eldest scion of the Nutt family decided on a more land-based career. He gained his commission as an ensign with the 33rd Foot on 28 August 1771 and was promoted to lieutenant after the outbreak of hostilities in North America.

Likely due to his junior status within the 33rd's officer corps, Nutt was one of the men, like Captain Kerr and Captain Burnett, selected to remain in Britain with the Additional Companies, responsible for ongoing recruitment and training. Towards the middle of 1776 those efforts were progressing well. Between 50 and 75 men were deemed fit to travel to North American to reinforce the 33rd, some of them new recruits and some more experienced soldiers who had been drafted in from other regiments. The prospective company was further augmented by the addition of 101 soldiers of German origin who had recently arrived in Britain. These men, not to be confused with the soldiers of the separate armies of German states sent to assist Britain, had been recruited directly into the British Army by British officers sent to Germany. Almost 2,000 had been raised, and the 101 assigned to the 33rd was one of the biggest single intakes of soldiers of German origin into a British regiment during the war.[94]

This somewhat disparate force was deemed fit for service. In 1776 it was placed under Lieutenant Nutt's command and was assigned to a convoy of reinforcements and supplies bound for America, where the recruits would join up with the rest of the 33rd. The convoy's destination was Quebec. Unfortunately for Nutt and his recruits, Quebec was not where the 33rd currently were.

Due to the slow nature of communication across the Atlantic, planners in London were unaware that the 33rd's initial orders in mid-1776 – to journey to Canada following the siege of Charleston – had been superseded. Rather than go to Quebec, Cornwallis and the 33rd had instead joined Howe's main army and participated in the campaigning through New York and New Jersey. This information was slow to reach the 33rd's recruits, too slow, in fact, to stop them from boarding ships bound for Quebec. Thus, by administrative oddity, a company-sized contingent of the 33rd found itself bound for a different theatre of operations from the rest of the regiment.

94 Hagist, *British Soldiers American War*, pp.132–133.

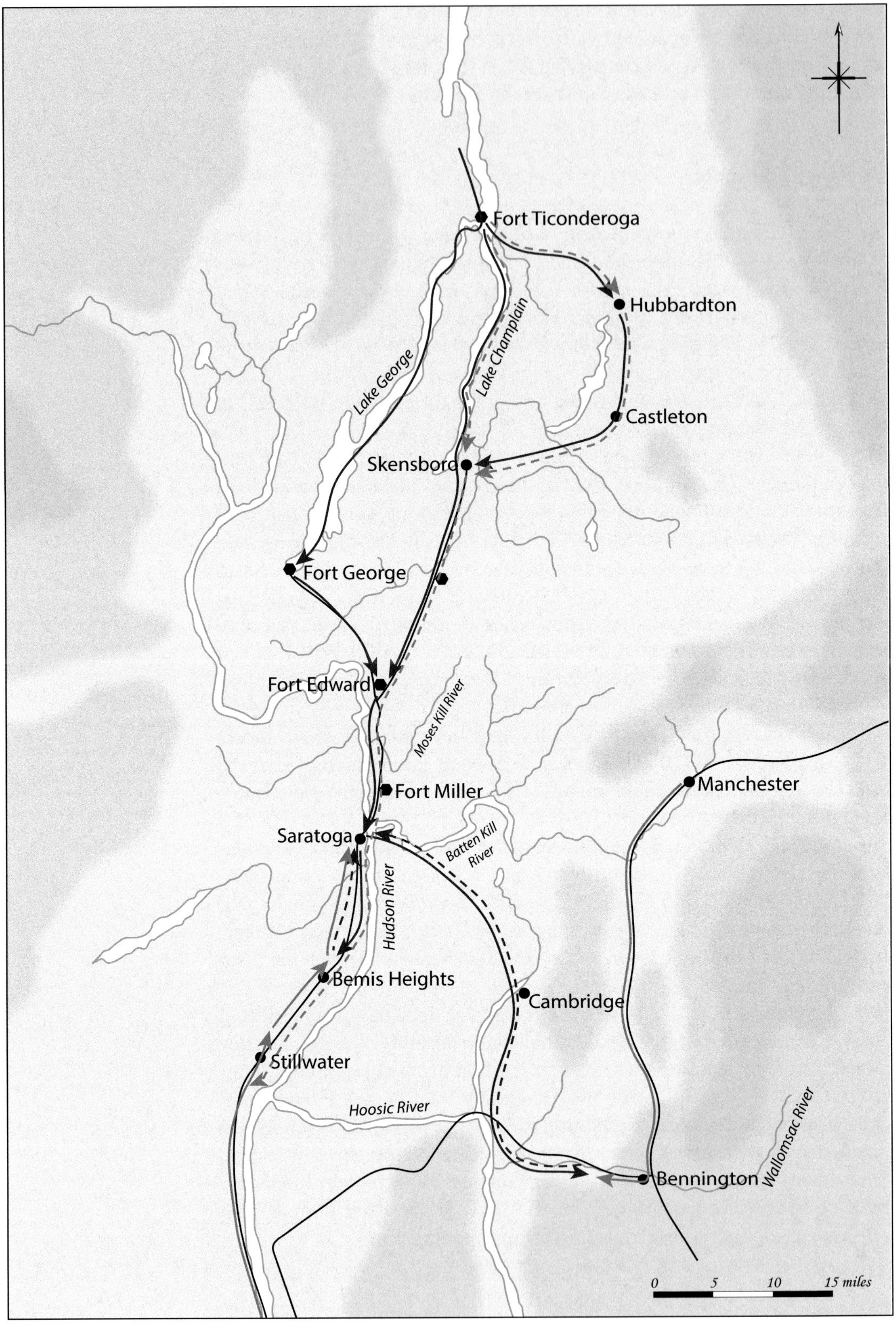

Burgoyne's invasion along the Hudson River, 1777.

Nutt's detachment reached Quebec late in 1776, too late, in fact, to journey south to New York. Normally this was no great issue. The realities of eighteenth-century travel and communication meant that parts of regiments, especially new recruits, could quite often become separated from the larger whole. When this occurred, it was standard practice to simply absorb the recruits into other regiments present in the theatre they had wound up in. For the 33rd's men, however, this proved more easier said than done. The commander of British forces in Canada, General Guy Carleton, indicated the problem with breaking up Nutt's detachment in a letter to the Secretary at War, William Barrington.

> It having been represented to me the English recruits for the 33d regiment, sent to Quebec with Lieutenant Nutt, were raised in the Neighbourhood of Lord Cornwallis's, and inlisted in Confidence of their serving in that Corps, therefore the disposing of the men otherwise than in his Lordships own regiment might prejudice its recruiting in those parts hereafter; that greater expense had been incurred in fitting them out than other Colonel might chuse to reimburse; and indeed uncommon pains had been taken with them in other respects; from these considerations, I shall therefore defer turning over both these and the German recruits, to the Regiments here, in hopes they may have an Opportunity of Joyning their own Regiment in the Spring.[95]

In short, the letter indicates the 33rd's status as something a little more than a regular line regiment. The particular attachment to Yorkshire and the pride in being commanded by Cornwallis has already been established, and was strong enough to be noteworthy to Carleton, who did not want to hamper further recruiting efforts with the fear that men who signed on specifically to serve in the 33rd would find themselves drafted into other regiments. It is also telling that the quality of the 33rd's uniforms and equipment was superior enough to mean that their new colonels in whatever regiments the detachment was dispersed to may not want to cover the cost of replacement. Carleton also hints at further unique aspects of the 33rd's recruits, though he does not elaborate – it may be the general deportment and drill that was noted as being exceptional in the build-up to war. It is likely that, given Cornwallis's relatively senior position in the army, Carleton also had no desire to risk his displeasure by breaking up part of the regiment he had put so much money, time and effort into. All of this ensured that Nutt and the other recruits of the 33rd found themselves in a very unique position; considered too valuable to redistribute.

Nutt's detachment spent eight months in Canada as Burgoyne prepared his invasion force. The strategic plan was to strike south through the wilderness, following the Hudson River, and ultimately link up with Howe in New York. In doing so the British would capture the vital Fort Ticonderoga and split the heartland of the rebellion, New England, off from the other colonies. The plan assumed a degree of assistance from Howe to the south,

95 Hagist, *British Soldiers American War*, pp.133–134.

assistance that Burgoyne was ultimately to find himself without. As the plan was to link up with Howe's army, which included the main body of the 33rd, Burgoyne decided to include Nutt's detachment with his expedition.

The exact composition of Nutt's company as it set off, beyond the fact it included 154 men, is unclear, but it may have included recruits from the 15th, 27th, 33rd, 35th and 54th Regiments. How it was uniformed is also largely unknown. Recruits typically did not receive their coats until joining their regiment but wore shorter jackets. On the other hand, soldiers drafted into the unit from other regiments would have their original coats until they could be supplied with the correct new ones. To further complicate matters, Burgoyne had ordered that his army ape the fashionable style of the light infantry, with shortened coats and felt caps with horsehair crests. Burgoyne's taste for light infantry uniforms and tactics did not extend far, as despite knowing that he would be campaigning in some of the most impregnable wilderness on the Eastern Seaboard, he insisted on a vast and cumbersome artillery train, which he believed he required for the anticipated siege of Fort Ticonderoga. How Nutt's men were uniformed therefore remains a point of conjecture.

As the main part of the 33rd left their New Jersey billets in June 1777 in an attempt to again draw Washington into battle, 370 miles further north Nutt's recruits set off with Burgoyne's army down Lake Champlain. Borne as they were on a flotilla, on 28 June it was noted that the 33rd detachment were 'for the present to serve on board the Fleet.'[96] Further specifics were not forthcoming and seem to have hinted at the place of Nutt's men within the army – not as undesirables as such, but as a unit too small, disparate and untried to be given a firm frontline role. Upon landing the 33rd found the duty that would occupy them for the rest of the campaign – they were to assist Burgoyne's three brigades of artillery, providing the raw muscles necessary in moving heavy weaponry and equipment over rough terrain.

Much to everyone's surprise, Ticonderoga fell almost without a shot being fired. This easy success did nothing to dissipate Burgoyne's overconfidence. He continued to press south even as his supply lines became stretched and it grew apparent that there would be little help from Howe. A detachment of Brunswick, Loyalist and Native troops were defeated at Bennington, after which many of the Native Americans that Burgoyne relied upon for scouting purposes decided to go home. On 19 September Burgoyne's army advanced towards rebel defences on Bemis Heights and were met head-on by forces led by Major General Benedict Arnold, who had probed forward to intercept them. Nutt's detachment spent an anxious afternoon with the artillery train, listening to the rising crackle of musketry as what began as a meeting engagement developed into a furious general action that swept back and forth over a clearing occupied by the farm of a local Loyalist, John Freeman. That anxiety doubtless grew as the other troops guarding the train, most of them Brunswickers, marched to the sound of the guns at around 5:00 p.m., their commander realising that only with his intervention could the battle be saved.

96 Hadden, *Hadden's Journal and Orderly Books*, p.67.

A soldier of the 33rd Foot as he might have appeared at the battle of Camden. The 33rd's clothing, here modified for fighting in the Carolinas, was in a steadily deteriorating state by the time of the battle, and in need of the replacements that would eventually arrive three months later. (Alexandr Chernushkin © Helion and Company 2023)

William Dansey, who served as the captain of the 33rd Foot's light company for much of the American Revolution, and later commanded the regiment following the losses at Yorktown. This portrait was painted in late 1780 while Dansey was on leave, at home in England. It was at this time that he also married his fiancée. (Courtesy of the Duke of Wellington's Regiment Museum)

The standard 'position of a soldier' saw the enlisted man standing straight, shoulders back, head inclined slightly to the right, arms by the sides but without the fingers clenched or rigid. (Photo by Henry Gage)

The style of lace was unique to each regiment in the British Army. The 33rd's consisted of what were later known as 'bastion ended loops' of lace with a red thread through the centre. (Photo by Henry Gage)

The kit of a soldier in full marching order, equipped with haversack, knapsack, canteen, bayonet and bayonet scabbard and, on the right hip (unseen here), cartridge pouch, along with the relevant belts. (Photo by Henry Gage)

A sergeant's uniform. The sergeant's rank was denoted by the fact that he had plain white lace (in the case of the 33rd, lacking the red thread in the middle of the lace), a slightly brighter shade of red wool for his coat, a silver belt plate, and a waist sash that was coloured red and whichever colour matched the facings of that particular regiment. Because the 33rd's facings were the same red as a rest of the coat, a stripe of white was used instead, to demarcate a sergeant's sash from an officer's all-red one. (Photo by Henry Gage)

Corporals and sergeants were the lifeblood of the British Army, typically responsible for overseeing all aspects of military life. A number of the 33rd's sergeants, such as the here-recreated Sergeant Crabtree, served for many decades. (Photo by Henry Gage)

An officer's formal hat was edged with silver or gold lace, depending on his regiment. (Photo by Henry Gage)

Officers purchased most of their own equipment, including their swords. The expense of maintaining the correct, uniformed appearance was lamented by a number of soldiers including the 33rd's William Dansey. (Photo by Henry Gage)

Here we see the sword belt also holding the sheath of a bayonet that could be fixed to the officer's fusil. Unlike the bastion-shaped white lace of the enlisted men, the lace of the 33rd's officers was silver, square-ended, and seems to have been grouped along with the buttons in twos on the breast turnbacks. (Photo by Henry Gage)

Top left: British officers tended to modify their uniforms for campaign in America, and sometimes used fusils in combat. Here we see Captain Campbell has donned a cartridge pouch to go with his own fusil and bayonet, and has replaced his expensive silver-taped cocked hat with a simpler one for the rigors of the field. (Photo by Henry Gage)

Top right: Most, though not all, drummers in the British Army of the period wore uniforms that reversed the colours of the facings from the rest of the regiment. Since the 33rd's facings were also red, however, the drummers instead wore off-white trimmed with red. (Photo by Henry Gage)

Right: One Continental Army soldier commented on how a drum belonging to the 33rd – abandoned after it was shot through – was of superior quality to his own. Drums tended to bear the number or crest of the regiment they belonged to. (Photo by Henry Gage)

While conducting recruiting efforts, NCOs such as this sergeant often decorated their hats with more colourful cockades than the black one worn as standard. John Robert Shaw describes a set worn to celebrate the battle of Long Island. (Photo courtesy of The Pattern: HM 33rd Regiment of Foot 1770–1785)

Recruiting parties offered a bounty to those who would enlist, though much of this was lost to paying for clothing and equipment. Men were not typically inveigled into joining though – the Army wanted willing volunteers. The bearskin cap worn by the drummer was usually discarded on campaign in favour of a regular cocked hat. (Photo by Henry Gage)

The typical contents of a soldier's knapsack, including spare shirts, socks and shoes, a leather and horsehair neck stock, blackball, a cleaning kit for buttons, a spoon, fork and mug, a shaving kit and mittens. As well as biscuits, meat was also often pre-cooked and then carried for around three days in the soldier's haversack, to enable him to operate for a short while independent of camp supplies. (Photo by Henry Gage)

Soldiers presenting, about to give fire. While the Army had usually operated in three ranks up until the Revolutionary War, in North America they adopted two, with open files, to account for the nature of the terrain. (Photo by Henry Gage)

A soldier of the 33rd in full kit, including knapsack, as he would appear for much of the Revolutionary War. Note that the breeches, stockings and half-gaiters have been swapped for more practical trousered gaiters, especially popular during summer months. (Photo by Henry Gage)

It has been suggested that the edges of cocked hats were partly let down in warmer climates, such as the Carolinas, to protect against the sun. Whether an officer as conscious of his regiment's smartness as Cornwallis would have permitted the 33rd to conduct this practice is another matter. (Photo by Henry Gage)

From left to right, a corporal, company officer, and sergeant of the 33rd Regiment. Note the differences in the shade of the coats, the style of lace and the hats, among other things. (Photo by Henry Gage)

At the end of the day the British held the field, but at a high cost. The Royal Artillery in particular had suffered, with 36 of the 48 matreosses operating the guns killed or wounded over the course of the action, giving Nutt's detachment even more work to do. For almost three weeks the British licked their wounds, until finally Burgoyne decided to press on and attack the rebel army holding Bemis Heights.

This engagement proved even more ruinous than the one at Freeman's Farm. Among those engaged was John Dyke Acland, who had first purchased his commission into the 33rd and had departed for America with the 20th Foot after lobbying for promotion within Cornwallis's regiment. The 20th had proved more amenable to his interests, and Acland was now a major and commander of their grenadier company. A friend of Burgoyne, he was with the composite grenadier battalion as it struck out against the rebel lines at Bemis Heights. During a bayonet charge he was shot through both legs and lay where he fell, abandoned by his men as they retreated. He was taken prisoner and nursed back to health by his wife, Harriet.

Nutt's detachment seems to have been on the left wing of the Crown force, again assisting as best they could with the artillery. Over the course of the campaign the detachment suffered nine wounded and 10 captured, prior to Burgoyne's final surrender after the defeat at Bemis Heights. At this point wherein the whole detachment of Nutt, four NCOs and 95 privates, marched into captivity with the rest of what became Convention Army, a massed force of prisoners.[97]

While Burgoyne's army was doomed to remain in captivity for the rest of the war, desertion and escape was rampant. A return from 17 February 1779 showed that only 60 percent of Nutt's detachment were still accounted for in the captive force, and it seems highly likely that well under half were still imprisoned by the end of hostilities. Ultimately, the tale of the misfortune of Nutt's detachment was a foretaste of what was to come for part of the wider regiment. For his own part, Anson Nutt would still play a vital part in the 33rd in the final years of the war.

The Battle of Germantown

Germantown was described by General Howe as a village which 'forms one continued street for two miles.'[98] On 4 October, while Burgoyne's forces were still recovering from the bloodletting at Freeman's Farm and prior to their assault on Bemis Heights, Howe's army was encamped 'in a line at right angles near a mile from the head' of Germantown, five miles north of Philadelphia.[99] The surrounding countryside consisted of small woods and fields bordered by rail fencing. The 33rd were with the rest of the 4th Brigade under Lieutenant Colonel Agnew on the army's left wing, under the overall command of *Generallieutenant* Wilhelm von Knyphausen. Dansey and the

97 Hagist, *British Soldiers American War*, pp.135–138.
98 TNA: CO 5/94: No. 68. Howe to Germain, 10 October 1777, p.639.
99 TNA: CO 5/94: No. 68. Howe to Germain, 10 October 1777, p.639.

light company were still with the 1st Light Infantry battalion covering the right side of the main encampment, while Captain Oakes' grenadiers, with his newly-appointed lieutenants, were with the 1st Grenadier battalion – and Cornwallis – in Philadelphia.

Due to the fact that their tents were still with the fleet at Head of Elk, the army were encamped for the most part in brush huts, which the soldiers walled wigwams, constructed from branches and foliage. This sort of encampment was typical of British forces on the move in America. Besides the huts, fire pits were dug for cooking, and firelocks were stacked along simple frames made from two Y-shaped sticks with a branch laid between them, against which the muskets could be rested, keeping them up out of the damp and within easy reach. When not stored in this way – or, during periods of close contact with the enemy, actually kept to hand by each soldier individually – they were sometimes stacked upright in 'triangles' of three. Cuthbertson described this as 'the method generally practised by the German troops,' and advised that 'when perhaps the dustiness of the road or wetness of the grass may render it prejudicial to the arms to have them grounded,' muskets could be fixed 'in files [of three], by locking the bayonets and ramrod tops together, and spreading out the buts to an exact triangle, at such distance as to form a steady foundation: on service, the advantage of this method over grounding is much to be considered, as by it many accidents may be prevented in the course of a campaign, when a Battalion always marches with loaded arms.'[100]

The ability of British soldiers to get at their weapons quickly was to prove vitally important at Germantown. For the 33rd, the night of 3 October and the early hours of 4 October passed uneventfully, beset by a heavy fog. Unbeknownst to the rank-and-file, a number of rebel deserters had been brought in and had informed senior British officers that something dire was afoot. Howe failed to act until the crackle of musketry sounded through the fog at around 5:30 a.m. The 33rd would have heard that initial exchange, with confirmation that it was more than the scrapping of pickets or a raid on the sentries by rebel bushwhackers coming as the sound grew louder and more sustained. The regiment, along with the rest of the army, was stood to, pulling on kit, grasping firelocks, quitting their wigwams and hastily forming into their ranks as officers sought direction and information.

The sound of firing from the morning fog was soon intense and included not only the rattle of musketry but the thump of artillery. It was also growing closer. Around 7:00 a.m. the light infantry of the 2nd battalion emerged, seemingly on the run from an overwhelming force of rebels attacking from the north-west. The sight of light infantry retreating en-masse was something the 33rd had only witnessed once before, at Harlem Heights.

Washington was on the offensive. Recalling the surprise attack on Trenton at the close of 1776, the commander-in-chief of the Continental Army had chosen to mount an ambitious four-pronged assault against Howe's forces while they were split between Germantown and Philadelphia. In the captured capital, messengers from Howe had alerted Cornwallis, who set the British

100 Cuthbertson, *Cuthbertson's System*, p.172.

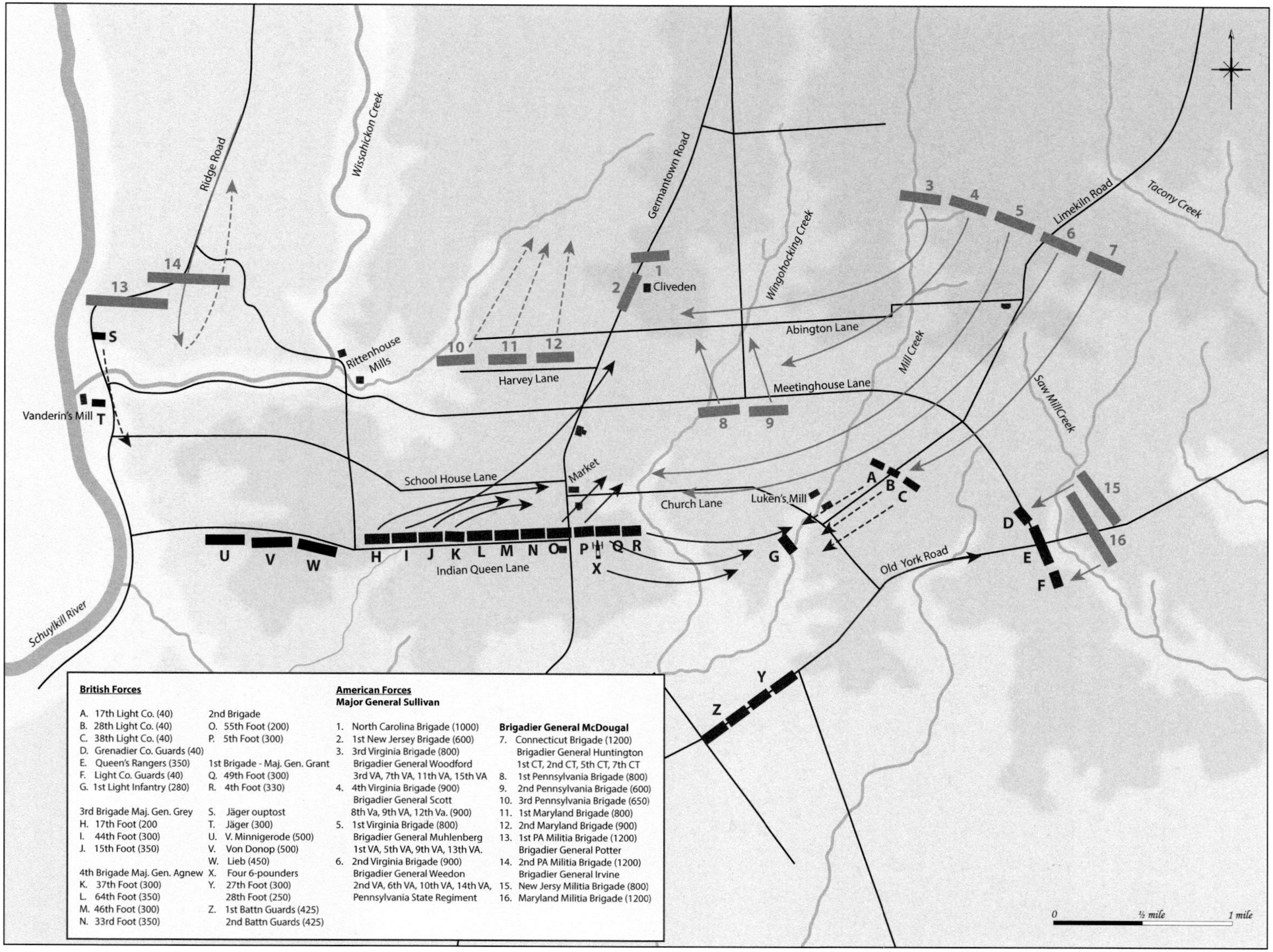

The Battle of Germantown, 4 October 1777.

grenadiers in motion, running Oakes and his fellow flank company men north along the road to Philadelphia in a desperate bid to reach Howe's force before it was overwhelmed by the surprise rebel offensive.

The intense fighting the 33rd could hear in the fog ahead of them was the sound of the 40th Foot stalling Washington's advance. Alongside the 2nd Light Infantry battalion, the 40th had been posted as an advance guard beyond the main encampment. The light infantry had been apprehensive about an attack for days, and when the shooting started at the advance pickets they had been out of their wigwams and formed up in a minute.[101] The light infantry twice charged the oncoming enemy column before being overwhelmed and forced to retire.

While the light infantry fell back, six companies of the 40th occupied a stone house astride the road through the village. This building, Cliveden House, had been built in 1767 by local attorney Benjamin Chew. Washington vacillated, not knowing whether to maintain his momentum by leaving just a small force to keep the 40th contained while pushing on, or stall his central column and attempt to storm the building. The latter option had worked well at Princeton at the start of the year – ironically against the same commander of the 40th, Lieutenant Colonel Thomas Musgrave – and so Washington chose to invest the manse with two brigades and most of his artillery. The building's thick stone walls proved impervious even to cannon fire, and the 40th refused to surrender, repelling repeated charges.

While the 40th were making their stand, the remaining five brigades of Washington's central column not directly attacking the manse became stalled. On the right flank, a second Continental column struck home, driving into the 1st battalion light infantry and then neighbouring units from the 1st Brigade. Dansey and the other lights became surrounded, their wigwams and their baggage wagon overrun, but with the help of the nearby 4th Foot they were able to fight through the rebels and recapture their camp. The engagement became a close-quarters scrap, with bayonets being used in and around the wigwams. Some rebels, confident the British had been routed, were killed while dividing captured bread among themselves.[102]

The Congressional offensive was coming undone, stymied by the stern opposition of the 40th and the fog.[103] Orders finally came through for the main body of the 33rd. Alongside the rest of the 4th Brigade, they began to advance, keeping the Germantown road and houses on their right. They soon encountered the stalled Continentals of the central column. Facing the 33rd directly was Colonel Moses Hazen's 2nd Maryland Brigade, which had been among the first units to break at Birmingham Hill. The two lines engaged in an exchange of musketry, the fog so dense that they may have been as little as 20 yards apart.[104] The Marylanders stood for longer than they had on Birmingham Hill, but the result was the same. They had been blazing away blindly into the fog for much of the attack, and so were short

101 Hagist, *These Distinguished Corps*, p.125.
102 Hagist, *These Distinguished Corps*, p.125.
103 Hagist, *These Distinguished Corps*, pp.125–126.
104 Hagist, *These Distinguished Corps*, p.125.

on ammunition, and the confusion of the firing off to the flank and from the rear at Cliveden combined with the pressure of the British advance to cause them to retreat. The 4th Brigade carried on. It was around this time that Lieutenant Colonel Agnew was fatally wounded by a Continental volley – not, as was later claimed, by a lone sharpshooter from behind the wall of the graveyard of the nearby Mennonite meetinghouse. As the 4th Brigade's next most senior officer, the 33rd's Lieutenant Colonel Webster may have taken over command of the brigade following the loss of Agnew.

Howe wrote that 'the 4th brigade, by a vigorous attack repulsed the enemy that had penetrated into the upper part [of Germantown] which was done with much slaughter.'[105] The 4th and 3rd Brigades reached Cliveden House as the rebels fell back before them, relieving the embattled companies of the 40th. The manse's stone walls were scarred by cannon and musket balls, the ground around it littered with rebel dead and wounded. At this point the grenadiers arrived, having completed their impressive jog from Philadelphia. While the 33rd and the other line battalions pausing to collect themselves, the grenadiers and the rallied 2nd Light Infantry battalion took over pursuit of the enemy, chasing them for another eight miles.[106]

Washington's attack had failed. In the relatively brief encounter, the 33rd had actually suffered more heavily than it had done at Brandywine, indicating the close-range intensity of the battle in the fog. Two sergeants and two privates had been killed and one lieutenant and 20 privates wounded.[107]

The 33rd stayed with most of the army in their wigwams at Germantown throughout October. In a series of letters to his mother, Dansey described how writing was difficult as the wound to his hand sustained at Brandywine was still healing. He wrote that 'it will bring great News to England, Philadelphia taken and the Rebels twice defeated, I was in the Heat of both Engagements and thank God received no other hurt than I have mention'd.'[108] He covered the hardships of campaigning, specifically where food was concerned;

> Your talking of Ribs of Beef makes me wish to be at home now I shou'd so much enjoy a good Joint of meat well dress'd clear set down and good Company, for we here literally eat to live and all we get is a Scramble, sometimes good meat ill dress'd nothing to eat or drink with it, other times plenty to drink and nothing good to eat, in short things are never all of a Piece with us except when we have nothing at all but thank God that seldom happens.[109]

He addressed local worries back home at Brinsop, unhappy that one of his tenants seemed intent on leaving and equally worried at the stress it was causing his mother – 'am very sorry as it must involve you in trouble about it and I had rather it was a'fire than give any of us any more trouble or

105 TNA: CO 5/94: No. 68. Howe to Germain, 10 October 1777, p.640.
106 Hagist, *These Distinguished Corps*, p.126.
107 *London Gazette Extraordinary*, 2 December 1777, p.5.
108 Dansey (ed.), *Captured Rebel Flag*, p.35.
109 Dansey (ed.), *Captured Rebel Flag*, p.39. Editor Paul Dansey describes a scramble as torn pieces of beef, milk and eggs.

uneasiness, I hope to be able to come Home next Spring and settle it for good some how or other.' He requested that his letters be sent by the post office, which was the most reliable means of getting word to him, and that he was pleased his mother and fiancée were writing to one another. He asked his mother to 'please to remember my Christmas Present to Mary Colley,' his old nurse who had been recently married.[110] He related news that his own young servant Ben, writing that he 'is grown amazingly, he begs his Duty to his Father and Mother,' and that 'he wishes to give his Parents two Guineas to help them in the Winter.'[111] He was saddened by news that his aunt was ill, asking that his mother pass on 'respectful Compliments to my Aunt [and] remember in kind Compliments to all my Friends in Hereford.' He whimsically reminisced about how he and an old friend had once vied to be married first, a race he had now lost due to the war, and looked forward to when he could see him again and 'vie with him and from the Experience I have learnt in Wars Alarms enjoy with double Happiness the Blessings of a peaceful Dwelling and a good Wife.' Likewise, he related how with another family friend 'I hope one of these Days to bring Mrs. Dansey to drink tea with my old Acquaintance Mrs. Child, while I recount the Feats of War to the Parson over a Jug of his best Cider.' He hoped that his mother would 'soon be over not being a Grandmother as soon as I wish'd as it being but the cruel Fate of War prevented it and as long as it pleases God to spare you a Son you must trust for a Grandson a little longer.'[112] He related the good news about Lieutenant Gorges' transfer to Captain Oakes' grenadiers, and the good stead he was in regarding possible promotion;

> I shall not be wanting in my Attention to Lieut. Gorges whenever it will be of Service, who is a most deserving young man, he is now Lieut. of Grenadiers being appointed since the Battle of the Brandywine where both our Lieuts. of Grenadiers were wounded and are since dead, so that he will be continued with the Grenadiers which he is very happy at, he is a fine spirited young Officer and whoever lives to see it will one Day or other cut a fine Figure and his good Temper gains him the Esteem of every Body, I hope there's no doubt of his getting a Company when the Campaign is over and People get Leave to sell [their commissions] for I believe that he must be now among the first in the General's List and is well recommended by Lord Cornwallis. I wish I had as good a Chance for a Majority.[113]

Here then we see the thoughts that preoccupied British officers during the Revolutionary War – concern and longing for friends, family and the comforts of home, hopes and fears for the future, and the mundane challenges of finances and promotion. Dansey seems to have been tired of the American War, or at least hopeful that it would soon be over, stating 'I look upon the Glory of this War over, I have been at the Beating of the Rebels

110 Dansey (ed.), *Captured Rebel Flag*, p.35.
111 Dansey (ed.), *Captured Rebel Flag*, pp.35, 39.
112 Dansey (ed.), *Captured Rebel Flag*, p.39.
113 Dansey (ed.), *Captured Rebel Flag*, p.38.

in two general Engagements and have seen their Capital taken.'[114] But in spite of the victories won, the end was nowhere in sight.

The Occupation of Philadelphia

Philadelphia was now secure, but the area around it, specifically the Delaware River, was not. Two forts, controlled by the Continental Army, made getting supplies and maintaining communication via the waterways difficult. Elements of the 1st Grenadier battalion laboured on the siege works necessary to force the capitulation of the forts, working at times up to their waists in mud and rainwater.[115] One of the forts was attacked by German grenadiers on 22 October, but the assault was driven back. Eventually, starved out and bombarded, the forts surrendered.

Throughout November Crown forces and Washington's army continued to skirmish with one another in small raids and foraging expeditions. On 17 November a force commanded by Cornwallis, consisting of the 1st Light and 1st Grenadier battalions, the 27th, 33rd and a battalion of Hessians, crossed over the Schuylkill and marched to Chester with the intention of linking up with more troops and seizing Red Bank, north-east of Philadelphia. While passing through the settlement of Darby a group of rebels fired on the 33rd. The regiment's sergeant major, John Yates, was killed. In response the soldiers rushed the buildings where the shots had come from and killed a dozen of the rebels, as well as taking over 20 prisoners.[116]

On 21 November four rebel ships on the Delaware were torched to prevent their capture by the British. On 22 November 11 houses in and around Germantown belonging to known rebels were torched on Howe's orders. That same day a minor earthquake struck Philadelphia, and five days later the skies were lit by the aurora borealis, viewed as strange portents by soldiers and civilians on both sides.

Redoubts had been constructed defending Philadelphia, and British forces had begun to set up encampments around the city, their baggage finally brought up from the Head of Elk. In early December Howe embarked on a final effort to lure the Continental Army into a battle of annihilation before the campaign season ended. Just before midnight on 4 December the 33rd were part of a 10,000-strong force that marched from Philadelphia, headed by Cornwallis' advance corps. At midnight on 5 December the light infantry pushed in rebel pickets as the column moved through Germantown, Beggarstown, and Flourtown. The British halted on Chestnut Hill, close to Washington's positions, and the light infantry resisted an attack before taking St Thomas' Episcopal Church. Howe ascended the church's spire to view the enemy positions and decided to hold the ground he had taken.

Both sides spent 6 December observing one another. On 7 December Howe chose to resume the offensive. He undertook what was by now his

114 Dansey (ed.), *Captured Rebel Flag*, p.35.
115 Hagist, *These Distinguished Corps*, p.125.
116 Peebles, *John Peebles' American War*, p.149.

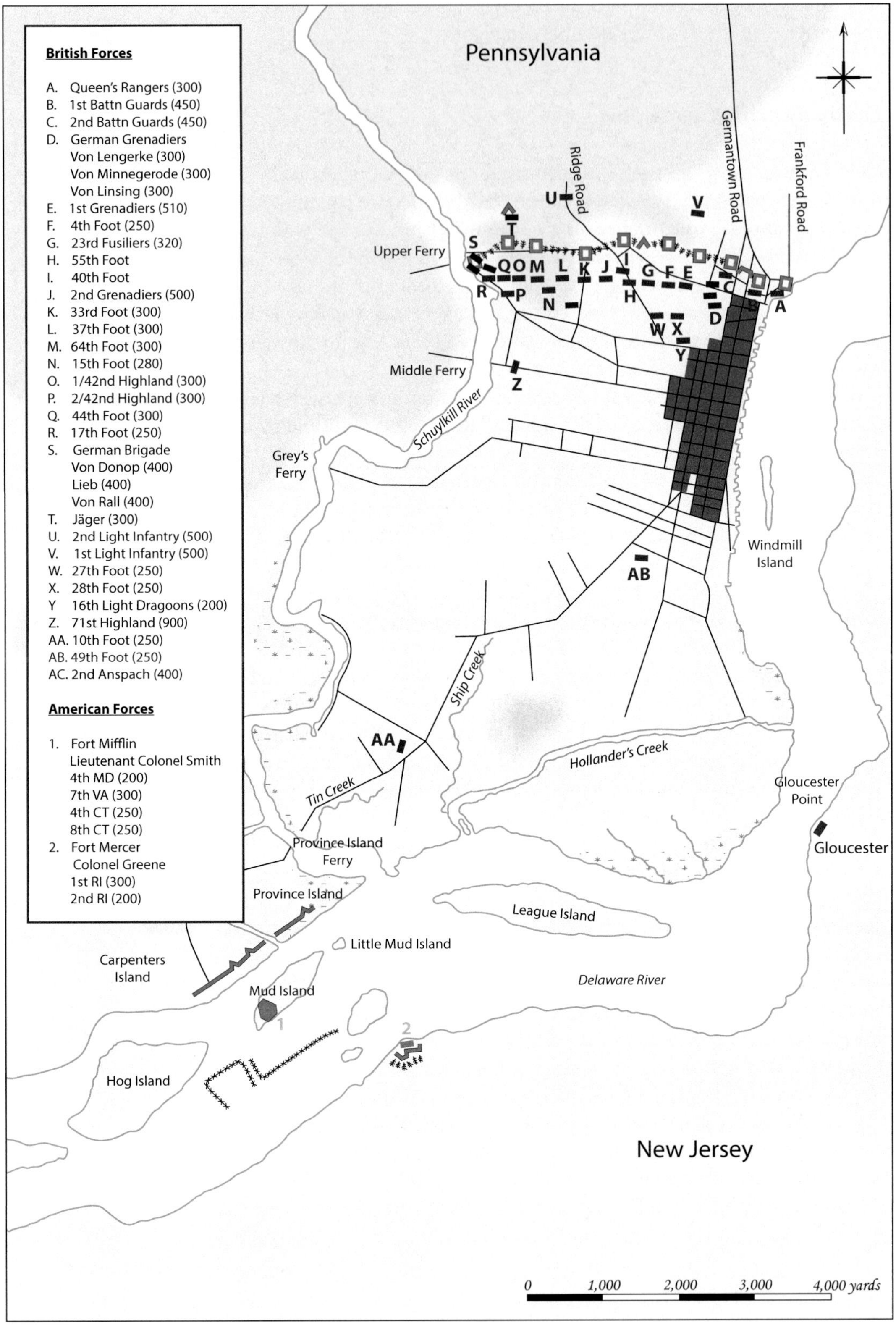

British cantonments around Philadelphia, late 1777 to early 1778.

standard flanking movement, taking the main body of the army in a march that he hoped would turn Washington's left while Major General Charles Grey kept the enemy occupied with a pinning force. This diversion ended up making some headway, while Howe's column, including the 33rd, encountered Continental riflemen and light infantry in dense woodland, protecting Washington's flank. Major John André wrote that:

> The second battalion light infantry had also a skirmish with Morgan's [rebel] Battalion of riflemen. Only five companies were brought to action, and of these from circumstances of ground, &c., which we are unacquainted with, three only could act with vigor; these drove them a considerable distance and threw them into confusion, but being unsupported and being called off, the rebels made their retreat without suffering much. The 4th regiment received a very heavy fire a little time after this, from a flying party probably of the same corps. The whole of the affair took place in a very thick wood. Our loss was between 30 and 40 men killed and wounded; that of the rebels was probably no greater.[117]

Around midday 'the 1st Battalion of Light Infantry and the 33rd Regiment attacked and defeated a strong enemy posted on a hill.'[118] During the fighting the 33rd were sent forward to support the light troops pressing the enemy on a promontory called Edge Hill. It is to be wondered, given that they were operating alongside light infantry, engaged in heavy woodland against skirmishing enemy riflemen, and may have been for a time under Cornwallis's direct command, whether or not the 33rd themselves employed the light infantry tactics they so thoroughly practiced in the build-up to the war. As we shall see, documentation from later in the war certainly implies the occasional use of the 33rd as light infantry.

Casualties were not high – a later history recorded three rank-and-file from the battalion companies wounded – but the lights suffered a stinging loss.[119] Sergeant Joseph Palmer, who also acted as the light company's paymaster, was killed during the fighting. Dansey lamented the death in a letter home; 'I met with an irreparable Loss in having my Paymaster Serjt. kill'd, which you know very well is always the Captain's right hand man in the Companies Business, indeed in the course of last year I lost three of the best Serjts. in the 33d Regiment out of my Company.'[120]

The privation of three days spent closely engaged with the enemy was also telling. The troops had no time to eat on 7 December, and again, for the sake of speed, had carried no baggage with them.[121] The nights were turning cold and this, combined with the fact that Howe's manoeuvring had gained him only a minor advantage over the enemy, convinced the Crown

117 André, *André's Journal*, pp.127–128.
118 Hagist, *These Distinguished Corps*, p.128.
119 Anon., 'Record of the Services of the 33rd (The Duke of Wellington's) Regiment of Foot,' *Colburn's United Service Magazine, and Naval and Military Journal*, 1869, Part III, pp.233–245.
120 DHS: William Dansey Letters: 19 January 1778.
121 Hagist, *These Distinguished Corps*, pp.128–129.

forces commander to give up on his final attempt to engage Washington. A withdrawal was ordered, back to Philadelphia, to see out the winter.

It was quite apparent that if the army was to occupy Philadelphia throughout the colder months, a large amount of food and forage would need to be brought in at regular intervals. On 10 December a pontoon bridge was erected across the Schuylkill, a tributary of the Delaware River that ran west of the city. At 3:00 a.m. on 11 December, four days after the aborted action against Washington's forces, Cornwallis led the light infantry, grenadiers, Guards, 100 German Chasseurs, the Hessian von Lengerke grenadier battalion, detachments of the 16th and 17th Light Dragoons, six six-pounders, and the 23rd, 27th, 28th, 33rd and 49th Regiments on a strong foraging expedition across the Schuylkill.[122] They intended to strip bare the area south of Matson's Ford over the river. Coincidentally, Washington had determined to shift the Continental Army west of the Schuylkill to see out the winter. Their route likewise led them to Matson's Ford.

The 33rd, along with the other foragers, set to rounding up cattle and supplies. According to Major John André 'it was said that great depredations had been committed by the soldiers on this march.'[123] However, their prey proved a little deadlier than bovine herds or the houses they pillaged along the route. Militia at Black Horse Inn initially met the British expedition but were forced to retreat. The local militia commander deployed five regiments in an effort to slow the Crown forces, but they too were overrun and routed. The regulars, with the guidance of a local man, John Roberts, who was later hanged by the rebels for the assistance he provided to the British, took up positions overlooking Matson's Ford.

The next day lead elements of the Continental Army began to cross the river, before discovering the presence of Cornwallis's corps and quickly withdrawing back to the other bank. For his own part, Cornwallis did not intend to bring on a general engagement. Forage collected, the 33rd and the other regiments on the expedition marched via a circuitous route back to Philadelphia, allowing Washington to cross the Schuylkill. When the Crown troops reached the bridge leading back to the city the cattle which they had taken was stopped 'and delivered to the commissary, to the great disappointment of many people' – presumably the regiments responsible for rounding up such a feast had hoped to have their pick before handing it over to the rest of the army.[124]

From 16 December onwards the army's quartermasters busied themselves with 'distributing quarters to the troops in Philadelphia.'[125] Warehouses and the abandoned properties of known rebels were requisitioned to house soldiers. The 33rd found most of their companies assigned to the buildings bordering onto the city's ropewalks, next to the docks that projected into the Delaware's cold waters.

122 André, *André's Journal*, p.130.
123 André, *André's Journal*, p.131.
124 André, *André's Journal*, p.131.
125 André, *André's Journal*, p.131.

The foraging continued. On 22 December troops again crossed the Schuylkill 'and hutted [in wigwams] to an extent of three miles from Derby to Grey's Ferry. The wagons were employed in the rear collecting forage, which was conveyed to the Philadelphia side of the Schuylkill.'[126] The expedition remained west of the city for a week, protecting foragers who sent wagonloads of hay back every day, all the while enduring lack of shelter and increasing cold.[127] On 24 December 'a few shots were fired by sentries of the 1st light infantry, at a party of the rebels who passed along their front.'[128] On Christmas Day, Captain Dansey found himself lamenting the lack of peace and goodwill, though he still found himself appreciating the thrill of combat as his troops guarded the foraging operations against opportunistic rebel attacks. He and his officers and men;

> Had Musket Balls flying about our Ears for a Minuit as thick as anytime during the War, a drole Way of keeping Christmas but thank God neither Officers or Men were hurt and we kill'd three of the Enemy and took five Prisoners, it is very good fun fighting when all the kill'd and wounded are on the Side of the Enemy. I like it prodigiously, it is better than a Fox Chace. As I have said in former Letters I have the greatest reason to thank God for my good Fortune in escaping almost untouched these two years past, for as to my Thumb it is now none the worse.[129]

The fighting was being conducted on the south side of Derby Creek, another passage over the Schuylkill, with the light infantry and regular battalions, including the 33rd, 'covering a quantity of meadowland from which the forage was taken.' The work continued the next day about three miles from Derby, west of the city. The 33rd were brigaded with the 46th and 68th Regiments, posted ahead of the British grenadiers and facing Cobb's Creek and, beyond it, the village of Derby. On 27 December 'the remainder of the forage within our compass was brought in, and in the evening the corps on the south side of Derby Creek were withdrawn across the bridges.' That day it began to snow heavily, continuing the next day prior to a 'very hard frost' on 29 December. The day before, with the foraging finally completed, 'the army marched towards Philadelphia … the whole crossed the Schuylkill and repaired to their several encampments and quarters.' At last, on 30 December, it was reported 'The Army came into winter quarters in Philadelphia.'[130]

With the army now safely ensconced in the captured capital, Cornwallis was finally granted permission to return home to visit his dying wife, Jemima, a whole year after his first leave was granted and then rescinded. Jemima lived long enough to see her husband again, passing away in February 1779. While travelling home, Cornwallis's first servant, James Forty, carried with him a letter from Dansey to his mother, having agreed to visit her while passing through Herefordshire.

126 André, *André's Journal*, p.132.
127 Hagist, *These Distinguished Corps*, p.129.
128 André, *André's Journal*, p.132.
129 DHS: William Dansey Letters: 19 January 1778.
130 André, *André's Journal*, pp.133–135.

While Christmas Day 1777 had passed full of action, the captain of the 33rd's light infantry could not help reflect on the fact that one year on from when he had sat down to Christmas dinner with Captain Oakes, and Lieutenants Drummond, Harris and Gorges, two of them – Drummond and Harris – were now dead, and the other three had all been wounded at some point. The year 1776 had finished with some hope – it seemed certain that over the course of the next 12 months the rebellion would collapse. But the stubborn resilience of the revolutionaries, and the brutal fighting at Brandywine, Germantown, Freeman's Farm, Bemis Heights and many smaller, wearing engagements had shown that the desire for American independence was strong, perhaps unwaveringly so. The conflict had not been resolved; it had only grown more entrenched, more violent, more desperate. 'We have taken Philadelphia,' Dansey wrote. 'And here we are, and think the War only beginning.'[131] He was right.

131 DHS: William Dansey Letters: 19 January 1778.

Chapter 8

What Havock War Makes

1778

To those struggling to keep the American revolutionary flame alight during the winter of late 1777 and early 1778, it seemed as though the British were taunting them. One supporter of Congress raged against the Crown forces who he believed were living in stolen luxury in Philadelphia, holding balls and parties and making free use of homes abandoned by the escaped Whigs, not to mention looting, raping and burning the surrounding countryside.[1]

In reality the captured city hardly proved to be a more pleasant place to be quartered than the Continental encampment at neighbouring Valley Forge. From a strategic perspective, Howe struggled to maintain the city. It drained British resources and focus, forcing Howe to govern it, overseeing civil matters such as the civil courts, trade and commerce and sanitation, none of which contributed to destroying the Continental Army.[2]

Even worse was the supply situation. Maintaining the army in the city required no small amount of food and fodder, more than the immediate surrounding countryside could readily provide. Despite the efforts to bring in enough sustenance in December, foraging expeditions remained regular activities throughout the winter months, with patrols leaving the city and its surrounding countryside to scour the locale for supplies or protect traders travelling into the city to sell their produce. Some of these were far-reaching, even plunging back into hostile, fertile New Jersey. Rebel forces attempted to interdict these expeditions, and so early 1778 settled into the same routine as early 1777, with small-scale raids and ambushes conducted by both sides. The 33rd did duty protecting forage parties, at least when the weather allowed – the diary of Captain John Peebles of the 42nd recorded on 11 February, for example, 'the 33d. Regt. went out this morng. to cover some foragers but the

1 Hugh Bicheno, *Rebels & Redcoats: The American Revolutionary War* (London: Harper Collins, 2003), p.117.

2 Mark Edward Lender and Garry Wheeler Stone, *Fatal Sunday: George Washington, the Monmouth Campaign, and the Politics of Battle* (Norman: University of Oklahoma Press, 2016), p.7.

badness of the weather render'd the jaunt fruitless.'[3] The rate of attrition was not as intense as it had been in New Jersey, but it nevertheless ensured the British stay in Philadelphia was not as comfortable as some of their enemies believed.

While the food coming in was enough to keep both the army and the city's remaining population from starving, it was far from plentiful, and consequently became extremely expensive. Dansey described how purchasing food was 'extravagantly dear, Beef 15 or 18 pence Sterling pr. Pound and everything in proportion except Liquor, Butter 2/4 a pound Eggs 2½ a piece Ster. things are dearer here than an Egg a penny one really can't live comfortably upon Captns. Pay had we not saved a little in the Summer.'[4]

With only the foraging to occupy themselves on a semi-regular basis, soldiers of all ranks turned to other activities to kill boredom. Public houses saw a great deal of trade, as did the courts martial dealing with drunkenness and vandalism, while officers enjoyed Philadelphian society and pursued interests ranging from reading and gambling to mistresses, cockfights and cricket.[5] Some put on amateur dramatics each Monday night between January and May at the city's Southwark Theatre.

The 33rd experienced all of this as part of the garrison. The regiment's commanders did their best to keep both themselves and their men busy. For his own part, Dansey found plenty of work in January ensuring his company's accounts were in order, a task made more difficult by the death of his paymaster sergeant, Joseph Palmer. In a letter written on 19 January he discussed his hope that he might be able to purchase a major's commission without delving into his financial savings, related that both Ben and the recently promoted Captain Gorges were well, and noted that ice in the Delaware River was blocking ships. He also grimly described how his light company had been all-but wiped out in the course of two years' fighting, sending a return of the losses 'to shew what havock War makes.' Of the one captain, two lieutenants, three sergeants, three corporals, one drummer and 36 privates that he listed as having been at Cork on 1 January 1776, the company had since suffered one captain (himself), three lieutenants, one sergeant, two corporals and 20 privates wounded, one corporal and four privates taken prisoner and two corporals and 13 Privates dead or killed – a distinction presumably made between those who had died in action and those out of it, from disease or mishap. The original company of 46 men had therefore suffered 47 casualties, a figure that Dansey explained; 'You see that the Casualties in the Company exceed the Original Strength of it which is by getting fresh Men for those kill'd and disabled.' He added rather drolly 'Observe the kill'd and wounded amount to 33 the Number of the Regiment.' Despite all this, he sought to reassure his family, writing that 'I still enjoy my Health and Spirits, and tho' I most heartily wish the War over I am not tired as I still persevere in the Light Infantry.'[6]

3 Peebles, *John Peebles' American War*, p.164.
4 DHS: William Dansey Letters: 4 March 1778.
5 Lender and Stone, *Fatal Sunday*, pp.9–10.
6 DHS: William Dansey Letters: 19 January 1778.

His sanguine attitude did not endure for much longer. In March he wrote with a bitter edge of the difficulties faced by officers in the light infantry and the fact that, even in the wartime army, promotion was not necessarily based on merit or competence, but involved the ability to make use of the web of personal relationships that helped the officer corps function;

> There is nothing to be gained by fighting with Light Infantry but Lord knows broken Bones, and as to the honor of it if it was not for self satisfaction it is all a farce. Merit goes by Favor, and we are only tools for the favorites to work with, consequently generally fall into ignorant, unskillful Hands, and like the mechanics's Tools we suffer, and if the Work does not succeed we are blamed, if it does we have no more merit than the Carpenter's Ax or Saw, in short an Officer of the Light Infantry's Character is always at Stake and if he does ever so well the merit becomes other peoples, whose Impudence or Sycophancy gains them the Ears of People in power, but I'll persevere.[7]

While continuing their sojourn, the army made little effort to engage Washington's forces as they saw out the winter at Valley Forge. This was not due to being seduced by the city's luxuries, indeed the activities undertaken in Philadelphia were not much removed from garrison life anywhere else in the eighteenth century.[8] Nevertheless, Washington's defensive positions at Valley Forge were strong, and there were no attempts to engage him that winter or for most of the spring.

None of this was helped by the fact that the British commander-in-chief in North America no longer wished to be there. Howe had sent his resignation letter to Britain in October 1777. In April 1778, he finally received confirmation that it had been accepted. His successor was to be the subordinate who had worked so closely with him almost since the war's beginning, Sir Henry Clinton. Appointed to his new role in March, Clinton sailed from New York and took command in Philadelphia in May. The officer corps took it upon themselves to throw a grand fete, called the Meschianza (Italian for 'medley'), to honour Howe's departure. On 18 May a crowd of 400 officers along with the great and the good of Loyalist Philadelphian society attended or participated in the biggest party Philadelphia had ever seen. A grand regatta was held featuring banners, cannons, martial music and a medieval-themed joust followed by a ball and supper, much of it viewed by thousands of spectators.[9]

Much is made of the Meschianza and its extravagance, less of the fact that even as it ended British soldiers were once more marching into action. Late on 19 May Major General James Grant and a detachment of 5,000 men headed out of the city. Their objective was to outflank and pincer Lafayette's Continental forces at Barren Hill. However, the Congressional troops were able to withdraw before they were caught. In the same month the 33rd put

7 DHS: William Dansey Letters: 20 March 1778.

8 Lender and Stone, *Fatal Sunday*, p.10.

9 Benson John Lossing, *Our Country: A Household History for all Readers, from the Discovery of America to the Present Time* (New York: The Amies Publishing Company, 1888), p.186.

A contemporary image of a British light infantryman as he would have appeared in the early years of the Revolutionary War. Note the shorter jacket, cap instead of hat, shoulder wings and powder horn. (Anne S. K. Brown Military Collection)

on their new clothing for the year. It seemed as though the war would drag on much as it had done for the past three years.

Things, however, had changed irrevocably. The war that had consumed eastern North America was now set to spread across the globe. In February France had signed a formal alliance with the fledgling United States, forcing Britain's hand. On 17 March, Britain declared war on France. What had been a conflict over a few colonies now became a conflict over the entire empire.

It also heavily altered the dynamics of the fighting in North America. Previously the British Army had operated along the coastline with impunity, knowing that the Royal Navy dominated the seas and offered a near-constant link in terms of supply and, if necessary, retreat. With France's own powerful navy now ranged against them, that was no longer necessarily the case. There was the potential for British forces to become cut off by both land and sea, and for British posts in far-flung places to be struck by seaborne enemies.

Clinton was acutely aware of this. His new army's eight-month occupation of Philadelphia had yielded nothing whatsoever. Congress was functioning elsewhere, the revolutionaries had not lost heart over the loss of their capital, and few local Loyalists had rallied to the royal standard. Now the news that France was once again at war with Britain meant that, if a French expeditionary force were landed to the east, Philadelphia could be cut off and surrounded by the Continental Army on one side and a French one on the other. Almost as disastrously, French forces could strike at New York while the main army was in Philadelphia. These factors combined to convince Clinton to abandon the city.

The Evacuation of Philadelphia

In early June Crown forces began to lay the groundwork for a movement across the Delaware and into New Jersey, with the intention of marching overland to the safety of New York. The main activities occurred on 17 and 18 June. On the 17th the majority of the army marched from their billets in the city and formed at their brigade parade areas at 6:00 p.m. From there they were moved out to the defensive works that had been thrown up around Philadelphia, where they spent the night laying on their arms. The 33rd, however, were not with them. Besides a few other small units, they alone remained in the rebel capital for the time being, given the task of policing the city for the last few hours of British rule. It seems likely that the 33rd were singled out for the task owing to their reputation for good discipline – as the last troops out, they could be trusted not to set about looting.

It can only have been a nervous few hours for the regiment, suddenly all-but alone in what was ultimately an enemy city. Word finally came for the regiment to march, and they departed to join the main body of the army as it passed over the Delaware at Gloucester Point, the last British regiment to leave Philadelphia. By midmorning, with the crossing guarded by a Royal Navy vessel and the light and grenadier battalions, the 33rd had re-joined the 4th Brigade across the Delaware. Philadelphia had been evacuated.

The army now faced a daunting task. Heavily encumbered by its supplies and baggage, it had to attempt what Howe had deemed too risky in 1777 – an overland march between Philadelphia and New York. Progress would necessarily have to be slow and methodical; the weather was alternating between intense heat and intense rainstorms, and the terrain less than ideal. Though most of the countryside was flat, the army would still have to divide to make the best use of the road network, which was bisected by numerous creeks and streams that would need to be forded when the rebels inevitably broke the bridges over them. All the while the columns would be subject to rebel sniping, along with the even greater threat posed by Washington's main army once it roused itself in pursuit.

Before daybreak on 19 June the 33rd, along with the rest of the 4th Brigade, the 3rd Brigade, the Guards, light infantry and grenadiers, marched under Cornwallis's command through the settlement of Haddonfield, where the army's baggage had halted, and on to Evesham. They formed part of one of the army's two total divisions, some 10,470 individuals, including 355 female camp followers.[10] The weather was poor, a heavy rain turning the roads to mud and soaking the soldiers through. There was minor skirmishing around the British columns of march.

At 4:00 a.m. the army rose and was on the march again an hour later, as was customary. In general, throughout the withdrawal the army marched as early as possible each day to avoid the intense afternoon temperatures. The divisions united at Mount Holly, where they remained for a day to rest. On 22 June the army was again divided and ordered to be ready to march at 3:00 a.m. It moved off, is it did throughout the retreat, in a carefully specified order, designed to ensure the greatest security. The division to which the 33rd belonged was spearheaded by 20 mounted jäger, then the Queen's Rangers, and 20 black pioneers who worked to ensure the roads and bridges for the rest of the column were navigable. Behind them came infantry and cavalry, baggiage and equipment, cattle, the artillery train and the 5th Brigade as a rearguard. One battalion from the 4th Brigade were detached to protect the column's vulnerable left flank.[11] Clinton's instructions did not specify which battalion from the 4th Brigade would act as flankers, only 'one Battalion from the 4th Brigade is to flank the baggage upon the left.'[12] Presumably the brigade's four battalions took it in turns, and the 33rd spent time moving through the terrain – often boggy or marshy – to the side of the column.

Rebel forces shadowed them but did not mount a major attack. Papers were left for the passing Crown soldiers to read, warning ominously that they might be 'Burgoyned,' as the rebels now called the surrounding and cutting off a British army. One British deserter who had been captured while wearing a rebel uniform was executed as Clinton sought to keep a tight grip on the army's discipline during the march.

---

10 Lender and Stone, *Fatal Sunday*, pp.126–127.

11 Lender and Stone, *Fatal Sunday*, pp.131–132.

12 'Head Quarters, Mount Holly, 21st. June, 1778', in Anon. (ed.), *Collections of the New-York Historical Society for the Year 1883* (New York: New York Historical Society, 1884), p.597.

On 23 June the column that included the 33rd was forced to stop near an inn called the Rising Sun, where the rebels had destroyed a bridge. Repairs were undertaken. Throughout the day the regiment would have been aware of the occasional thump of cannon fire, and perhaps the fainter crackle of muskets. The Queen's Rangers, the grenadiers, the light infantry and the 16th Light Dragoons skirmished with small parties of rebels, while a Royal Artillery 3-pounder overlooking a bridge being repaired at Crosswicks Creek helped drive off the enemy. Later on, rebel artillery cannonaded troops of the 5th Brigade from a distance, without doing any damage. André noted the next day that 'a good deal of attention was paid to enforcing the orders respecting plunder, and also the Battalion horses and followers of the army not mixing in the line of march.'[13] Despite these initial efforts, it did not take the army long to engage in its usual activities during a long march. There was looting, the destruction of fences for fuel, the seizure of livestock and poultry, as well as various personal belongings, either appropriated for use or to be sold on.[14] One Continental Army soldier in pursuit recalled his anger at seeing cattle lying dead in the surrounding fields, some with steaks cut from them.[15]

The other common occurrences of a march – and the less common experience of a solar eclipse – took place on 24 June. As well as bridge repairs there was more minor skirmishing, with the light artillery supporting the rearguard or screening troops usually sufficient to cause the rebels to scatter. British light dragoons set an ambush, but failed to lure any rebels in. Rumours spread that Morgan's feared riflemen were nearby. The baggage train had been moved to the front of the line of march that morning, to better protect it. The long column of supplies made the whole operation exceptionally vulnerable. It consisted around 5,000 horses and 1,500 wagons stretching the length of twelve miles.[16]

By this point the weather had turned, becoming 'very sultry.'[17] The rebels had stopped up wells along the way, and this scarcity of water combined with the hot weather to increase the hardship of the operation. Soldiers endured temperatures that broke 30°C.[18] Men perished from heat exhaustion, including as many as 20 on 26 June.[19] Brief bouts of torrential rain and thunder only made the situation worse. The sandy soil and the many streams caused transports to become stuck or broken, while swarms of mosquitos from the neighbouring swamplands were a plague upon the soldiers.[20] The 33rd suffered perhaps the most sweltering, uncomfortable experience since their stay on Long Island outside Charleston in mid-1776. André described the roads as 'in a general way sandy, and the land, except in

13 André, *André's Journal*, p.8.
14 Lender and Stone, *Fatal Sunday*, pp.145–147.
15 Lender and Stone, *Fatal Sunday*, p.147.
16 Lender and Stone, *Fatal Sunday*, pp.97–98.
17 André, *André's Journal*, p.10.
18 Lender and Stone, *Fatal Sunday*, p.141.
19 Lender and Stone, *Fatal Sunday*, p.142.
20 Lender and Stone, *Fatal Sunday*, p.142.

the neighbourhood of Allentown, deemed poor.'[21] Rumours that Washington was in close pursuit increased.

It was undeniably tough campaigning, but by this point in the war the army was not unaccustomed to it. Later histories claimed that the heat had a particular effect on Crown forces and 'was not favourable to the progress of the heavily accoutred British.'[22] This seems to have been a product of the idea that the British troops were not well-prepared to fight in North America, a concept that has been repeatedly disproven. Lender and Stone argue that by 1778, 'the British were experienced campaigners and certainly understood the need to adapt to adverse weather conditions.'[23] Knapsacks and other unnecessary baggage were left in the wagons, and the troops were possibly still wearing the uniforms they had modified for the operations in 1777, with cut-down hats and shortened coats. The short, early-morning marches undertaken by Clinton also helped. Despite the difficult conditions of the retreat, the army remained fully cohesive and battle-ready.

On 25 June the troops marched from Allentown and headed towards Sandy Hook, where they would embark for New York. The road networks meant that for once the divisions were forced to use the same route, forming a column 12 miles long, moving painfully slowly. Washington was gaining ground, and the likelihood of a general engagement was increasing. The army closed in on Monmouth Court House, the chief settlement in Monmouth County. Skirmishing between the light infantry and rebel parties intensified. On 26 June the main part of the army reached Monmouth and encamped in an arc covered around four and a half miles between the town's western and northern sides.[24]

The Battle of Monmouth

Clinton chose to pause at Monmouth. His army had marched 67 miles in a little over the week and, besides near-constant sniping and skirmishing, had faced inimical weather and difficult roads.[25] The men took the opportunity to rest and recuperate before the final push to Sandy Hook – at least, those not assigned to foraging, picket duty, or driving off the incessantly harassing rebels, or choosing to plunder Monmouth itself, which was ransacked and partially burned. It seems Clinton was happy to linger for a while at the township, harbouring ambitions that Washington might finally risk a general engagement.

While there, the 33rd's reported strength was 365 men. This was recorded alongside 16 women and no children, the official strength of the camp followers permitted with the regiment, but this was unlikely to be the

21 André, *André's Journal*, p.10.
22 Anon., 'Record of the Services,' p.238.
23 Lender and Stone, *Fatal Sunday*, p.142.
24 Lender and Stone, *Fatal Sunday*, p.157.
25 Lender and Stone, *Fatal Sunday*, p.209.

reality.[26] Most of the woman and children had been ordered to accompany the part of the army's baggage being evacuated from Philadelphia to New York via sea, but accounts indicate that many simply ignored these instructions and participated in the overland withdrawal alongside their husbands and partners.

While it seemed the main body of the Continental Army was certainly close, an attack was not forthcoming, and so on 28 June the British moved out once again. The 33rd broke camp early in the morning with the rest of the army, though a mistake in the order of march and the movement of the artillery delayed the start of the day's passage. It is unlikely that most of the enlisted men in the regiment would have anticipated a major battle that same day, but that would be exactly what they would get. Washington's vanguard had come up, and Clinton's position was 'very critical, for victory only could ensure a moderate degree of safety; defeat meant the destruction of his whole army.'[27]

The 33rd had barely set out when orders came to counter-march, back along the road they had just come down. The morning was turning into another swelteringly hot day, and the crackle of musketry and the thudding of artillery betrayed the fact that it was about to get even hotter. Information was likely scant for the men in the ranks, but the portents were all there. It was not just the 33rd being ordered back on itself – Cornwallis's whole division had come about. Using two roads, it began to move west towards an area of creeks and marshland with small forests and fields, and a low hill rising beyond. It was from this terrain that the gunfire was emanating from. The column of march received orders to spread out into line of battle, another sure indication that they were moving into an engagement. The grenadier battalion ahead did likewise.

Somewhere a little north of a homestead, the 33rd, along with the rest of the 4th Brigade, halted. The house in question belonged to William Ker, whose family had been long-time residents of the area and had founded the local Presbyterian congregation.[28] There the regiment waited in the sweltering heat, as ahead of them the battle unfolded.

The engagement had started when the vanguard of the main Continental army had opportunistically attacked the rear of the British column. Clinton had turned at bay, and the rebels had retreated before him. Now Washington himself was on the field, the main body of his force occupying Perrine's Hill, ahead of the British. Both sides were looking for a fight.

The battle developed on two wings, with the 3rd Brigade, light infantry and Queen's Rangers driving back the rebels on the right while the grenadiers and Guards, ahead of the 4th Brigade, pushed them back on the left. The progress of both advances ceased when Clinton decided against trying to take Perrine's Hill, where Washington was posted in strength. Throughout it all the 4th and 5th Brigades remained in reserve.

26 Lender and Stone, *Fatal Sunday*, p.470.
27 Anon., 'Record of the Services,' p.238.
28 Lender and Stone, *Fatal Sunday*, p.516.

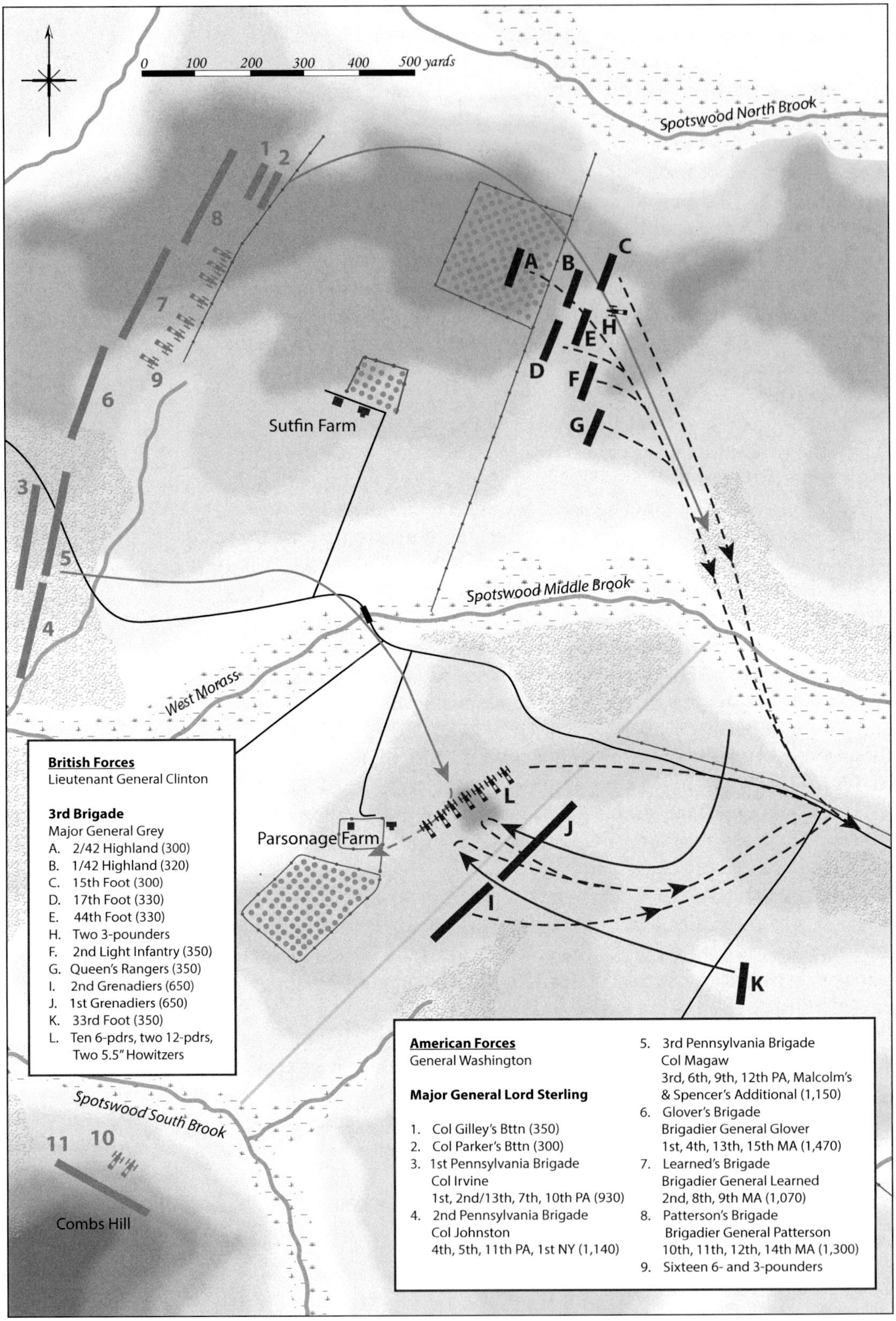

The latter stages of the Battle of Monmouth, 28 June 1778.

For those units engaged, the fighting was intense. A British newspaper spoke of soldiers 'spent with heat, thirst and fatigue' and claimed that 'they expended from eighty to ninety rounds in a short time.'[29] During an aborted flanking attack along Spotswood North Brook the 33rd's light infantry, operating with the 1st light infantry battalion, had to make use of their alacrity when they were almost caught short by the sudden appearance of rebel light dragoons. Captain Dansey admitted that 'I had a very narrow Escape from being taken Prisoner with my whole Company. We were obliged to run up to our middles in a Bog to get away from the Rebel Light Horse and I had only one man taken.'[30] The company, running the risk of being cut off, made it back exhausted, but without having suffered any men killed.[31]

The 33rd's grenadiers had a hotter time of it. The regiment's former colonel, Hildebrand Oakes, would surely have been proud of his namesake son as he led the grenadier company advancing on the rebels as part of the 1st grenadier battalion. With volleys and bayonets, they pushed the Continental vanguard back, urged on by Clinton himself.

From about 1:30 p.m. a lull in offensive operations occurred, and both sides held their positions and conducted a long-range cannonade that did little damage. Clinton, believing that Washington would not move from the hill, and knowing that he could not simply remain watching him, decided to order a staggered withdrawal. His primary objective remained to protect the supply column and reach Sandy Hook with his army intact. Consequently, around 3:30 p.m. the right wing was ordered back towards the left, the highlanders of the 42nd Foot covering that flank amidst sharp fighting. However, much of the left wing, which was intended to hold its ground as the right withdrew behind it, misunderstood its orders. They began retreating as well, with only the 1st Grenadier battalion maintaining their position just west of a small waterway and boggy ground known as the Middle Morass.

Washington had already ordered forward a series of probing attacks. One, consisting of the Pennsylvania brigade of Brigadier General Anthony Wayne, discovered the grenadiers, alone now but for a single six-pounder as they moved south along a lane in search of a passage over the Middle Morass. The 1st Grenadier battalion, which included the 33rd's company under Captain Oakes, had already been heavily engaged in the day's fighting, in extreme temperatures, and were exhausted.

Wayne, one of the most experienced and aggressive Continental commanders, attacked them immediately. The grenadiers were possibly caught still on the march, and hastily formed to meet the assault, likely along a fence line.[32] Clinton, drawn to the sound of the sudden engagement, found the battalion being cut down.

It was at this point that the 33rd arrived. It is unclear whether the regiment was ordered forward, or whether Lieutenant Colonel Webster took it upon

29 *General Advertiser and Morning Intelligencer*, 18 September 1778, p.2.

30 DHS: William Dansey Letters: 28 July 1778.

31 Hagist, *These Distinguished Corps*, p.137.

32 Lender and Stone, *Fatal Sunday*, p.344.

himself to leave behind the rest of the 4th Brigade and march towards battle.[33] Clinton noted only that regiment made a movement towards the enemy. Whether it was a brigade order or Webster's idea, the 33rd's arrival saved the grenadiers. The 33rd crossed over the Middle Morass and, deploying into line, added their volleys to those of the flank battalion.

Now it was the turn of the Pennsylvanians to waver. Formed in open order, the grenadiers and 33rd began to outflank the shorter Continental line. Going toe-to-toe, the firefight was as intense as any eighteenth-century linear engagement. A Continental Army officer, Alexander Dow, described the desperate carnage as men, including both senior and junior officers, fell killed and wounded around him;

> Lt Coll Bunner fell near me [and] Coll Barber much wounded. Four subalterns of our Regt [were] wounded one of which [was] Adjintant Talman Closs by my side. I Commanded the platun on the left of our partey and being Closs prest by the right of the Enemy in frunt Lost three of my men the English Comanding Officer on the right of the Enemy holoring Com on my brave boyes for the honour of Great Briton.[34]

Wayne's forces began to retreat, driven back through a long hedgerow that had already been cut up by fighting earlier in the day. Beyond it was Parsonage's Farm, a house, barns and outhouses abutted by a fenced orchard. The Pennsylvanians hurried to occupy the position as the grenadiers and 33rd forced their way through the shot-scarred hedge and reformed on the other side. They began to once more to close with Wayne's men, the grenadiers charging the orchard.

The echoing thunder of artillery, rolling out through the unbearably hot air, announced a shift in the engagement. Four Continental 3 or 4-pounder cannons had unlimbered just to the south-west, on Combs Hill. Commanded by a Frenchman serving in the Continental Army, Lieutenant Colonel DuPlessis, they opened fire, sending their shot whipping along the British line. Even worse, the position of the artillery meant they were able to enfilade the regulars from their left, an ideal target for the gunners.

Outflanked and with Wayne's men now ensconced in Parsonage farm, the position for the 33rd and the grenadiers had become untenable. A hasty retreat was conducted back through the hedgerow, which helped to conceal the two battalions from the withering fire emanating from Combs Hill. The grenadiers and the 33rd suffered the enfilading fire, but were able to stop any disruption of their retreat.[35] The withdrawl continued for about a mile, back to roughly where the 33rd had started their advance from, on higher ground close to the homestead of William Ker. Back in Britain the *General Advertiser and Morning Intelligencer* reported that the withdrawal 'was covered by the 33d regiment of infantry; the steady behaviour of which corps, on this occasion, will always add to their former reputation.'[36]

---

33 Lender and Stone, *Fatal Sunday*, p.345.

34 John U. Rees, 'Eyewitness to Battle: Alexander Dow's Account of a 1777 Skirmish and the 1778 Battle of Monmouth', *Brigade Dispatch*, vol.XXIX, no.1, Spring 1999, pp.15–16.

35 Lender and Stone, *Fatal Sunday*, p.404.

36 *General Advertiser and Morning Intelligencer*, 18 September 1778, p.2.

As the last booming reports of the Continental artillery faded into the evening heat, the battle came to a close. The 33rd's rescue of the grenadiers had been the final action of the day. As the sun began to set the exhausted regulars took stock. It seemed likely that the engagement would be renewed the next day. Clinton, however, had different plans. Washington's position was a strong one, centred on Perrine's Hill. The strategic situation offered Clinton no leeway. Attacking would risk the destruction of his army, and he could not remain in place with Washington likely to receive reinforcement – his forces could very quickly become surrounded and 'Burgoyned.'

A little after 11:00 p.m., after about four hours of much-needed rest, Clinton's army began to withdraw. They did so in the dark, silently, not wishing to alert the Continentals to their movements. The 33rd pulled themselves to their feet, fell in, and joined the rest of the 4th Brigade as they shifted north-east towards Nut Swamp, where von Knyphausen's column and the precious baggage train were safely encamped. From there they marched to the settlement of Middletown, and then the Navesink Highlands, which looked out onto New York Bay. Beyond the hills lay Sandy Hook and salvation; a fleet of Royal Navy ships to safely transport the weary army to New York.

Withdrawal to New York

By this point it seemed Washington did not intend to pursue another battle immediately, and most of the rebel militia had drifted back to their homes. Sandy Hook was a Loyalist enclave, and reasonably well fortified. Nevertheless, military embarkations were always fraught processes, and Clinton still had no way of knowing if a French fleet might appear off the Hook and pen him in with Washington bearing down on him from the other side.

Earlier in the year the actual Sandy Hook peninsula had been cut off by a storm that had created a channel 60 yards wide. This consequently had to be crossed on flatboats before the soldiers and camp followers could then embark for the Royal Navy transports beyond. Most of the infantry remained on the Navesink Highlands, protecting the baggage and artillery as it was brought aboard first, enduring mosquitos and bouts of intense heat and torrential rain as they did so. On 4 July – with distant gunfire signalling rebel Independence Day celebrations – the Royal Navy constructed a pontoon bridge over the waterway, speeding up the embarkation process. Soldiers were forced to cross in single file as the army continued to filter down from its defensive posture on the heights above. Finally on 6 July the last of the rearguard made it onboard.[37]

The ships set sail unopposed, ferrying troops across the New York Bay to Manhattan, Staten Island and Long Island. The 33rd landed on Long Island, the sight of their victory just under two years earlier. The havoc of war had brought the army full circle, and for next to no appreciable gain.

37 Lender and Stone, *Fatal Sunday*, pp.374–375.

While the evacuation from Philadelphia all the way to New York had been strategically successful, it had come even closer to disaster than any at the time had realised. On 11 July, just five days after the Royal Navy had moved the army from Sandy Hook to New York, a powerful fleet appeared off the coast. It flew the white standards of the King of France. Dispatched from Toulon in April, the 12 ships of the line and six frigates had arrived just too late to cut the British off from New York.

The appearance of the old enemy's fleet caused a considerable stir throughout both the British army and navy. Vice Admiral Lord Richard Howe, the Royal Navy commander-in-chief for North America and the general's brother, appealed for volunteers from merchant shipping in the harbour to help crew his outnumbered vessels, and likewise asked for the infantry to bolster the ranks of his marines. While on land batteries were laid to bombard the French if they made an effort to enter the bay, Howe set his ships to rake any of the enemy that dared cross over the bar of Sandy Hook.

Volunteers from the army were so plentiful that they were required to draw lots to see who would board. Both the 33rd's light and grenadier companies were among the eight flank companies selected from four regiments to act as marines. Assuming that Washington was able to coordinate with the French, it seemed as if the decisive moment of the war might suddenly be at hand, a combined assault from land and sea against the British fastness at New York. The fatigues of the recent campaign apparently now forgotten, Dansey described the passion of the moment;

> The glorious Spirit of our Officers and Seamen on board the Ships of War, the prudent and active Conduct of Lord Howe back'd by every body of People here, shew'd most conspiciously the brave Character of the English in times of the greatest danger, which never cou'd be more apparent than on this Occasion. One of the most powerful of Fleets that ever sail'd from France at the Harbour's Mouth ready to come and crush us to Atoms on the first fair Wind, Our Army block'd up on Islands after three years being victorious and unable to do anything, this instead of dismaying caused such a Spirit of Bravery, unanimity and Resolution ... the Glory of the British Empire never sullied before, a British Admiral pent up in an Harbour. History never furnishes such an Instance. How every Englishman heart felt the Indignity the Event shew'd... The Army no[t] forgetful of the many Services it had experienced from the Fleet embraced with Ardor this Opportunity of shewing their sense of it and anzious for their Country's Honor and to share the Glory of its Defence, offer'd their Service on the Occasion to act on board the Men of War as Marines.[38]

The 33rd's light bobs were assigned to Captain Sir James Wallace's *Experiment*, a 50-gun 4th rate ship of the line. Its muster books showed that at the time Dansey had under his command only two other officers, one sergeant, two corporals and 30 private soldiers fit for duty.[39] They waited onboard, expecting a French attack, but finding instead that the enemy appeared content to wait

38 DHS: Dansey Letters: William Dansey 28 July 1778.
39 Hagist, *These Distinguished Corps*, p.140.

beyond the bay. Writing from the *Experiment* on 28 July, Dansey informed his mother that;

> On Wednesday the 22d both Wind and Tide favored the French, they got under Way and stood in for the Harbour to near Canon Shot when discovering the warm Reception they were to meet with they put about and sheered off and we have seen no more of them since but are now in hourly Expectation of Comodore Biron when we make no doubt Lord Howe will have his Revenge and make the French repent coming here. Was the Spirit, Bravery and Unanimity to reign in the Councils of Great Britain as manifested itself in her Fleets and Armies She may yet be Great.[40]

The abrupt disappearance of the French was something of an anti-climax. New York was not to be the target of the first joint Franco-American operation, but rather the smaller British base at Newport, further north off Rhode Island. Resolving to assist the garrison there, Clinton made preparations to also take an expedition in pursuit of the French.

While the main body of the 33rd had been conducting the difficult withdrawal from Philadelphia and clashing with the enemy at Monmouth Courthouse, John Robert Shaw and a detachment of the regiment's newest recruits had just arrived in North America. Following in the footsteps of thousands of other soldiers who served in the American colonies, Shaw had marched from Chatham Barracks to Portsmouth, sailed to the Isle of Wight, and from there on to Cork, Ireland. The fleet then travelled to Madeira in the Atlantic, eventually making it to Rhode Island three months after sailing from Cork. Once there Shaw described 'doing duty, while the British army were on their march from Philadelphia.'[41]

The recruits finally joined the rest of the 33rd at Gravesend on Long Island, not long after the successful evacuation via Sandy Hook. Shaw's first experiences with the regiment involved marching north to Bedford, above New York. They did not remain there for long. At the beginning of autumn the regiment, according to Shaw, 'was called out, to perform as we supposed, some great exploit.'[42] On 26 August the 33rd, along with the rest of the 4th Brigade, the 3rd Brigade and the 1st Light Infantry and 1st Grenadier battalions (which included the 33rd's flank companies) moved from their encampment at Bedford to Flushing, back on Long Island. Under the immediate command of Major General Charles Grey, they then marched from Flushing to Whitestone, three miles away, where they embarked on transport ships that set sail on 27 August.[43]

Contrary winds bedevilled the expedition, which arrived at Rhode Island on 1 September to find both the rebel and French forces gone following their brief and unsuccessful siege of Newport. Clinton decided to carry on and burn the rebel supply base at nearby New London, but the attempt was foiled by the bad weather and the belief that most of the enemy's stockpiles had

40 DHS: Dansey Letters: William Dansey 28 July 1778.
41 Shaw, *A Narrative*, p.17.
42 Shaw, *A Narrative*, pp.17–18.
43 André, *André's Journal*, p.21.

probably already been moved to safety. Clinton himself sailed back to New York, leaving Grey in command of the expedition.

On 5 September sails were spotted on the horizon. Could this be the French fleet that had so recently menaced New York? It turned out to be Vice Admiral Howe. Grey resolved to raid the coast around Buzzards Bay, on the southern edge of Massachusetts further east from New London. Branching north from the bay lay the Acushnet River, with the town of New Bedford (not to be confused with Bedford above New York) on the west bank and the settlement of Fairhaven on the east. The area was known to be a base for rebel privateers and included a large amount of captured shipping.

The Royal Navy frigate *Carysfort* led the fleet into Buzzards Bay, initially being grounded twice upon the bay's rocks, but getting off without any lasting damage. As they sailed, the transport ships lowered their flatboats over the sides, which were soon filled with light infantry and grenadiers. Tasked with securing a landing place, the flank battalions were ferried to Clark's Cove, just below New Bedford, where they disembarked unopposed as the sun was setting. The rest of the expedition, including the 33rd, were then brought ashore.

Six flank companies, later supplemented by three companies of 42nd Foot, entered New Bedford 'to burn the vessels at the wharves, the stores, &c' and afterwards 'proceeded up the banks of the river destroying everything at McPherson's and other wharves.'[44] While this was happening the rest of the flank battalions moved up beyond New Bedford, securing high ground near Crane's Mill, overlooking a bridge that crossed the Acushnet close to the river's head.

The 33rd along with the 64th then marched north past this advanced guard, passing over the bridge to the Acushnet's east side. From there they turned south, the blaze of warehouses and ships on the opposite bank illuminating the night. Major André wrote that 'everything being consumed on the west side of the river, the troops marched down the other shore, and in passing Fair Haven the 33rd entered that place and destroyed everything of stores and shipping.'[45] John Robert Shaw remembered the expedition, 'where we landed, marched to the town [Fairhaven], plundered and burned it, with all the shipping in the harbor.'[46] Along with the destruction at New Bedford, a total of almost 30 storehouses as well as a number of private properties were reduced to ash, along with their contents, described by Major André as 'great quantities of rum, sugar, molasses, coffee, tea, tobacco, medicines, cotton, gunpowder, sail cloth, cordage, &c.'[47] Shaw's first military operation had been, according to him, one of a number of 'predatory excursions.'[48] With Fairhaven blazing behind them, a twin for New Bedford across the river, the 33rd carried on south, intending to reach a narrow spit of land called Skonticut Neck, where the transports were waiting to pick them up. However, a mistake by their local guide took them down the wrong road, leading them instead to the mouth of the Acushnet.

44 André, *André's Journal*, p.28.
45 André, *André's Journal*, p.28.
46 André, *André's Journal*, p.19.
47 André, *André's Journal*, p.42.
48 Shaw, *A Narrative*, p.19.

Throughout southern Massachusetts the militia were stirring, alerted by church bells ringing the alarm and the conflagration lighting up the night sky. Shaw recalled 'the next day we marched into the country without opposition, except from a few of the militia who brought on a skirmish; but they were soon dispersed.'[49] Major André similarly noted that 'we had a few men wounded by people lurking in the swamps behind stone fences … The rebels carried from New Bedford four pieces of brass cannon from which they fired a shot or two as they retired on the Boston Road.' The flank battalions in the vanguard had done their usual vicious work, with three or four militiamen found by André 'bayoneted, one an officer. They had fired at the advanced party and were not alert enough to get off.'[50] But despite the feeble efforts of the local militia to stop the incursion, more were certainly flocking to the now-misdirected Crown troops.

The expedition's guide led them down to the beach, hoping to follow it east and thereby reach Skonticut Neck. Instead, they ran into the rear of a rebel artillery battery that had been set up overlooking the bay. As the British ships had begun their landing the evening before they had briefly fired on them, before the crew spiked the guns and abandoned them, leaving their colours flying. The British therefore stumbled across the deserted battery during their efforts to reach Skonticut.

Pausing briefly to destroy it, along with the adjoining barracks and magazine, they 'followed the course of the shore over trackless ground until stopped by a run of water which obliged us to turn to our left to search and fall into the road which headed the run.'[51] This detour had the unwelcome effect of bringing them all the way back to Fairhaven, which was still burning. Had the militia arrived in any numbers, the column could well have been in danger.

As it was, however, few militiamen had yet arrived. There was a brief exchange of shots before the column turned south again, this time along the correct road. They reached Skonticut Neck, and the safety of the ships beyond. Throughout the expedition the 33rd had suffered a single loss; one soldier missing.[52] They began to embark just as the sun was rising, fighting through the plumes of smoke and ash rising along the length of the Acushnet behind them. During the raid 70 ships were destroyed along with magazines, warehouses and their stores and the rope walks.[53]

The next day the navy set about destroying several more rebel vessels along the banks of the bay. On 8 September they sailed for Martha's Vineyard, an island rich with livestock and produce that lay south of Buzzards Bay. The weather was still set against the expedition, and with supplies running low Major General Grey was forced to reduce rations to two-thirds the normal allowance.

After anchoring off Martha's Vineyard on 10 September, the inhabitants agreed to supply 10,000 sheep and 300 head of cattle. Grey demanded

49 Shaw, *A Narrative*, p.19.
50 André, *André's Journal*, p.30.
51 André, *André's Journal*, p.29.
52 André, *André's Journal*, p.44.
53 Lee, *History of the Thirty-third*, p.115.

'the inhabitants to drive in their sheep and cattle, or that troops should be marched thro' the island; likewise to being in their arms, or that the colonel and captains of the militia should be sent prisoners to New York.'[54] Over the next four days detachments were landed on the island to speed along the process. By 12 September 6,000 sheep and 130 oxen had been secured onboard. On 13 and 14 September, as more livestock were seized, a salt works was destroyed, a number of vessels burned and captured, and the weapons of the militia taken. A colonel and five captains of the militia were confined, along with a number of prominent local rebels who had attempted to conceal a store of ammunition. Money intended to be supplied to Congress was also seized. Two British soldiers having deserted, Grey threatened to kidnap a number of the inhabitants if they were not returned to their regiments by whoever was hiding them.

The tribute taken, the fleet prepared to sail on 15 September. The two deserters were apprehended, and the captured rebels were released after swearing they would 'abstain from taking part any more in the war or persecuting others for their political opinions.'[55] Grey promised to pay for the 10,000 sheep and 300 cattle now crammed into the fleet's stinking holds but advised the islanders that they would have to travel to New York to collect the payment. The islanders duly sent a delegate, only for him to be refused, and required to travel all the way to London to pursue the claim. Eventually there was a degree of compensation paid, though not as much as the islanders had claimed for.

The 33rd missed all of this. When the fleet first arrived at Martha's Vineyard on 10 September the transports carrying the regiment remained outside the harbour, along with those bearing the light infantry and grenadiers. Grey intended to sail on to neighbouring Nantucket Island, which was believed to be sheltering up to 200 ships, including many privateers and their prizes. The 33rd were consequently once again brigaded with the army's elite.[56]

Still, however, the weather confounded them. No opportunity could be found to chart a course from Martha's Vineyard to Nantucket, despite the island lying just three hours sail away. Consequently, the 33rd remained onboard while their fellow bloodybacks brought in Grey's tribute from across the Vineyard.

On 15 September the entire fleet set sail, leaving Nantucket undisturbed. Over the next few days they fought their way through buffeting gales, being scattered at one point, before eventually making it back to New York. By 22 September the 33rd were back with the main body of the army, at Bergen in New Jersey, just across the Hudson from Manhattan.

During the Massachusetts excursion, Shaw recorded with humour the plight of one particular camp follower;

> We took a store of molasses, the hogsheads being rolled out and their heads knocked in, a soldier's wife went to dip her camp-kettle in a hogshead of molasses and while she was stooping in order to fill her kettle, a soldier slipped behind her

54 André, *André's Journal*, p.34.
55 André, *André's Journal*, p.36.
56 André, *André's Journal*, p.32.

> and threw her into the hogshead: when she was hauled out, a bystander threw a parcel of feathers on her, which adhering to the molasses, made her appear frightful enough – this little circumstance afforded us a good deal of amusement.[57]

Besides being an example of the age-old, crass mischievousness of serving soldiers, the woman's misfortune reminds us that whether they were serving in Massachusetts or South Carolina, the 33rd, like all regiments in the British Army, went on campaign accompanied by a host of both official and unofficial followers, most of them women and children. Indeed, without such an accompanying train, the army could scarce have functioned. Contrary to some popular beliefs, soldiers were responsible for their own cooking and darning, though there is some evidence that pointed to the work of women in auxiliary roles, from washing and tailoring to cooking and nursing.[58]

When the 33rd first sailed from Ireland to America in February 1776, included on the transports were 60 women and 12 children. These wives and offspring of the serving soldiery were officially included on the books of the army. This meant the women were entitled to draw half rations and the children quarter rations. This expense, and the cost of spaces in transports overseas, unsurprisingly resulted in the military attempting to cut costs by applying strict limits to the number of women and children that could accompany their partners, but even then, it can be assumed that where a regiment settled for any length of time there would be plenty of others not listed on the official strength. When the 33rd sailed from New York at the end of 1779 the listed returns show 76 women 42 children in attendance, a fairly substantial growth in the official side of the regimental family in a little over three years.[59] These women and children shared in the privations of campaigning, enduring hard marches, outbreaks of disease, inclement weather and lack of food. Their fortitude went largely unremarked upon.

Even less remarked upon was the potential presence of women serving as soldiers. Like almost all eighteenth-century militaries, the British Army forbade women from joining on as soldiers and regarded the concept of females serving in combat as unwelcome and borderline unnatural.[60] However, the eighteenth century is littered with accounts of women being discovered disguised as males while attempting to join the British military or, in three confirmed cases, actually already serving in it. Indeed, the 33rd had their own short case of a covert woman warrior just prior to the revolution. The *Public Advertiser* reported on 8 April 1772 that;

> A Worcestershire Lass who, by an unlucky Slip, had hurt her Character, and could not get a place in her own Country, being driven to great Necessity, procured the Disguise of Man's Cloaths [*sic*], and came and enlisted in the 33d Regiment quartered here. She appeared to be such a clever and tight Fellow, that the Officer

57 Shaw, *A Narrative*, pp.19–20.

58 Conway, *The British Army*, p.128.

59 John Dillon, *All at Sea: Naval Support for the British Army during the American Revolutionary War* (Warwick: Helion, 2019), p.105.

60 Conway, *The British Army*, p.117.

> gave her an extraordinary Gratuity; nor was her Sex discovered for two or three Days, 'till she was to undergo the usual Ceremony of Examination by the Surgeon. Although she had slept several Nights with a Comrade, she gave not the least Room to suspect her Sex. She seemed concerned at being rejected, and professed that she would do her Duty as well as any Man in the Regiment.[61]

While the standard physical examination undoubtedly ensured that the presence of women serving clandestinely was almost non-existent, the attempts by some to serve in the line of battle is worth mentioning.

While dozens if not hundreds of wives followed their menfolk on many of their excursions throughout North America, and one or two may have even served for a time in the ranks, there were also many left behind, either back in Britain or in places such as New York, where a permanent Crown garrison existed for almost the entire length of the war. Though some might have found secret relief in separation from unwanted partners, a great many expressed their distress both at the absence of their loved ones, and at the potential hardship that could befall a woman whose husband had left her behind. The letters of Captain Dansey to his fiancée back in Britain speak as frequently about his affection and concern for her wellbeing – as well as that of his mother and their country home – as they do about the struggles of life campaigning in America. Writing from near New York in November 1778, he lamented the war's interruption of their plans to be wed;

> How little did we then think what to happen before our Union, which was to take Place almost immediately and now three years are gone and the happy time still at an uncertain distance. Remember I told you it was a bold undertaking to accept a Soldier, wedded as I am to my Profession. Fortune in the Events of the World sports with our private happiness.[62]

Another letter opened with a declaration that 'I don't know how it is but I am more in Love than ever. You are never a Moment from my Thoughts, and I indulge myself in a pleasing Melancholy that the Cruelty of our Situation may have its reward.'[63] Such thoughts occupied the minds of officers and enlisted men alike, as the tides of war swept them apart from their wives and sweethearts.

The 33rd's return to the vicinity of New York in September 1778 likely brought them back to wives and offspring, but the campaigning season was not yet done. Clinton conducted a grand forage into New Jersey, and also wished to create a diversion for another raid, this time against rebel forces at Little Egg Harbor. Intelligence had reached British headquarters that a small force of a little over 100 Continental Army dragoons, supported by nearby militia, were billeted in barns and houses along the road at Old Tappan, near the border between New Jersey and New York. Despite occupying a Loyalist neighbourhood that lay dangerously close to British lines, it seemed that the dragoons were undertaking little in the way of security measures.

---

61 *Public Advertiser*, 8 April 1772, p.4.
62 DHS: William Dansey Letters: 16 November 1778.
63 DHS: William Dansey Letters: 26 March 1781.

A trap was laid involving two columns and a third, smaller blocking force, with the whole moving off late on 27 September. The first column, consisting of the 2nd Light Infantry and 2nd Grenadier battalions, the 33rd and 64th Foot, led by a vanguard of 50 British dragoons, were placed under the command of Major General Grey, with orders to march through the night up the west side of the Hackensack River, which flowed just below the rebel positions. Two hours after this column set out, Cornwallis moved off along an alternative road with the 1st Grenadier battalion, the Brigade of Guards, and the 37th and 42nd Foot. The third force, intended to block off the rebel escape, consisted of several groups of Loyalists and the 71st Foot, commanded by *Generallieutenant* von Knyphausen.

Major André described how Grey's column was 'successful enough to come unperceived within a mile of the place [Old Tappan], so as to enable him to detach six companies of light infantry by 3 in the morning to spread round the houses and barns where they lay, whilst the rest, after a little halt, marched on upon the road to them.'[64] Showing their deadly efficiency, the light infantry moved from barn to barn where the rebel dragoons were quartered, putting them to the bayonet before they could fully awake and resist. Surrendering men were also killed, not only in a fit of bloodlust from the enlisted men, but – according to the depositions of survivors – on the orders of junior officers. Some of the dragoons were stabbed up to 16 times.[65]

The 33rd's light company were not in the composite battalion involved in the immediate attack, but the main body of the regiment itself came upon the scene just as the bloody business was coming to a close. John Robert Shaw had yet to witness combat up close and personal, and the sights he saw, illuminated by torchlight in the dead of night, clearly left a vivid impression on the young soldier;

> As we approached, the shrieks and screams of the hapless victims whom our savage fellow soldiers were butchering, were sufficient to have melted into compassion the heart of a Turk or a Tartar – Tongue cannot tell nor pen unfold the horrors of that dismal night – Some were seen having their arms cut off, and others with their bowels hanging out crying for mercy.[66]

The rebels decried the attack as a massacre. Such accusations held little concern for the 33rd or, it seemed, most British soldiers, who now scarcely seemed to view the American colonists as fellow-subjects, or even proper enemies deserving of the rules of war.

Regardless of the outrage the attack at Old Tappan generated, it failed to draw Washington into battle. Operations began to wind down, with the British devoting most of their time to foraging, bringing supplies in and around New York ahead of the impending winter.

---

64 André, *André's Journal*, p.47.

65 Holger Hoock, *Scars of Independence: America's Violent Birth* (New York: Crown, 2017), p.257.

66 Shaw, *A Narrative*, pp.20–21.

At the start of October, encamped with the rest of the light infantry at Newbridge in New Jersey, Captain William Dansey was preparing to make his play. In a letter to his mother, he set out how he was hoping to marshal his finances in an attempt to take the next step up the promotional ladder of the officer corps – £650 from stock owned jointly by Dansey and his mother, another £500 loaned directly from her, and the rest from the 33rd's agent, Mr Meyrick. Should any of the sum miscarry, Dansey was in contact with a Mr Toldervey, who was under instructions to raise £2,000 from the £5,000 tied up in Dansey's country home at Brinsop. Dansey had initially viewed this as a last resort, but the fact that France was now involved in the war had left him feeling more bullish. The prospect of a longer struggle with higher casualties improved the odds of promotion without needing to purchase.

Dansey's hopes were to be realised. He received his promotion, being raised up from the captain of the 33rd's light company to the rank of major on 14 October 1778. It cost him £1,850, and came despite the fact that he was, as far as seniority was concerned, not the first in line for the job. Dansey reported happily back to his mother that he was 'endorsed by Lord Cornwallis, from whom I have experienced such distinguish'd marks of his Friendship and Patronage as are very flattering to my future Prospects in the Army. By this Step I have gain'd Rank of above forty Captns in the Army in general and I hope tho' the Price is large you will approve of what I have done under such Encouragement.'[67]

Dansey's advancement did not take him far from his old company. Although now the 33rd's major and thus its third most senior officer, he remained assigned to the 1st Light Infantry battalion, an auspicious appointment for any enterprising officer. John Kerr, the captain who had first recruited young John Robert Shaw in Leeds, was initially supposed to command of the 33rd's light company but did not join the regiment from Britain until the latter half of 1780 – in reality the light company fell to Captain William Gore. During this period a number of light infantrymen were supplied with horses and utilised like dragoons, with the detachment seemingly led by Lieutenant Thomas Nicoll of the 33rd. Another of the light company's officer alumni, Captain (formerly Lieutenant) Thomas Gorges, was mentioned with dissatisfaction by Dansey as he wrote home about his successful promotion. It seemed as though the relationship between the former Herefordshire friends had soured – Dansey confided initially that Gorges, now serving with 10th Foot, was to sail 'for England in a few Days and I am angry that he never call'd upon me before he goes home. I have hardly seen him since we left Philadelphia.'[68] A few weeks later he informed his mother that 'I believe Captn. Gorges is sail'd if you see him tell him I took it very unkind his never coming to see me before he went home.' He never gave the reason for the apparent cooling of their friendship. In better news, Dansey reported that his young servant Ben was still with him and, though 'has got the Ague but not very bad. I have great Reason to be thankful for the Blessing of Health thro' the great Fatugues and Hardships I experienced in the Light Infantry as a Captain.'[69]

---

67 DHS: William Dansey Letters: 21 October 1778.

68 DHS: William Dansey Letters: 3 October 1778.

69 DHS: William Dansey Letters: 21 October 1778.

On 15 November the army entered its winter quarters in and around New York, thus bringing the 1778 campaign season to a close. At this point, over two years into the 33rd's service in the war, it is worth looking at the composition of one of the regiment's companies and seeing how it had changed – and continued to change – as the war dragged on. The following table shows those soldiers who served in the colonel's company in the 33rd, showing a snapshot of men present in Dublin in 1775, on Staten Island before the battle of Long Island in August 1776, at Bedford near New York in December 1778, and then in North Carolina in June 1781.

33rd Foot: The Colonel's Company, 1776–1781.[70]

Dublin Jul. 1775	Staten Is. Aug. 1776	Bedford Dec. 1778	Carolina Jun. 1781
Allen, Edward	Allen, Edward	Broadbent, John	Abercrobie, John
Atkenson, Joshua	Bentcliff, John	Brown, Stephen	Armstrong, Joseph
Bencliff, John	Bolland, John	Caldwell, John	Atkinson, William
Bollden, Joseph	Broadbent, Francis	Canbey, Christopher	Brown, Stephen
Broadbent, Francis	Broadbent, John	Cockell, William	Browne, Alexander
Caldwell, John	Caldwell, John	Collins, John	Canby, Christopher
Cranshaw, Richard	Cockill, William	Duckworth, John	Cass, John
Duckworth, John	Collins, John	Duggan, Thomas	Cockell, William
Fawthrop, Enoch	Croshaw, Richard	Dunn, John	Crabtree, James
Greenward, James	Duckworth, John	Erskine, William	Denby, George
Hammons, John	Duggan, Thomas	Erskine, James	Duckworth, John
Hannad, Simon	Dunn, John	Fauthorp, Enoch	Duggan, Thomas
Hazzard, Richard	Farnley, John	Fitzpatrick, John	Farnall, George
Heariden, Owen	Faytrop, Enoch	Foster, William	Foster, William
Henshaw, Willian	Fitzpatrick, John	Gallagher, George	Gillespie, William
Illes, Samuel	Freeman, Michael	Gaukrodgers,Samuel	Graham, William
Jealley, William	Gallaugher, George	Halroyd, Aaron	Halroyd, Aaron
Mackey, James	Hammonds, John	Hammonds, William	Hammonds, William
Magee, Robert	Hammonds, William	Hansell, John	Hansall, John
Magee, Thomas	Harrison, James	Harrisson, James	Hay, David
Mains, William	Hassard, Richard	Hays, David	Hazzard, Richard
Mains, John	Hays, David	Hazzard, Richard	Hebden, Thomas
Montain	Henshaw, William	Heald, David	Herridon, Owen
Mellor, Robert	Herridon, Owen	Henshaw, William	Howard, Robert
Morlidge, Roger	Howard, Robert	Herridon, Owen	Hughes, John
Nicholes, Robert	Ingledow, Thomas	Howard, Robert	Ingledew, Thomas
Powell, James	Isles, Samuel	Howarth, James	Jones, William
Robarts, Joseph	Lahee, Patrick	Howlings, Andrew	Kelly, John
Savage, John	Lahee, James	Ingledow, Thomas	Lahee, James
Smith, Patrick	Mains, William	Lahee, James	Mathews, James
Smith, Joshua	M'Gee, Robert	Lahee, Patrick	Mathews, Bryan
Underhill, John	Middleditch,Michael	McGee, Robert	McGee, Robert
Walsh, William	Morlidge, Roger	McIntire, Samuel	Monaghan, Arthur
Whitham, Thomas	Murphy, Cormick	Middleditch,Michael	Morlidge, Roger
Yeomans, Thomas	Powell, James	Monaghon, Arthur	Morton, John
	Richy, Mungo	Morlidge, Roger	Patrick, John
	Savage, John	Murphy, Patrick	Pearson, Thomas
	Smith, Joshua	Nicoll, Joseph	Pickles, Jonas
	Taylor, Thomas	Pearson, Thomas	Pindar, John
	Teetham, James	Pender, John	Powell, James
	Thomas, William	Powell, James	Richardson, Samuel
	Titly, John	Ritchy, Mongo	Savage, John
	Undrill, John	Savage, John	Smith, John
	Walsh, William	Squires, Richard	Squires, Richard
	Webster, Daniel	Taylor, Thomas	Tate, Robert
	Weeks, Richard	Tetlow, John	Webster, Daniel
		Webster, Daniel	
Totals: 35	46	47	47

70 Lodge, *To What Extent*, pp.11–13.

At the end of 1778 the colonel's company of the 33rd therefore had at least 14 men who had been serving since Staten Island 1776; John Broadbent, John Caldwell, John Collins, Thomas Duggan, John Dunn, John Fitzpatrick, George Gallagher, William Hammonds, David Hays, Robert Howard, Thomas Ingledow, Michael Middleditch and Thomas Taylor. There were another eight who had been in the company since Dublin, 1775; Roger Morlidge, John Duckworth, Enoch Fauthorp, Richard Hazzard, William Henshaw, Robert McGee, James Powell and John Savage. A total of 22 men at the end of 1778 – 46 percent of the company's rank-and-file – had thus served from Long Island to Brandywine, Germantown and Monmouth. It is also important to note that this does not track the likely not-inconsiderable number of men who transferred within the regiment from one company to another.

Veterans or new arrivals alike, the 33rd likely spent their first nights shivering in old tents, while their days were occupied in constructing huts for their winter accommodation. Built from scratch, these were the army's primary means of housing soldiers during the colder months when there were insufficient existing structures at hand. The huts in question were built into hillsides, with thatched roofs and fireplaces built into the dugout end walls. These were arranged row-by-row, generally on the south-facing sides of hills, with officers' huts behind and above those of the enlisted men.[71]

Like the rooms of the more formal barracks the 33rd had occupied in Amboy, each individual hut was usually built to house between 12 and 16 soldiers, though larger ones were also constructed. While all regiments had no shortage of skilled tradesmen such as carpenters, thatchers, glaziers and many laborers who possessed the necessary expertise and manpower, construction still took time due to a scarcity of both tools and materials, most of which had to be supplied from New York.[72] One officer in a grenadier battalion reported a lack of nails and straw, with the latter being substituted for thatch brought from Flushing, and there was also a lack of boarding for doors, beds and windows.[73]

By the end of November most of the huts were completed. Captain Hildebrand Oakes of the 33rd's grenadiers, writing from Long Island, reported that;

> Most of the Army are Hutted … which I think far more comfortable than if they were in Houses – Some of the Officers are in the Town but most of us in the Farms contiguous to it: upon the whole our Quarters would be very good, if it was not for the very great scarcity and Dearness of every kind of Provisions…[74]

71 Hagist, *Noble Volunteers*, pp.121–122.

72 Hagist, *Noble Volunteers*, p.122.

73 Hagist, *Noble Volunteers*, p.123.

74 Hildebrand Oakes to Henry Seymour Conway, Jamaica Long Island, from a collection of letters sold in May 2008 at a private auction. Transcript courtesy of Don Hagist.

As they prepared to see out the winter, Oakes recorded the usual rumours circulating through the regiment and the army as a whole. He believed that the publications of the rebels pointed towards;

> Great Dissensions among them ... Every body here is [illegible] to know what will become of us in the Spring, as it is impossible for us to take the Field with the small Number of Troops we have at Present. The two prevailing opinion are, that we shall abandoned this Part of the Country for Canada, or carry on the War by Excursions against their Sea Port Towns, and put the Threats of the Commissioners in Execution...[75]

Despite his recent promotion to major, Dansey, was of a similarly morose opinion, though he was still fired with patriotic fervour following France's entry into the war. He railed against Clinton and the possibility of years of more fighting, writing to his fiancée;

> That Lord Howe may be bless'd with Success against our natural Enemies in all his Undertakings as his unequal'd Abilities deserve, had our General [Clinton] been equal to our Admiral we shou'd have had no French War and our turbulent [American] Bretheren, wou'd have been sensible of their Error. Armies can't conquer without Officers, tho' they may beat the Enemy. I have fought hard for Peace this three Years past, and may for seven to come when Battles are only fought for the few Acres the Armies occupy.[76]

Dansey's predictions were not wholly without merit. In three years in North America the 33rd had fought in four major pitched battles (six if counting Lieutenant Nutt's unfortunates at Freeman's Farm and Bemis Heights) as well as dozens of skirmishes, raids, ambushes and rearguard actions. Yet, its American odyssey was not even half-way complete.

75 Oakes to Conway.
76 DHS: William Dansey Letters: 16 November 1778.

Chapter 9

Surrounded by Great Numbers

1779

The year 1779 is popularly misremembered as one of the least violent of the American Revolutionary War. While it is true that there were no major battles in the northern theatre of the conflict, there was still action there, as well as hard-fought engagements in the south that ensured the capricious tide of the war swung ponderously back in Britain's favour. It was also the year when the 33rd came closest yet to near-total annihilation.

Initially there were few alarms to disturb the regiment from their huts. The time spent wintering outside New York was certainly quieter than the first few months of 1777, when the 33rd had been bedevilled in constant skirmishes around Bonhamtown and Amboy. Dansey wrote home, displaying some sorrow and concern that no letters from his mother had reached him for the past 12 months and wondering how his young cousin Richard was doing with his studies. He closed with good news about his servant Ben.

> I have the Pleasure to tell you that Ben goes on very well and is in a way to learn to be a most useful Servant this Winter as I live with Colonel Abercromby who has the best Servants I ever saw. Upon turning over the Paper I find I am writing on a sheet I have drawing on, but as it is a Draft of the Dansey Tent, pitch'd with a Firelock and four Bayonets of which I gave you a Description last Spring, I will send the Letter as it is, perhaps it may please you as well as if the Page had been full of writing, and I have nothing so material to say as to assure you I am with every Respect Affection and Regard, which I have room enough now to do.[1]

From February onwards the army went through its customary preparations for the coming campaign season. The descriptions of a grenadier officer of the 42nd Foot detailing the activities of his company would have been common to most in the army during the period. His men conducted several marches to raise fitness levels, practiced firing at targets and set to fitting

1 DHS: William Dansey Letters: 20 February 1779.

and sewing materials newly arrived for the making of the new year's supply of regimental coats and summer trousers, which had now been adopted in place of breeches, stockings and half-gaiters.

As these preparations gathered pace, the 33rd found themselves busier than most. Along with the 42nd and the light company of the Guards, they were picked for a special operation in late February, another of the activities described by John Robert Shaw as 'predatory excursions,' in the vein of the burning of New Brunswick and Fairhaven the year before.

Elizabethtown, which lay west of Staten Island, had once been the colonial capital of New Jersey, before Amboy assumed the title. In 1779 it was serving as a Continental outpost commanded by General William Maxwell. Situated as it was at the mouth of Newark Bay, it was vulnerable to amphibious operations. British commanders in New York resolved to mount a raid against the town.

On Tuesday, 23 February the 42nd and the Guards light infantry 'embarked in flat Boats,' and sailed to Newark just as the day began to grow dark. The 33rd were to be part of the expedition but became unaccountably delayed. Missing the rendezvous point, it took them over an hour to catch up with the main force, which landed at Crane's Ferry on the New Jersey shore at around 2:00 a.m.[2] According to Shaw the regiment were bedevilled by the treachery of a local guide after making landfall.

> We marched about a mile through the marsh, before we discovered the trick; – our pilot had left us in the snare; some times up to the middle in mud and water; some times over our head and ears in ditches, crawling one over another, in the greatest confusion. At length and with much difficulty we made our appearance near Elizabethtown, just at day break, in woeful pickle, all bedaubed with mud and mire, as black as chimney-sweepers; we looked more like frightening the people out of the town, than making them run for fear of the sword or bayonet. In this plight we advanced up to the town and took it.[3]

Such were the realities of soldiering in any age – it was a mucky business.

Reaching Elizabethtown around 4:00 a.m., the British found its defenders had evacuated, forewarned by a local resident. They torched the barracks and the courthouse, and 'this being the day the continental troops were to draw their provisions,' demanded the town's bakers hand over their supplies of bread. The bakers 'very boldly answered: "This bread is for gentlemen and not for you d---d bloody backs." – Bread was therefore taken by force.'[4]

The operation appeared complete – all that remained to do was return to the flatboats. This, however, did not go to plan. The expedition 'found their Boats aground, which delayed their reembarking until 10 in the morning,

2 Kemble, *Journals of Lieut. Col. Stephen Kemble*, p.173.

3 Shaw, *A Narrative*, p.18.

4 Shaw, *A Narrative*, p.18. Bloodybacks was contemporary slang for British soldiers, as was lobsters, though the phrase sometimes used by historians, lobersterbacks, is a later conflation of the two.

by which time the Rebels had Assembled.'[5] A large rebel force closed in and attacked the British rearguard, consisting of the light company of the Guards, as the expedition attempted to re-float their boats. Things went from bad to worse when Continental artillery came up and opened fire on the men as they tried to embark. Shaw emphasises panic, stating the men 'took to our heels, and made our way to the boats in the utmost disorder.'[6]

The Guards were taking casualties, one killed and 15 wounded. One of the 33rd's boats, used by Captain Campbell's company, was beached too high. As the men struggled to get it down to the shore, they were struck by rebel artillery fire. Two soldiers, William Proctor and John Keith, both of whom had served with the regiment since before its arrival in America in 1776, were killed in the flatboat. The rest decided it was wiser to abandon it that remain stranded under the enemy's cannon fire. Dispersing to the other transports, the regiment set out with the rest of the expedition. Their casualties, along with Keith and Proctor, included two men wounded and five taken prisoner. They returned to their cantonments outside New York.

Securing the Lower Hudson

As the year progressed, it became apparent that Clinton's strategy remained unchanged from that of his predecessor. Just as Howe had unsuccessfully attempted in 1776 and 1777, and as he himself had tried in 1778, Clinton's primary goal was to draw Washington and the main body of the Continental Army into a battle of annihilation.

By the middle of the year Washington had withdrawn to the Hudson Highlands, his army divided between the east and west banks of the Hudson River, north of New York. Clinton resolved to move up the river, seize the strategic crossing point at King's Ferry, and threaten the rebel forts around West Point, which Washington now considered the lynchpin of Congress's grip on the Hudson. By taking the ferry, Clinton would be severing the most important link between the northernmost colonies and everything south of New York. He hoped this would encourage Washington to give battle.

Stony Point in particular was a highly defensible position. A rocky promontory that jutted out into the west bank of the Hudson, Washington described how it, 'from its peninsular and commanding form, is naturally strong, and which, from the narrowness of the neck, that connects it to the main land, may be insulated and maintained without any great difficulty.'[7] Opposite Stony Point, guarding the other half of King's Ferry, was Verplanck's Point which, though not as elevated as Stony Point across the river, was still fit for defence.

Continental forces had started fortifying both Stony Point and Verplanck's, but the work was in its infancy. On 30 May Clinton moved north with the

5 Kemble, *Journals of Lieut. Col. Stephen Kemble*, p.173.

6 Shaw, *A Narrative*, p.19.

7 Jared Sparks (ed.), *The Writings of George Washington* (Boston: Russel et al, 1834), vol.IV, p.127.

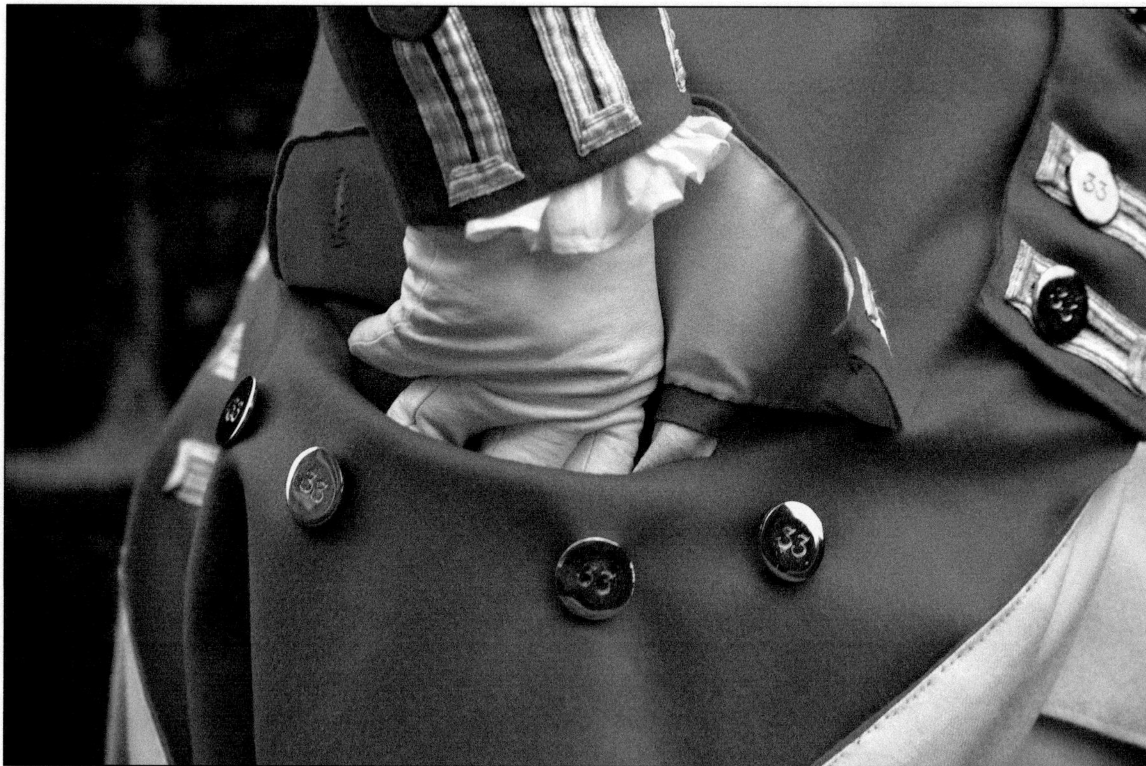

While pocket flaps on the coats of officers were sometimes practical, the pockets seen on the outsides of most enlisted men's coats were for display only. However, they did have interior breast pockets in the lining. (Photo by Henry Gage)

British and German grenadier battalions, the light infantry battalions, 300 German jäger, a force of Loyalists and the 17th, 63rd, 64th and 33rd Foot.[8] The expedition was divided into two, so as to attack the rebel positions at Stony Point and Verplanck's simultaneously. The 33rd were on the eastern bank, under the command of Major General Vaughan. They made landfall from their transports on the river eight miles below Verplanck's before marching the rest of the way.

The small Continental work details present at both forts were caught by surprise. The force at Stony Point abandoned it after destroying the breastworks and torching the blockhouse, though the garrison of Verplanck's, consisting of a captain and 60 men, refused to either withdraw or surrender immediately. Artillery was brought up to Stony Point and from there 'kept up a constant fire upon it [Verplanck's] in conjunction with their ships, till four in the afternoon, when the party station in it, finding that it was also invested on the land side in force, surrendered.'[9] According to a later history, the 33rd conducted 'a difficult climb among the hills, especially with artillery, which had to be dragged from a bad landing-place up a precipitous slope, but it was done during the night' in order to get the guns into position at Stony Point, but if they were indeed part of Major General Vaughan's force on the east bank it is not explained why they would be shifted across the river to

8 Kemble, *Journals of Lieut. Col. Stephen Kemble*, p.179.
9 Sparks (ed.), *The Writings of George Washington*, vol.IV, p.127.

move artillery when there were troops already there who could do the job.[10] Regardless, by the end of 1 June King's Ferry was once more in the hands of the King's forces. Over the next few days there was little movement, besides a brief and inconsequential threatening of a Continental supply depot further north.

On 5 June Clinton noted an unusual request from the 33rd. The army's headquarters recorded that 'the 33d Regiment, having solicited to be employed as a Light Corps, the Commander in Chief grants this request, and directs Lt Col Emmerichs corps of Chasseurs to be attached to it til further orders.'[11] Lieutenant Colonel Andreas Emmerich was a German soldier who had initially asked to raise a force in Germany for service with the British in America. This was rejected, but Clinton permitted him to form a company of marksmen from Loyalists in America. This company was then expanded into a corps known commonly as Emmerich's Chasseurs, a composite regiment of Loyalist light troops, namely light infantry (some of whom may have been mounted) and light dragoons.

The diary of the 42nd Regiment's Captain Peebles likewise recorded on 6 June that 'the 33d. Regt. to act as Light Iny. At Col: Websters request.'[12] The fact that the 33rd specifically requested to perform the duties of a light infantry battalion, and the fact that this request was granted and saw them paired with another light corps, shows that the years between 1770 and 1775 spent developing light infantry tactics and drills had not been wholly abandoned by the regiment during their American service. Indeed, evidence from later campaigns implies that it continued in this role for at least the next year. It seems that the 33rd's assumption of the mantle of light infantry was part of what historian Don Hagist points to as 'the continued evolution of the army by increasing the numbers of light troops.'[13]

From 12 June the army set to finishing and improving the captured defensive positions at Stony Point and Verplanck's. The 33rd also received and donned their new year's uniforms. John Robert Shaw described the work at Verplanck's, where the 33rd were stationed, in some detail;

> A range of batteries was erected, with two block-houses, one on the right, and the other on the left side of the batteries, so as to command both the land and the river... there was a deep ditch in front of the works with three rows of abbatis, 40 yards apart, and three large piles of tar-barrels between the rows of abbatis, where stood a man with a slow match ready to set fire at the approach of the enemy.[14]

Besides this, a further blockhouse was raised as an outpost one mile east of the fort. This was garrisoned, according to Shaw, by a company consisting of a captain, lieutenant, ensign, two sergeants, four corporals, a drummer and fifer, and 50 privates, with a further '100 yards in front, the guard consisting

10 Lee, *History of the Thirty-third*, p.117.
11 CL: Henry Clinton Papers: Vol. 266, Head Quarters Verplancks Point, 5 June 1779.
12 Peebles, *John Peebles' American War*, p.267.
13 Hagist, *These Distinguished Corps*, p.153.
14 Shaw, *A Narrative*, pp.22–23.

of one sergeant, one corporal, and twelve privates, forming a line of four centinels.'[15]

The fort had a modest amount of artillery to aid in its defence – a 6-pounder, two 4-pounders and a somewhat more impressive 18-pounder covered the approaches to the main redoubts, while Shaw also mentioned the presence of swivel-guns, presumably provided by British shipping on the river. The roof of the largest blockhouse, which overlooked the river, had also been removed and another 6-pounder placed on the upper floor, which consequently had an excellent line of fire out over the entire fort. Lastly, the upper blockhouse acting as an outpost a mile to the east also had its own 6-pounder in place, besides its company-strength garrison.

To complete this work over the course of a little over two weeks, the 33rd worked half-on half-off, with 'one half on duty and the other on fatigue.'[16] Ever mindful of a surprise attack, the men 'generally lay at night with our accoutrements on, and with our firelocks in our arms.'[17]

On 27 June the main part of the army sailed south after General Clinton. The 33rd were left behind, to finish the fortification of Verplanck's and garrison it. With them and the Royal Artillery gunners manning the cannon was a detachment of green-coated Loyalists from the Loyal American Regiment, whose colonel, Beverley Robinson, had a farmstead a little further upriver, as well as the energetic Major Patrick Ferguson, who commanded a small reconnaissance detachment. Meanwhile, Stony Point across the river was left with the 17th Foot and the two grenadier companies of the 71st Foot's two battalions, as well as another detachment of Loyalists. There was also a Royal Navy gunboat and a sloop, the *Vulture*, occupying the river between the forts. The 17th's lieutenant colonel, Henry Johnson, was junior in terms of commission date to the 33rd's Lieutenant Colonel Webster, and it was therefore the Scotsman who had the overall leadership of the twin ferry garrisons, totalling nearly 1,100 men.[18] It was the largest command Webster had yet received. It would also be one of his most fraught. Washington was formulating plans to strike back against the British possession of King's Ferry. The Corps of Light Infantry, the seasonal elite Continental Army force modelled after the British composite light battalions, was reformed for that year with the intention of mounting an assault.

Verplanck's Point Surrounded

The first hint of trouble came at midnight on 16 July 1779. Soldiers on duty at Verplanck's caught the rising crackle of musketry drifting across the river from the heights at Stony Point. It rapidly grew too intense and sustained to be dismissed as the popping of pickets at the odd skulking militiaman. The boom of cannon fire only confirmed it – the neighbouring fort was under

15 Shaw, *A Narrative*, p.22.
16 Shaw, *A Narrative*, p.23.
17 Shaw, *A Narrative*, p.23.
18 Kemble, *Journals of Lieut. Col. Stephen Kemble*, p.179.

attack. 'First from the picket a running fire was heard, which occasioned some alarm,' Shaw wrote.[19] Not only was Stony Point being assaulted, but the company occupying the upper blockhouse, that acted as a forward outpost for Verplanck's, had also been attacked. The rebels were bearing down on Verplanck's too. The garrison was stood to. As the men formed in the fort's parade officers dashed to and fro, seeking orders and clarity. What exactly was happening at Stony Point? Should they attempt to support the garrison there? Were they expecting to be attacked as well?

Webster reacted quickly and effectively. Shaw recalled that 'there you will not find a *colonel Johnson*, lying snug in his tent as at Stony-Point; but you will find old colonel Webster, the Scotchman, ready cut and dry for you, with the action commenced at the opposite fort.'[20] Another account recorded that Webster 'instantly set to work and closed in the batteries, which rendered his work respectable, and enabled him to defy the enemy.'[21]

Webster had four men from every company detailed as a reserve at the riverside blockhouse, in order to protect Verplanck's from the water in case an attack was launched from the opposite bank. The rest of the 33rd and its detachments of Loyalists and Royal Artillery gunners manned the breastworks and blockhouses, priming and loading muskets and cannons, eyes straining in the night as the terrible sounds from Stony Point drifted down to them from across the Hudson. The noise lasted only about 25 minutes before it began to fade. By 1:00 a.m. an ominous silence had fallen.

Still, there was no attack upon the 33rd's positions. Besides the scattered shots at the blockhouse, the rebels failed to show themselves outside Verplanck's. This was, in fact, all part of the plan. The Continental force on the east side of the Hudson was under orders to create a diversion for the main attack at Stony Point. Having successfully done this, they had no intention of trying to storm the work that night. Washington had considered a simultaneous assault, much as Clinton had done when first capturing the ferry but had deemed it too risky. Whether Webster would indeed have been able to resist the same type of surprise assault that had beset Stony Point will therefore never be known.

As dawn broke over the Hudson, the disaster that had unfolded through the night became more apparent to the 33rd. The British flag no longer flew over Stony Point. The fort had been stormed by the bayonet-wielding Continental light infantry under the command of the ever-active General Anthony Wayne, a success modelled on the deadly night-time assaults conducted by British light infantry at engagements like Paoli and Old Tappan. The garrison of Stony Point, taken completely by surprise, had been killed or captured, spelling disaster for the 17th Foot and the grenadier companies of the 71st.

The 33rd were next. The sun rose to show Continental forces moving to pen them in. One rebel, who had already faced the 33rd at Monmouth, recorded the high spirits, writing 'our officers were all on tiptoe to show their

19 Shaw, *A Narrative*, p.23.
20 Shaw, *A Narrative*, p.24.
21 Anon., 'For the Political Magazine', p.342.

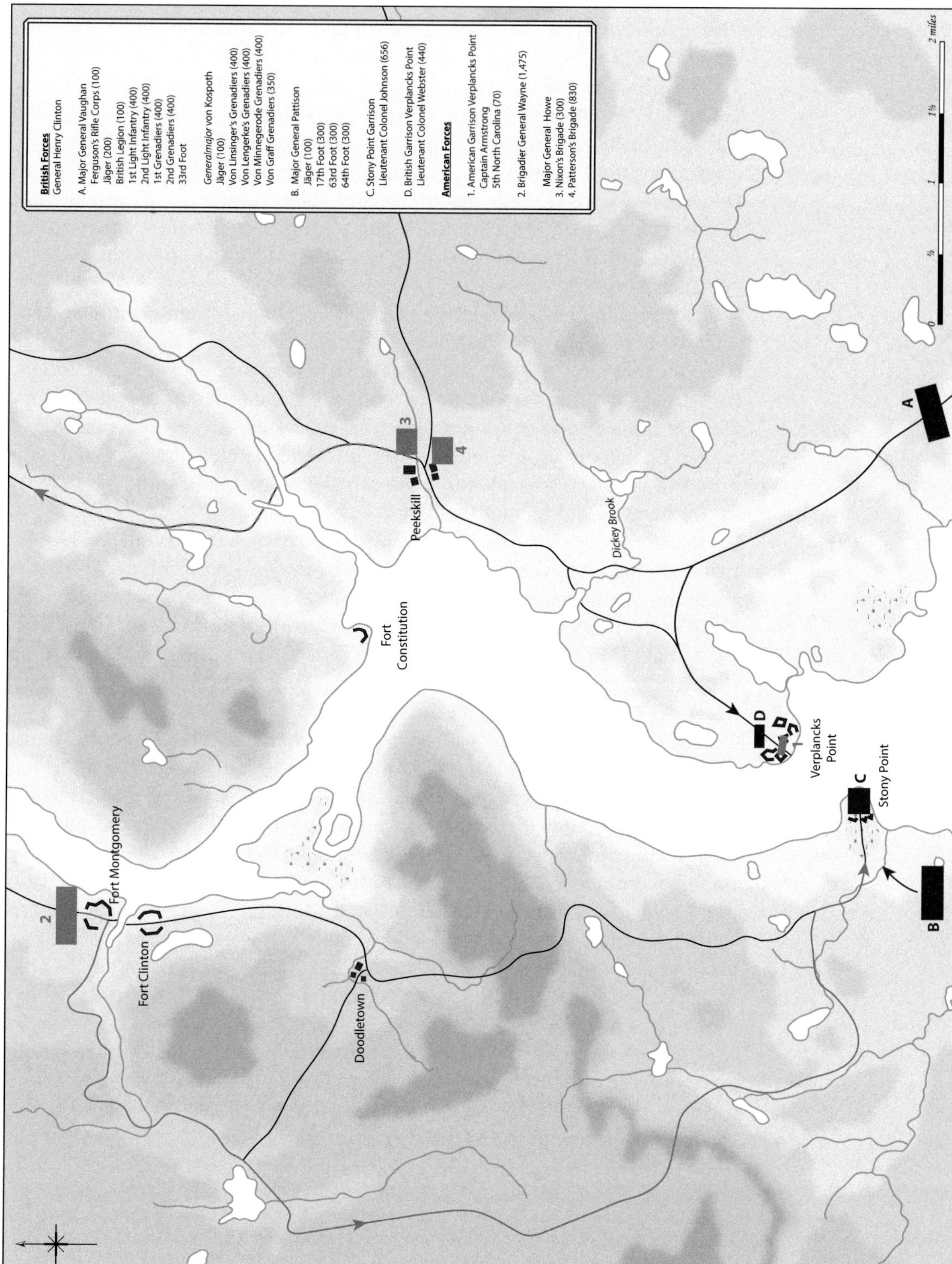

The attacks on Stony Point and Verplanck's, 16 July 1779.

abilities in executing some extraordinary exploit. Verplank's point was the word; "shall the Light Infantry get all the honor, and we do nothing!" said they. Accordingly, we set off, full tilt, to take Verplank's point; we marched directly for the Peekskill, and arrived near there early in the day.'[22]

The situation for the 33rd continued to grow more precarious. Having taken Stony Point, the rebels on the opposite side of the river now controlled the fort's artillery, including four 12-pounders and an 8-inch howitzer. They also had the advantage of elevation, with Stony Point rising about 150 feet above the river, considerably higher than Verplanck's. Consequently, they opened fire on the fort, and began to rain shot and shell down on the embattled garrison while also obliging the British shipping on the river 'to cut their cables and sail down.'[23]

By this point, news of the unfolding disaster had reached Clinton and the main body of the army downriver. A grenadier captain in the 42nd wrote in his diary that 'Col: Webster still holds out tho' surrounded by great numbers, his retreat cut off, a heavy fire from Stony Point but only one man woundd.'[24] Clinton rushed to save the garrison. He embarked a strong relief force and set sail once more up the Hudson River. However, the winds were not with him, and the ships struggled to make any headway. There would be no relief for Verplanck's, at least not that day.

Washington gave orders for a show of force outside Verplanck's, hoping that the shock of what had happened at Stony Point combined with the apparent untenableness of his position would convince Webster to surrender. The Continental troops on that side, however, full of ardour as they might be, were unable to do much that day either. They lacked artillery and, according to their commander, were short of food, wagons and the entrenching tools necessary to make even the show of a siege.

The 33rd spent their second uncomfortable night without support, doubtless anticipating an attack at any moment. While the Continentals did not attempt it, they were heavily reinforced, and the next day moved closer to Verplanck's defences. Shaw recalled seeing 'the Yankey army lay in our front eating molasses instead of attacking us.'[25] The bombarding from Stony Point recommenced, and while the Royal Navy shipping in the Hudson attempted to answer it, Webster refused to allow Verplanck's artillery to return fire. The guns under Webster's command were only half the calibre of those at Stony Point, or smaller, and opening fire with them would only have rendered them ideal targets for the enemy, who also possessed the advantage of elevation.

On the same day, the advance elements of Clinton's relief force finally arrived in the vicinity, prompting concern in the rebel ranks – while Verplanck's was cut off, Continental troops blockading it could likewise find themselves pinned between the garrison and a relief force if they were not

22 Joseph Plumb Martin, *A Narrative of a Revolutionary War Soldier: Some of the Adventures, Dangers, and Sufferings of Joseph Plumb Martin* (New York: Signet Classics, 2010), p.141.

23 Shaw, *A Narrative*, p.24.

24 Peebles, *John Peebles' American War*, p.278.

25 Shaw, *A Narrative*, p.24.

careful. Washington consequently authorised a withdrawal back towards the Hudson Highlands.

The 33rd undoubtedly watched the withdrawal of the enemy with great relief. Webster, however, still had a part to play. Washington was also evacuating Stony Point, not willing to risk troops in its defence. As they left they took anything of value with them. To assist in this, a number of small vessels were rowed downriver. Presumably, the Continental forces assumed that, as there had been no answer to their bombardment from Stony Point, Verplanck's was without meaningful artillery. Webster soon disabused the enemy of such a notion. Having held his fire until then, one of the vessels proved too tempting and exposed a target. Verplanck ordered the garrison's lone piece of heavy ordinance, the 18-pounder, to open fire. Shaw recalled how;

> Among the number of small vessels that came to carry off the booty, was a row-galley laden with cannon and other stores, on our side of the river. Against this galley we directed our artillery, and poured in a volley of grape and chain shot, which obliged the officers on board to desist from loading any farther, and finding it impracticable to save the vessel, they spiked their cannon, and set fire to the galley which having burned to the water, sunk her cargo to the bottom.[26]

Another account wrote of how the unexpected barrage had 'sunk a vessel on board of which they [the Continentals] were carrying off the artillery they had taken.'[27] Clinton's report to George Germain carried the most detailed description of the feat;

> Lieutenant Colonel Webster, who had with great Firmness supported the heavy Fire of the Enemy, had not during the whole Time, deigned to return a single Shot, being sensible that it would have been of no material Effect. The Enemy possible supposing from this Circumstance that he might have no heavy Cannon, brought down a Galley to carry off from Stoney Point Part of the Artillery which would have found Difficulty in retiring through the Roads of that Country. As soon as the Cannon were aboard the Galley, Lieutenant-Colonel Webster turned upon her an Eighteen Pounder, the only piece of heavy Ordnance he had, which raked her with such Effect, that, to prevent her sinking, the Crew ran her ashore, and there set Fire to her. Such of the Cannon as remained upon Stoney Point were buried, or thrown into the River by the Enemy, who immediately made a most precipitate Retreat.[28]

The little garrison of Verplanck's had the final say in the exchange of the past three days.

The arrival of Clinton's forces heralded relief in every sense for the 33rd. Stony Point was re-occupied and a new, stronger fort constructed there. British forces remained in place until October. By then it was apparent

26 Shaw, *A Narrative*, pp.24–25.
27 Anon., 'For the Political Magazine', p.342.
28 *London Gazette*, 5 October 1779, p.1.

that Washington could not be drawn down from the Hudson Highlands. A new strategy was being formulated by the British high command, and it no longer included holding King's Ferry. Consequently, both Stony Point and Verplanck's were evacuated.

In mid-October the 33rd, along with the 7th, 23rd and 57th Foot and the Provincials of the Queen's Rangers and Volunteers of Ireland, were earmarked for an expedition, to be commanded by Cornwallis. At Yellow Hook they prepared to embark, 'it was supposed to be intended for Jamaica, at that time presumed to be threatened with an invasion from [French admiral] M. D'Estaing. On Intelligence being received, that his designs were pointed elsewhere, the troops were re-landed; and were ordered to continue in readiness to embark at the shortest notice.'[29]

Ultimately, there was to be no expedition to Jamaica. In mid-November the 33rd shifted to winter quarters on western Long Island, at Denyse's Ferry, where they had landed before the Battle of Long Island in 1776. During this time, and like the rest of the army when it went into winter quarters, they received winter clothing from Britain, such as mittens, the cloth necessary to make woollen leggings, blankets, shirt linen, Russia drill to be used for breeches, yarn hose and other such necessities.[30]

In August sickness began to spread among the troops encamped around New York, possibly arriving on board troop transports carrying reinforcements from Britain. What appears to have been a dysentery epidemic spread rapidly to Staten and Long Island, raging throughout both the army and local inhabitants through September, October and November. Over 5,000 soldiers were struck down, and fatalities ranged from 25 to 60 men per regiment.[31]

While the 1779 outbreak was grievous, illnesses and diseases of varying severity were constant companions for all eighteenth-century militaries. From the crowded holds of ships, to sharing beds in barracks or living five to a tent in camps – and often in less-than-ideal weather conditions – armies were a natural breeding ground for a plethora of diseases. Soldiers from Britain also struggled to acclimatise to the different diseases and climates found in the colonies. Those who arrived in spring or autumn generally had the best chance of adjusting without serious illness, but both winter and summer were febrile seasons for infections.

Sir John Pringle, who served for a time as physician general to the British Army, documented his medical experiences in a 1757 publication. In it he identified two broad categories of disease, namely inflammatory fevers and putrid or bilious fevers. Inflammatory diseases, such as inflammation of the brain and bowels, rheumatism or pleurisies occurred only infrequently among soldiers by the revolutionary period, but what he termed putrid or bilious fevers were far more widespread.[32] Thomas Reide, serving as surgeon

29 John Graves Simcoe, *Simcoe's Military Journal: A History of the Operations of a Partisan Corps Called the Queen's Rangers* (New York: Bartlett & Welford, 1844), pp.108–109.

30 Hagist, *These Distinguished Corps*, p.155.

31 Frey, *The British Soldier in America*, p.42.

32 Frey, *The British Soldier in America*, pp.41–42.

to the 29th Foot during the American Revolution, made similar observations to Pringle. He classed most diseases as fevers of two kind, remitting and inflammatory. Remitting fevers were often malaria (known as ague), which accounted for about a quarter of all fevers contracted by soldiers during the war. These occurred exclusively in the warmer months of the year, and were rarely fatal, but could be debilitating. Conversely, inflammatory diseases such as scurvy, rheumatism and tuberculosis (known as consumption), did not reoccur, were contracted during the colder months, and at a rate of about half of the remitting fevers.[33]

Dysentery (known as the bloody flux) was almost as common as malaria, and was a year-round problem. Easily communicated in crowded camps, it was also the deadliest of the diseases regularly contracted.[34] Typhus and smallpox also reared their heads at various times and in various locations occupied by the army. Besides these, during his service with the 29th Foot, Reide recorded all manner of lesser ailments, the plethora of disorders and complaints that have always afflicted humanity, which Hagist sums up as 'sore throats, jaundice, cholera morbus, epilepsy, sore eyes, earache, venereal diseases, inflammation of the bladder, cough, erysipelas, worms, stomach complaints, vertigo, cutaneous eruptions, haemorrhoids, pain in the side, scrofula, headaches, dropsy, asthma, stones, gravel, colic, palsy.'[35] It is safe to say that scarcely a soldier in the 33rd who served for more than one campaign would have avoided an illness of some sort. Despite this, while deaths from disease were far higher than the number of men killed in actual combat, and while debilitation brought on by outbreaks certainly affected the course of the war, the vast majority of those struck down by sickness recovered eventually. Extremely fatal outbreaks such as the one at New York in 1779, which accounted for, at most, 15 percent of a regiment's strength, were rare. Diseases aside, after the scare at Verplanck's it seemed as though another quiet winter was in the offing for the 33rd. In reality, it would be anything but.

In mid-October, Crown forces holding Savannah in Georgia had repelled a powerful attempt by a combined Franco-American army to take the town. The news was greeted joyously by the army at New York, as recorded by Captain Hildebrand Oakes of the 33rd's grenadiers, who wrote;

> Upon our great Success in Georgia; which has been celebrated here by the Whole army firing a Few de Jose! [a *feu de joie* or fire of joy, a celebratory rolling musket volley] a Mode of rejoicing, which has never been practiced by us before since the Commencement of the War: and it is now put upon the Footing of having gained a Victory over the French; assisted by the rebellious Colonys [*sic*]. We have also an Account from the West Indies, of Admiral Parker having taken and destroyed the whole of the Reinforcement consisting of twelve Sail of the Line, that was coming to D'Estaing, which joined to our Success in Georgia, seems to have totally changed the face of Affairs in this Part the World; which before wore

33 Hagist, *Noble Volunteers*, pp.141, 144.
34 Hagist, *Noble Volunteers*, p.144.
35 Hagist, *Noble Volunteers*, p.144.

> a very gloomy Aspect. It is said that the Congress have taken great Offence at the Garrison of Savannah being summon'd [several words lost] ...The Army have been in their Winter Quarters a fortnight, which are much the same as last Year; only more crowded on Account of the Rhode Island Garrison.[36]

The successes in the south helped to convince British strategists that the interminable deadlock which had developed in the northern colonies would best be broken by shifting the centre of operations towards the Carolinas. It was generally believed that there was still a substantial Loyalist presence in those colonies, one which could provide sufficient support once a royal army arrived to reclaim everything south of Virginia.

In early December rumours became orders. Regiments earmarked for the southern expedition received instructions 'to be in readiness to Embark on the shortest notice with Camp Equipage & field Baggage only, the heavy Baggage to be sent to store on further orders, no horses for the Capts.'[37] On 19 December, amidst freezing conditions, the embarkation process began. The 33rd, including the 76 women 42 children on the regimental books, boarded the fleet with Clinton and a strong portion of the army. They remained onboard 'until the breaking up of the ice' before sailing the day after Christmas, 26 December.[38]

What awaited them was some of the hardest campaigning that they had yet endured in America, and included both the regiment's greatest triumph, and their most grievous defeat.

---

36 Oakes to Conway, 30 November, from a collection of letters sold in May 2008.

37 Peebles, *John Peebles' American War*, p.313.

38 Shaw, *A Narrative*, p.25.

Chapter 10

The Services Which They Rendered

1780

Much as their first voyage to Charleston had, the 33rd's journey southward soon turned inauspicious. After sailing from Sandy Hook outside New York, the fleet was struck within 48 hours by a fearsome storm. Initially it resulted in 'a good deal of tossing & tumbling which affects the Stomachs of several in the Cabbin & many between decks had a scrambling breakfast no dinner.'[1] Things quickly grew even worse. Much as they had been when they had first sailed from Ireland, the ships of the fleet became scattered. Captain Oakes wrote that 'the Ship I sailed in was so very leaky that for several Days we were obliged to pump every quarter of an hour.'[2] Shaw had an even worse experience, describing the tribulations of the journey with the 33rd in some detail;

> We set sail in very lord spirits – our prospects were gloomy indeed – the very elements seemed to conspire against us, and threatened us with destruction … the ship in which I was, being accidentally separated from the fleet in a storm, we were all in danger of being lost. The tempest blew with violence for about six hours – We had 400 soldiers on board, and by the heaving and rolling of the ship, all the beds in which we lay broke loose from the sides of the vessel to which they were fastened; and the ship was so agitated by the wind and waves, that she changed her position, so the gunnels ran under water, and the guns on the same side broke loose on the quarter deck. The storm, however, having somewhat abated, we refreshed ourselves, and cheered our hearts with a good can of grog, and pursued our voyage, hoping the worst was over and that we should soon get in sight of the fleet.[3]

1 Peebles, *John Peebles' American War*, p.319.
2 Oakes to Conway, 13 May 1780, from a collection of letters sold in May 2008.
3 Shaw, *A Narrative*, pp.25–26.

Shaw was mistaken, for the ordeal was not yet over. The transport failed to locate the rest of the fleet. An argument broke out between the 33rd's officers and the officers of the ship, resulting in an accidental fire. This caused even more danger, compounded by yet another storm;

> Fire fell into the steerage and communicated into the hold, from which the smoke was immediately perceived to issue in curling volumes, so that we expected every moment to be blow up. In this critical & perilous situation the cries of the women & children were truly distressing: & to render our danger still greater, we were again assailed with a violent squall: the waves rose like mountains, and threatened to overwhelm us: the ocean seemed to open its bosom to receive us: the swelling surges broke upon us, until we had five feet water in the hold; our pumps were choked, and for a while refused to perform our office – Our condition was desperate – But it pleased God to prolong our existence: – the fire was extinguished; and by repeated attempts and strenuous exertions, we at length brought the pumps to work; the tempest ceased and we continued our voyage, still hoping to come up with the fleet.[4]

Shaw recalled the boredom that attended seafaring between the bouts of life-threatening danger, writing of the hours whiled away while doing duty on the ship's foretop, looking for any sign of a sail on the horizon.

Eventually the transport did indeed link up with the rest of the fleet, which was reassembling off Tybee Island, at the mouth of the Savannah River and south of Charleston. The place was described by a captain of the 64th Foot as having 'a miserable appearance, being a Bank of Sand with a few Trees and no Water.'[5] Another officer was slightly kinder, calling it 'a Sandy island with Pine wood & some Cabbage Trees some wild deer & Hogs on the Island.'[6] Regardless, the veterans among the 33rd must have had in recollection the hard voyage followed by the grim weeks enduring heat, thirst and flies on Charleston's Long Island, four years earlier.

There was to be no repeat of the debacle that had occurred the last time Charleston had been attacked. The expedition was to land south of the town and work its way overland, intending to cut off the Charleston peninsular and thus besiege it. After a time spent reassembling the scattered fleet, where the 33rd went ashore for brief periods on Tybee Island to stretch legs and wash clothes, the expedition set sail on 10 February, and by noon the next day had passed into the North Edisto inlet, not far south of Charleston. Light infantry and grenadiers went ashore that evening at Simmons Point. The 33rd, German grenadiers and a detachment of jäger, all carrying enough provisions for three days, followed in the second disembarkation amidst heavy fog and rain.

The next day was similar, with rain during the night and heavy cloud. The 33rd were paired with a force of German jäger and joined the British

4 Shaw, *A Narrative*, p.26.

5 James Bain Jr., 'The Siege of Charleston: Journal of Captain Peter Russell, December 25, 1779 to May 2, 1780', *The American Historical Review*, April, 1899, vol.4, no.3, p.481.

6 Peebles, *John Peebles' American War*, p.331.

light infantry that day before carrying on, probing the countryside towards Stono Ferry. *Kapitän* Johann Ewald, the jäger commander, noted in his writings that the 33rd 'were to perform the service of light infantry' under Lieutenant Colonel Webster, whom Ewald called 'a very meritorious man.'[7] It is clear therefore that the 33rd were still operating as light infantry, working in the army's vanguard alongside other light troops under the command of Lieutenant Colonel Webster, who has, as historian Hugh Bicheno notes, been 'singled out for praise by every important memorialist of this campaign.'[8]

The countryside certainly appeared to warrant their work as light troops. One officer described the terrain as 'a light sandy soil flat woody Country the woods mostly pines, when cleared, produces corn & calavances … the Country here about is so intersected with creeks & water courses that they go several ways by water up to Chas. Town.'[9] Ewald put what the 33rd faced on their first excursion more bluntly; 'the troops set out through a pathless and marshy wood, which continued with the greatest difficulty until five o'clock in the evening. A path often had to be cut through the bushes with axes and bayonets in water up to the waist.'[10]

At length the vanguard reached the Simmons plantation. The 33rd carried on, crossing a creek that divided Simmons Island in two, then crossed a second creek onto neighbouring Johns Island. With the jäger they then occupied the road leading to Stono Ferry, a vital point of communication. Soldiers marvelled at how 'the trees are covered with a sort of grass which hangs down from the highest point over all branches like horses' tails. This phenomenon absorbed our complete attention because of its rarity.'[11]

The next day the 33rd and jäger moved on to the Wilson family plantation. On 14 February they marched towards Stono Ferry, cautious of reports that the rebels were present in force on the far bank. Ewald narrated the struggles that soon beset the expedition;

> Since all the country people, especially the males, had run away, spies and guides were very scarce. With the utmost effort we had gotten hold of a Negro boy of eleven or twelve years who knew the way there. To our ill luck, however, this boy spoke such a poor dialect that he was extremely hard to understand, which predicament worsened because none of us was provided with a map of this area.[12]

Led by their young and incomprehensible guide, the jäger and 33rd soon discovered a stone and log causeway that appeared to 'zigzag through an impenetrable morass without its end being visible.'[13] The detachment began to follow it through the marsh, the jäger in front and the 33rd following. After around an hour the vanguard discovered 'high ground and several

7 Joseph P. Tustin (ed.), *Diary of the American War: A Hessian Journal* (New Haven: Yale University Press, 1979), p.195.
8 Bicheno, *Rebels & Redcoats*, p.170.
9 Peebles, *John Peebles' American War*, p.339.
10 Tustin (ed.), *Diary of the American War*, p.196.
11 Tustin (ed.), *Diary of the American War*, p.197.
12 Tustin (ed.), *Diary of the American War*, p.197.
13 Tustin (ed.), *Diary of the American War*, p.197.

Though some officers carried fusils, swords were still wielded during the Revolutionary War and, according to some accounts, were even occasionally used to deadly effect. (Photo by Henry Gage)

houses' and realised soon after that they were occupied by a strong rebel force.[14] The detachment had stumbled upon the Stono Ferry guard, which they had believed to be on the other side of the river. They were now within rifle range.

The British and Germans abruptly found themselves in a precarious position, strung out on a long causeway in the midst of a marsh. Webster, also seeing that the rebel post was at least partially fortified, prudently ordered a withdrawal back along the causeway; 'we marched back safely; the enemy did not fire a shot, and we certainly didn't want to fire any! We reached the causeway safely, laughed heartily, and were astonished over the strange behaviour of the enemy.'[15]

The next day the rebels abandoned their position and withdrew across the river – Stono Ferry was now under the control of the Crown forces. Ewald's map of the area shows his jäger acting as pickets beyond the works on the opposite bank of the ferry, while the 33rd's companies were split, with four posted outside the defences and the other four within.

While occupying the area, the usual activities were undertaken, with 'Negroes, Horses & Cattle' brought in (horses were in particular supply after most of the expedition's had perished onboard ship during the storms), two days of fresh meat were issued to the men, and several sloops with rice on the Stono River were captured.[16] Cornwallis issued strict verbal orders 'against plundering & killing of Cattle.'[17]

On 16 February the 33rd and jäger, now joined by the 1st Light Infantry battalion and the 7th and 23rd Foot crossed over the ferry onto Johns Island and occupied a series of old, makeshift fortifications that had been built by British forces campaigning in the area the previous summer. Two days later a party of rebels were sighted, but they remained at a distance.

Seemingly jealous of the activities of the light troops and the 33rd, 'several officers of the 7th and 23rd regiments… begged General Leslie to allow them to go out on patrol to share the glory of the service of the light troops.'[18] The request was granted, and three officers and 50 men were assigned to go out 'to collect Negroes and livestock, if any were still left.'[19] It quickly emerged that the duties of the light infantry were not suited to regiments that had not been trained in them. Ewald related that the detachment from the 7th and 23rd initially went 'marching like a changing of the guard' on the way out and, as they returned, due to not having spotted any of the enemy, 'they marched in all tranquillity and without formation.'[20] Little did they realise that they were being stalked by a rebel detachment which fell upon them in an ambush. Nineteen of their party were killed or wounded, and the rest were only saved by the timely intervention of Ewald's jäger. Given that the 33rd were at the leading edge of light infantry innovation in the first half

14 Tustin (ed.), *Diary of the American War*, p.197.
15 Tustin (ed.), *Diary of the American War*, p.198.
16 Peebles, *John Peebles' American War*, pp.339–340.
17 Peebles, *John Peebles' American War*, p.340.
18 Tustin (ed.), *Diary of the American War*, p.202.
19 Tustin (ed.), *Diary of the American War*, p.202.
20 Tustin (ed.), *Diary of the American War*, p.209.

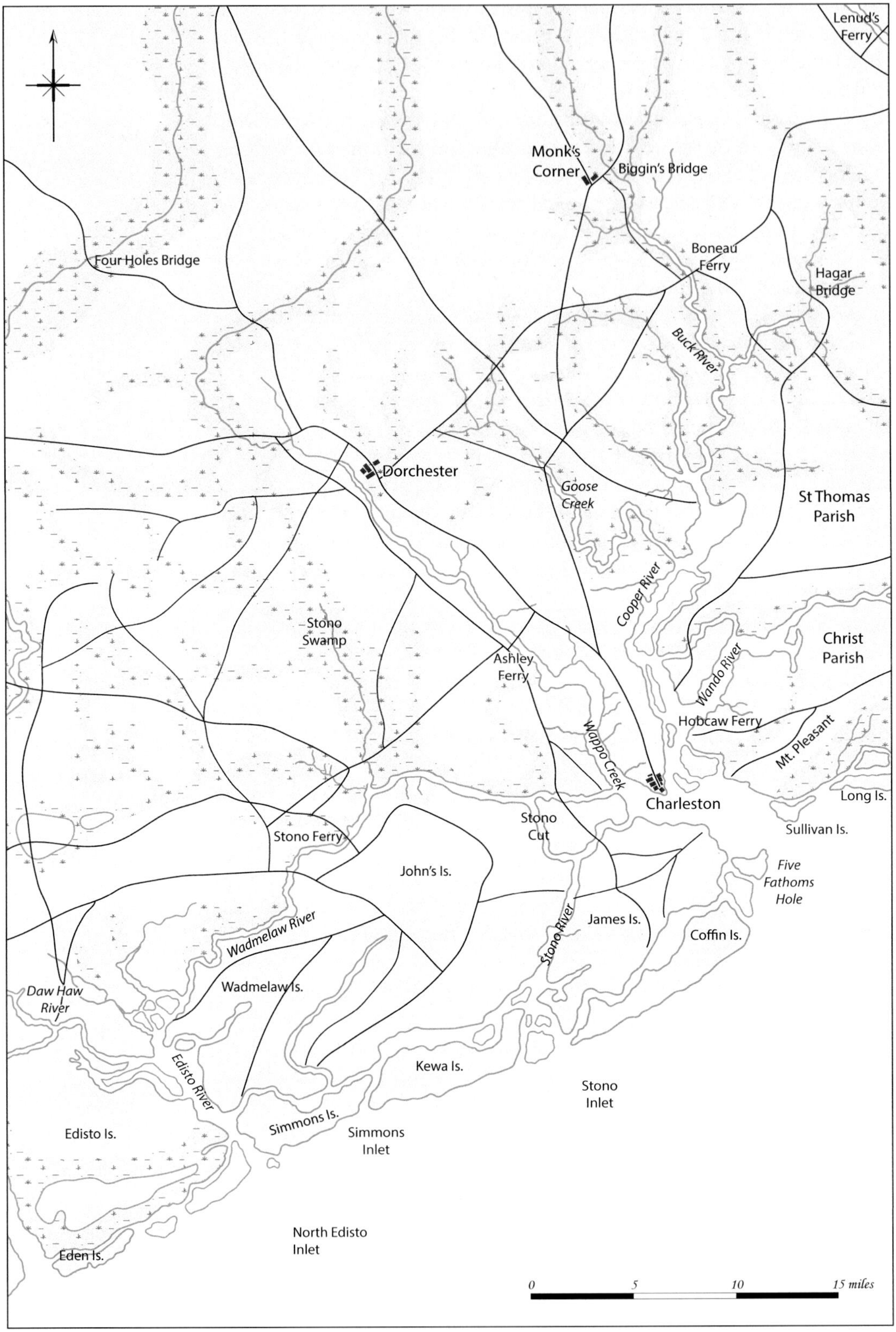

The Charleston region, 1780.

of the 1770s, it seems clear that acting in the role of light infantry was not as simple as operating in open or extended order or going 'to tree.' It is also notable that, with the long service of many of the 33rd's NCOs and with most commissioned officers coming from within the regiment rather than from outside, it appears the leadership cadre from the early to mid-1770s helped ensure that the 33rd could be properly and safely employed as light troops even late in the war.

The advance continued, the British moving across the islands dotting the coast until their vanguard reached the last one overlooking Charleston harbour, James Island, on 24 February. Three days later the 33rd occupied a plantation belonging to William Ashely on John's Island, where they were joined the next day by a battalion of the 71st. By this point there had been minor skirmishing, but nothing involving the regiment.

At the start of March, the army largely paused for five days while heavy artillery was landed and brought up, along with the tools necessary for siege work. On 7 March the 33rd, still operating with the jäger and the 71st, marched at 3:00 a.m. to Matthew's Ferry, which allowed them to cross over to James Island if need be. This they did on 9 March, the crossing taking half an hour due to the river having broken its banks and spread into the surrounding marshland. The force shifted to the bridge at New Cut. The next day they crossed the bridge over the Wappoo River along with the light infantry, grenadiers, the 7th and 23rd and, commanded by Cornwallis 'encamped in a thick wood mostly pine, flat & watery as usual.'[21]

The noose continued to tighten on Charleston, as the islands and rivers that provided access to the town were occupied and cut off, one by one. The methodical advance had allowed the defenders to prepare strong works, but they had underestimated the ability of the British to bring heavy artillery to the landward side of the town.

The 33rd shifted to the plantation of Thomas Rose, close to Fenwick's Point overlooking the Wappoo Cut, a tributary that ran between the Stono and Ashley rivers. An officer and 20 men of the regiment helped the jäger in providing a picket in the rice fields around the upper side of the plantation, while the main body of the regiment lay below it. From here they moved on to Lowndes plantation on the flank of the royal advance, 'to forage there and divide the enemy forces.'[22]

On 22 March the 33rd, jäger, and light infantry shifted themselves to St Andrew's Church, next to a bridge that passed over St Andrew's Creek, where minor skirmishing took place. The next day they moved on to Drayton Hall, which included a particular large garden planted by the hall's builder, John Drayton. Here Ewald recalled that 'the *jägers* and the 33d Regiment, under Colonel Webster, took their post in a thicket opposite the zoological garden on the road to Dorchester.'[23]

---

21 Peebles, *John Peebles' American War*, p.347.

22 Tustin (ed.), *Diary of the American War*, p.209.

23 Tustin (ed.), *Diary of the American War*, p.214.

On 24 March the 33rd, jäger and light infantry received 'four days Bread and rum and one days pork.'[24] They were part of the initial thrust across the Ashley River that cut off the neck of land upon which Charleston itself stood. Marching with the grenadiers, Captain Oakes declared 'we got our first View of the Town, which from the Number and force of their Vessels of different kinds, and the Strength of their Batterys appeared very formidable…'[25]

At daybreak on 29 March troops began loading into boats to cross the Ashley. The 33rd were brigaded with the 71st in the fourth embarking, with the whole landing 13 miles from the town. An officer of the 64th noted that 'this important event was effected without giving the least Alarm with the Boats, or suffering the least Opposition on our landing or in our March.'[26]

The next day the British advanced on the town, with the 33rd, 7th and 71st acting as a corps de reserve with the baggage. The head of the column made contact with Charleston's defenders two and a half miles from the town, driving them in after a brisk skirmish. That evening the army 'encamped in three lines extending from one Side of the Neck to the other,' basing their flanks on the Ashley and Cooper rivers. The 33rd remained with the 7th and 71st under Webster's overall command, occupying the third line, which was 'faced outwards to cover the Camp from an attack from the Country.'[27] On 1 April the 33rd acted as a covering party for foragers, with an orderly book recording that 'a Corps Commanded by Liut Coll Webster, to Morrow Morning at day break towards the Contry, Under Cover of which Forrageing parteys May be Sent out.'[28]

On 1 April the construction of the first siege works began. Captain Peebles described 'frames erecting on the road in front of the 1st Lt. Infantry for the purpose of making works with expedition, they are faced with boards nail'd to right angled timbers parapet height, in divisions about 18 feet long.' The light infantry worked in the night to erect the first redoubts a little over 700 yards from the rebel fortifications, which were 'strong & well made with a very wide & deep wet ditch or canal from River to River, & a thick abbattis.'[29] A group of 400 men from the reserve, quite probably including men from the 33rd, were detailed as a work party to speed the construction.

Over the coming days the troops laboured to raise up redoubts and batteries, doing so under what Captain Oakes of the 33rd's grenadiers recalled as 'a constant fire of Canon and small Arms upon us.'[30] Work was done night and day, with a barrage of roundshot and shells from both the town and rebel shipping in the inner harbour doing little to impede efforts. Detachments of the 33rd laboured with the rest, but on 3 April received special orders from Clinton;

24 Paul L. Pace, *Capt. Eyre Coote's 37th Light Infantry Company Order Book, 1778–1781*, RevWar'75, <http://www.revwar75.com/library/pace/37-light-OB.pdf>, p.58, accessed January 2023.
25 Oakes to Conway, 13 May 1780, from a collection of letters sold in May 2008.
26 Russell, 'The Siege of Charleston', p.493.
27 Russell, 'The Siege of Charleston', pp.493–494.
28 Pace, *Capt. Eyre Coote's 37th Light Infantry Company Order Book*, p.60.
29 Peebles, *John Peebles' American War*, p.355.
30 Oakes to Conway, 13 May 1780,' from a collection of letters sold in May 2008.

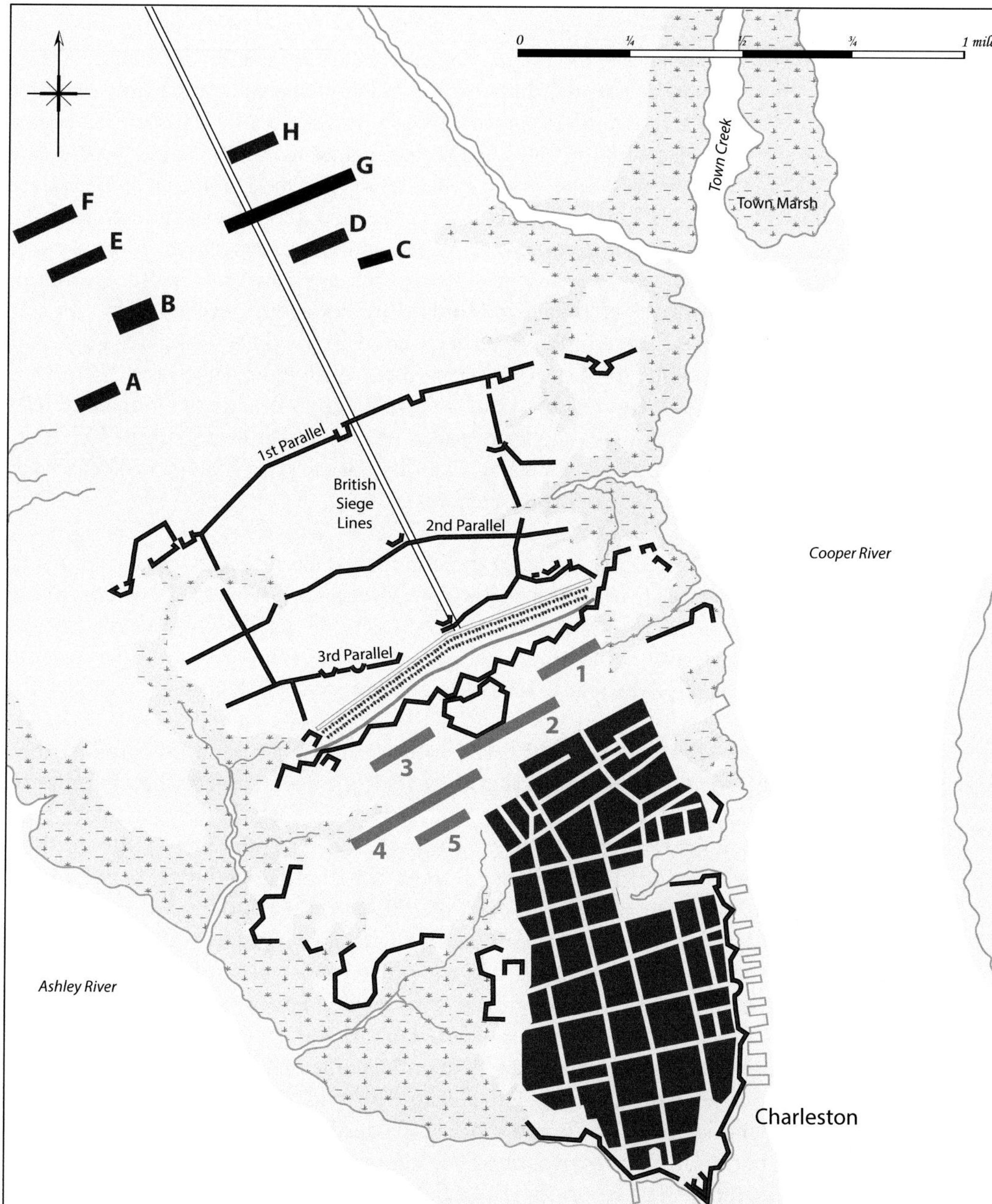

April 25 Dispositions

British Forces

A. 1 & 2/42nd Highlanders (780)
B. Artillery Park
C. Jäger (224)
D. 1st & 2nd Light Infantry (1,277)
E. 1st & 2nd Grenadiers (1,139)
F. 1 & 2/71st Highlanders (869)
G. German Grenadiers (1,525)
H. 7th Fusiliers (463)

American Forces

1. NC Continental Brigade
   Brigadier General Hogun
   1st NC Continental Regt. (260)
   2nd NC Continental Regt. (240)
   3rd NC Continental Regt. (160)
2. VA Continental Brigade
   Colonel Parker
   1st VA Detachment (260)
   2nd VA Detachment (305)
   2nd SC (266)
   3rd SC Rangers (300)
3. 1st VA Continental Brigade
   Brigadier General Woodford
   1st VA Continental Regt. (260)
   2nd VA Continental Regt. (305)
   3rd VA Continental Regt. (252)
4. NC Militia Brigade
   Brigadier General Harrington
   1st NC (305)
   2nd NC (355)
   3rd NC (476)
   4th NC (291)
5. SC Militia Brigade (300)
   Brigadier General McIntosh

The siege of Charleston, 29 March–12 May 1780.

> The several dutys of this night are to be by Detachment from the whole army, Excepting the 33d Regt. maj Grahams Lt Infantry and Hessian Yegars… The 33d Regiment, Excepting (at Lt Colonel Websters direction) such men as have been resently submitted to purculiar Fatigues are to parade for A particular service on the right of the whole – The 33d Regt. not being Included in the Gen Detail for to night, Maj Dansey is of course to do durty in the 33d and not on Detachment – The place of parade is the same as Yesterday According to the directions of the Engineers, the troops are to be put in motion and disposed of.[31]

The purpose of this mysterious duty soon became apparent. As Captain Peebles of the 42nd's grenadiers noted in his diary, 'the 33d. Regt. as Light troops make the Covering party' for that night's excavations.[32] The 33rd had once again been singled out for the dangerous activities normally reserved for light infantry. The night was a wet one, with heavy rain. While the 33rd kept watch, the work parties laboured to erect a battery just 600 yards out from the town's defences. Peebles wrote;

> We broke ground & filled them up [frames for the battery] pretty well but not sufficiently to resist battering, towards morng. It rain'd hard & the men being much fatigued we left off about 4 & came to Camp; five Negroes came in to us having made their escape over the works The enemy did not fire a shot during the night, & we work'd in such silence that they did not discover us.[33]

The 33rd undoubtedly spent an uncomfortable night, exposed in the rain, but could be thankful that they had not been subjected to bombardment. That quickly changed however. As the sun rose the rebel artillery began to open fire, and during the morning the two 32-gun rebel frigates in the inner harbour sailed a little way up the Cooper and added their broadsides to the barrage for an hour. Captain Peter Russell of the 64th recorded the rebel ships came up 'to enfilade the Redoubt erected last night by which one man Of 33d was killed.'[34] This death was the only combat loss suffered by the regiment during the siege, though the barrage also left three men wounded, one an officer, Arthur Beavor, a lieutenant in the grenadier company. A British newspaper reported that Beavor, the son of a gentleman named Thomas Beavor who lived at Hethel near Norfolk, 'was wounded at the attack on Charlestown, by a grape shot, which destroyed or took away seven teeth with part of his lower jaw; but we are happy to hear that he is otherwise in perfect health.'[35] The wound was not debilitating, as he continued to serve. At least one other man in the 33rd, William Clarkson, died from an illness onboard one of the fleet's hospital ships on 18 February, but it is unknown how many others succumbed to sickness.[36]

---

31 Pace, *Capt. Eyre Coote's 37th Light Infantry Company Order Book*, p.63.
32 Peebles, *John Peebles' American War*, p.356.
33 Peebles, *John Peebles' American War*, p.356.
34 Russell, 'The Siege of Charleston', p.495.
35 *Norfolk Chronicle*, 1 July 1780, p.2.
36 CL: Henry Clinton Papers: Vol. 86, p.14.

Clinton's orders on 4 April noted that 'the 33d and Yagers are to Give No men for the Duty to Night,' though whether that was because they were again sequestered as a covering force, or whether it was to give them time to recover from the previous night's activities, is unclear.[37]

On 7 April rebel shipping sailed unopposed down the Wando River, bringing a further 750 men into the Charleston garrison. In the trenches and encampments, Crown forces listened to cheering and celebratory musket volleys from the town. On 8 April the noise was even more pronounced, with the battering thunderclaps of artillery coming from beyond the town signalling that the Royal Navy was attempting to do what it had failed so spectacularly at in 1776 – pass Fort Moultrie on Sullivan's Island and gain Charleston's middle harbour. Three ships-of-the-line and four frigates sailed past Fort Moultrie, disdaining its firepower and suffering little in the way of damage. The noose was drawing ever tighter.

Clinton wanted it tighter still. Charleston was not yet entirely cut off – communication with the outside was still possible via the Cooper River. Indeed, a force of Continental cavalry and militia had gathered in the vicinity of Monck's Corner, a small settlement north of Charleston that controlled 'the forks and passes of Cooper River, and maintained a communication with Charles town; by which, supplies of men, arms, ammunition, and provision, might be conveyed to the garrison during the siege.'[38] John Robert Shaw recalled that;

> The town had still kept up a communication with the country on the farther side of Cooper's river, and some bodies of militia, cavalry and infantry began to assemble on the higher parts of that river, who, by keeping possesion of the bridges might, at least, by cutting off supplies, and molesting our foraging parties, having considerably retarded and disturbed the operations of our army.[39]

The presence of a rebel force inland was also something Clinton could not tolerate, as it raised the spectre of being trapped between Charleston's garrison and the forces in the interior. Consequently, after the regiment had spent a period in the trenches, Clinton detached the 33rd, the Loyalists of the British Legion, a small force of the 17th Light Dragoons and Major Patrick Ferguson's company of marksmen and placed them under the command of Lieutenant Colonel Webster. Their orders were, according to the dashing commander of the British Legion, Lieutenant Colonel Banastre Tarleton, 'to counteract the designs of the Americans, and to break in upon the remaining communications of Charles town.'[40] The diary of Captain Peebles recorded on 12 April 'the 33d. Regt. the Legion & Fergusons Corps are march'd back in the Country to scour our neighborhood.'[41]

---

37 Pace, *Capt. Eyre Coote's 37th Light Infantry Company Order Book*, p.63.

38 Banastre Tarleton, *A History of the Campaigns of 1780 and 1781 in the Southern Provinces of North America* (Dublin: Colles et al, 1787), p.15.

39 Shaw, *A Narrative*, p.27.

40 Tarleton, *A History*, p.16.

41 Peebles, *John Peebles' American War*, p.359.

The detachment moved swiftly. The vanguard, consisting of Tarleton's green-coated Loyalists and Ferguson's sharpshooters, reached Goose Creek bridge, 15 miles south of Monck's Corner, by the evening of 12 April. The 33rd, marching after them, arrived the next day. Tarleton intercepted a man carrying a letter from the commander of the rebel forces at Monck's corner, which allowed him to learn the enemy's dispositions. Finding them split between the banks of the Cooper River, on either side of a crossing known as Biggin Bridge, he resolved to strike while the enemy were unawares. In the first of many such incidents during the southern campaigns, Tarleton raced ahead, caught his enemies napping, and entirely routed them.

Webster and the 33rd arrived in the vicinity of Monck's Corner the next day. Shaw recorded the previous night's skirmish as 'bloody work,' though much as at Old Tappan in 1778, the 33rd did not arrive until after the killing was done.[42] Webster was approached by a trio of ladies who had been violently assaulted by three British Legion dragoons who had broken into a plantation owned by a local Loyalist in the aftermath of the action the day before. The ladies had gone to Webster for protection, and their assailants were immediately arrested, court-martialled and, in the case of three of them, suffered floggings.[43] It was a foretaste of the indiscipline that was to plague Crown forces in the south over the coming year.

As per their orders, Webster's detachment set about securing the Cooper River and then moving on towards the Wando River. The 33rd crossed a branch of the Cooper at Strawberry Ferry, about seven miles south of Monck's Corner, on 16 April. They were reinforced by the 64th Foot before pushing on over another crossing called Bono Ferry, and then securing Miller's Bridge, which ran across a branch of the Wando. The 33rd took post at St Thomas' Church, intending to continue to sweep south towards the Wando River, which was now the last rebel-controlled waterway leading to Charleston.

Aware that this was their last route of both supply and possible retreat, rebel forces had been dispatched up the Wando to attempt to fortify it, raising defences at the settlement of Cainhoy on the north bank and constructing an artillery battery at Lempriere's Point, overlooking the ferry there, a place described by one Loyalist as 'a very disagreeable post ... being nothing but a bank of sand, where, in a windy day, you must keep your eyes shut or have them filled with sand.'[44] Webster's command post was initially in Cainhoy, but when a scouting party received the full fury of the Lampriere battery's artillery, it was decided that the post was too strong to storm. While waiting for support, the 33rd assisted in fortifying their post at Miller's Bridge, with a blockhouse constructed by 20 April. A detachment of regulars and Loyalists, including 20 soldiers of the 33rd led by a subaltern, were posted to hold the bridge while the main body of the regiment returned to St Thomas' Church.[45]

42 Shaw, *A Narrative*, p.27.

43 Anthony J. Scotti Jr, *Brutal Virtue: The Myth and Reality of Banastre Tarleton* (Westminster: Heritage Books, 2007), p.168.

44 Diary of Lieutenant Anthony Allaire, in Lyman Copeland Draper, *Kings Mountain and its Heroes* (Cincinnati: Peter G. Thomson, 1881), p.493.

45 Diary of Lieutenant Anthony Allaire, in Draper, *Kings Mountain*, p.492.

With more reinforcements arriving from New York, Clinton detached Cornwallis with more troops to move over the Cooper and reinforce Webster. The Continentals occupying Lampriere's Point abandoned it with such haste that one boat sailed in the wrong direction and was captured. A detachment of marines and sailors occupied the position, thus seizing control of the Wando, and completing the encirclement of Charleston. In doing so, according to Peebles, they took 'a great many stores of considerable Value, tobacco Indigo, dry goods, Liquors plate &ca & live in midst of plenty.'[46]

On 6 May Tarleton routed another force of Continental cavalry and militia at Lenud's Ferry. Two days later Fort Moultrie, which had failed to stop the Royal Navy passing its guns and was now also threatened from the landward side following the capture of the Wando, surrendered. Piece by piece, Charleston's defences had been methodically stripped away, while the foremost British siegeworks, which had first broken ground 800 yards from the town's redoubts, were now just 60 yards away.

On 12 May Charleston surrendered. Over 5,000 Continentals, militiamen and sailors laid down their arms, and likewise gave up 311 cannon, tens of thousands of rounds of ammunition, hundreds of barrels of supplies, and 49 vessels. These numbers, combined with the fact that Crown forces had suffered less than 200 casualties over the entire course of the campaign, ensured that Clinton had just won the greatest British victory of the war.

A 1781 publication noted that Webster 'received the thanks of Sir Henry Clinton, for his good conduct' during the advance on Charleston and particularly for leading the corps that moved off into the interior to cut off the last of the town's communications.[47] Indeed in his detailed letter to George Germain following the surrender of Charleston, Clinton wrote that 'I have especially to express my obligation to Lieutenant-colonel Webster, and the corps which acted under him.'[48] In the address to the army the day after Charleston's surrender, Clinton likewise expressed 'his Great Obligation to Liut. Coln Webster And The Corps With Which he broke in Upon the Most Essensual of the reable [reliable] Communication's.'[49]

Word of Charleston's surrender reached the 33rd on the same day, encamped around Silkhope plantation further north. Dansey found the time to sit down and pen a letter to his mother for the first time in six months; 'We have just heard of the Surrender of Charlestown and as we are up the Country almost 50 Miles If I don't embrace the first moment I may not have an Opportunity of sending time enough for the Packet that will sail with the News home.' He was hopeful that the victory would allow him to return home for a while and help settle financial and legal matters, as well as see his family and fiancée. Concerned about the legal business that awaited him at Brinsop, he admitted that 'war is a much pleasanter thing to me than Law. I

46 Peebles, *John Peebles' American War*, pp.368–369.
47 Anon., 'For the Political Magazine', p.342.
48 Tarleton, *A History of the Campaigns*, p.45.
49 Pace, *Capt. Eyre Coote's 37th Light Infantry Company Order Book*, p.81.

was born to my share of both, and from what Experience I have had in this World am now equal to either but prefer War of the two.'[50]

Captain Oakes, still serving with the grenadier battalion, was even more positive, believing that the tide of the war had turned. In a letter to a friend he claimed that 'we expect to march into the County immediately, and I am credibly informed that when we make our Appearance in North Carolina, there will be five Thousand Men in Arms who will join us; so that I hope I shall soon be able to tell your Lordship that the Southern Colonys [*sic*]are all ours.'[51]

Oakes was mistaken, for while the victory seemed to have laid South Carolina bare to royal occupation, it was not quite as absolute as it first seemed. While over 2,000 of the prisoners were Continental Army soldiers who marched into captivity, the remainder were militiamen, too numerous to keep in Charleston or even consign to the overcrowded prison hulks around New York. They were consequently released on parole, after swearing not to fight against the crown. This undermined British authority in the long term, as Clinton later chose to demand not just that these former rebels forebear from waging war against the king, but that they actually take up arms against their former revolutionary comrades. This had the opposite effect, driving paroled militiamen to once again join the fight against Crown forces in the south. In that sense the success at Charleston was, like so many other British victories throughout the war, a hollow one.

March to the Interior

While Charleston was being occupied the 33rd remained with the rest of the detachment now commanded by Cornwallis on the far side of the Cooper at Silkhope plantation and Huger's bridge. In mid-May orders came for Cornwallis to chase down the last Continental troops in South Carolina, who were withdrawing northwards. Setting out from Huger's bridge on 18 May, the corps reached Lenud's Ferry over the Santee. Rebels had destroyed or hidden the ferry's boats, but more were collected with the aid of some escaped slaves, and others repaired. By 22 May the force had crossed in its entirety and marched to Nelson's Ferry. Once there, it was clear that the Continentals would escape unless drastic action was taken. Cornwallis subsequently detached the British Legion and a small number of the 17th Light Dragoons under Tarleton and unleashed them on the rebels. Tarleton, with typical ferocity, hunted down and caught the Continentals near the settlement of Waxhaws, decimating them and ending, if only for a brief while, all organised resistance to the crown's authority in South Carolina.

Despite the belief that turning the southern colonies into a Loyalist enclave could win the war for Britain, Clinton did not share the same strategic priorities. Still convinced that a battle of annihilation against Washington was the best course of action, at the end of May the main body of the army he had

50 DHS: William Dansey Letters: 12 May 1780.

51 Oakes to Conway, 13 May 1780, from a collection of letters sold in May 2008.

brought to Charleston began to embark. Clinton left on 5 June, once again concentrating the bulk of Crown forces in North America – over 20,000 men – in the vicinity of New York. He left Cornwallis behind with instructions to continue to oversee the expansion of royal authority in the south. Among the small force of regulars left for Cornwallis to bolster his southern Loyalists with were the 33rd. Oakes and the grenadiers as well as Gore and the lights were taken back to New York as part of the composite flank battalions. In his parting instructions to Cornwallis, Clinton closed with 'your Lordship will observe that on the above arrangement I have not named the 33rd. You will of course dispose of them as you please, but wherever you are, I shall naturally expect to find them.'[52] It is clear that the regiment was still very much Cornwallis's corps.

At the end of May the regiment marched into Camden, the largest settlement in South Carolina's interior. A trade hub located beside the Wateree River, it was earmarked to become a vital supply base and staging post for further Crown forces expansion west into the uplands and north into the neighbouring colony of North Carolina. South Carolina possessed good communications, with numerous wagon roads built to service the plantation economy, as well as a large number of rivers and streams that could be traversed by boat.[53] This enabled military forces, especially small groups, to traverse the countryside more rapidly than they did in the northern colonies, rendering outposts vulnerable to attack. To help garrison the developing string of strongholds, it appears a detachment of the 33rd was sent to the settlement of Ninety-Six, Shaw describing how 'when we arrived at Camden, a detachment was ordered to Ninety-six; but it fell to my lot to continue at Camden.'[54]

Along with the 23rd Foot, the Volunteers of Ireland, several pieces of artillery, the infantry of the British Legion and various other small Loyalist corps, the rest of the 33rd were left as a garrison force in Camden under the command of Colonel Francis Rawdon. Here they constructed 'huts of proper materials to resist the hot weather.'[55] It was not only the summer weather that was hot. By July a vicious civil war was raging throughout South Carolina as Loyalists, emboldened by the return of Crown forces, rose up against their rebel counterparts. While having Loyalists take up the slack in terms of front-line operations was one of the major reasons for the British shift south – especially with so many regulars being redeployed to other parts of the globe following France's entry into the war – the explosion of violence, with tit-for-tat killings and home burnings, threatened to create a spiral of destruction that would undermine the rule of law that Cornwallis was hoping to re-establish.

52 Ian Saberton (ed.), *The Cornwallis Papers: The Campaigns of 1780 and 1781 in the Southern Theatre of the American Revolutionary War* (Uckfield: The Naval & Military Press, 2010), vol.1, p.62.

53 J.R. McNeill, *Mosquito Empires: Ecology and War in the Greater Caribbean, 1620–1914* (Cambridge: Cambridge University Press, 2010), p.214.

54 Shaw, *A Narrative*, p.28.

55 Tarleton, *A History*, p.89.

While Crown forces were attempting to return South Carolina to what they termed good governance, Washington had already dispatched Continental Army regiments south. In July Horatio Gates, victor of Saratoga, took command of the army, which was built around two Continental Maryland brigades and one Delaware regiment as well as one Continental legion (Armand's, formerly Pulaski's), along with seven pieces of artillery. Both Maryland regiments had been raised in 1776 and the Delaware regiment in 1775 – while the nature of Continental Army enlistments meant few of the soldiers had been serving since the beginning, all three regiments as a whole were experienced. Indeed, the 2nd Maryland had already encountered the 33rd in a sharp, close-range firefight in the heavy fog at Germantown in 1777. In late July the Continentals pushed into North Carolina, intending to march onwards to Camden. Their numbers were swelled by 2,700 militia from North Carolina and Virginia. The Camden garrison, including the 33rd, was outnumbered more than three to one. Rawdon began to assemble his meagre forces to meet the expected attack, with the 33rd marching at 10:00 p.m. on 12 July to the Robertson plantation at the west branch of Lynches Creek, north-east of the town. With them went the Volunteers of Ireland and two 6-pounders. Later in July they shifted to the east branch of Lynches Creek to support the nearby 71st, with the Volunteers of Ireland and the artillery remaining at Robertson's to provide a link to the neighbouring outpost of Hanging Rock.

At Camden, John Robert Shaw had fallen ill, writing laconically 'I fell sick for the first and last time, that is, with common sickness; for I have often times indisposed with the bottle-fever, and by wounds, bruises and broken bones.'[56] His experience was normal, especially in the south, where disease ran riot among Europeans unaccustomed to environment. The climate in South Carolina hampered British efforts, reducing the number of soldiers fit for service in an area where the number of Crown troops was already dangerously low. In August that year the 71st had two out of every three men struck down by a remitting fever – as Gates bore down on them it was reported that from their two battalions they had only 274 men under arms. The 63rd likewise was so sickly when they later arrived at Camden that the regiment as a whole was deemed unfit for service. Though most men recovered time and momentum during a vital campaign had been squandered.[57] There were also outbreaks of smallpox in the army in 1780 both at Charleston and Camden, despite the army's earlier, voluntary inoculation against the disease.[58]

Hearing about Gates's impending arrival, Cornwallis rushed with reinforcements to Camden, but it seemed that a defence of the settlement was doomed. The hospital was overrun with soldiers who, like Shaw, had fallen sick, an estimated 800 in total, mostly afflicted by malaria. Army regulations of the period included practical measures for alleviating illness and avoiding epidemics, requiring that hospitals be thoroughly cleaned, the interior washed with soap and vinegar and fumigated with substances

56 Shaw, *A Narrative*, p.28.

57 Hagist, *Noble Volunteers*, pp.143–144.

58 Frey, *The British Soldier in America*, p.44.

A soldier of the 33rd as he likely would have appeared going into action in the southern colonies during the latter years of the Revolutionary War. Bayonets were fixed as standard practice. (Photo by Henry Gage)

like wet gunpowder or incense, juniper wood or berries. Flux or fever patients were segregated and the victims of smallpox quarantined. Despite these efforts, conditions were still often far from ideal, especially in the south, where hospitals lacked basic items such as brooms and rakes for cleaning, which only worsened as overcrowding took hold, leaving many of the sick sharing small straw pallets rather than beds.[59] Overwhelmed by patients, there was no hope that the hospital at Camden would be capable of dealing with the sick, even more so given that doctors and surgeons were also falling ill.

Cornwallis was left with barely 2,000 effectives in his army, and not all of them fully recovered. Gates outnumbered him two-to-one. To make matters worse, retreat was not an option. The sick could not be evacuated in time from Camden, so withdrawing the part of his army that could still walk would mean surrendering those who could not to the oncoming Gates, along with the supplies that had been stockpiled in the town. Cornwallis would have to stand and fight with what he had, and in doing so risk losing control over South Carolina as quickly as it had been gained.

The Battle of Camden

When Cornwallis arrived to take command in Camden on the night of 13 August, he was furnished with a list of the garrison's strength. Not including officers, the 33rd's total was listed as 305 rank-and-file, 16 sergeants, and just one drummer. Of that, 44 rank-and-file and three sergeants were too sick to do duty, leaving a total of 275 men capable of bearing arms. Given the on-paper strength of even the eight hat companies in a battalion by this point was supposed to be over 500 men, the level of attrition endured by the regiments serving in America, and the difficulties associated with reinforcing them, was stark. Like all regiments under Cornwallis's command, the 33rd would be expected to go into battle at well below half its nominal strength. To make matters worse, the detachment sent to Ninety-Six were captured on their way back to Camden by Sumter's partisans, with a Continental Colonel relating how 'a Detachment of 70 men of the 71st & 33d Regts came from Ninety Six to join the Enemy at Camden, were likewise taken Prisoners by Genl Sumpter.'[60]

In fact, in a way the situation was even more severe. A return of the regiment taken just two days later – and the night before the ensuing battle – listed a total force of 13 sergeants, one drummer and 209 rank-and-file, 52 private soldiers less than the first assessment 48 hours earlier. Besides the possibility that a few more men had fallen ill or the fact that one headcount was simply incorrect, there is a chance this number belonged to a detachment left behind to guard the supplies left in Camden, an event related by Shaw

59 Frey, *The British Soldier in America*, pp.45–46.

60 John Christian Senf, in Jim Piecuch, *The Battle of Camden: A Documentary History* (Charleston: The History Press, 2006), p.23.

when he wrote that 'we all turned out except a few who were left to guard the sick and military stores.'[61]

Commanding this probable force of 209 rank-and-file on 16 August was one lieutenant colonel (James Webster), one adjutant (John Fox, who had been promoted from sergeant on 22 October 1778 and would serve as adjutant until 1790), five captains (Frederick Cornwallis, Allen Malcolm, James Campbell, John Manley and Richard Cotton), four lieutenants, two ensigns and, awaiting the wounded, one surgeon and his mate. Webster was in fact acting as a brigadier, in command of both the 23rd and 33rd, so presumably the tactical minutia of battalion command would have fallen to the most senior captain, James Campbell. The companies that ordinarily would have been commanded by the colonel, lieutenant colonel and major were presumably commanded by a single lieutenant each, if indeed the regiment fought using a company structure rather than dividing into divisions.

At 10:00 p.m. orders came through for the army to form up on the road heading north. At the front were 20 British Legion dragoons and another 20 British Legion light infantry mounted on horses, followed by the 23rd and 33rd. Behind them came the Volunteers of Ireland, the rest of the British Legion's infantry, the North Carolina Volunteers and the two much-reduced battalions of the 71st highlanders, acting as the reserve. The rest of Tarleton's British Legion dragoons brought up the rearguard, with a few wagons, while six pieces of artillery interspersed the divisions of march.

In this way the 33rd marched off into the night. At midnight there was some difficulty in passing over Saunders' Creek about five miles north of Camden, and 'the line of march was somewhat broken … a short halt remedied this inconvenience, and the royal army proceeded in a compact state with most profound silence.'[62] At about 2:00 a.m., close to a plantation owned by the Sutton family, a lone pistol shot rang out. There was a brief, uncertain pause, the men surely eyeing the scattering of pine trees spread around the road. Then, from ahead, the 33rd would have been able to hear a trumpet call the charge, and the terrible yelling and whooping of Native American war cries. The sound was made by the British Legion dragoons in the vanguard, who had adopted the shrieking as their own over the course of four months spent harrying and terrifying southern militia. One rebel officer who encountered the British vanguard that night, Guilford Dudley, recalled how the Loyalists charged, 'every officer and soldier with the yell of an Indian savage – at every leap their horses took, crying out, "charge, charge, charge," so that their own voices and the echoes resounded in every direction through the pine forest.'[63]

The yelling was accompanied by the crash of pistols, and then the clash of sabres. The 23rd and 33rd formed from column of march, fanning out to either side of the road but still remaining compact as they waited to see the

61 Shaw, *A Narrative*, p.28.

62 Tarleton, *A History*, p.107.

63 Guildford Dudley, in Piecuch, *The Battle of Camden*, p.74.

outcome of the skirmish. If enemy scouts were this far advanced, the chances of taking the enemy camp by surprise seemed slim.

The Loyalists got the better of the clash, at least initially, before the crash of a volley of musketry – and not the disjointed rattle of cavalrymen's pistols – announced the fact that there was something more up the road than a cavalry patrol. Now it was the turn of the Loyalists to withdraw, galloping hard back upon their infantry, the officer leading them wounded.

The 23rd and 33rd swung into action, advancing in column up the road towards the enemy infantry. Tarleton related that 'the weight of the enemy's fire made the detachment of the legion give way … and occasioned the [Legion] light infantry, the 23d and 33d regiments, to form across the road.'[64] Guilford Dudley recalled 'the moon was at full and shone beautifully … Consequently, we could see to fight in the open piney wood plains … as well in night as in day.'[65]

The British infantry and the rebels began to trade musketry through the trees and moonlight. The royal governor of North Carolina, Josiah Martin, was travelling with the Crown forces and recalled 'the advanced guard was fired upon and fell back on the 33rd regiment, which steadily supported it and returned the enemy's fire.'[66] Dudley, with the rebels, recounted 'both sides being simultaneously prepared, poured in upon each other the heaviest fire.'[67] He recalled a fellow Continental officer being hit in the leg and, as he struggled to help him away, 'we received another fire from a platoon of the enemy just in our front.'[68]

After about 15 minutes of firing, the rebels gave way and withdrew back up the road, with the British advancing a short way to secure the location. Francis Rawdon, who had been riding in the rear of the lead battalion (either the 33rd or 23rd) came forward. He suspected, from the weight of fire and its sustained nature, that the opposition the leading brigade had just driven off were Continental infantry, rather than militia. He dismounted and felt the uniforms of the nearest bodies in the dark.[69]

It was as he had feared. The infantry were indeed Continentals, not a roving band of militia or a mere scouting party. It became apparent that, at the exact same time Cornwallis had set out with his army with the intention of striking a surprise attack on the enemy camp, Gates had done the same with his own force, hoping to reach Saunders' Creek and establish a line of defences there in an effort to recreate the battle of Bemis Heights and subsequent Saratoga surrender. The two armies had, in effect, bumped into each other going in opposite directions on the same road at around 2:00 a.m.

Cornwallis examined what Tarleton called 'the guides, and the people of the country' and established that the section of the road his army had halted on was flanked on both the left and the right by marshes impassable to an

64 Tarleton, *A History*, p.107.
65 Guildford Dudley, in Piecuch, *The Battle of Camden*, p.73.
66 Guildford Dudley, in Piecuch, *The Battle of Camden*, p.69.
67 Guildford Dudley, in Piecuch, *The Battle of Camden*, p.76.
68 Guildford Dudley, in Piecuch, *The Battle of Camden*, p.77.
69 Francis Rawdon, in Piecuch, *The Battle of Camden*, p.60.

army.[70] The firm ground in between was dotted with pine trees and dense with wiregrass, but suitable for an engagement. Cornwallis realised that with both armies hemmed in by the marshes on either side, the superior numbers of the rebels would be curtailed, since they would be unable to outflank the Crown forces. This helped convince Cornwallis to make a stand the next day, confident that Gates would likewise meet him in open battle. Pickets were deployed and the men were ordered to lay on their arms. It is doubtful that much sleep was had. Tarleton recalled that 'except a few occasional shots from the advanced sentries of each army, a silent expectation ushered in the morning.'[71]

The troops had perhaps two hours of rest before they were roused once more, before the sun rose at 6:45 a.m. They formed column and advanced a little under a mile, to contact with the enemy.[72] Cornwallis made his dispositions, deploying his lines just beyond where the vanguard of the two armies had clashed the night before. He arrayed his small force in two wings, on either side of the road running north-south. The right wing, commanded by Webster who was again acting in the role of brigadier, consisted of the small light infantry battalion, the 23rd Foot and, next to the roadway, the 33rd. Beside the 33rd on the opposite side of the road was the left wing commanded by Rawdon, consisting of the Volunteers of Ireland, the British Legion's light infantry and the North Carolina Volunteers. On the road between the two wings were two 3 and two 6-pounder cannon manned by the Royal Artillery. Behind this first line was a reserve consisting of another small group of Loyalist militia, the two under-strength battalions of the 71st and Tarleton's mounted dragoons, waiting in column to the right of the road due to the thickness of the wood, ready to be unleashed.

The deployment displayed the stark danger the royal army was in. In a later report to George Washington, Thomas Jefferson related that he was told that the royal infantry 'from a defect in Numbers were only a Single file five feet apart.'[73] Even by the standards of the looser formations usually employed by crown troops in North America, the line was spread exceedingly thin, a necessity brought on by the fact that while the royal front consisted of under 1,300 men, that of the rebels opposing them was close to 3,000-strong. Cornwallis was forced to take up all the ground he could in order to meet the marshes he hoped would guard his left and right, and even then, the light infantry on the far right of the line were unable to reach the swampy ground and found themselves slightly outflanked.

Roger Lamb, by now a sergeant with the 23rd, related that during the battle he carried one of his regiment's two colours. The practice of actually carrying colours into battle was relatively uncommon among British troops in North America, due to the rapid pace they tended to set, the broken nature of the terrain fought over, and the fact that less compact formations rendered

70 Tarleton, *A History*, p.108.

71 Tarleton, *A History*, p.108.

72 Piecuch, *The Battle of Camden*, p.94.

73 Thomas Jefferson, in Piecuch, *The Battle of Camden*, p.105. It is possible he means rank or line, rather than file.

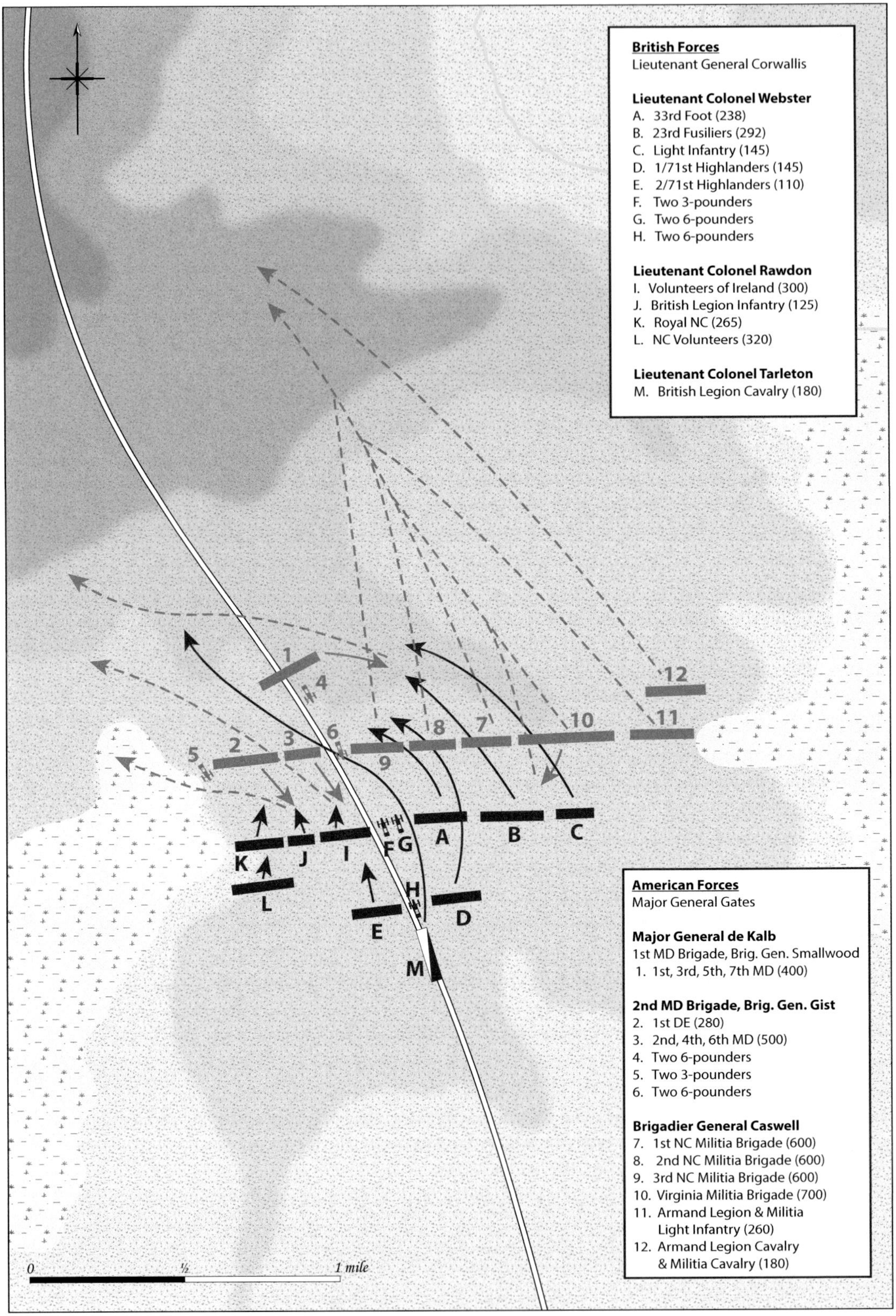

The Battle of Camden, 16 August 1780.

the standards more liable to capture. Despite the looseness of the formation at Camden however, it seems both the Volunteers of Ireland and the 23rd were willing to risk fighting beneath the silk of the regimental colours. It is unknown whether the 33rd did likewise. Having operated closely with the 23rd since arriving in the south, the 33rd had built a close rapport with the Royal Welsh Fusiliers, who were widely considered to be another excellent regiment. Lamb related how; 'The Royal Welch fuzileers were brigaded with the 33d during the entire of the campaign in South Carolina; both regiments were well united together, and furnished an example for cleanliness, martial spirit, and good behaviour ... we were not in any thing inferior to the 33d.'[74] They would once again be going into battle side-by-side. In his history of the 23rd, Mark Urban describes how 'so well did they mix that the two understrength corps that formed Webster's 'brigade' might have been assumed to be a single regiment of two wings or halves.'[75]

In spite of the high regard in which they were held, both the 33rd and the 71st in were likely particularly ragged-looking, as well as being hard-hit by sickness – letters from Cornwallis a little over two months later describe them as almost naked for want of new clothing, as they had been wearing their garments since putting them on at Verplanck's over a year before. Nevertheless, the men were determined to again prove themselves in combat. Shaw described how, fired up by the skirmish in the early morning, 'we were eager for a general engagement.'[76] He also recorded a short speech Cornwallis had given just prior to marching out of Camden the day before;

> Now, my brave soldiers, now an opportunity is offered for displaying your valour, and sustaining the glory of the British arms; – all you who are ambitious of military fame stand forward; for there are eight or ten to one coming against; – Let the man who cannot bear the smell of gun-powder stand back, and all you who are determined to conquer or die turn out.[77]

About 300 yards away from the thin line of Crown infantry, through the scattered pine trees and springy grass, the rebels likewise formed for battle. Gates deployed the Continentals of the 2nd Maryland Brigade and the Delaware regiment on his right, and the North Carolina militia and the Virginia militia on his left, with Armand's Legion behind them and some Continental light infantry covering his far left flank. He held the 1st Maryland Regiment in reserve, and spaced his seven artillery pieces, mostly brass 3- and 4-pounders, across his front line. The sun began to rise onto a morning fog that drifted between the pine trees, the air still and heavy ahead of what promised to be a hot day.

The rebels made the first move. Thinking that the British right wing was still deploying and that a rapid advance might catch them out, the Virginia

74 Lamb, *Memoire*, pp.90–91.
75 Urban, *Fusiliers*, p.205.
76 Shaw, *A Narrative*, p.29.
77 Shaw, *A Narrative*, p.28.

militia were ordered to advance. Ahead of them went 40 or 50 volunteers who, according to one Continental officer;

> would run forward of the brigade, and commence the attack. They were led forward, within forty or fifty yards of the enemy, and ordered to take trees, and keep up as brisk a fire as possible. The desired effect of this expedient, to exhort the enemy's fire at some distance, in order to the rendering it less terrible to the militia, was not gained.[78]

At about the same time, Gates ordered his artillery to open fire, shattering the dawn stillness and sending roundshot whipping between the trees. The Crown forces response was immediate. Cornwallis, spotting the advance of the Virginian militia, believed it was an effort to redeploy their own line and, much as Gates had done, ordered an advance in an effort to catch them before they were ready. Cornwallis rode personally to Webster and ordered him forward, an aide likewise going to Rawdon to order the same. As the British artillery answered their rebel counterparts, a general advance was conducted by the entire royal front line.

The skirmishers thrown out by the Virginian militia retired without having succeeded in drawing a premature volley from the light infantry or the 23rd opposing them. The Crown troops employed what had become their regular mode of warfare in the Americas, their open-order line advancing at a brisk pace through the trees.

The 33rd soon began to suffer casualties. The rebels had artillery on the roadway, which the regiment were immediately to the right of. As they closed the distance the Continental gunners switched to case shot, blasting cylinders of musket balls, like giant shotguns, towards the 33rd and the regiment to their immediate left, Rawdon's Volunteers of Ireland. One of the officers of the Volunteers vividly recalled;

> The enemy surpassed us in artillery, and threw in horrid showers of grape: this chiefly fell on ours, and the 33d regiment, (they having the post of honour), who were cut off amazingly. I commanded a company, and lost more than half the number I took into the field, and the company next me lost two thirds.[79]

It was the heaviest fire the 33rd had been under since Monmouth. Regardless, they pressed on.

Directly opposite the 33rd were the North Carolina militia, while the 23rd on their right were largely facing the Virginian militia. As Shaw went forward with his red-coated compatriots, moving at a brisk pace into the galling fire of the rebel artillery, one of the militiamen facing him left behind an account rare for its truthfulness and frankness. Williams Gipson recalled how the militia, almost none of whom had been in a pitched battle before, were suffering the aftereffects of their recent meal of molasses, were perspiring

---

78 Otho Williams, in Piecuch, *The Battle of Camden*, p.31.

79 Anon., 'Baltimore, Maryland, Aug. 29', *The Scots Magazine*, Volume XLII. (1780), pp.533–535.

in the rising heat, and had been ordered to operate in platoons rather than companies, a tactical distinction they were unused to.[80] Most saliently, they were unnerved by the rapid and confident approach of the British regulars who, Gipson recalled, 'appeared to manoeuvre in contempt of us.'[81]

The militia were under instruction to reserve their fire until they were given the word of command, but with the 33rd bearing down on him, Gipson panicked. In a later pension claim he recounted that; 'I can state on oath that I believed my gun was the first gun fired ... and I fired without thinking except that I might prevent the man opposite from killing me. The discharge and loud roar soon became general from one end of the lines to the other.'[82] Panicking, the militiamen blazed away too early. While Shaw recalled this fire as deadly, it is likely the vast majority of the shots missed their targets, and most of the casualties suffered at this point came from the rebel artillery on the militiamen's flank.

The 33rd did not make the same mistake by throwing away their shots. Shaw remembered how they approached to 100 yards of the militia line, writing 'we returned their fire, and immediately charged on them with the bayonet.'[83] The single volley was well delivered, with William Gipson admitting to 'a great many killed and wounded even on the first firing.'[84] Without pausing to reload, the British levelled their bayonets and charged forward. These were the same shock and awe tactics that had broken rebel armies from Canada to Georgia over the past five years, and they proved potent once again.

The militia ran. Gipson, again admitting to personal failings, left a vivid account of the panic and confusion that lies at the heart of almost every military engagement;

> I confess I was amongst the first that fled. The cause of that I cannot tell, except that everyone I saw was about to do the same. It was instantaneous. There was no effort to rally, no encouragement to fight. Officers and men joined in the flight. I threw away my gun, and, reflecting I might be punished for being found without arms, I picked up a drum, which gave forth such sounds when touched by the twigs I cast it away.[85]

The same had happened just to the 33rd's right, where the sudden and ferocious onset of the 23rd and the light infantry had immediately put the Virginian militia to flight. Their commander had attempted to 'put his men in mind of their bayonets' which, relatively unusually for militia, they were equipped with.[86] He cried out 'my brave fellows, you have bayonets as well as they, we'll charge them.' The militia did not seem to share his boldness – 'at that moment the British infantry charged bayonet with a shout: the Virginians

80 William Gipson, in Piecuch, *The Battle of Camden*, p.92.
81 William Gipson, in Piecuch, *The Battle of Camden*, p.91.
82 William Gipson, in Piecuch, *The Battle of Camden*, p.91.
83 Shaw, *A Narrative*, p.29.
84 William Gipson, in Piecuch, *The Battle of Camden*, p.91.
85 William Gipson, in Piecuch, *The Battle of Camden*, p.91.
86 Otho Williams, in Piecuch, *The Battle of Camden*, p.31.

threw down their arms, and run off as fast as possible.'[87] On the opposite side, one light infantry officer wrote of how his men 'regardless of their numbers, and with their usual bravery and undauntedness, gave a screech, that made the woods and vallies re-echo, and dashed with their bayonets into the center of them, as lions and tigers do at their prey.'[88]

One Continental lieutenant recalled that the British 'made a furious attack on our weakest position, where the militia were posted, being on the left of the front line. After the first fire they gave way and left the field, although they were commanded by officers of the Virginia [Continental] line, who had ever exertion to rally them, but all in vain; they left the field helter-skelter.'[89] Gates's deputy adjutant general, Colonel Otho Williams, witnessed how one militia officer;

> General Stevens, observing the enemy rush on, put his men in mind of their bayonets; but, the impetuosity with which they advanced, firing and huzzaing, threw the whole body of the militia into such a panic, that they generally threw down their loaded arms and fled, in the utmost consternation. The unworthy example of the Virginians was almost instantly followed by the North Carolinians.'[90]

Gates himself wrote 'the Militia had taken the woods in all direction.'[91] Some were so confused they actually ran into the British.

Gates and his staff were behind the militia line when the British fired and charged, and were consequently caught up in the stampede towards the rear. Gates reported rather lamely how the militia 'ran like a Torrent, and bore all before them … we were obliged to retreat with them … I concluded with General Caswell to retire towards Charlotte.'[92] Gates infamously proceeded to cover 180 miles in three days, beating his entire army to safety.

In reality, despite the collapse of the rebel left flank, the action was far from decided. Not quite all of the militia had given way. The North Carolinian rebels, closest to the Delaware Continentals and artillery just across the road from them, took heart from their regulars and stood their ground, firing three or so volleys. They could not stand for long though. The 33rd and possibly the left of the 23rd fell upon them with their fixed bayonets. Lamb wrote that their commander 'was twice wounded by a bayonet in bringing off his men: several of his regiment, and many of his brigade who were made prisoners had no wound except from bayonets.'[93]

By this point the conditions of the action had made it extremely difficult for anyone to discern what was actually happening. 'The morning being hazy,' Tarleton recollected, 'the smoke hung over, and involved both armies in such a cloud, that it was difficult to see or estimate the destruction on

87 William Moultrie, in Piecuch, *The Battle of Camden*, p.101.
88 Anon., Piecuch, *The Battle of Camden*, pp.95–96.
89 C.P. Bennett, in Piecuch, *The Battle of Camden*, p.70.
90 Otho Williams, in Piecuch, *The Battle of Camden*, p.31.
91 Horatio Gates, in Piecuch, *The Battle of Camden*, p.20.
92 Horatio Gates, in Piecuch, *The Battle of Camden*, p.20.
93 Lamb, *An Original and Authentic Journal*, p.304.

either side'[94] In his after-action report Cornwallis described 'a dead calm,' during the battle 'with a little haziness in the air, which prevented the smoke from rising, occasioned so thick a darkness, this it was difficult to see the effect of a very heavy and well-supported fire on both sides.'[95]

Through the smoke, stabbed through by the flames of musketry and cannon fire, it became apparent that while the royal troops had routed the enemy's left wing, on their right the opposite was close to occurring. There the Loyalist Provincials of the Volunteers of Ireland and the British Legion infantry, flanked by the Loyalist North Carolina Volunteers, were wavering in the face of the firepower of the Maryland and Delaware Continentals. The Congressional regulars actually advanced with the bayonet, driving the Loyalists back and possibly capturing an artillery piece. Likely sensing as much as actually seeing the danger, Cornwallis dashed to the point of decision. According to one of the Volunteers of Ireland he cried out to the regiment, 'Volunteers of Ireland, you are fine fellows! Charge the rascals – by heaven you behave nobly!'[96] With the Continentals threatening their flag, the Loyalists pushed back, and furious, close-range combat developed. Tarleton wrote of how the Continentals, with 'small arms and artillery, continued a heavy and well-directed fire upon the 33d regiment and the whole of the left division.'[97]

The 33rd and 23rd had caved the enemy's left, but now they had to salvage their own left. This was easier said than done, as the initial firing and charging that had driven off the militia would undoubtedly had left the widely-spaced ranks even more scattered. Reforming the line, wheeling left, and then pressing onto a further attack in the midst of stifling heat and smoke required the steadiness that regulars were renowned for. Cornwallis wrote that 'our line continued to advance in good order, and with the cool intrepidity of experienced British soldiers, keeping up a constant fire, or making use of bayonets as opportunities offered.'[98]

The 33rd assailed the left flank of the Continentals, who brought up their reserve and attempted to refuse the left of their line. The engagement lasted about half an hour, a crashing crescendo to a hard-fought battle. By the end of it the Continental resistance had collapsed, and the commander left behind by Gates, Major General Johann de Kalb, had been both shot three and bayonetted eight times in the wild melee. In the end, after a stubborn resistance, the Continentals were broken as thoroughly as the militia had been before them.

At this point, Cornwallis unleashed Tarleton and his British Legion dragoons. Camden was one of the only pitched battles of the Revolutionary War that was followed by a vigorous and ruthless cavalry pursuit, the convention in more standard European warfare. Shaw recalled the 33rd opening their ranks to the left and right to allow the cavalry to pass through

94 Tarleton, *A History*, p.110.
95 Charles Cornwallis, in Piecuch, *The Battle of Camden*, p.54.
96 Anon., 'Baltimore', p.533.
97 Tarleton, *A History*, p.110.
98 Charles Cornwallis, in Piecuch, *The Battle of Camden*, pp.54–55.

without disrupting the formation. The Legion lived up to its deadly reputation as it pursued the scattering militia and Continentals for miles, looting Gates's baggage as they went. 'Victory declared in our favour,' Shaw wrote.[99]

Consolidation

It was indeed a victory, perhaps the most complete won by the Crown in a pitched battle during the war. Cornwallis's after-action report listed 68 men dead, 245 wounded and 11 missing. Congressional losses are more difficult to tabulate, but likely stood at around 900 killed and wounded and 1,000 missing. All the artillery and baggage fell into the hands of the royal army.

The 33rd suffered more than any other regiment. Advancing into the teeth of the Continental artillery, and then going toe-to-toe with Continental infantry for a half hour resulted in 18 men killed and 81 wounded, as well as one man missing. The Volunteers of Ireland, who had fought next to them and suffered the second-highest losses, listed 17 men killed and 70 wounded.[100] The two regiments combined accounted for over half the casualties suffered by the royal army – indeed, nearly half the 33rd had been killed or wounded, a casualty rate of 42 percent. For the regiment, it was the bloodiest battle of the war.

The losses suffered by the 33rd's officer cadre also indicate the fury of the fighting. Captain Allen Malcom, formerly a lieutenant in the 43rd's light company who had only joined the regiment two months earlier, was killed, and lieutenants George Wynyard and James L. Harvey and Ensign John-Wheeler Collington were wounded. Lieutenant Colonel Webster was lightly wounded. Captain Richard Cotton, who had previously served as a lieutenant in the light company under Dansey, was also badly wounded. Despite a newspaper report claiming hopefully that he 'was in a fair way to recover,' he eventually died on 30 September.[101] However, the losses had earned a victory. Roger Lamb of the 23rd later wrote that 'in the account of the battle of Camden, particular mention ought to have been made of the 33d regiment. The services which they rendered on that day, were long the theme of the soldiers and officers present.'[102]

The destruction of Gates's grand army wrecked Congressional plans in South Carolina for the second time in three months. Cornwallis, however, was unable to capitalise. In the aftermath of the battle he complained to Clinton that sickness was still so prevalent that every officer on his staff was incapable of doing duty. Nor did it simply mean that some troops were temporarily out of action. While Gates had been moving south, rebel militia had captured 100 sick soldiers being moved down the Peedee River to receive treatment at Georgetown.[103] When soldiers were left behind, they became

99 Shaw, *A Narrative*, p.29.

100 Tarleton, *A History*, p.196.

101 *Morning Post*, 11 October 1780, p.2.

102 Lamb, *An Original and Authentic Journal*, p.438.

103 Peter McCandless, *Slavery, Disease, and Suffering in the Southern Lowcountry* (Cambridge: Cambridge University Press, 2011), p.96.

easy prey for the groups of partisans that constantly shadowed Crown forces. Cornwallis found he was forced to guard his sick men, who were vulnerable to capture at the hands of rebel partisans, and so could not move forward to take advantage of his victory.[104]

Consequently, rather than striking north after his defeated enemy, Cornwallis moved first to Waxhaws, which he was informed would provide a healthier environment and a possible reprieve from the fevers plaguing the army. It was to no avail. A potential advance into North Carolina was delayed not only because of a lack of wagons to transport sick soldiers, but also because Tarleton himself was struck down with what one of his subordinates described as yellow fever. In the Carolina countryside, cavalry was king, and without Tarleton – who was quickly acquiring a talismanic reputation with Cornwallis – there could be little in the way of offensive operations.

In late September Cornwallis decided to move on the settlement of Charlotte, which lay close to the border between North and South Carolina. He laid out his plans to Clinton:

> I mean, as soon as Lieutenant-colonel Tarleton can be removed, to proceed with the 23d, 33d, volunteers of Ireland, and legion, to Charlotte town, and leave the 71st here [at Waxhaws] until the sick can be brought on to us. I then mean to make some redoubts, and establish a fixed post at that place, and give the command of it to Major Wemyss, whose regiments [the 63rd] is so totally demolished by sickness, that it will not be fit for actual service for some months.[105]

At Charlotte militia forces put up a short but sharp resistance before melting away, leaving the settlement to the Crown. Worse was to come. Major Patrick Ferguson, who had served alongside the 33rd on several occasions, including at Verplanck's and during the siege of Charleston, had been dispatched west to help raise Loyalist militia forces. On 7 October he was surrounded by rebel militia at Kings Mountain. After a desperate stand his force was killed or captured, and Ferguson himself was shot dead as he attempted one last charge. The defeat convinced Cornwallis that a move into North Carolina would be premature. He requested reinforcements from Clinton and moved the army into winter quarters at the settlement of Winnsboro, south of Charlotte and north-west of Camden.

Time to rest and refit was much needed. The regiment's clothing was in a particularly sorry state. Late November through early December saw Cornwallis exchange a flurry of anxious letters with Rawdon regarding the arrival of new materials from Britain to garb his men. On 25 November Cornwallis wrote that 'in regard to the cloathing coming up I can only say that the regiments are in the utmost want of it. Therefore the safest and speediest method will be best. The 71st are quite naked.'[106] The next day he added 'in regard to the cloathing, you know the greatest importance it is to us. If it was to be lost, the 33rd and 71st Regiments would be rendered

104 McNeill, *Mosquito Empires*, p.214.
105 Tarleton, *A History*, p.196.
106 Saberton (ed.), *The Cornwallis Papers*, vol.3, p.172.

totally unfit for service. I cannot guess how many waggons would be wanted to bring it by land.'[107] Rawdon reported on 27 November that 'the necessaries for the 33rd and 71st are arrived and shall be forwarded as soon as possible. Seven puncheons of rum have likewise come up, four of which are on their road to your Lordship' and the next day 'the cloathing for the 33rd is arrived at McChord's [ferry over the Santee]. As many waggons as can be collected shall be sent for it without delay.'[108] In the event 10 wagons were required, setting out at daybreak for Winnsboro on 29 November. They may have miscarried, and five wagons sent by Cornwallis for the 71st clothing actually returned with that of the 33rd's. Cornwallis complained that unless the 71st's clothing was found he was 'much afraid it [the regiment] will soon be unfit for service.'[109] A possible solution presented itself, with a suggestion that 'some men of the 71st who are reported to be in such a state as to be unfit for service this winter but who by quiet quarters may be rendered usefull by the spring' could be redeployed to Charleston, to garrison Sullivan's Island, where no hard campaigning was expected. On 4 December Cornwallis wrote that 'the cloathing of the 33rd and rum is arrived. The twelve waggons return tomorrow to McChord's in quest of the 71st cloathing and any thing else that my offer.'[110] Finally on 11 December it was reported that 'the cloathing of the 71st is arrived and every regiment here has received its winter appointments.'[111] All that remained was the arrival of reinforcements.

Fresh forces arrived under the command of Lieutenant Colonel Alexander Leslie who, at the end of October, had led a strong raiding force from New York down the coast to Virginia. He did this on Clinton's orders, to divert rebel attention away from Cornwallis's activities in South Carolina. After news of the loss of Ferguson and his Loyalists at Kings Mountain reached British commanders, however, Leslie was ordered south to join Cornwallis directly, providing a reinforcement of over 2,000 men. It was a desperately needed addition, as Washington had dispatched arguably his most able subordinate, Nathanael Greene, south with a fresh force of Continentals to end British progress once and for all. Leslie's detachment landed at Charleston on 16 December and marched for the interior.

Ahead of Leslie's forces also came new recruits. Back in Britain the 33rd's Additional Companies had been busy as ever, with a detachment of four officers, two sergeants, one drummer and 114 newly-trained private men arriving as part of the fresh deployment, the largest provided for any one regiment at the end of 1780. Cornwallis wrote that 'the recruits I should wish to join their regiments as soon as they conveniently can, but with good cloaths on their back and a good supply of necessaries.'[112] As far as the 33rd were concerned the latter two points were a guarantee. The recruits of the new regiments variously arrived from Britain were inspected upon their arrival

107 Saberton (ed.), *The Cornwallis Papers*, vol.3, p.172.
108 Saberton (ed.), *The Cornwallis Papers*, vol.3, pp.179–180.
109 Saberton (ed.), *The Cornwallis Papers*, vol.3, p.192.
110 Saberton (ed.), *The Cornwallis Papers*, vol.3, p.193.
111 Saberton (ed.), *The Cornwallis Papers*, vol.3, p.194.
112 Saberton (ed.), *The Cornwallis Papers*, vol.3, p.218.

The cartridge pouch, worn on the right hip, should not be confused with the smaller cartridge box typically worn on the belly or slung under one arm. Most pouches held 29 or 36 rounds. Photo Credit: Henry Gage.

in America in October 1780 by a board of field officers. The state of each regiment's recruits was recorded, marked with comments such as 'indifferent,' or 'some good some very bad,' or 'one suit bad, rest indifft' depending on how well they were uniformed. Only one regiment was described as 'very good' – the 33rd.[113] This shows that even late in the war, the regiment was maintaining the same high standard of dress that had led to General Guy Carleton to state that recruits of the 33rd who had arrived at Quebec instead of New York in 1777 could not be drafted into other regiments, as paying to replace their uniforms would be cost-prohibitive.

The replacements were much-needed. As the 33rd set to fitting their new clothes and welcoming the new arrivals ahead of their next campaign, the influx combined with the recovery of the sick and wounded after Camden brought their numbers up to 328 rank-and-file fit for duty.[114]

They would need every man ahead of their final major campaign in America.

113 TNA: WO 1/10: State of Recruits Inspected by a Board of Field Officers, Long Island, October 24, 1780.

114 Paul E. Kopperman, 'The Medical Dimension in Cornwallis's Army, 1780–1781' *The North Carolina Historical Review*, vol.89, no.4, 2012, pp.367–398.

Chapter 11

To the End of the World

1781

The weather in the Carolinas meant that armies were not confined to winter quarters for as long as they were in the northern colonies, but the beginning of Cornwallis's 1781 campaign still took longer to get underway than the British commander had hoped. A desire to strike out north was tempered by the need to wait for Leslie's reinforcements.

On New Year's Day Cornwallis dispatched Tarleton in an effort to pin partisan commander Daniel Morgan, who had been sent by Nathanael Greene to threaten the British line of supply. Cornwallis wished to support Tarleton, but still had to wait for Leslie, who reached Camden on 4 January and then turned north after Cornwallis. The 33rd were shifted with what remained of Cornwallis's force along Broad River to Bull Run.

Deciding he had waited long enough, Cornwallis set off on 8 January from Winnsborough after Tarleton and Morgan. On 18 January the army was at Turkey Creek, a branch of the Broad River, when Leslie and his forces finally reached them. The good news was heavily tempered, for by then disaster had struck. Tarleton, convinced as ever in his own abilities, had hunted down Morgan and thrown himself against the rebel's combined force of militia and Continentals without waiting for Cornwallis. The result was the Battle of Cowpens, where Tarleton's command of just over 1,000 men was routed. A clash of such modest size might hardly have constituted a skirmish in the northern colonies, but in the south, where the tiny number of Crown forces were already spread desperately thin, it was a grievous blow. Leslie's fresh troops reached Cornwallis at much the same time as Tarleton and his survivors were straggling in. Realising that the loss at Cowpens had to be avenged quickly if the reputation of the royal army was to be maintained, and that Morgan was now attempting to escape with about 600 prisoners, Cornwallis launched himself after the rebel partisan leader.

The only problem was that, initially, he launched himself in the wrong direction. Believing that Morgan was circling south, Cornwallis set off over Buffalo Creek and the Little Broad River, whereas Morgan in fact headed over the Catawba and into western North Carolina. After discovering the mistake,

After the first few years of the war, goatskin knapsacks like this one seem to have been largely replaced by canvas or cloth ones. (Photo by Henry Gage)

Cornwallis changed course but struggled to make headway with his baggage in an area that was little more than wilderness. The Crown forces' pace was ponderous, managing only 72 miles in a week compared to Morgan's 100 in five days.[1] Heavy rains made the march even more difficult, swelling the numerous waterways that intersected the route of the royal army. Tarleton reported that 'the train of waggons that now attended them [the army] met with great obstacles on the march, which considerably impeded the progress of the army.'[2] While Cornwallis, writing to Germain, partially blamed 'the swelling of the numberless creeks in our way.'[3]

The army paused to collect itself at Ramseur's Mill, north-west of Charlotte, finding that Morgan was two days ahead. Cornwallis decided upon a bold expedient. He ordered the army's baggage train to be torched. Only wagons with hospital stores, salt, ammunition, and four reserved for carrying the sick and wounded, were spared. Cornwallis wrote that 'though at the expense of a great deal of officers' baggage, and of all prospect in future of rum, and even a regular supply of provisions to the soldiers, I must, in justice to this army, say that there was the most general and cheerful acquiescence.'[4] One Loyalist officer commented that 'such was the ardour both of officers and soldiers, and their willingness to submit to any hardship for the promotion of the service; that this arrangement, which deprived them of all future prospect of spiritous liquors, and even hazarded a regular supply of provisions, was acquiesced in without a murmur.'[5] That Cornwallis was willing to torch his own baggage and that of his officers cemented his reputation as a fighting general who was willing to share in the hardships of the most difficult form of campaigning – operating in winter, in wooded and sparsley populated country, with next to no supply train.[6] Cornwallis responded with speed to the defeat and Cowpens and, in the opinion of Stanley D.M. Carpenter, 'simply converted his entire army into a light, highly manoeuvrable, and agile striking force.'[7]

The royal army remained at Ramseur's Mill for three days, preparing itself for the trial ahead. Brigade orders issued on 26 January advised;

> There being a sufficient quantity of leather to complete the brigade in shoes in this village, it is recommended to, (and expected) the commanding officers of companies see their men's shoes immediately soled and repaired, and if possible, that every man, when they move from this ground, take in his blanket, one pair of spare soles, as the like opportunity may not happen for some time.[8]

1 Stanley D.M. Carpenter, *Southern Gambit: Cornwallis and the British March to Yorktown* (Norman: University of Oklahoma Press, 2019), p.175.
2 Tarleton, *A History*, p.267.
3 Tarleton, *A History*, p.267.
4 Tarleton, *A History*, p.268.
5 Charles Stedman, *The History of the Origin, Progress, and Termination of the American War* (London: Murray, Debrett, Kerby: 1794), vol.II, p.326.
6 Stedman, *The History of the Origin*, vol.II, p.325.
7 Carpenter, *Southern Gambit*, p.177.
8 E.W. Caruthers, *Interesting Revolutionary Incidents* (Philadelphia: Hayes and Zell, 1856), p.395.

A return 'of such sick men as are absolutely unable to march, and a return of such men as are by lameness bad marchers' was made. As well as shoes, gaiters were made or repaired and the men were ordered to 'clean and wash themselves thoroughly.' They were reminded that 'when, upon any occasion, the troops may be ordered to march without their packs, it is not intended they should leave their camp-kettles and tomahawks behind them' – items that could not be abandoned if the army was to live off the land.[9] The 33rd provided their share of guard details to cover foraging parties that ranged the surrounding countryside. John Robert Shaw recalled how he 'turned baker for the guard, *(and a little for myself)*,' assigned to turning the flour being collected by the army into bread.[10] The excess that he ate would be the last good quantity of food he received for some time.

A letter from George Germain bearing the king's praise following the news about the victory at Camden five months earlier was read to the men. On the 27 January an extra gill of rum was issued, prior to the destruction of the supply along with the rest of the baggage.

At 11:00 a.m. on 28 January, the army moved out. Continental general Nathanael Greene was moving in close support of Morgan, and the militia had been called out to contest the river crossings that awaited the royal army. Cornwallis's intention now was not just to catch Morgan, but to chase down Greene and win a second Camden before the Continentals could cross the Dan River and reach the safety of Virginia. Charles O'Hara, an officer in the Guards who had joined the main army with Leslie's reinforcements, summed up the grim determination that suffused the Crown army ahead of arguably their most difficult campaign, in an oft-quoted passage; 'without baggage, necessaries, or provisions of any sort for officer of soldier, in the most barren, inhospitable, unhealthy part of North America, opposed to the most savage, inveterate, perfidious, cruel enemy, with zeal and with bayonets only, it was resolved to follow Greene's army to the end of the world.'[11]

The Race to the Dan

The army approached the fords over the Catawba and found them already occupied by rebel militia covering Greene's withdrawal. Cornwallis addressed the troops with instructions regarding the expected difficulties of keeping the army supplied;

> Lord Cornwallis has so often experienced the zeal and good will of the troops, that he has not the smallest doubt that the officers and soldiers will most cheerfully submit to the inconveniences which must naturally attend a war so remote from water-carriage and the magazines of the army. The supply of rum for a time will be absolutely impossible, and that of meal very uncertain. To

9 Caruthers, *Interesting Revolutionary Incidents*, pp.394–396.
10 Shaw, *A Narrative*, p.34.
11 Spring, *Zeal*, p.24.

> remedy the latter, it is recommended either to bruise Indian corn, or to rasp it after it has been soaked.[12]

On 29 January the men received 'any portion of salt they can conveniently carry with them,' which was predicted to last them for 20 days. It was warned that 'the delivery of provisions will probably be very irregular.' Expecting a fight, the men were directed to 'wash, clean and repair their necessaries, and that the ammunition is properly inspected and dried on the men's blankets in the sun, at a distance from the fire, and return per battalion given in of all damaged cartridges.'[13]

Cornwallis resolved to cross the Catawba at Cowan's ford. Hoping to distract the militia defending it with a diversion, he detached Webster with the 33rd, a battalion of the 71st, a force of Loyalists, jäger, several 6-pounder cannon and all the remaining wagons towards Beattie's ford, six miles above Cowan's. They marched out at daybreak on a dark and rainy morning on 1 February. It was not long before they realised that their effort at deception was in vain – despite the hoped-for distraction of cannon fire over Beattie's, the militia had concentrated at Cowan's, where Cornwallis, bold and aggressive as ever, decided to force the crossing over the rain-swollen river.

As the main body of the army fought its way over at Cowan's, the 33rd's crossing at Beattie's was uncontested. Getting not only the men but the wagons across 'had become tedious and difficult by the continuance of the rain and the swelling of the river,' but eventually the Catawba was crossed, and the 33rd re-joined the main body of the army which had successfully fought its way over Cowan's, reaching them soon after dark.[14]

The chase continued, now towards the next swollen waterway, the Yadkin. On the way, troops used rail fences for firewood and burned several houses, much to Cornwallis's frustration. The rebels were narrowly able to get across the Yadkin before being caught, taking all available boats and ferries with them. Forced to pause once again, the royal army remained for a while at the settlement of Salisbury. Shaw remembered finding the place deserted by the enemy, 'leaving only a few sick tories [Loyalists] in jail, to die for want of water; and all the provisions they had were a few pounds of salt beef.'[15] In Salisbury Cornwallis again reproached his army for 'the most shocking complaints of the excesses committed by the troops.'[16] The difficulties of living off the land were starting to tell as, at times, foraging gave way to outright looting.[17]

After two days at Salisbury the army set off again at 6:00 a.m. on 6 February. A captain and 100 men from Webster's brigade were detailed with an officer and 50 Hessians from the Regiment von Bose and 13 dragoons were ordered to form a rearguard to sweep up stragglers. Orders specified

12 Caruthers, *Interesting Revolutionary Incidents*, p.397.
13 Caruthers, *Interesting Revolutionary Incidents*, p.399.
14 Tarleton, *A History*, p.270.
15 Shaw, *A Narrative*, p.31.
16 Tarleton, *A History*, p.405.
17 Urban, *Fusiliers*, p.230.

that 'any officer who looks on with indifference, and does not do his utmost to prevent the shameful marauding which has of late prevailed in the army, will be considered in a more criminal light than the persons who commit those scandalous crimes.'[18] On the evening of 7 February the army forded the Yadkin.

At this point the royal force was passing through an area of North Carolina that had been settled by Moravians, a group of German and Czech Protestants – the descendants of famed medieval Czech reformer Jan Hus – who had worked hard to remain neutral during the conflagration of the American Revolution. The Moravians were particularly famed for their distilling of whisky, and John Robert Shaw recalled that the 33rd were encamped 'one night on a rising ground contiguous to one of these [Moravian] towns, the inhabitants of which were very generous in rolling out their whiskey-barrels to make us drunk.' The regiment's discipline, strained by hard marches through mud and rain and the interminable crossings of rivers and creeks, appears to have momentarily broken down, with Shaw supposing 'that there were not fifty sober men among us; for it was a very rainy night, and we had suffered much for want of drink, as well as through fatigue.'[19] The problem was born out by orders from Cornwallis who, 'having perceived that many soldiers from different corps are coming into town, and seemingly for the purpose of getting liquor; He begs it may be told to the men that if they commit such irregularities, he shall not think it necessary to trouble the Commissaries in providing any more rum for them.'[20]

Alcohol, and indeed outright alcoholism, was a recurring problem not just for the British Army but eighteenth-century British society in general. Drunkenness was a socially accepted form of relaxation among all classes of people during the period, and these intemperate attitudes carried over into the military.[21] From 1777 onwards rum was issued daily as standard practice, resulting in the consumption by the army in North America of 360,000 gallons a year.[22] Officers had to balance alcohol consumption, widely considered a soldier's just reward, with excesses that harmed the service. Soldiers' pay was carefully regulated so that they did not receive large lump sums, primarily because officers knew much of it would be immediately spent on alcohol. Despite these efforts, days when soldiers were paid tended to be marred by drunkenness, and while regiments rarely became so as heavily intoxicated as Shaw claimed the 33rd were in early February 1781, infractions relating to – and most often, caused by – alcohol were commonplace.[23]

The stumbling misfortunates of one intoxicated soldier of the 33rd illustrates the issue. At the end of August 1777, not long before the Battle of Brandywine, one of the 33rd's light infantrymen under Captain Dansey, Daniel Hallewell, was confined to the quarter guard for 'irregular behaviour.'

18 Tarleton, *A History*, pp.407–408.
19 Shaw, *A Narrative*, pp.33–34.
20 Tarleton, *A History*, p.408.
21 Frey, *The British Soldier in America*, p.63.
22 Frey, *The British Soldier in America*, p.63.
23 Conway, *The British Army*, p.88.

He somehow succeeded in escaping, and was later seen by a picket collapsing in the road. When challenged 'what he was doing there at that time of the Night, he said he was come down with grog for his Comrade Freeman, and asked if he … knew where he was posted Centry.' The picket said he was uncertain, but believed it to be further right along the line. Shortly afterwards, the same picket 'heard a Noise among the leaves.' Having issued a challenge that went unanswered, he attempted to fire, but the flint of his musket failed to strike sparks. Deciding to investigate further rather than try to fire again, the picket discovered Hallewell once more – 'he asked him what he was about, and he told him he was endeavoring to find his way to the Battalion. That as he had no suspicion of his having an intention to desert, he advised him to go straight home and shewed him the way… And he adds that [Hallewell] was in liquor.' A little later, as the sun was coming up, the intoxicated Hallewell appeared before another group of pickets and, on being challenged, claimed variously that he 'had come down to wash a Shirt' and that 'he had come down in the Night to get a Canteen full of Water & had lost his way.'[24] He was promptly seized and restrained.

The details of Hallewell's drunken escapades are recorded in his subsequent trial for desertion. Fortunately for Hallewell, the officers acting a judge and jury decided that he had not been attempting to desert while he had wandered out of camp, influenced by the fact that he had at least attempted to return, and that he, by his own admission, 'was so much in liquor that he did not know what he was about 'till Monday morning [the next day].'[25] The decision appears to have been the correct one, as Hallewell continued to serve in the 33rd until 1791 before spending a further six years in another regiment. Not without reason did Shaw write that 'all the world knows that a soldier's chief delight is in drinking.'[26]

Fortunately, rebel forces were in no position to take advantage of the inebriated state of parts of Cornwallis's army in early February 1781. Greene was still intent on escaping across the Dan, but Cornwallis was now bearing down on him. The royal army marched 24 miles on 13 February and 22 the next day. Baggage and knapsacks – every encumbrance bar weapons and canteens – were left to those who were too sick or lame to carry on, who were in turn instructed to give their shoes to those who could still march and whose footwear had come apart, and so, in the words of historian Mark Urban, 'those who could march did so, in many cases in the shoes of those who could not.'[27] Shaw recalled the desperate circumstances, highlighted by the want of food – 'no forage – no provisions for our men, though marching day and night. At this time I saw an English guinea offered for a bit of corn-bread, no larger than my two fingers – Hard times with us indeed – 16 days without a morsel of bread.'[28]

24 TNA: WO 71/84: Courts Martial Proceedings, pp.209–214.

25 TNA: WO 71/84: Courts Martial Proceedings, pp.209–214.

26 Shaw, *A Narrative*, p.33.

27 Urban, *Fusiliers*, p.231.

28 Shaw, *A Narrative*, p.34. Shaw's narrative after Camden becomes somewhat garbled and non-linear for a time, and he misremembers several place names. It seems this description falls either during the race to the Dan, or just after it.

Ultimately, the efforts of the small royal army were in vain. On 15 February they arrived at the Dan and discovered that Green had made it over the day before. Having marched his army almost to breaking point, Cornwallis finally conceded the race. After a day's rest he turned back into the interior of North Carolina, marching 50 miles south to the settlement of Hillsborough. Here Cornwallis hoped to gather supplies and, most importantly, rally Loyalists to the Crown's cause.

The efforts proved in vain. It was not that North Carolina was avowedly pro-Congress – Hillsborough was the seat of the old Regulator movement, whose adherents had no love for the colonial elite now leading the rebellion, and the response from the North Carolina militia in support of Greene had hardly been overwhelming. However, after five years of fighting and suppression, most of North Carolina's inhabitants would rather wait and see who emerged victorious before lending their assistance. Some claimed that the exhausted appearance of the royal army further dissuaded support. Tarleton wrote bitterly that;

> Soon after the King's standard was erected at Hillsborough, many hundred inhabitants of the surrounding districts rode into the British camp to talk over the proclamation, inquire the news of the day, and take a view of the King's troops. The generality of these visitants seemed desirous of peace but averse to every exertion that might tend to procure it. They acknowledged the Continentals were chased out of the province, but they declared they soon expected them to return and the dread of violence and persecution prevented their taking a decided part in a cause which yet appeared dangerous.[29]

Hillsborough would not be the epicentre of royal revival in North Carolina. The only positive was that the army had at least left behind the sickness that had so literally plagued it during the summer in South Carolina. A surgeon of the 71st wrote that;

> The army travelled over a great extent of country, and was considered by many as performing very hard service; but I have the satisfaction to add, that notwithstanding occasional forced marches, wading of rivers, exposure to rain, accidental scarcity of bread, and no great profusion of beef, with the total want of rum, the troops enjoyed in general a most perfect state of health.[30]

While living in their brush wigwams just outside Hillsborough, Shaw related an incident that would have been familiar to fighting men in armies all through the ages. The account, a small window into the day-to-day life and camaraderie of ordinary British soldiers during the Revolution, deserves to be told in full;

29 Tarleton, *A History*, p.237.

30 Robert Jackson, *A Treatise on the Fevers of Jamaica* (Philadelphia: Robert Campbell, 1795), p.198.

> There was a certain Bill Airton, a butcher, who was a mess-mate of mine, and had often endeavoured to provoke me to a fight; but as I always considered him a stouter man than myself, and being besides unacquainted with the art of boxing, (as it is called) I had constantly declined his invitations, and endeavoured to keep clear of all private quarrels. It happened, however, one day, when myself and several of my companions had made a fire before our wigwam, that Mr. Airton, who had been absent while the fuel was gathering, came up to the fire, and in a very abrubt manner, says to me, 'Shaw, d--n you stand back, you have no right here; d--n you stand back.' – giving me at the same time such a blow in the eye, as made my head sing psalms for some time. The sergeant then coming up, and understanding the circumstance, says 'Shaw you must fight and whip him, or else I will whip you.' So we buckled to it in our buff; and having a good second helped the cause very much on my side; for a good officer makes a good soldier. Inspired with confidence through the encouragement of the sergeant, I soon gave Mr. Airton an Irishman's coat of arms, i.e. '*Two black eyes and a bloody nose*,' which made him a good friend ever after.[31]

The regiment would be in need of such rough-and-tumble esprit de corps, for by mid-February the balance of power was tipping once more. Greene had not only escaped, but had drawn Cornwallis deep into hostile territory, his baggage destroyed and his army now isolated at Hillsborough. As reinforcements flocked to him, Greene re-crossed the Dan, cautiously switching from hunted to hunter. Lack of support and provisions meant Cornwallis could remain in Hillsborough no longer, with the men reduced to killing and eating a number of the draught horses. On 26 February Cornwallis crossed the Haw River and made camp near Alamance Creek, in such a position as to both threaten Greene and withdraw towards the British-held costal town of Wilmington, as the need arose.

With a battle now looming, both armies jockeyed for position. Greene hoped to draw Cornwallis into a pitched battle on ground he had already assessed near Guildford Courthouse, though not before the arrival of further reinforcements. Lack of provisions continued to afflict the royal army. Shaw left an account of the efforts of soldiers in the 33rd to make ends meet;

> The scarcity of provisions was so great that we had but one pound of flour for six men per day with very little beef, and no salt the half of the time. With this allowance my mess-mates and I made two meals a day, which we managed by first boiling our beef, and then taking it out, and having mixed our pound of flour with some water, we put it into the kettle in which the beef had been boiled; and when sufficiently heated we took it off the fire, and let it stand until it cooled. This served us for breakfast, and the beef we kept for dinner; and as for supper we were obliged to do without it.[32]

Greene continued to manoeuvre his forces to keep Cornwallis guessing about their exact size and location. Otho Williams, one of the survivors of Camden,

31 Shaw, *A Narrative*, p.35.
32 Shaw, *A Narrative*, p.37.

Among their many other duties, NCOs oversaw the dolling out of food and rations on a daily basis. (Photo by Henry Gage)

was sent with a strong detachment to keep close to the royal army and harass it. There were a number of small skirmishes. On 2 March foraging British Legion dragoons detected Williams's vanguard, consisting of Henry Lee's Continental cavalry and supporting riflemen, near Clapp's Mill, on the same side of the Alamance. Aggressive as ever, Tarleton assembled a detachment consisting of the British Legion, the light company of the Guards, and 150 men of Webster's brigade. Exactly what regiments from the brigade this detachment was comprised of was not recorded, but it was led by the 33rd's Captain James Ingram, who had taken over from the fallen Allan Malcolm, and presumably therefore included a number of other men from the 33rd.

The small force marched towards Clapp's Mill in column, the Guards' light infantry in front, followed by Ingram's men, then the British Legion cavalry, who were hemmed in by woodland and thick undergrowth. Alerted to the Crown forces approach, Lee laid an ambush, hitting the light company from the trees on either side. Tarleton related the action which followed. 'The guards formed with their usual alacrity, and Captain Ingram, of the 33d regiment, who commanded the hundred and fifty men of Webster's brigade, was directed to dress his left by their right, whilst the cavalry moved to his right, where the country appeared more favourable for their exertions.'[33]

With Ingram's men forming up to the right of the light infantry, and the cavalry taking to the less heavily wooded ground to their right in turn, a

33 Tarleton, *A History*, p.242.

short firefight ensued. One rebel described being 'so hampered with thick underbrush' and noted 'a smart firing commenced and after 3 or 4 rounds, our line gave way.'[34] The rebels withdrew to the succour of Williams's main force, the royal troops pursuing only 500 yards through the difficult terrain. The royal losses amounted to 21 killed and wounded – including one soldier of the 33rd killed, John Bowes – the enemy likely similar, with Tarleton reporting higher losses among their riflemen, who were abandoned by the enemy cavalry. The regulars foraged the area then withdrew back to Cornwallis's main body.

The next day the detachment was again sent out, with more cavalry and 80 jäger, two 6-pounders and the Hessian Regiment von Bose. They formed an advanced post that could forage in close proximity to the enemy and spent an uncomfortable night in what Tarleton described as a 'delicate and ticklish situation,' with skirmishes occurring between the sentries throughout the hours of darkness.[35] They pulled back to the main force the next day.

On 6 March Cornwallis resolved to probe in Greene's direction in force. Webster's brigade comprised the core of the force sent against Williams at Whitesell's (often spelled Wetzell's) Mill. In thick fog, the 23rd, 33rd and 71st got close to the rebel pickets and initially drove them in. Riflemen and dragoons under Lee were dispatched to give the royal offensive pause, which they succeeded in doing until the pickets had withdrawn over Reedy Fork, where Williams was preparing for battle. Deciding the waterway was indefensible, Williams began to withdraw, leaving a rearguard to contest the Crown forces crossing. Webster was ordered into line, with the Guards' light infantry and jäger providing support. This force attacked the last of the rebel rearguard, consisting of about 150 Virginian militia. Shaw was in amongst the action with the 33rd, and remembered 'we came up with the enemy by the river side, and having formed a line, we [ex]changed a few shots, and then advanced to give them the bayonet; but they retreated and crossed the river.'[36]

Over the river, Lee's rearguard stood its ground. Among them were veteran riflemen of the action at Kings Mountain, whom Lee had posted in a log schoolhouse to the right of the ford. The regulars began to push over the creek, but were driven back on their first attempt by a fusillade of musket and rifle fire. 'We had a standing fight,' Shaw recalled.[37] The Crown infantry reformed, covered by artillery firing from a hillside overlooking their bank of the creek. They pushed once more into the waters.

The Kings Mountain riflemen in the schoolhouse had ripped the mud from between the log walls, allowing them to slide their long-barrelled weapons through and take aim without exposing themselves. In an account related by Lee, they watched as a British general officer, assumed to be Lieutenant Colonel Webster, 'rode up, and in a loud voice addressing his

34 Joseph Graham, in J.D. Lewis, *NC Patriots 1775–1783: Their Own Words* (Little River: J.D. Lewis, 2012), vol.2, pt.1, p.347.

35 Tarleton, *A History*, p.243.

36 Shaw, *A Narrative*, p.37.

37 Shaw, *A Narrative*, p.37.

soldiers, then rushed down the hill at their head, and plunged into the water, our fire pouring upon him.'[38]

The riflemen in the schoolhouse had been ordered to wait for just such an opportunity. They 'singled him [the officer] out as their mark. The stream being deep, and the bottom rugged, he advanced slowly; his soldiers on each side of him, and apparently some of them holding his stirrup leathers.'[39] As Webster and the rallied 33rd struggled through the water the riflemen began to fire 'one by one, each man sure of knocking him over; and having reloaded, eight or nine of them emptied their guns a second time at the same object. Strange to tell, though in a condition so perilous, himself and horse were untouched; and having crossed the creek, he soon formed his troops and advanced upon us.'[40]

Shaw wrote that 'we had orders not to cross the river, yet… would not be stopped by anything. So we crossed the Rocky Ford, and hot work we had; but we beat them off and formed a line on the same side of the river which they had occupied.'[41] Further to the right the 23rd and 71st had managed to ford the creek with only minimal opposition, but the schoolhouse and woods directly opposite the 33rd proved a sterner test. Under Webster's direction however and with the support of the Guards' light infantry, the regiment advanced and drove off the enemy. Shaw reported they 'soon put them to flight, and pursued them for 14 miles, until we lost sight of them.'[42] Lee admitted that 'the enemy's column being now formed, soon dislodged our centre … the British halted on the ground selected by Williams for our use, which he had abandoned.'[43] A Loyalist officer recounted that the rebels 'were dislodged with considerable slaughter by the brigade under lieutenant-colonel Webster.'[44] Tarleton wrote that 'the ardent bravery of the 33d and the light company of the guards soon dislodged them from their strong position.'[45] One soldier of the 33rd, John Caldwell, who had been with the regiment since before departing to America, was killed.

Greene declined to turn the clash at Whitesell's into a more general engagement. Realising that Greene was continuing to be reinforced even as his own army suffered from hunger and increasing bouts of sickness and desertion, Cornwallis decided that he had to attack the Continental forces at Guildford Courthouse, even though they were occupying chosen ground.

Hunger continued to beset the royal army. Seeking relief, John Robert Shaw joined a private of the 23rd, Richard Tattersall, who had served with the Royal Welsh Fusiliers for almost 11 years. 'Impelled by hunger we took the blessed opportunity of going out in search of something to satisfy our craving appetite,' Shaw wrote. They 'made a push for the country,' and after

38 Henry Lee, *Memoirs of the War in the Southern Department of the United States* (Washington DC: Peter Force, 1827), p.163.
39 Lee, *Memoirs*, p.163.
40 Lee, *Memoirs*, pp.163–164.
41 Shaw, *A Narrative*, p.37.
42 Shaw, *A Narrative*, p.37.
43 Lee, *Memoirs*, p.164.
44 Stedman, *The History*, p.336.
45 Tarleton, *A History*, pp.244–245.

about a mile approached a house, only to find it already full of British soldiers who had had the same idea. With the house's owner threatening to go and tell their officers, Shaw and Tattersall carried on another two or three miles, where they discovered 'a fine open plantation, and an elegant framed house belonging to a major Bell of the American army.' Entering, they found an elderly woman and her two daughters. 'We saluted them with as much politeness as our awkward manners would admit of; and the old lady very civilly asked us to sit down.' She provided them with flour for their knapsacks and the immediate remedy of 'truly delicious' Jonny-cakes, a cake made from fried cornmeal.[46] After this the woman attempted to inveigle the two soldiers to switch sides by offering them a new set of clothing and marriage to her two daughters. Shaw was more than tempted, but fear of the punishment that awaited deserters, should they be caught, convinced him to turn the offer down.

In the end it made little difference. Not long after leaving the house they found themselves approached by seven dragoons. Tattersall assumed fearfully that they belong to the British Legion, and that they would be flogged for plundering, but in fact the horsemen were rebels of Lee's Legion, a circumstance Tattersall apparently considered even worse, as he burst into tears.[47] The two men knelt in the dirt and begged for quarter, which was granted. They were taken to the rebel camp where they were initially interrogated, then stripped of most of their clothes and belongings by the rebels – 'God knows, they wanted them badly; for such ragged mortals I never saw in my life before, to pass under the character of soldiers.'[48]

Had Shaw deserted, or been captured? The line was a thin one but, unlike Tattersall, he admitted to a sense of relief when he discovered his fate. It seems as though the hard campaigning he had endured had eroded his will to carry on. The two prisoners were questioned by Greene, then conducted into captivity.

The 33rd suffered about 100 desertions over the eight years they spent in North America, a figure largely in line with other British regiments during the war. There were cases like that of William Walsh, who deserted and then joined the Continental Army. Others chose simply to disappear into the American countryside. The reasons for desertion are as multifarious and unique as men's reasons for enlisting in the first place. Some grew tired of the hardships or drudgery of military life, or chafed at the army's firm discipline. Some were lured by the bounties rebels offered to men willing to flee, or the promise of a better life in America, or indeed the promise of female companionship that had delayed Shaw and Tattersall long enough for the rebel dragoons to catch them. Another soldier of the 33rd, Robert Young, who served with the party under Lieutenant Nutt that ended up

46 Shaw, *A Narrative*, p.38.

47 Shaw, *A Narrative*, p.39. Mix-ups between Tarleton's British Legion and Lee's Continental Legion were common, as both generally wore green uniforms. Most infamously, this resulted in the massacre of Loyalists at Haw River on 24 February 1781. The Loyalists believed Lee's cavalry to be Tarleton's, a fatal mistake that Lee took full advantage of.

48 Shaw, *A Narrative*, p.40.

joining Burgoyne's expedition in 1777, recalled that after his capture 'I became acquainted with a girl, who advised me to desert; I spent a night with her, and agreed to go.'[49] Ironically, Young had first enlisted partly because he 'was much inclined to the company of women.'[50] Ultimately, desertion was a plague to both sides during the war, and its level of frequency was dependent not only on the mood of individuals but on the probable ease of escape – successfully fleeing from the cantonments on one of the islands outside New York, for example, was an unlikelier prospect than slipping away while foraging on campaign or serving picket duty.

Shaw was therefore no longer with the 33rd, though captured soldiers remained on the regiment's books and were expected to return when they either escaped or were released. As we will see, Shaw would not. His service in the 33rd was over.

The end of Shaw's service had come at a fortuitous time, for him. Cornwallis, realising that his army was slowly wasting away and that Greene was conversely being constantly reinforced, resolved to force the issue and end the impasse that had developed. For his own part, Greene was concerned that the militia that had swelled his ranks would as quickly depart when their period of service ended – he too now wished for a decisive pitched battle, believing he had laid the groundwork necessary to crush the royal army. He believed himself on the cusp of a second Saratoga, and not without reason – his strategies had lured Cornwallis far from resupply or reinforcement, into a make-or-break showdown that, if it resulted in defeat, would almost certainly lead to the ruination of the small, tired and hungry royal force.

The Battle of Guildford Courthouse

On 13 March the royal army encamped at the meetinghouse at the Quaker settlement of New Garden, between the forks of Deep River and four miles west of Guildford Courthouse, where Greene had concentrated his strength. On 15 March, having verified Greene's location, Cornwallis set the army in motion at daybreak. The vanguards of the two armies clashed early in the morning, the rebels withdrawing as Greene finished his dispositions. Cornwallis deployed to engage him, 'and both sides prepared … with tranquillity and order.'[51]

The 33rd filed off the road to the left, through the trees on either side, as the sound of two cannon opening fire boomed through the air. With Webster again assuming the duties of brigadier, Captain Campbell once more had command of the regiment. They can have had little idea what awaited them, yet. The 23rd once again were deployed on their right, Webster commanding the small brigade, while their left initially appeared to be in the air, before being covered by the ever-dependable Guards light infantry and jäger, who moved into the deep woods there. This combined force composed the left

49 Hagist, *British Soldiers*, p.141.
50 Hagist, *British Soldiers*, p.140.
51 Tarleton, *A History*, p.280.

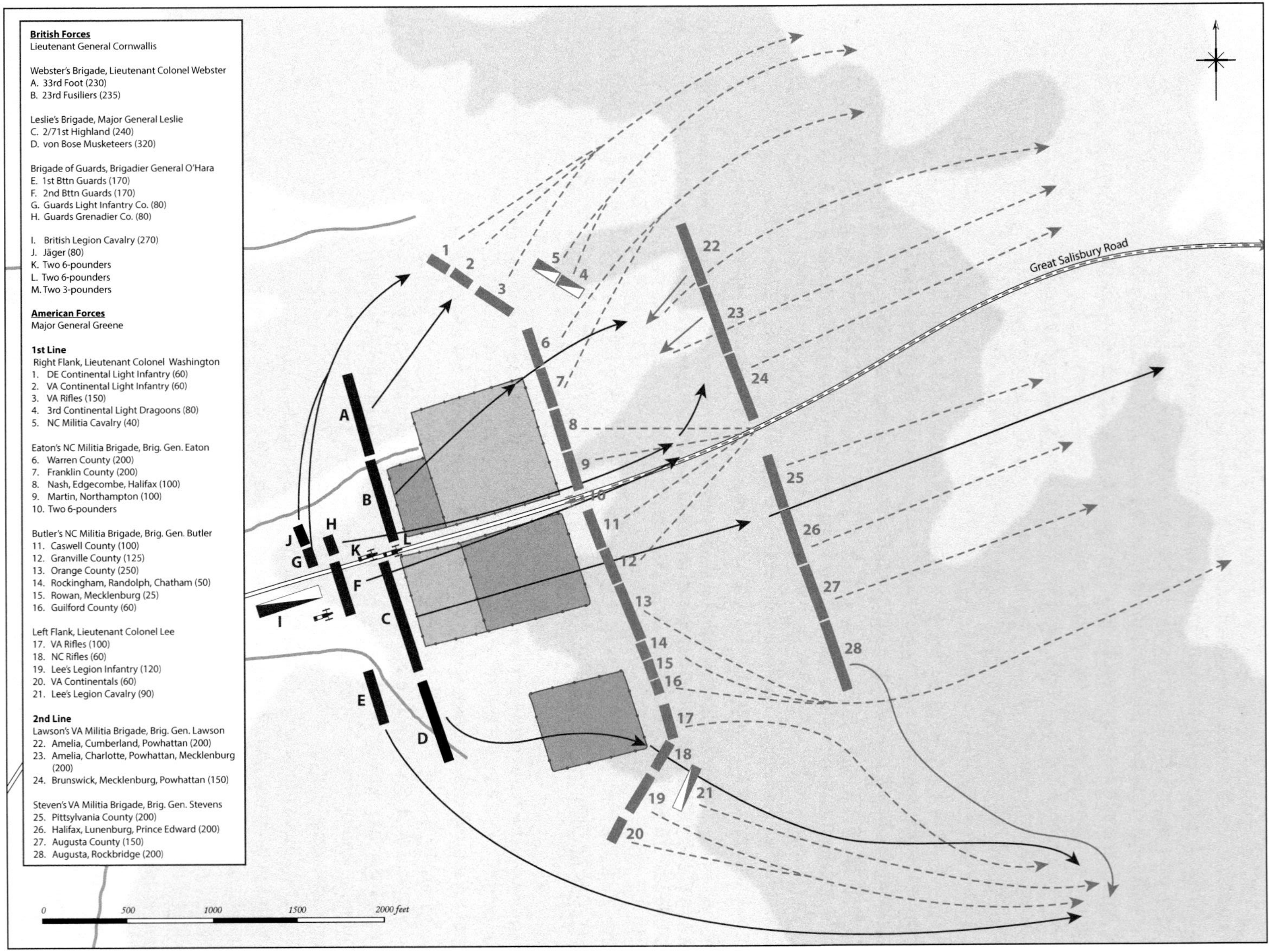

The Battle of Guildford Courthouse, 15 March 1781.

wing of the army, while the right consisted of the 71st Foot, the 1st battalion of the Brigade of Guards and the Hessian Regiment von Bose, with the 2nd battalion of the Guards and the Guards grenadier company, along with Tarleton's British Legion, in reserve.

Two Continental guns had opened fire, and the cannon Cornwallis had deployed on the roadway to the right of the 23rd now responded, a little before 2:00 p.m. As soon as the Crown troops were formed, they stepped off. Tarleton described how the veteran British and Hessian infantry 'marched forwards with steadiness and composure.'[52] The woods gave way to a clearing comprised of a number of fields, split in half by the roadway and hemmed in around the edges by rail fences, but the 33rd remained in the trees to the left of the open space, the 23rd advancing across it with the 71st to their right. Opposite them they got their first view of the rebels. Greene had formed a front line of militiamen, occupying the fences at the far side of the fields. Almost every account of the battle reprints the words of Roger Lamb at this moment, and with good reason, as they give a vivid first-hand view of the brutality and heroism of eighteenth-century warfare:

> When arrived within forty yards of the enemy's line, it was perceived that their whole force had their arms presented, and resting on a rail fence, the common partitions in America. They were taking aim with the nicest precision … At this awful period a general pause took place; both parties surveyed each other for the moment with the most anxious suspense. Nothing speaks, *the general* more than seizing on decisive moments: colonel Webster rode forward in front of the 23d regiment, and said, with more than even his usual commanding voice (which was well known to his Brigade,) '*Come on, my brave Fuzileers*.' This operated like an inspiring voice, they rushed forward amidst the enemy's fire; dreadful was the havoc on both sides.[53]

The 23rd and 71st suffered heavily from the militia's fusillade, but returned it and charged with the bayonet. As Webster was leading the 23rd, to the left his own regiment were pushing through the trees into where the militia line extended beyond the edge of the fields. It was not only militia either, but riflemen and a small force of Continentals, both infantry and cavalry. The 33rd, with the Guards' light company and jäger on their left, engaged this force amidst the trees, but found themselves outflanked by the extent of the enemy's line. They had the unenviable duty of trying to hold onto contact with the 23rd Foot on their right while keeping skirmishing Virginia riflemen at bay to their front and left.[54]

The 33rd were forced to shift left to make up for this disparity as they pressed the attack. An account written a year later talked of how Webster, presumably racing from the 23rd to his own regiment, 'in the heat of the engagement under a heavy fire from the enemy, who flanked his left …

52 Tarleton, *A History*, p.280.

53 Lamb, *An Original and Authentic Journal*, p.361.

54 Lawrence E. Babits and Joshua B. Howard, *Long, Obstinate, and Bloody: The Battle of Guildford Courthouse* (Chapel Hill: University of North Carolina Press, 2009), p.117.

executed with such success, a very delicate and dangerous manoeuvre, that of changing his front in time of action. When formed to the left, he attacked and routed the enemy.'[55] In the process of this difficult manoeuvre the 33rd had to push over a stream and drive along a ridgeline – once taking the crest they shifted towards their east and continued to drive the enemy flank before them.[56] In a later report Cornwallis wrote 'when, on finding that the left of the 33d was exposed to a heavy fire from the right wing of the enemy, he changed his front to the left, and, being supported by the yagers and light infantry of the guards, attacked and routed it.'[57]

Onwards the 33rd drove the enemy, having now lost contact with the 23rd to the right, who had also entered the woodland that covered the entire stretch of this part of the battlefield. With command and control beyond the regimental level now almost impossible, each regiment could only push forward as best as possible. With the 33rd forced to move left to deal with being outflanked, a dangerous gap had opened in the centre of the Crown line between them and the 23rd, but it was plugged by the 2nd battalion of the Guards, who moved up from reserve.

It quickly became apparent that a second line of militia was drawn up in the woodland, and 400 yards beyond the first. The fighting devolved into vicious skirmishing between small groups of British and Virginian infantry in and amongst the trees and undergrowth.[58] The action was so bloody and confusing that Cornwallis rode forward into the fray in an effort to maintain his army's coherence, much as he had done at Camden. He had two horses shot from beneath him and at one point had to be rescued by Sergeant Roger Lamb of the 23rd.

The 33rd, continuing forward on the left flank, were in the thick deadly action of their own. The presence of the jäger allowed the Crown troops to match the enemy's riflemen and, as experienced soldiers often did, both the Germans and British aimed low, as recorded by US military pension records;

> Private Henry Brown of Moon's company fell with 'a wound in the thick part of my thigh.' His cousin, Hubbard Brown, was shot through the hand 'leaving me a cripple.' Sixteen-year-old Moses Hendricks received a ball in the left leg, while Isaac Ready and Robert Church were both crippled with gunshot wounds to their hips.[59]

Once again showing their experience, the 33rd employed their bayonets to clear the trees of enemy riflemen, but the Continentals opposing them put up a few minutes of stubborn resistance before retreating.[60] What followed was, much as with the engagement against the first line, a back-and-forth through difficult terrain as they continued pushing the rebels east.[61]

55 Anon., 'For the Political Magazine', p.342.
56 Babits and Howard, *Long, Obstinate, and Bloody*, p.117.
57 Tarleton, *A History*, p.313.
58 Babits and Howard, *Long, Obstinate, and Bloody*, p.119.
59 Babits and Howard, *Long, Obstinate, and Bloody*, p.123.
60 Babits and Howard, *Long, Obstinate, and Bloody*, p.123.
61 Babits and Howard, *Long, Obstinate, and Bloody*, p.128.

On the battle raged. The 33rd emerged from the trees for the first time since the initial shots, finding before themselves a gentle vale and, at the far end, seemingly nothing more than two pieces of enemy artillery. Webster, likely lightly wounded at this point, could see nothing of the rest of the army emerging from the treeline to his right, but he could doubtless still hear the furious engagement as it continued to hang in the balance in the battlefield's centre and right.

Hoping that the apparently exposed cannon would be easy pickings after the exhausting combat in the woods, the 33rd descended into the vale towards them. About halfway across, their hopes were painfully disabused. Multiple regiments of Virginian and Maryland Continentals were concealed behind the slope or in the woods further to the left, and as the 33rd went forward they moved to engage them. They were hit by Continental musketry and case shot from the artillery, in the front and also in the right flank as they were partially enfiladed. A retreat was quickly ordered.[62] It may also be at this point that Webster suffered a serious leg wound, reportedly 'through the joint of the knee.' [63]

The 33rd were thrown back but did not lose their coherence. They rallied on the edge of the woods. There, 'Webster seemingly ordered his men to lie down, possibly to avoid case shot fired by Finley.'[64] The Continentals attempted a counterattack, though without much enthusiasm, causing a long-range firefight to develop over the vale between the 33rd and the rebel regulars. One Continental recalled seeing the British 'concealed in ambush, rise up, and pouring in a very heavy fire on them, in which they were obliged to retreat, having suffered very much by the last fire of the enemy.'[65]

Though they had stymied the Continental advance, it was clear any effort by the 33rd to advance again would meet with the same result as their first attempt. Fortunately, it was around this time that other Crown forces regiments finally began to appear through the woods to the right, having fought their way through the centre of the enemy's second line.

The first to do so was the 2nd battalion of the Guards. Like the 33rd, instead of waiting to see if further support materialised, they threw themselves into an assault on the Continentals. The 2nd Maryland, caught out of position, were broken, and the artillery pieces captured. The 1st Maryland counterattacked in turn along with Continental dragoons. What ensued was one of the most ferocious moments in the war, as both side's infantry and the Continental cavalry fought a desperate melee with bayonets and sabres. What Babits and Howard describe as 'two of the best, perhaps finest, veteran battalions in both the British and Continental armies' clashed in a desperate melee.[66] Both sides gave way, the Continentals supposedly only because Cornwallis had ordered

---

62 Babits and Howard, *Long, Obstinate, and Bloody*, p.145.
63 Anon., 'For the Political Magazine', p.342.
64 William Seymour, in Babits and Howard, *Long, Obstinate, and Bloody*, p.146.
65 Babits and Howard, *Long, Obstinate, and Bloody*, p.146.
66 Babits and Howard, *Long, Obstinate, and Bloody*, p.155.

his artillery to fire indiscriminately into the melee – a claim that is almost certainly a later invention.[67]

With the rest of the Crown troops beginning to emerge from the tree line, Greene had seen enough – he pulled his Continentals and the remaining militia back, leaving Cornwallis in possession of the field following one of the closest and most bitterly-fought engagements of the war.

Retreat to the Coast

The butcher's bill for the 33rd's losses at Guildford was almost as brutal as it had been at Camden. One ensign, Talbot, had been killed along with one sergeant and nine rank-and-file. Lieutenant Colonel James Webster, Lieutenants Anthony Salvin and George Wynyard, Ensigns John Kelly, Ralph Gore (not to be confused with Captain William Gore of the light company) and John Hughes, Adjutant John Fox, one sergeant and 55 rank-and-file had been wounded.[68] Among them were men of the regiment such as Joseph Bates, who had suffered a compound fracture in his leg and endured an amputation, Robert Yeald, who was shot in the thigh, John Yeald, also wounded in the thigh, John Martin, who was injured in the arm and back, William Hoyd, who was shot through the chest. It seems all of the above survived, but others were less fortunate. Thomas Needham had been shot through the lungs and died on 20 March, while John Bateman, who had suffered a badly fractured thigh, perished 10 days later.[69]

Most prominent of all those who died in the days after the battle was Lieutenant Colonel James Webster. The shot to the joint of his knee proved fatal. Despite briefly looking as though he might recover, he succumbed two weeks after the action, at Elizabethtown, at the age of 41. Sergeant Roger Lamb of the 23rd later wrote that 'it was reported in the army, that when lord Cornwallis received the news of colonel Webster's death, his lordship was struck with such pungent sorrow, that turning himself, he looked on his sword, and emphatically exclaimed, "I have lost my scabbard."'[70] In a letter to a friend, Cornwallis himself lamented 'I have lost poor Webster.'[71]

The Earl sent his condolences to Webster's father in Edinburgh, a tribute that, though particular to his regiment's lieutenant colonel, could have spoken to a number of the men killed during active service in America;

> It gives me great concern to undertake a task which is not only a bitter renewal of my own grief, but must be a violent shock to an affectionate parent.
>
> You have for your support the assistance of religion, good sense, and an experience of the uncertainty of all human happiness. You have for your satisfaction, that your son fell nobly in the cause of his country, honoured and

67 Babits and Howard, *Long, Obstinate, and Bloody*, p.162.
68 Tarleton, *A History*, pp.310–311.
69 TNA: PRO 30/11/5: Cornwallis papers, ff.180.
70 Lamb, *An Original and Authentic Journal*, p.360.
71 TNA: PRO 30/11/85: Cornwallis papers, ff.33.

> lamented by all his fellow soldiers; that he led a life of honour and virtue, which must secure him everlasting happiness. When the keen sensibility of the passions begins a little to subside, these considerations will give you real comfort.
>
> That the Almighty may give you fortitude to bear this severest of trials, is the earnest wish of your companion in affliction, and most faithful servant. CORNWALLIS.[72]

Beyond the personal and human loss, the 33rd, not to mention Cornwallis's southern army as a whole, had been deprived of one of its most capable officers. As usual when it came to his own regiment, the Earl looked for the best, and found his able replacement in one of the 33rd's former officers.

John Yorke, who had served in the 33rd since 1761, was the regiment's major during their early years in America, prior to transferring to the 22nd Regiment on 19 October 1778, where he assumed the rank of lieutenant colonel. He also commanded one of composite grenadier battalions. With the death of Webster, Cornwallis needed a new lieutenant colonel for his regiment, and with Major Dansey on leave in Britain and seemingly not in contention for the role, strings were again pulled to make sure the 33rd had the best officer cadre available. The diary of Captain Peebles of the 42nd Regiment, stationed in New York, recorded on 29 April 1781 that 'Yorke is going to the Southward to join the 33d. by particular request of Lord Cornwallis.'[73] He transferred back to his old regiment in the role of lieutenant colonel on 4 April 1781, and would arrive in time to provide experienced leadership in the field for most of their final American campaign. The change in leadership also affected the veteran officer who had been leading the 33rd in the field for the past two campaigns. In a letter to Clinton, Cornwallis mentioned; 'That Captain Campbell of the 33rd has commanded the regiment in two important actions [Camden and Guildford Courthouse] and that on both occasions he behaved with the greatest bravery and distinguished himself very much. He is an old captain and very deserving of a share in the promotion occasioned by the death of his late lt colonel.'[74] Campbell received his reward, though it meant depriving the 33rd of their most experienced captain. For his gallantry at Camden and Guildford Courthouse he was promoted to major in the 71st.

The immediate aftermath of the action near Guildford Courthouse was a grim one. The heavens opened while the Crown troops were left to sleep on the battlefield with no shelter, among the darkness, the rain, the wounded and the dying. Charles O'Hara, who had himself been wounded and whose son had been killed during the fighting, wrote;

> I never did, and I hope I never shall, experience two such days and Nights, as these immediately after the Battle. We remained on the very ground on which it had been fought, covered with Dead with Dying and Hundreds of Wounded, rebels as well as our own. A violent and constant rain that lasted above forty hours

72 Anon., 'For the Political Magazine', pp.342–343.

73 Peebles, *John Peebles' American War*, p.440.

74 TNA: PRO 30/11/75: Cornwallis Papers, ff.111–112.

> made it equally impractical to remove or administer the smallest comfort to our wounded.[75]

Guildford Courthouse is often portrayed as the beginning of the end for the Crown's strategy in the south, but this is an oversimplification. While Cornwallis's army had been mauled, Greene's was little better, particularly following the loss of much of his artillery and the flight of his militia in the battle's aftermath. In reality North Carolina had proven to be an infertile conquest for both sides. Regardless of the outcome of the battle, both Greene and Cornwallis would have to decide whether to stick or twist, to push north or south. In the end, they chose the opposite from each other.

In the immediate aftermath of the battle, Greene pulled his forces back. Cornwallis, knowing his army was in no fit state to reengage, also broke contact. He moved to Cross Creek, which had a large community of Scottish highlanders, who were typically loyal to the Crown. In doing so he had to abandon the worst of his wounded, 64 men, including seven from the 33rd, at New Garden, leaving them to be captured. After his initial withdrawal, Greene pursued, and now it was the turn of the Crown forces to hurriedly attempt a crossing over Broad River using a makeshift bridge. The army was able to get to safety and destroy the bridge behind them just before Greene's arrival. Knowing that the district ahead was Loyalist territory, and with his own militia either on the cusp of leaving or already gone, Greene declined to continue the pursuit.

Cross Creek could not provide the succour Cornwallis had hoped for. The area lay at the head of the Fear River, and it had been initially believed that supplies and reinforcements could be ferried up from the British base at the river's mouth, Wilmington. That proved impractical however, and there was little in the way of supplies that could be provided for the royal force. The locals proved as unwilling to turn out as anyone else in North Carolina, for either side of the divide. Consequently, Cornwallis took his weary, bloodied, hungry army south-east, to Wilmington, and in doing so abandoned his attempted conquest of North Carolina. Rather than marching on Wilmington, Greene decided to turn his efforts towards South Carolina, essentially leaving Cornwallis to his own devices.

The campaign from the start of January to when Cornwallis approached the safety on Wilmington on 7 April was probably the most difficult the 33rd had faced in North America. The race to the Dan had seen them cover just shy of 250 miles, the weather perpetually cold and wet, the meagre roads muddy. Numerous waterways had been crossed, supplies had run low, and several sharp skirmishes culminating in one of the most brutal battles of the war had been fought. British arms remained undefeated, but strategically, they were adrift. Ironically, the 33rd were now at a post adjacent to where they had first made landfall in America, on Cape Fear, five long years before.

Cornwallis had lost the initiative. His army, however, remained intact. Taking on supplies at Wilmington, the 33rd's colonel once more showed that

75 George C. Rogers Jr., 'Letters of Charles O'Hara to the Duke of Grafton,' *Historical Magazine*, vol.65, 1964, p.177.

side of his personality that has been alternately described as bold or foolish. Rather than shadow Greene back south and repeat the campaign that had won him South Carolina, Cornwallis resolved to head in the opposite direction. In late April, he marched for the heartland of rebellion in the south – Virginia.

A contemporary image of a British grenadier as he likely would have appeared in the early years of the Revolutionary War. Unlike more formal images of grenadiers, this figure wears a cocked hat not dissimilar to those of the battalion companies, and has discarded unnecessary items like the match case formerly used for lighting grenades. (Anne S. K. Brown Military Collection)

Advance into Virginia

The reasoning behind Cornwallis's decision to march with his small force into Virginia without the strategic acquiesce of Clinton has long been debated. In a candid letter on 10 April to his friend and fellow-officer, William Phillips, Cornwallis seems to give as clear a set of reasons as could be hoped for by spelling out the conundrums he faced;

> The idea of our friends rising in any number and to any purpose totally failed as expected … now, my dear friend, what is our plan? Without one we cannot succeed and I assure you that I am quite tired of marching about the country in quest of adventures. If we mean an offensive war in America, we must abandon New York, bring our whole force into Virginia; we then have a stake to fight for and a successful battle may give us America. If our plan is defensive … let us quit the Carolinas (which can not be held defensively, whilst Virginia can be so easily armed against us) and stick to our salt pork at New York sending now and then a detachment to steal tobacco &c … I can come by land to you, but whether after we have joined we shall have sufficient force for a war of conquest, I should think very doubtful. By a war of conquest, I mean to possess the country sufficiently to overturn the rebel government, and to establish a militia, and some kind of mixed authority of our own. If no reinforcement comes, so that I am obliged to march with my present force to the upper frontiers of South Carolina, my situation will be truly distressing. If I was to embark from hence the loss of the upper posts in South Carolina would be inevitable. I have as yet received no orders; if the reinforcement arrives I must move from hence, where the men will be sickly and the horses starved: if I am sure that you are to remain in the Chesapeake, perhaps I may come directly to you.[76]

76 TNA: PRO 30/11/85: ff.31–34.

Phillips was commanding a British expedition into Virginia which Cornwallis resolved to link up with. On 15 April the army under Cornwallis mustered 127 officers, including the regimental chaplains and surgeons, 230 sergeants and drummers and 1,829 rank-and-file. A further 436 were sick and 397 wounded.[77] Orders 'were given to the principal officers to prepare their troops as well as they could for a long march.'[78] Supplies of 'rum, salt, and flour' were secured.[79] Evacuating his sick by boat to Charleston, Cornwallis set out on 25 April, after just a few weeks rest. It marked the beginning of the 33rd's last campaign in North America.

The first obstacle faced by the army was a familiar one – the passage over a river, in this case a branch of Cape Fear. Light troops collected boats, the Royal Navy provided assistance, and 'the stores, waggons, cannon, and troopers, were brought over' with speed and efficiency.[80] Conscious of further waterways ahead, two of the boats used to effect the passage were mounted 'upon carriages, which could proceed with the army, and might facilitate the passage of any waters.'[81]

The march north was initially no more pleasant than the last campaign. The northern and eastern reaches of North Carolina 'were found more barren than they were described, and much assistance of provisions to save the stock upon the waggons could not be taken or bought from the inhabitants.'[82] The army advanced with almost no intelligence about its surroundings, and concerning rumours circulated that Phillips's forces had already evacuated Virginia, leaving the little expedition to march into the enemy's heartland alone. As they went, the army acquired a set routine, marching from midnight until early morning to avoid the worst of the heat. Once encamped they would eat, then rest. Another meal at dusk, a few hours of sleep, reveille at 11:00 p.m., and the march would resume.[83]

In early May the countryside began to prove more prosperous. The army's vanguard drove off rebel forces and successfully occupied the settlement of Halifax. A short, anxious period was spent by the main body near Vivaret's Mill waiting on news from Phillips, which was eventually received – the existing British expedition already in Virginia had not withdrawn and was still present at Petersburg.

Cornwallis marched with haste, aware that should a more powerful rebel army appear, both himself and Phillips might be defeated in detail. The 33rd, numbering 209 men, marched with the rest of the army to Petersburg on 19 May, where their arrival caused quite amongst those Crown forces already present.[84] Mark Urban describes how 'Cornwallis's men had, after all, fought repeatedly against intimidating odds, marched 1,500 miles and had weaned

77 Charles Ross (ed.), *Correspondence of Charles, First Marquis Cornwallis* (London: John Murray, 1859), vol.I, p.88.
78 Tarleton, *A History*, p.292.
79 Tarleton, *A History*, p.293.
80 Tarleton, *A History*, p.293.
81 Tarleton, *A History*, p.293.
82 Tarleton, *A History*, p.293.
83 Urban, *Fusiliers*, p.258.
84 Urban, *Fusiliers*, p.259.

themselves from many of the comforts other redcoats took for granted. As the 23rd, 33rd and Guards trooped into camp, they cut quite a figure.'[85] One officer already in Petersburg recalled 'words can ill describe the admiration in which this band of heroes was held by the two Scotch regiments [the recently-raised 76th and 80th Regiments], and even by the battalions of light infantry – the elite of the army, who had fought and generally led in every action during the war … the gallant earl and his brave officers who shared with him in his long and arduous marches, as well as in his laurels, were almost idolised.'[86]

Like many of the other regiments that marched with Cornwallis, the 33rd had certainly seen a great deal of fighting. Using the colonel's company as an example, 11 of the 47 rank-and-file and drummers present at the end of the North Carolina campaign had been with the regiment since mid-August 1776.[87] These men, John Duckworth, Thomas Duggan, William Hammonds, David Hay, Richard Hazzard, Robert Howard, Robert McGee, Roger Morlidge, James Powell, John Savage and Daniel Webster, had experienced the ferocity of combat at Long Island, Brandywine, Germantown, Monmouth, Camden, Guildford Courthouse and a host of other engagements and had served in over half-a-dozen campaigns from South Carolina to New York. Some, like John Duckworth, would not survive the war. Others, like Thomas Duggan and William Hammonds, would choose desertion following a period of captivity, likely settling down in America. Others, like Robert McGee and John Savage, would see out the war and continue to serve for years in the army, eventually claiming pensions. Extrapolating the colonel's company veterans across the regiment as a whole, by mid-1781 around 23 percent of the 33rd had served through almost the entirety of the American Revolutionary War.

Among them were men like James Brown, born in Strabane in Ireland in 1751 and listed as 5' 9½" tall. After working as a labourer he enlisted in the army in 1774, being promoted to sergeant, then reduced for an unnamed infraction on 9 June 1777. He quickly made amends, was raised to corporal on 22 November 1777 and then to sergeant on 14 December 1778. He suffered 'a severe Wound in the right Knee at the Battle of Guilford in North Carolina' but continued to serve until 1793.[88] There was also Martin Elliott, born in Dollanstown, Ireland. Formerly a labourer, he was appointed a drummer on 4 August 1775, then promoted to corporal in 1776. He transferred to the grenadier company while being reduced to private on 24 June 1777, going on to serve a total of 21 years in the army. It was noted that during the American Revolution 'he distinguished himself as a good Soldier.'[89] There was Mathew Collier, who enlisted in the regiment at the age of 17 on 10 April 1777 as a drummer and continued to do so despite 'having a dislocated Shoulder which

85 Urban, *Fusiliers*, p.259.

86 S. Graham, 'An English Officer's Account of His Services in America, 1779–1781: Memoirs of Lt.-General Samuel Graham' in *Historical Magazine*, 9 (1865), quoted in Spring, *With Zeal* (p.114) and Urban, *Fusiliers* (p.259).

87 Lodge, *To What Extent*, pp.11–13.

88 TNA: WO 97/510/78: James Brown discharge papers. The discharge papers quoted in this section were kindly provided to the author by Don Hagist.

89 TNA: WO 97/511/54: Martin Elliott discharge papers.

he received when on a Fatigue party at Kings Bridge North America,' an injury that would eventually contribute to his pension application in 1792.[90] At the other end of the scale regarding age was William Smith, born in Barming, Kent in 1739. After pursuing a career as a labourer, he enlisted in the 33rd in 1758, during the Seven Years War. Standing at 5' 11", it is little surprise that by 1776 the 38-year-old was a sergeant in the regiment's grenadier company. In 1777 he was transferred to one of the regiment's battalion companies and reduced to corporal, then private soldier, but worked his way both back up to sergeant and back into the grenadier company, transferring on 25 February 1779 and being promoted on 27 May 1780. He served a total of 23 years, taking his discharge in 1781 due to 'being worn out and having violent Rheumatic Complaints.'[91] These records give only the smallest insight into the lives and experiences of the hundreds of ordinary soldiers who served in the 33rd throughout its American War.

Upon nearing Petersburg, Cornwallis discovered that Phillips had died of a fever. This personal loss aside, further reinforcement from New York left the gallant Earl with over 7,000 men at his disposal. To the south, Greene had been driven off by Rawdon, while news had also arrived of further reinforcements being sent from Cork to Charleston. It seemed as though there was yet the possibility of renewed British success in the south.

The first order of business was to hunt down the largest organised rebel force in Virginia, commanded by the Marquis de Lafayette. The rebels initially withdrew until they too were reinforced, at which point they attempted to shadow Cornwallis's progress. It quickly became apparent that the Earl's intention was to bring economic ruination down upon the rebels in the most prosperous of North American colonies.

The 33rd, along with the other regiments that had campaigned through the barren stretches of North Carolina, found Virginia to be a fertile target. A surgeon with the army recalled 'the camp abounded with a profusion of the best provisions; and the marches were seldom long or fatiguing.'[92] Horses in particular were easily secured, and Crown forces were also soon rapidly inundated with thousands of escaped slaves, who were either directly liberated from the plantations of rebel owners by Crown troopers, or fled to them seeking the emancipation the king's army offered. What this produced was described vividly by *Kapitän* Ewald; 'the army appeared similar to a wandering Arabian or Tartar horde … Each officer had four to six horses and three or four Negroes, as well as one or two Negresses for cook and maid. Every soldier's woman was mounted and also had a Negro and Negress on horseback for her servants …'[93]

While Ewald's account might hint at an undisciplined rabble, in reality British officers mostly succeeded in retaining control over their men's proclivities, in contrast to certain periods earlier in the war. Measures such as the curtailing of private foraging and the close monitoring of officers

90 TNA: WO 97/510/133: Mathew Collier discharge papers.
91 TNA: WO 97/514/113: William Smith discharge papers.
92 Jackson, *A Treatise on the Fevers of Jamaica*, p.198.
93 Tustin (ed.), *Diary of the American War*, p.305.

Sometimes, knapsacks were replaced in favour of blanket rolls and slings, with the men's possessions wrapped up in the roll. Note also this soldier is carrying his mess group's hatchet. (Photo by Henry Gage)

remaining amongst their men both on and off duty combined with a series of orders to guard against irregular behavior, as well as bring discipline to the many runaway slaves accompanying the British and acquire fresh horses. Gregory Urwin characterises the objective as 'to undermine Virginia's economic ability to buttress the rebel war effort without sullying the British Army's honour.'[94] Both of these objectives were largely achieved, with atrocities and outrages kept to a minimum even while stores were burned and Virginia's economy strangled. Arms and military stores were destroyed, plantations burned and slaves freed, and everything considered to have a value to the colony's economy was either seized or wrecked, principally by a force of 800 mounted infantry who spread out through the Virginian countryside.[95]

After about a month of ferocious raiding, Cornwallis marched for the colonial capital at Williamsburg. There, receiving contradictory orders from Sir Henry Clinton, he shifted his field army away from prime ground on the Williamsburg Neck.[96] They marched first to Portsmouth, a settlement at the mouth of the James River already occupied by a small Crown garrison. The 33rd had been brigaded with their old comrades in the 23rd and 71st as well as the 17th Regiment, with overall command falling to the 33rd's Lieutenant Colonel Yorke. Once at Portsmouth they 'encamped in front of the redoubts which covered the town … the infantry constructed huts as soon as they arrived on their ground, to shelter them from the scorching heat of the climate.'[97]

Cornwallis did not think Portsmouth a suitable garrison. Besides its geographic vulnerability, it lay next to a particularly noisome swampland that was soon being blamed for spreading sickness among the troops. Indeed, disease remained a problem during much of the Virginia campaign and would only become more pronounced. In September Ewald wrote that the 23rd, 33rd, 43rd, 71st and Guards 'number scarcely five hundred men fit for duty … the illness results from the great heat, which has decomposed our blood too much, and from the continued and frequent drinking of bad water. To this must be added that all medicines are lacking.'[98]

As an alternative to the unwholesome and exposed dispositions as Portsmouth, Cornwallis began to shift forces along to Yorktown, a small settlement further north, on the banks of the York River, one of the branches of the Chesapeake. While its sandy soil was scarcely more defendable, both bases showed evidence that the apparent resurgence in British fortunes was bearing out in terms of local willingness to interact with and assist the Crown's soldiers. As a centre of operations, Virginia had plenty in the way of resources for the royal army, and gold drew in a large number of farmers willing to work with them. Urwin describes how 'at Portsmouth, and then

94 Urwin, 'To bring the American Army under strict Discipline', pp.22–23.
95 Carpenter, *Southern Gambit*, pp.231–232.
96 Urwin, 'To bring the American Army under strict Discipline', p.25.
97 Tarleton, *A History*, p.370.
98 Tustin (ed.), *Diary of the American War*, p.328.

at Yorktown, the marketplace supplanted confiscation as the means for sustaining the earl's Army.'[99]

Though these positives gave cause for hope, Yorktown hardly looked to be any more auspicious from a defensive standpoint than Portsmouth had. Still, Clinton had urged Cornwallis to the coast, to provide an easy link with the Royal Navy, and so the Earl began to dig in. Redoubts were constructed around the settlement and on the small peninsular across the river from, it, Gloucester Point.

The 33rd remained initially at Portsmouth under the command of Brigadier General Charles O'Hara. On 2 August Cornwallis sent him a letter from Yorktown complaining 'the position is bad' and requesting cattle drivers, 'labouring Negroes' and engineering tools, as well as reinforcements in the form of the Legion and 'the 71st or, if that regiment is too strong for the boats, either the 23rd or 33rd.'[100] The Earl clearly wished to have his veteran southern regiments with him as quickly as possible. He closed, possibly somewhat sarcastically, with the line 'I shall be happy to embrace you on the delightfull banks of the York River.'[101] Apparently the 71st were sent first, as four days later Cornwallis wrote again stating that he 'shall be glad to have either the 23rd or 33rd before your final evacuation.'[102]

The regiments transferred from Portsmouth to Yorktown 'by the row boats of the army and fleet.'[103] By 22 August Portsmouth had been fully evacuated, its defences demolished, and the army lay in its entirety in and around Yorktown and neighbouring Gloucester Point, still accompanied by thousands of escaped slaves as well as Loyalist refugees.

Work on the defences began in earnest. The 33rd, like every other regiment besides the British Legion, provided details to assist in the construction of redoubts. Cornwallis wrote to Clinton of 'the fatigue and difficulty of constructing works in this warm season.'[104] *Kapitän* Ewald described it in more memorable terms when he called the heat 'so unbearable that many men have been lost by sunstroke or their reason has been impaired. Everything that one has on his body is soaked as with water from the constant perspiration.'[105] Work they did though, as word began to spread that Washington himself was on his way south.

By early September the seriousness of the situation faced by Cornwallis's army was growing ever-more apparent. Washington had indeed come south from New York to nearby Williamsburg not only with the main body of the Continental Army, but with French troops as well. Even worse, a powerful French fleet had appeared off the coast, cutting the Crown's land forces off from vital support – and the possibility of evacuation – via the Royal Navy. A battle off the Virginia Capes on 5 September saw the British fleet of Rear Admiral Thomas Graves driven off. Cornwallis sent a series of increasingly

99 Urwin, 'To bring the American Army under strict Discipline', p.26.
100 Saberton (ed.), *The Cornwallis Papers*, vol.6, p.43.
101 Saberton (ed.), *The Cornwallis Papers*, vol.6, p.43.
102 Saberton (ed.), *The Cornwallis Papers*, vol.6, p.46.
103 Tarleton, *A History*, p.371.
104 Saberton (ed.), *The Cornwallis Papers*, vol.6, p.28.
105 Tustin (ed.), *Diary of the American War*, p.314.

concerned dispatches to Clinton in New York as it became clear that there was another British army about to be 'Burgoyned.' Clinton promised prompt aid, but acted slowly.

On 28 September, with work on Yorktown's defences still ongoing, pickets reported the approach of Washington's combined army. Crown forces stood to, arraying themselves before the redoubts. Despite being outnumbered two-to-one, Cornwallis hoped to fight a pitched battle, rather than a siege, relying only on the outermost works.

French grenadiers and light infantry arrived in sight first, before noon, forming at a distance across the Williamsburg road. Rebel troops followed soon after, with some long-range cannon fire being directed towards the British Legion's videttes. The combined army advanced no further, and the two forces spent a restless night facing one another. The next day Continental infantry began to move in column to the right, over a morass via causeways they had constructed in the dark, and the armies exchanged cannon and rifle fire. 'The two armies observed each other with cautious attention, and nothing material occurred within or without the lines till evening,' when news from Clinton reached Cornwallis.[106]

The commander-in-chief in North America promised that assistance would be sent from New York by 5 October. Reassured, Cornwallis broke contact and drew his forces back within Yorktown's inner defences. In his reply to Clinton he wrote that 'I have ventured these two last days to look General Washington's whole force in the face, in the position on the outside of my works, and I have the pleasure to assure your Excellency that there was but one wish throughout the whole army, which was that the enemy would advance.'[107]

Such high spirits would not last. The next day Washington's combined army broke ground, beginning to dig their siege works. The 33rd found themselves initially placed alongside the Hessian Regiment von Bose on the far side of town, on the banks of the York River facing towards the small British garrison on Gloucester Point.

On 30 September the French attacked the 23rd Regiment, holding an extended redoubt on the western tip of the defences. The Royal Welsh Fusiliers repulsed the surprise assault. Crown artillery bombarded Washington's forces as they attempted to dig their way forward, doing damage to the combined army. On 3 October there was a sharp skirmish in front of the lines on Gloucester point between foraging Crown troops and French cavalry.

On 7 October the combined army began to excavate their first parallel. Siege artillery was mounted in the face of the ongoing British barrage. On 9 October Washington ordered the bombardment of Yorktown to begin. Badly outgunned, the defenders soon found their artillery being silenced. On 11 October, with Clinton's reinforcements nowhere to be seen, Cornwallis wrote a stark letter to his superior reporting 'we have lost about seventy men, and many of our works are seriously damaged. With such works, on disadvantageous ground, against so powerful an attack, we cannot hope to

106 Tarleton, *A History*, p.384.
107 Saberton (ed.), *The Cornwallis Papers*, vol.6, p.36.

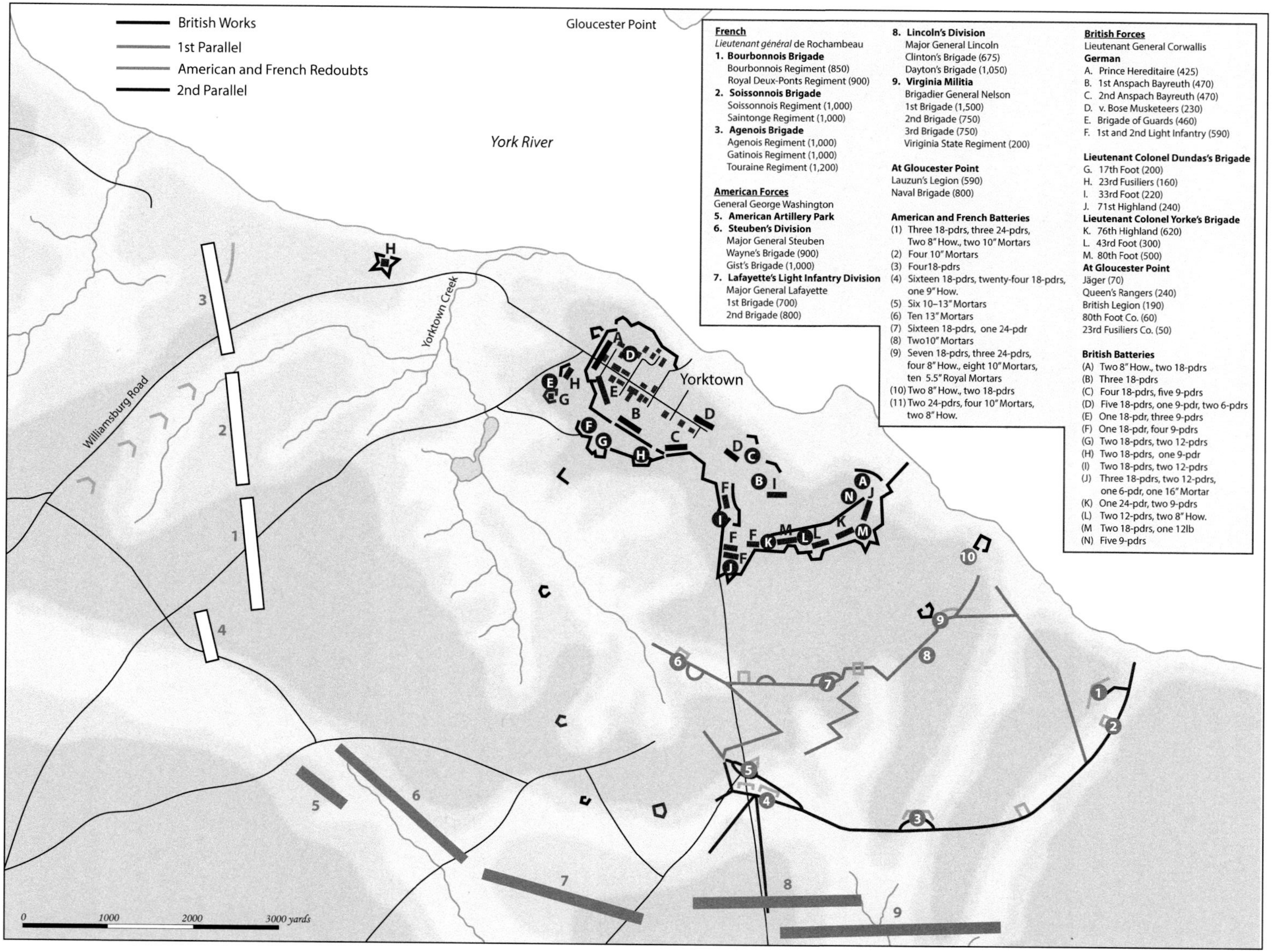

The Siege of Yorktown, 28 September–19 October 1781.

make a very long resistance.'[108] He updated the number to 90 men before sending the letter and noted 'we continue to lose men very fast.'[109]

Among them was Captain John Kerr of the 33rd. The same officer who had first recruited John Robert Shaw in Leeds and had joined the regiment in the field just after Camden, was killed by shell or roundshot while 'sitting with some friends drinking a glass of wine.'[110]

Besides the cannonade, disease and desertion also began taking its toll on the garrison. The 33rd were no exception – by the siege's end 15 percent of the already-undersized regiment were too ill to do duty, and the rest were undoubtedly suffering the effects of disease, fatigue and hunger. One letter reported that 2,500 of Cornwallis's soldiers and sailors were sick.[111] Cornwallis himself believed that up to half of his garrison were suffering from malaria, which was endemic at that time of year in the swamps of eastern Virginia.

The privation was as relentless as the bombardment, which continued all day and into the night, lighting up the darkness and denying any rest to the besieged. Tarleton wrote that 'every hour both day and night, was an hour of watching and danger to the officer and soldier; where every gun was dismounted as soon as shown; and where a long defence, against superior numbers and superior artillery, was utterly hopeless.'[112] Soldiers and sailors laboured to open new embrasures in their redoubts to remount guns that had been knocked out by the enemy. One British frigate at anchor in the river was driven aground by cannon fire and set alight to prevent its capture. Other ships were likewise deliberately scuttled. Civilians and refugees huddled under a cliff on the riverbank in an effort to avoid the continual shelling. The settlement's houses were wrecked. Surgeons laboured to tend to both the sick and wounded while under fire. In an effort to save resources, most of the garrison's horses were slaughtered, their bodies dumped in the river. Escaped slaves who had fled to the Crown army for protection were ejected into no-man's-land as food ran out and smallpox became rampant.

On 11 October the besiegers dug a new parallel. On the night of 14 October a ferocious bombardment was opened on two of the outermost redoubts. The larger of the pair, Redoubt Number 9, was held by between 120 and 140 troops, which included a detachment of the 33rd. The redoubt and its abatis endured roundshot and shell relatively unscathed, but in the moonless darkness that followed a shout of alarm went up. Elements from four French regiments, mostly light infantry and grenadiers, were launching a surprise assault on the redoubt in tandem with a Continental light infantry attack on the smaller neighbouring fortification. The little garrison resisted. One German serving in the French Régiment de Royal Deux-Ponts recalled;

> Anyone can imagine what happened once we were inside the redoubt. People of four nations were thrown together: Frenchmen, English, Scots, and Germans…

---

108 Ross (ed.), *Correspondence of Charles, First Marquis Cornwallis*, vol.I, p.124.
109 Ross (ed.), *Correspondence of Charles, First Marquis Cornwallis*, vol.I, p.124.
110 *London Chronicle*, 3 January 1782, p.2.
111 *London Chronicle*, 3 January 1782, p.2.
112 Tarleton, *A History*, p.390.

> the soldiers … were so furious that our people were killing one another … The French were striking down everyone in a blue coat. Since the Deux-Ponts wore blue, many of us were stabbed to death … One screamed here, the other there, that for the grace of God we should kill him off completely. The whole redoubt was so full of dead and wounded that one had to walk on top of them.[113]

In panic, the remaining British and Hessian soldiers fled out of the rear of the redoubt to the safety of the main lines. Both redoubt 9 and 10 had been taken, and the besiegers could complete their latest parallel trench. The next day Cornwallis wrote to Clinton, stating gravely that 'we shall soon be exposed to an assault in ruined works, in a bad position, and with weakened numbers … I cannot recommend that the fleet and army should run great risk in endeavouring to save us.'[114]

Despite acknowledging the doom of his post, Cornwallis refused to give up. In the early hours of 16 October a force of grenadiers and light infantry, likely including the 33rd's light company, mounted a sortie, sallying forth against a section of the besiegers' trenches. The attack was initially successful, and 11 guns were spiked, but after the British withdrew they were quickly repaired and back in operation.

Besides surrender, Cornwallis had one, desperate option remaining. He determined to attempt to ferry the main body of the army across the York River to Gloucester Point and try a breakout, hoping to march the 400 miles to the safety of New York. Ferrying of the troops across the river began that night, the operation spearheaded by the 23rd Foot. However, the movement had scarcely started before a tempest blew up, making the crossing impassable.

Cornwallis held a council of war with his officers. With food low, ammunition almost completely expended, the defences pounded to ruination, and the garrison ravaged by injury and sickness, it was agreed that there was nothing left to do besides surrender. A drummer appeared atop one of Yorktown's smoking redoubts, accompanied by a white flag, and beat a 'parle.' The siege was over and, with it, the 33rd's last campaign in America.

The Surrender

On the afternoon of 19 October, those Crown troops who were still able to marched from Yorktown's ruined defences, passing between the armies of France and the United States and into an open meadow that became known as the surrender field. They did so dressed in new uniforms, which had arrived not long before the commencement of the siege. Colours remained cased and bayonets unfixed.

Apocryphal tradition suggests the 33rd's regimental colours were torn up by the officers after the surrender and hidden in their coats, the pieces

---

113 Kim Burdick, 'What they Saw and Did at Yorktown's Redoubts 9 and 10', *Journal of the American Revolution*, <https://allthingsliberty.com/2020/04/what-they-saw-and-did-at-yorktowns-redoubts-9-and-10/>, accessed 31 January 2023.

114 Ross (ed.), *Correspondence of Charles, First Marquis Cornwallis*, vol.I, p.124.

then smuggled to safety. In reality however Dansey's letters show that the flags were kept at the regiment's depot at Fort Johnston outside Charleston, possibly being put into storage after the Battle of Camden. This was common practice with British regiments during the Revolutionary War. Albert Lee's early twentieth century history of the regiment claims the flags flown during the Revolution were hung in the church of St Mary of Magdalen in Taunton, England.[115] In 1832 these flags were given to the descendant of the colonel who commanded the regiment at the Battle of Dettingen, Kemys-Tynte, who after some negotiation gave them to a descendant of William Dansey in exchange for another, older set of regimental colours. Dansey apparently wished the flags to be returned to St Mary of Magdalen. They were recorded in the 14 September 1895 issue of the *Army and Navy Gazette* as resting in the dining hall of Cefn Mably in Wales, seemingly their last known location.

Regiment by regiment, the Crown forces laid down their arms, some supposedly throwing them down in rage and frustration, hoping to break their weapons rather than surrender them. For the men of the 33rd and other veteran British regiments, some of whom had marched and fought every step of the way from their first actions in American to the present, it must have been a bitter experience.

Over the course of the siege the 33rd had suffered seven rank-and-file killed, seven missing and 10 wounded, as well as one sergeant wounded, one subaltern missing, and one officer killed and one wounded – the unfortunate Captain Kerr the former, and Lieutenant Carson the latter.[116] The casualties were comparatively light, and broadly in line with the losses suffered by other regiments, but did not include the devastation wreaked by disease. On 18 October the 33rd was listed as having 141 rank-and-file present and fit for duty, with another 37 sick and wounded, giving a total of just 178 men, not including drummers, sergeants and officers.[117] Although this did not include the light or grenadier companies, it left the regiment as the second smallest in the Yorktown garrison bar the 23rd.

The soldiers were given two days to recover from their ordeal, before being marched for prison camps in Virginia, North Carolina and Pennsylvania. The soldiers of the 33rd appear to have ended up in Pennsylvania, accompanied by junior officers who had drawn the short straw – most of the officers, including Cornwallis, were given their parole and returned to New York and Britain.

Almost 18 months of captivity awaited the greater portion of the regiment. The 33rd were seemingly first ordered to the barracks at Fort Frederick in Maryland, but ended up in Lancaster, Pennsylvania. Their number was listed as 225 men, which included the sick and wounded expected to join them later, the discrepancy between that and the 18 October review presumably

115 Lee, *History of the Thirty-third*, pp.140–141.

116 Tarleton, *A History*, p.446.

117 Saberton (ed.), *The Cornwallis Papers*, vol.6, p.116.

accounted for by the drummers, sergeants and remaining officers not listed in that first tally.[118]

John Robert Shaw had marched into similar captivity seven months before the rest of the regiment but, while he was not with the Yorktown contingent, his account remains the only one of a regular soldier of the 33rd in captivity, and undoubtedly bore many similarities to the experiences of his fellows. He recalled that;

> We suffered much: our houses had no covering to shelter us from the inclemency of the weather; and we were exposed to cold, hunger and want of clothing; and all manner of ill-treatment insult and abuse. Having thus for a considerable time (I cannot say with the patience of Job) endured many hardships, we formed a project for our escape, by means of one of the guards, who agreed for 3 half Joes, to conduct us to New York.[119]

The guard betrayed Shaw and his enterprising companions, 'so we had to continue in our confinement, and we were now worse treated than ever; for we had parted with our uniform, and were considered as refugees.'[120]

Shaw and the other prisoners taken before Yorktown were moved in the summer of 1781 from Winchester in Virginia to Lancaster in Pennsylvania, likely in part to avoid Cornwallis's then-marauding army. 'The cruelty of this new guard exceeded anything we had yet seed,' Shaw claimed;

> They drove us like so many bullocks… scarcely had we advanced three miles, before the captain broke his broad sword by cutting and slashing the prisoners, who were too much weakened by hunger, and former ill-treatment to keep up in the march. The lieutenant, a snotty-nosed stripling, just from the chimney corner, came up, raging like a madman, with his small sword in his hand, and pushed it with such violence into the back of one of my fellow-prisoners, that he broke it in the wound, where it remained till one of his comrades pulled it out.[121]

Shaw was reduced to shaking 'like a patient in a severe fit of the ague' due to lack of food. 'All we drew was but one ear of corn per man, and this was a sweet morsel to us: – we softened it in water, and grated it in the lid of our camp-kettle, and made bread of it.'[122]

Prisoners were often permitted to take employment in areas close to the camps where they were held. Shaw however failed to land himself a job. He related how 'I got a quarter of a dollar from a Mr. John Hoover, by dint of hard begging: I now fancied myself as rich as a king, and immediately sent for a loaf of bread and a pint of whisky; with which I and my comrade

118 James Linwood Carpenter, *The Yorktown Prisoners: A Narrative Account of the Disposition of the British Army Which Capitulated at Yorktown, October 19, 1781* (Williamsburg: College of William and Mary, 1950), <https://dx.doi.org/doi:10.21220/m2-0mfs-s403>, accessed January 2023

119 Shaw, *A Narrative*, p.43.

120 Shaw, *A Narrative*, p.43.

121 Shaw, *A Narrative*, pp.43–44.

122 Shaw, *A Narrative*, pp.45–46.

regaled ourselves, and sung some merry songs: being for a time as happy as princes.'[123]

Escape attempts were common. After his first effort, Shaw and a number of other comrades began 'undermining, from one of the cellars under the barrack-yard and stockades, about 100 yards, and coming out in the grave-yard – conveying the dirt in our pockets, and depositing it in the necessary house, and other private places.'[124] After this they intended to seize weapons and ammunition and, joined by a group of Loyalists, torch the town and link up with the main British army. The scheme was betrayed by a fellow-prisoner from the 71st Foot by the name of Burk. Undeterred, Shaw and another two others tried again later on, with more success – 'we procured a large knife with which about two o'clock in the morning we had dug about two feet under ground, where, to our great joy, we found the stockade rotten.'[125]

Rather than return to the British Army, Shaw spent time living and working among his erstwhile enemies and, in order to avoid suspicion, even enlisted in the Continental Army. Ironically, he was assigned to guard prisoners from the Yorktown capitulation, which included many of his old comrades from the 33rd. 'In a few days I was attacked by the sergeant major,' he wrote, 'who called me a d--d rebel … a cutlass was given me to enable me to stand in my own defence against the British officers, who often threatened to take me out of the ranks.'[126] Shaw was now viewed not only as a deserter, but as a traitor.

Dansey reported in 1783 that when the prisoners taken at Yorktown eventually re-joined the rest of the regiment, two corporals and 25 privates were listed as absent and were 'struck off the Strength by a Genl. Order for not returning from Captivity.'[127] Most of these men would have been either escapees who decided to settle down in America rather than make the arduous trek back to Crown lines, or soldiers who chose to flee once they were released from American prisons. Research remains to be done into how many, like Shaw, did not wholly disappear but actively went over to the other side. Dansey was careful to note that, when it came to his regiment's 27 deserters, 'I believe I may flatter the 33d. [that it is] a proportion as small as any Corps in the Service.[128]

The year 1781 closed with defeat for the 33rd and British arms. But while even the most stubborn advocates of the war were beginning to realise that the end was drawing inevitably closer, peace remained distant. For their own part, the 33rd as a regiment had not been fully destroyed. Though several hundred men marched into captivity at Yorktown, there was still the grenadier company in New York, and still dozens of sick and injured who had been left behind during previous campaigns, many in the southern

123 Shaw, *A Narrative*, p.46.
124 Shaw, *A Narrative*, p.46.
125 Shaw, *A Narrative*, p.47.
126 Shaw, *A Narrative*, p.56.
127 DHS: William Dansey Letters: 11 July 1783.
128 DHS: William Dansey Letters: 11 July 1783.

colonies. They began to be collected at Charleston, still held by Crown forces, where Major William Dansey had recently returned from leave.

He found himself with a thankless task – maintain and, if possible, rebuild the 33rd, with some semblance to the renowned force that had gone before. This he would have to do in the face of enemy action. The 33rd's fighting days were not yet done.

Chapter 12

A Broken Army

1782 and 1783

Many popular histories of the American Revolution War close after Cornwallis's capitulation at Yorktown, but this is a gross oversimplification of the final years of the conflict. While Yorktown brought home the reality of the situation to the British, and effectively ended major campaigning on the eastern seaboard of North America, the war carried on everywhere else.

In India the Kingdom of Mysore, backed by the French, was waging a campaign against the British presence in the Carnatic region. In Europe, the key British possession of Gibraltar was being besieged by a powerful joint Franco-Spanish army. In the Caribbean, France, Britain and Spain were vying for control of the vital sugar islands, a conflict only resolved by the crucial British naval victory at the Battle of the Saintes in April 1782. Even in North America, the fighting continued to rage ferociously along the frontiers as Native American tribes, backed by the British, continued to resist with notable success right up until 1783, laying the seeds for further conflicts in the following decades.

During all of this, skirmishes between rebel and Crown forces continued around areas such as New York and Charleston. It was in the latter that those remnants of the 33rd not in captivity found themselves stationed, besides the grenadier company still in New York. Major William Dansey had missed the fraught campaigns of 1780 and 1781. While on leave in England he had married his fiancée and had his portrait painted. Now he was ordered to James Island, just outside Charleston, where he was to assume command of the remnants of the 23rd, 33rd and 71st.

Dansey faced stark difficulties from the beginning, not only in maintaining the coherence, morale and discipline of the soldiers, but in quelling disaffection amongst the remnants of the officer corps. On his arrival at James Island in January 1782, he wrote that 'the first thing I heard from General Leslie & the Commandant was a Representation of the irregular Behaviour of the following Officers of the 33d. Lieuts. Wynyard, Innes, Gore and Kelly and this heighten'd by being told the same by some old Friends of the Regiment.'[1]

1 DHS: William Dansey Letters: 27 March 1782.

Dansey does not state just what the 'irregular Behaviour' was but, given that all four men were veterans of the southern campaigns – all but Innes had been wounded at Guildford Courthouse, and Wynyard had also been injured at Camden – it is not difficult to imagine that they had little time for their new commander, a man who, for all his earlier, active service in the light infantry, had spent the difficult, bloody years of 1780 and 1781 at home in England. Indeed, Dansey himself admitted to 'the honors I lost in not sharing the Laurels of the 33d. at Campden and Guilford.'[2]

Lieutenant John Kelly returned to Britain, described by Dansey as 'a terrible Fellow.' The Major attempted to take charge, writing in his report to Lieutenant Colonel Yorke that 'the other three I spoke to as their Commanding Officer and Friend and flatter'd myself I had been listen'd to.' In fact, he had not been. Whatever the problem was, it persisted to such an extent that Dansey felt himself forced into the rare expedient of not only reprimanding his fellow officers in front of the remnants of the regiment, but after another offence 'to go to Extremity and put them in Arrest, which they suffer'd to go such lengths to be reported to the General and put it out of the power to take any Apology.' Dansey hinted at the nature of their crimes when he wrote that at least one now realised 'there is no joking with Commanding Officers & Orders.' Wynyard, he believed, was finally repentant, while Gore showed 'little or no feeling and has put it out of my power ever to be his Friend except great Reformation which I hope for,' and Innes, 'is so much involved that if he has not some very extraordinary Assistance he must quit the service.'[3]

As though indiscipline and disrespect among his small officer cadre was not enough of a problem, Dansey found himself contending with a host of difficulties as he sought to keep the 33rd functioning while on James Island. The regiment's stores, including its clothing, had been neglected, the bales carrying the garments left on the floor without anything beneath them or without ever being moved or aired out. The bottoms of the bails had subsequently rotted away and the lowest garments were damaged. Dansey demanded a formal inquiry into the neglect.

Next, he had to deal with the issue of accoutrements, such as belts and cartridge pouches. Dansey refused to write an attestation of accoutrements lost during the previous campaign until he knew 'whether those the men of the Regiment had on when taken at York Town were paid for by the Government or not.' In his view there was no point in writing an attestation 'of the few I have Knowledge of,' adding that with the regiment's remains 'we have not an Accoutrement but what the Grenadier Company have.'[4] The grenadiers in question had been taken over by Captain Frederick Cornwallis, a distant relative of the Earl, in June of 1781, while their former captain, Hildebrand Oakes, became one of the regiment's few remaining hat company captains, joining Dansey at Charleston.

2 DHS: William Dansey Letters: April 1783.

3 DHS: William Dansey Letters: 27 March 1782.

4 DHS: William Dansey Letters: 27 March 1782.

Maintaining the Remnant

Besides troubles with stores and equipment, maintaining regular discipline among the rank-and-file also presented Dansey with yet further challenges. He noted that 'the Regiment is in a terrible State' and he had only a few reliable officers and NCOs to work with. Among the latter was Sergeant George Walker, who Dansey wrote 'is very useful to us and gives his Assistance towards keeping some small Appearance in the 33d.'[5] He was still with the regiment until at least 1790. Mentioned in similar terms was the adjutant, John Fox, himself a former sergeant who likewise served to 1790. A few other officers also proved their worth. Oakes, once he joined, was invaluable, and Dansey also spoke highly of Captain George Anson Nutt. The former lieutenant, best known for commanding the 33rd's unfortunate batch of recruits who ended up embroiled in Burgoyne's Saratoga debacle, had been exchanged, after four years a prisoner, for an enemy officer on 3 September 1781, and had finally joined the main body of the regiment, or at least what remained of it. Dansey noted that;

> Fox is very attentive and the Attention and Encouragement Nutt gives every Body keeps us a little on our Legs, I don't know what I shou'd do without him, it is very uphill Work keeping Order and Regularity here … The Zeal and attention of Oakes & Nutt are my only hopes of seeing the Regiment worthy to be remember'd as the 33d. I most sincerely wish we may leave this Country or we shall be annihilated with every Idea of what has been the Character of the Regiment.[6]

Reflecting on his first few months in command of the 33rd, Dansey lamented to Yorke that;

> As to the Situation of Affairs here, they are as bad as can be, nothing but a Siege can compleat it, a broken Army of all manner of Corps, of which the Debris of Lord Cornwallis's Army are the most respectable, amounting to about 300 wounded men and Recruits that never join'd. We are all much hurt at the seeming Indifference at home, concerning the Fall at York Town, Great Britain will not see such and Officer nor such an Army again soon. He closed the letter with the only good piece of news – 'we shall have a tolerable Band of Muisick I have got some of them in training with the Buffs [3rd Foot].'[7]

In May 1782, it was resolved that British Army infantry regiments not already bearing titles or distinctions were to have the geographic location they were most commonly associated with included in their regimental title. British regiments had been associated with their own specific areas for many years, but this was the first attempt to formally tie each to their own region, largely in a bid to aid recruitment. A total of 54 regiments were asked to provide the

5 DHS: William Dansey Letters: 27 March 1782.
6 DHS: William Dansey Letters: 27 March 1782.
7 DHS: William Dansey Letters: 27 March 1782.

Deputy Adjutant General with information about any pre-existing regional ties, and while not all regiments replied, Cornwallis seems to have been pleased to formalise the 33rd's long association with the west of Yorkshire. In his reply he wrote;

> I am to desire that you will please inform General Conway that the 33rd Regt. of Infantry has always recruited in the West Riding of Yorkshire, and has a very good interest & the general good will of the people, in that part of the Country:– I should therefore wish not only to be permitted to recruit in that county, but that my Regt. may bear the name of 33rd or West Yorkshire Regt. If that district is thought too extensive to give a name to one regt. only, I should desire to have my regt. called the 1st West Yorkshire; and am fully sure that no older Regt. can claim so long and intimate conection with the West Riding of Yorkshire.[8]

Cornwallis's choice of name was accepted, and in August 1782 the 33rd were formalised as the '33rd (or the 1st Yorkshire West Riding) Regiment of Foot.'[9]

While the close association with west Yorkshire would undoubtedly help the 33rd's recruiting efforts in the long term, in the short it made little difference to Dansey's situation. As the year wore on the 33rd's troubles continued. George Wynyard seems to have struggled with illness and possibly his finances. He obtained leave to go home, Dansey explained;

> On account of his Health as also his private Circumstances which has become exceedingly embarrass'd from the Situation he has been in for a Year past, altho' an error in his Conduct at my first joining the Regiment had put us on disagreeable Terms at the time of his sensibility of it, and the Opinion I must entertain of him as a Gentleman and an Officer made me interest myself in getting him leave, as I think he is a very fine young Man and should not be lost, it would be presumption to give my Opinion of him as an Officer to Your Lordship, who has seen much more of him and are a much better judge, I hope his coming home will enable him to settle his Affairs, and also get him Promotion which he has some Reason to flatter himself with.[10]

Dansey wrote of his concerns that the 33rd's numbers would be swollen by drafting soldiers in from other regiments, a practice he viewed with unease. He reported that 'from the Inclinations of the few Officers here two Years would make us hold up our Heads again, but if we are drafted into it will be very uphill Work as old men are not so easily managed as young.'[11] Better, he believed, to take the time to bring new, well-drilled recruits into the regiment.

More positively, a vital cadre of NCOs had by the summer of 1782 managed to escape captivity following the Yorktown surrender and make their way back to Charleston. Their number included a corporal, a drummer, a few privates, and six sergeants – Thomas Hill, John Crabtree, three others by

8 Brereton and Savory, *The History of the Duke of Wellington's Regiment*, pp.74–75.
9 Brereton and Savory, *The History of the Duke of Wellington's Regiment*, p.75.
10 DHS: Dansey Letters: William Dansey 21 June 1782.
11 DHS: Dansey Letters: William Dansey 21 June 1782.

the name of John Middleton, John Bentley and James Donnelly, and Samuel Coggill, the grey-eyed former drillmaster who had so impressed young John Robert Shaw when he was still a recruit. Whether they had escaped separately or all as part of a single successful escapade was not mentioned, but they undoubtedly brought vital experience and discipline back to the 33rd at a time when it needed it most.

While the war, at least in North America, had turned decisively against the British, Dansey still reported unrest among his fellow soldiers, and a desire to take the fight to the enemy; 'we can't help thinking we have a right to lay before our Sovereign our Feelings on this Occasion, however Policy may dictate a Submission to Rebels and Army while they have Arms in their Hands will not suffer an Insult.'[12] In fact, the 33rd would find themselves with a chance to vent their frustrations in combat. One final battle awaited the regiment in America.

While major operations had been suspended on the eastern seaboard, Crown forces in and around Charleston continued to mount small expeditions into the surrounding countryside in search of forage. Rebel forces sought to intercept them. A series of sharp skirmishes were fought between both sides in the latter months of 1782. Continental troops commanded by Polish military engineer Tadeusz Kościuszko detected the presence of a British woodcutting party who appeared regularly in the same area of James Island, at Dills Bluff. In November it was decided to attempt an attack on these foragers. Elements of the 1st Maryland and 2nd Pennsylvania Regiments of the Continental Army crossed to James Island from John's Island and attempted to snatch the small group.

What they failed to realise was that Dansey was in command of the foragers, based in nearby Fort Johnston, and was in the vicinity with at least the remnants of the 33rd and the Guards. Dansey had anticipated the possibility of an attack on the wood cutters, his watchfulness even giving rise to a belief among the Continentals that their plans had been betrayed. In a letter to his mother Dansey wrote 'my Caution prevented Surprise and my good Fortune gave them a Trimming for which I am indebted to the Bravery of Captn. Oakes and about twenty fine fellows that stood by him, who beat the Enemy on the first Onset and enabled me to drive them over a River eight miles from my Post.'[13]

Dansey also related an encounter with a personal acquaintance of his mother's, Richard Roberts, who had joined the regiment with the recruits that arrived at the end of 1780, and 'was one of these brave men, he is wounded in the Arm but doing very well, I can't help saying I was pleased to see him wounded it has open'd a road to my sincere Friendship for him, I shall take Care he never wants any Comforts his station of Life can admit of.'[14] A bullet broke Roberts's arm, and while the wound was being dressed one of the 33rd's ensigns, William Lockhart, was also carried in injured. Dansey related that 'being about my Size some of the Soldiers said it was the

12 DHS: Dansey Letters: William Dansey 21 June 1782.
13 DHS: William Dansey Letters: 4 December 1782.
14 DHS: William Dansey Letters: 4 December 1782.

Major upon which the poor Boy [Roberts] burst out a Crying not having flinch'd before but bore his Wound very patiently.'[15] By April the next year Dansey was reporting back to his mother that Roberts 'has hardly yet got the full Strength of his Arm, but the Spring will set him up, it was lucky Shot for him had it not been for it, I shoud have been a long time before I promoted him, for had I a Brother I wou'd not favour him before a deserving Soldier.'[16]

The British suffered two killed and three wounded during the skirmish at Dills Bluff, the Continentals five dead and five wounded, including a captain and a lieutenant killed. Dansey called the clash 'an unthought of Sprig of Laurel left on James Island for the poor Debris.'[17] He also noted that if peace was indeed forthcoming 'it will seal to Captn. Oakes and me honors in which we can have no Rivals, in having maintain'd the Superiority of His Majesty's Arms in the last serious Shot fired in this long and bloody Contest.'[18]

Dills Bluff was the 33rd's last engagement in America, and it had occurred just a few miles from their first involvement in a major action outside Charleston in 1776, six years and six months earlier. They had come full circle.

A month later, on 14 December 1782, Crown forces evacuated Charleston. Included with them were the 33rd onboard the transport ship *Peggy*, bound for New York. They totalled 82 men, 11 women and four children. They reached their destination on 6 January 1783 and were ordered to another old stomping ground, at Kingsbridge north of New York City. The change of climate brought the first of many improvements in the regiment's circumstances. Dansey wrote an explanation to Cornwallis, who had by then returned on England, noting that;

> I have the pleasure to inform you that we are much improved in health and other wise since our Arrival here from that horrid Climate of Carolina; I beg to represent to Your Lordship how much the Regiment will stand indebted to the Grenadier Company, for every Appearance we shall be able to maintain as the 33d. It is unnecessary for me to point you, my Lord, the state of the Debris I brought with me must be in, after a continuance of hard duty to the very last moment, unavoidably causing a Relaxation of that Dress and Regularity which ever distinguish'd us, and an almost total want of Noncommission'd Officers, that was it not for the Grenadier Company and the Serjeants who have escaped we must have been quite gone. I must beg leave further to represent to Your Lordship that the Grenadiers, have been equally as conspicuous for their good Behaviour as for every thing else and Captn. [Frederick] Cornwallis has done them great Justice.[19]

Just as positively, a new batch of recruits for the 33rd had arrived at Halifax in Nova Scotia, and had been drilling through the winter of early 1782 under

15 DHS: William Dansey Letters: 15 March 1783.
16 DHS: William Dansey Letters: 15 April 1783.
17 DHS: William Dansey Letters: 11 March 1783.
18 DHS: William Dansey Letters: 14 March 1783.
19 DHS: William Dansey Letters: 13 March 1783.

command of the 33rd's Lieutenant Arthur Beavor, who had lost seven teeth and part of his jaw to cannon fire during the 1780 siege of Charleston. Dansey expected them to join the rest of the force outside New York soon, returning their numbers to an operational level. In a letter to Lieutenant Colonel Yorke, he related the improved spirit;

> Our Situation at present does not admit of Regimental Mess, [Frederick] Cornwallis, Oakes and myself keep House in my Hutt, live as well and as hospitably as we can to which I am indebted for a much better share of Health and Spirits than I enjoy'd in Carolina, indeed we are all much better both Officers and Men of the Debris but have lost some of the finest Fellows in the General Hospital that came ill from Charlestown.[20]

Even better news awaited. On 19 May, after the regiment had moved to Fort Knyphausen (formerly Fort Washington) on Manhattan, they were joined by over 140 of the regiment's former Yorktown prisoners, released from their internment the month before. Led by Captain James Ingram and Lieutenant James Lee Harvey, they seemed no worse off for their 18 months of captivity. Dansey described how the 33rd's spirit and good discipline had seemingly survived the hardships of time spent in prison in Pennsylvania;

> Upwards of 140 Prisoners have join'd us in the handsomest manner and which has done great honor to the 33d. Nothing but the want of Arms seem'd to make the least difference in the Soldier. Ingram speaks in the highest terms of their good Behaviour, we expect between 30 & 40 more and depend on it shall loose very few, a very flattering circumstance different from many other Corps. Ours have come in the largest and most regular Body of the whole in proportion to our Numbers and in the best Order; depend on it Ingram has paid them great Attention and his merit highly deserving the notice of those in whose power it may be to reward it.[21]

Returning Home

At the end of May 1783 the regiment were seemingly able to muster 14 officers, 30 sergeants, 22 drummers and 399 rank-and-file.[22] This force, a startlingly impressive one considering the small remnant who travelled to New York from Charleston at the end of 1782, can be accounted for by the addition of the grenadier company, the large detachment of returned prisoners (plus the 30 or 40 Dansey spoke of arriving later) and the new recruits brought over from Halifax. It is a stark reversal of fortunes, and an indicator that the 33rd had survived. The hard work of officers like Dansey and Oakes in maintaining standards and discipline had paid off. The former wrote, with some justifiable pride, that;

20 DHS: William Dansey Letters: 13 March 1783.
21 DHS: William Dansey Letters: 20 May 1783.
22 Brereton and Savory, *The History of the Duke of Wellington's Regiment*, p.73.

> I shall not be afraid or ashamed to shew the 33d. to anybody, the zealous support I meet with from some Officers makes the whole unanimous in our Endeavours to get like ourselves again, I am pleased to find our improvement very conspicuous, that our ground Work is not quite gone and that Lord Cornwallis and Webster are not wore out of the 33d.[23]

The regiment had shifted from Fort Knyphausen to Flushing, on Long Island, where Dansey reported they had 'establish'd a Regiml. Mess and are living together very comfortably.'[24] Formal news of a declaration of peace was expected daily, with the mood seemingly alternating between relief that the trials and tribulations of war were over, and lingering resentment towards the American colonists and to those back home in Britain who had tacitly supported the revolution. However, while the 33rd had fired its last shots in anger in America, the regiment's more dangerous military duties were not quite yet behind them.

In August news of trouble reached Dansey. The 33rd's administrative processes involving settling back pay for soldiers entitled to their discharge at the end of the war were interrupted by a plea for assistance. Loyalists were still arriving in and around New York City in the desperate hope that they would be evacuated either to Britain or Canada, thus avoiding retaliation by those they had fought against during the war. A force described by Dansey as 'the Inhabitans of this Country assembling in Banditties' had gathered 'to rob and plunder the Loyalists' as they tried to reach the safety of British lines and the Royal Navy vessels sent to evacuate them.[25] In an effort to protect the refugees, the 33rd were mobilised alongside light infantry and grenadiers, two 6-pounders, and all the 17th Light Dragoons who could be mounted. This force, under Dansey's overall command, marched east on Long Island, heading into rebel territory for the last time.

There was certainly the potential for disaster. Dansey observed that 'this has been a very critical Service and had not I been very cautious and the Troops under my Command in high Discipline, it might have rekindled the Flames of War from the violent disposition of the inhabitants of this New Nation.'[26] Eventually, the Loyalist refugees were located and brought safely to a Royal Navy frigate, the *Grana*, without either side firing a shot. Dansey noted that 'the 33d. are employe'd to the last moment, and I believe I shall have added to the honor of holding the last hostile Post that of leading the last Column that moved in this Country.'[27]

The Peace of Paris, signed on 3 September 1783, brought an end to the conflict, at least in North America – fighting between Britain and the Dutch in the Fourth Anglo-Dutch War and between Britain and the Kingdom of Mysore in India would both continue until 1784. For Dansey and the 33rd however, peace beckoned. The number of men in the regiment dropped

23 DHS: William Dansey Letters: 11 July 1783.
24 DHS: William Dansey Letters: 11 July 1783.
25 DHS: William Dansey Letters: 30 August 1783.
26 DHS: William Dansey Letters: 30 August 1783.
27 DHS: William Dansey Letters: 30 August 1783.

drastically as those who had enlisted only to the end of the war took their discharges, the first in a series of measures designed to drastically reduce the size of the British Army and put it on a peacetime footing. Dansey did his best to keep the regiment fully stocked, but struggled for a number of reasons. He wrote to Cornwallis that 'we were employ'd on a kind of actual Service to the very last moment and were not in a Situation to take Advantage of Recruiting as other Corps, indeed my Attention was mostly engaged to re-enlisting our own men.'[28] He was also unsure as to whether the discharged men would have to be paid for by the regiment via the unit's non-effective fund. Soldiers from the flank battalions sharing a billet on Long Island could not be tempted to transfer into the 33rd due to the unsettled state of accounts, and Dansey likewise refused the opportunity of 'relaxing the Reins of Discipline necessary in Recruiting.'[29] He noted the effect the loss of men had on his burgeoning regimental band with some dismay;

> We loose two of the Musick, three are entitled to their Discharge viz. Collier, Lisk & Carey, the two latter will not enlist again (ungrateful Dogs) so my dear Colonel do enlist two Clarinets and what other Musick you think proper, especially a Horn or two I never wish to be without a Band as long as have a Penny to spare and the whole of us here are of that Opinion.[30]

The 33rd's musicians would have a good deal of time in which to practice. The regiment received new deployment orders. They embarked at Bedford on Long Island on 9 October 1783. Their destination was Halifax, Nova Scotia, part of Britain's Canadian territories, successfully retained following the war's close. Dansey, meanwhile, received leave to return for a while to England. Earlier he had written to his mother that 'I must acknowledge that after Seven long Years of War and trouble I cou'd enjoy a little domestic Rest with my Family, and be very well contented as Major of the 33d. in some Country Quarter or Barrack in England.'[31] He hoped that 'now the Blessings of Peace are return'd to the World, that we may spend many happy Years.'[32]

That hope was not without good cause. The 33rd's war was over.

28 DHS: William Dansey Letters: 29 November 1783.
29 DHS: William Dansey Letters: 29 November 1783.
30 DHS: William Dansey Letters: 29 November 1783.
31 DHS: William Dansey Letters: 15 March 1783.
32 DHS: William Dansey Letters: 13 April 1783.

13

Conclusion

While the 33rd was an exceptional regiment in terms of drill and appearance in the early 1770s, there is no argument to be made that they were the most effective regiment on operations during the American Revolution. While at times they stood out as a picked corps, such as when they joined the vanguard in the battles around New York in 1776, or acted as light infantry in the south in 1780, most of their time in North America was spent like any other solid, dependable line regiment. The most effective troops during the war were undoubtedly the composite flank battalions, and other units earned praise and appellations as well. During the southern campaigns Cornwallis himself described how the Brigade of Guards 'is become the Pattern of good Order, attention, and subordination, to the rest of the Army.'[1] He likewise assured an absent officer of the 23rd Royal Welsh Fusiliers in the aftermath of Guildford Courthouse that 'nothing could behave better than the 23rd.'[2]

While the 33rd could not be considered among the elite, they fought in every major battle apart from the retreat from Concord and the engagement at Bunker Hill, a record held by few other units. They often played a prominent role, as when they drove Continental troops before them on Long Island, came to the rescue of the grenadiers at Monmouth, or broke the enemy's resistance at Camden. They certainly performed their duties well, and their record of service offers an insight into the victories and defeats, trials and tribulations faced by ordinary British soldiers during the American Revolution.

After evacuating New York, the 33rd spent over two years in Nova Scotia, first at Halifax, then from July 1785 in the newly built barracks in Sydney, Cape Breton. The most notable occurrence of their stay appears to have been the reformed Captain George Wynyard's sighting of his brother's ghost, seemingly at the very moment of said brother's death back in England.[3] Cornwallis continued to monitor his regiment even as he pursued other duties, writing in

1 TNA: PRO 30/11/85: f.34.

2 TNA: PRO 30/11/85: f.24.

3 Brereton and Savory, *The History of the Duke of Wellington's Regiment*, p.74. This was not the only revolutionary-era encounter between a man of the 33rd and the supposed supernatural. John Robert Shaw's memoirs relate meeting what he called 'the ghost of Old Funk' in Pennsylvania.

1784 that 'I had a letter from Yorke to-day in good spirits, and giving a most excellent account of the appearance of discipline of the 33rd.'[4]

In 1786, after a decade's absence, the 33rd were ordered back to Britain. They spent time at Windsor Castle guarding the king, and from 1789 to 1792 were stationed back in Devon and Cornwall. With the French Revolution well underway, the army became overstretched, often serving onboard Royal Navy vessels as marines, and for a while the 33rd was the only full regiment stationed in the south of England.[5]

Cornwallis remained the 33rd's colonel, and for at least the next decade the regiment appears to have remained well-noted for its high standards. In 1787 the 33rd was still being described as 'the Pattern, or Lord Cornwallis' Corps.'[6] An inspection at Windsor in 1788 found that 'the Regiment appears founded upon the same system as in the last war and when complete, is likely to retain its usual Discipline.'[7] Another inspection a year later found that 'to report them fit for Service without adding that they were adequate to any active military Service whatsoever, would be too indifferent a representation of their gallant and warlike Deportment.'[8]

The 33rd transferred back to Dublin in 1792, partly to combat the efforts of a group of insurrectionists known as the Whiteboys. The regiment's flank companies were incorporated into six composite flank battalions and sent on campaign to the West Indies, where they suffered terribly, while in 1794 the main body of the regiment were deployed to Flanders as part of the ill-fated attempts to stifle revolutionary France.

It is perhaps ironic that the 33rd had for their colonels arguably (at least in modern times), the most famous British general of the eighteenth century, followed by the most famous British general of the nineteenth century. Arthur Wesley, who changed his name to Wellesley in 1798 and would later be known as the Duke of Wellington, purchased the rank of major then, within a few months, lieutenant colonel in the 33rd in 1793. It is worth noting that Wellesley's desire as lieutenant colonel was 'to maintain the system of discipline, subordination, and interior economy' that Cornwallis had created.[9]

With Cornwallis in poor health, having only just returned from leading a successful campaign in India, there was no prospect of him being involved in the next campaign the 33rd were assigned to. Wesley had command of the regiment in the field when they sailed from Cork in June 1794. He got his first taste of combat at the Battle of Boxtel on 15 September 1794, leading the 33rd well on what was otherwise a disastrous campaign. In one engagement;

> In retreating owing to the narrowness of the road a Regiment of Irish Dragoons, threw the First Guards into some confusion. Fortunately the Thirty-third

4 Ross (ed.), *Correspondence of Charles, First Marquis Cornwallis*, vol.I, pp.166–167.

5 Brereton and Savory, *The History of the Duke of Wellington's Regiment*, p.75.

6 H. E. Gatliff (ed.), *Stations, Gentlemen! Memoirs of James Gatliff* (London: Faber & Faber, 1938), p. 43.

7 TNA: WO 27/64/65, quoted in Lodge, *To What Extent*, p.43.

8 TNA: WO 27/69, quoted in Andrew Lodge, *To What Extent*, p.43.

9 Middleton, *Cornwallis*, p.18.

> regiment was formed in the rear, and opening to allow them to pass, wheeled up, and initially throwing a few cool and well-directed volleys into the enemy's squadrons obliged him to decamp precipitately, enabling [British commander] Abercrombie to retire without further molestation.[10]

It is worth noting that during this campaign there were still hardened veterans of the 'American War' serving in the ranks, such as sergeants Coggill and Crabtree. Major General Lord Cathcart 'considered them to be one of the better regiments with a good set of officers.'[11]

After the Flanders campaign the 33rd were sent to India with Wellesley, where they were notably involved in the war against the Tipu Sultan, emerging victorious in the Battle of Mallavelly and the siege of Seringapatam. The regiment spent a lengthy period stationed in India, missing much of the Napoleonic Wars. They returned to Britain in 1812 and saw action in Germany and, once again, in the Netherlands, before joining Wellington's Anglo-allied army at the Battle of Waterloo. Before the start of the Waterloo campaign, in early 1815, Major General Sir Henry Clinton, the son of the Revolutionary War commander-in-chief, wrote that 'upon the whole I consider this regiment [the 33rd] to be in the most advanced state of any in the army.'[12] Another officer considered 'it in a very high state of discipline, and that the high order of the men's appointments and their precision in moving do great credit to the officers of the corps.'[13]

The 33rd spent the decades between the end of the Napoleonic Wars and the start of the Crimean War alternating between garrisons in Britain, Jamaica, Gibraltar, the West Indies and Canada. In 1853, not long after the death of the Duke of Wellington, Queen Victoria had the regiment renamed to the 33rd (The Duke of Wellington's) Regiment making it the only regiment after 1782 to bear the name of a non-royal. The 33rd fought at Alma, Inkerman and Sevastopol in the Crimea and took part in the Abyssinia expedition of 1868. The regiment was merged in 1881 with the 76th Foot as part of the Childers Reforms, creating The Duke of Wellington's Regiment (West Riding).

After service in the Second Boer War, the World Wars saw battalions from the regiment serving in combat all over the globe. In 1953, during the Korean War, the Dukes won particular renown as part of the defence of the Hook, a series of strategic hills in North Korea. They performed tours of duty in Bosnia and in Northern Ireland during the Troubles, and were part of the 2003 invasion of Iraq. In 2006 the Dukes were amalgamated with other regiments to form the Yorkshire Regiment, which remains a part of the British Army to this day.

Many regimental accounts close with further monolithic discussions on their own particular formation's place in history. It seems remiss, however,

10 R.N.W. Thomas, 'Wellington in the Low Countries 1794–1795', *International History Review*, vol.11, 1989, p.18, quoted in Lodge, *To What Extent*, p.43.

11 Lodge, *To What Extent*, p.43.

12 Anon., 'Record of the Services of the 33rd (The Duke of Wellington's) Regiment of Foot,' *Colburn's United Service Magazine, and Naval and Military Journal*, 1869, Part III, p.518.

13 Anon., 'Record of the Services of the 33rd,', p.519.

to forget that fighting units are made up of individuals. A little under 1,000 men served in the 33rd Regiment of Foot over the course of the American Revolutionary War. Hundreds were killed in action or perished from disease, or suffered wounds and injury, some debilitating. Almost all endured hardship and privation, often not just the struggles common to eighteenth-century soldiering in general, but in campaigns that were notably hard and gruelling. It seems best, therefore, to end with some comments about the fate of some of the soldiers mentioned.

Charles Cornwallis might have become infamous in US school textbooks as the man who lost America, but in many ways his career only just started with defeat at Yorktown. An adept colonial administrator with the leanings of a reformer, he was knighted in 1786 and appointed as Governor-General in India. He enacted significant changes to the East India Company, and commanded British forces during their victory over the Tipu Sultan during the Third Anglo-Mysore War. He returned to Britain in 1794, becoming Lord Lieutenant of Ireland in 1798, where he defeated a major uprising and brought Ireland fully into the union with Great Britain in 1801. After taking part in negotiating a treaty with Napoleon, he was reassigned to India in 1805, where he died three months after his arrival. He is buried in a well-maintained tomb in Gauspur, overlooking the River Ganges. He was the 33rd's colonel right up until his death.

At the war's close John Robert Shaw left the Continental Army and eventually settled down in Kentucky as a frontier well-digger. While recovering from injuries sustained during an excavating explosion he began to write *The Life and Travels of John Robert Shaw: A Narrative of the Life and Travels of the Well-Digger, now resident of Lexington, Kentucky, Written by Himself.* In 1807 over 1,000 subscribers in the US helped pay for its printing. He had five children by several different women. Well-digging proved more hazardous an occupation than being a soldier, and Shaw was killed in an explosion in 1813.

George Anson Nutt, who had marched into captivity in 1777 and returned to the 33rd in 1781 to help get the regiment through its post-Yorktown difficulties, went on half-pay after the war, but returned to active service on 30 May 1787 when transferred to the 65th Foot. He married a woman named Mary Smith in 1793, with whom he had two sons and a daughter, then remarried one Mary Tymewell. He died in 1841.

John Dyke Acland, whose influence saw him rise rapidly through the ranks of the 33rd's officer corps before he transferred to the 20th Foot in time for active service, found his disdain for Americans misplaced. After being wounded and taken prisoner at Bemis Heights he was well-treated by his captors and nursed back to health by his loving wife, Harriet. He returned to Britain and, in an act of irony, fought a duel with an officer who disparaged the very colonies Acland himself had once spoken so vehemently against. He suffered a blow to the head from a fall during the duel and died from the injury on 22 November 1778.

Hildebrand Oakes, the young officer who led the 33rd's grenadier company for much of the war and was instrumental in helping keep the regiment's remnants together after Yorktown, was one of a number of 33rd officers who went on to have illustrious careers. He became deputy quartermaster-general in 1794, served in Portugal and Egypt, attained the role of Lieutenant-Governor of Portsmouth and then Civil Commissioner of Malta in 1810. He became colonel of the 52nd Foot, and died on 9 September 1822.

The exact fate of Sergeant Samuel Coggill is not currently known. The records of the Chelsea Pensioners show that he left the British Army at the age of 59 in 1812, after a service of 39 years and 11 months, 35 of them spent as a sergeant. His reason for leaving is listed simply as 'worn out,' a familiar complaint applied to old soldiers.[14] Hopefully he marched off into an easy retirement.

William Dansey got his wish for some years of peace and spent the greater part of the 1780s in England with his family. He transferred as lieutenant colonel to the 49th Foot in 1790. In 1793 he received the prestigious appointment of Aide de Camp to King George III. He had four children – three sons and a daughter – with Catherine Malet, whom he had married on 18 December 1780 while on leave in England. At least one son followed in the footsteps of his father and grandfather, joining the British Army and becoming colonel of the 76th Foot in 1839. With the outbreak of war with revolutionary France, William Dansey was posted to the Caribbean island of Domingo, where he commanded the post of Cape Nicola Mole. He died there on 18 November 1793, aged 48, 'a victim to the Zeal with which he discharged his Duty regardless of the effects of an insalubrious and destructive climate.'[15]

14 TNA: WO 116/19: Royal Hospital Chelsea, admissions books.
15 DHS: Dansey Letters: Obituary Notice of Mrs William Dansey.

Appendix

33rd Foot Locations and Marching Orders 1769–1776[1]

RHQ Location	Date	Coy & Detachment Location	Marching Orders (MO)	Remarks
St Phillips, Minorca	1764–1769			
			MO 1 May 69: on arrival at Portsmouth march to Salisbury, Lisherton, Farnham and Milford	
Salisbury	May–Jun 69	All		General Inspection Salisbury 22 Jun 69
Hounslow	Jul 69	Hartford Bridge & Hartley Row: 5 Coy Basingstoke: 4 Coy	MO 4 July 69 Hounslow: march in 2 Div to Derby & Leicester	King's Grand Review
Derby	Aug 69–May 70	Derby: 5 Coy Leicester: 4 Coy	MO 27 Feb 70: coys at Leicester to march on 9 Mar to Loughborough and Mt Sorrel and then to Derby	General Inspection Derby 22 May 70
Norwich	May–Dec 70	All: 9 Coy	MO 15 May 70: march in 2 div on 30 May to Norwich. MO 1 Jun 70: send det to Gt. Yarmouth, North Walsham & Holt. MO 13 Sep 70: send det to Lynn. MO 6 Oct 70: send dets to Beccles, Halesworth, Yarford, Loestoff, Southwolf & Blythebury. MO 11 Oct 70: Send det to Clay. MO 1 Dec 70: march regt to Bury on 10 Dec 70. MO 1 Dec 70 Bury: March regt to Chatham Bks (routes given for 2 div).	
Chatham Barracks	Jan–June 71	All	MO 8 June 71: move regt to Greenwich, Blackheath, Shooters Hill, Lee and Lewisham by any route and in an div.	Inspection 71 (no return) Dansey refers to Blackheath and Hyde Park.

1 TNA: WO 5/56, 5/57 and WO 17/142 in Lodge, *To What Extent*, pp.11–13.

RHQ Location	Date	Coy & Detachment Location	Marching Orders (MO)	Remarks
Greenwich	Jun 71	All: 10 Coy	MO 21 Jun 71: march on 25 June to Hammersmith, Chiswick & Turnham Green (2 Coy), Fulham, Parsons Green & Waltham Green (4 Coy), and Putney, Putney Bowling Green (4 Coy) from where to move in 2 div to Portsmouth and Portsmouth Common (routes given for 2 div). MO 25 June 71: Dover det to move to Portsmouth once relieved.	
Portsmouth	Jun-Nov 71	All	MO 25 June 71: on arrival a part of the regt to be stationed at Gosport. MO 25 Nov 71: march in 2 div to Gloucester (5 coy) and Cirencester (5 coy).	Dansey reports working on 'works' through winter if 71 to Mar 72
Gloucester Cheltenham Gloucester Gloucester Gloucester	Jan–May 72 Jun 72 July–Sep 72 Oct–Dec 72 Jan–Feb 73	All Cheltenham: 2 Coy Tewkesbury: 3 Coy Stroud: 2 Coy Baunton: 1 Coy Ross: 1 Coy Gloucester: 5 Coy Cirencester: 5 Coy Gloucester: 5 Coy Tewkesbury: 5 Coy Gloucester: 5 Coy Tewkesbury: 3 Coy Cheltenham: 2 Coy	MO 20 Mar 72: march regt to assemble at Gloucester. MO 8 Sep 72: move 5 coy at Cirencester to Tewksbury. MO 13 Feb 72: march regt in 2 div to Exeter.	General Inspection Gloucester May 72.
Wellington	Mar 73	Wellington: 5 Coy Taunton: 5 Coy	MO 10 Mar 73: move three coys or similar sized det to Penryn, Truro, Torquay, Falmouth and adjacent places to relieve 23rd Foot. MO 10 Mar 73: move three coys to Plymouth	Dansey writes from St Thomas nr. Execter. 12 & 13 Mar three coy marched out of Exeter to Cornwall & another three to Plymouth
Exeter	Apr 73	Exeter: 4 Coy Plymouth & Redruth: 3 Coy Penryn: 1 Coy Detachments at Penzance, St Nicholas Is, Helstone, St Ives	MO 7 Apr 73: move one coy from Plymouth to Truro. MO 21 Apr 73: move from Redruth to Falmouth. MO 5 May 73: move dets to Penzance, St Nicholas Is, Helstone and St Ives on relieved to Plymouth and Plymouth Barracks.	Dansey refers to an officer and 30 soldiers at Redruth to protect the market.

THE PATTERN

RHQ Location	Date	Coy & Detachment Location	Marching Orders (MO)	Remarks
Plymouth Barracks	May 73	Plymouth Barracks: 6 Coy Falmouth: 2 Coy Penryn: 1 Coy Truro: 1 Coy	MO 12 Aug 73: move 5 coy from Plymouth into county of Cornwall and replace dets of 3rd Foot. MO 27 Oct 73: Cpt Creed det to Penryn to assist revenue men. MO 10 Dec 73: Capt Creed det to be relieved.	Dansey touring dets. 16 May 73 Dansey reports marching his coy from Trutor to Plymouth (48 miles).
Plymouth Barracks	May–Aug 73	All	MO 5 Apr 74: It is HMP that you cause the 33rd Foot to march and embark on board the transports destined to carry them to Ireland.	General Inspection Plymouth 26 May 73 and 31 Mar 74.
Plymouth Barracks	Sept–Dec 73	Plymouth: 5 Coy Penryn: 2 Coy Trutor: 1 Coy Helstone: 1 Coy Padstow & Wardbridge: 1 Coy		
Plymouth Barracks	Mar 74	All		
Cork	Apr–Aug 74	All		
Cork	Oct 74–Jan 75	Cork: 3 Coy Inchequela: 2 Coy Clonakilty: 2 Coy Youghal: 3 Coy		
Dublin	Apr–Oct 75	All		General Inspection Dublin 1775
Cork	Jan 76	All		
Cork	Feb 76	All	Set sail for America	

Bibliography

Archival Sources

Delaware Historical Society (DHS)
William Dansey Letters, Delaware Historical Society, Wilmington, Delaware. With thanks to The Duke of Wellington's Regiment Museum, Halifax, UK

The National Archives (TNA)
CO 5/94: Military despatches, 1776–1777
PRO 30/11: Cornwallis Papers
SP 63/445–451: Miscellaneous State Papers Ireland
T 14/15: Treasury out-letters, Ireland
WO 1/10: Commanders-in-chief, North America
WO 26/29: Entry books of warrants, regulations and precedents
WO 12: General Muster Books and Pay Lists
WO 27/15–31: Inspection returns
WO 71/88: Courts-martial proceedings
WO 97: Royal Hospital Chelsea, soldiers' service documents
WO 121/10/48: Royal Hospital Chelsea, discharge papers
WO 116: Royal Hospital Chelsea, admission books

Clements Library, University of Michigan (CL)
Henry Clinton papers (1736-1850)

Library of Congress (LOC)
George Washington Papers, Series 4

Unpublished Materials

Cornwallis, Charles to Sackville Turner, 'Chatham, March 15, 1771' from a letter sold at auction on June 27, 2015 by Goldberg Coins & Collectibles (Lot 276)

Duke, George, 'German Town Camp Octr 13, 1777,' from a letter sold in May 2008 at a private auction, transcript courtesy of Don Hagist

Oakes, Hildebrand to Henry Seymour Conway, from a collection of letters sold in May 2008 at a private auction, transcript courtesy of Don Hagist

Newspapers

British Chronicle or Pugh's Hereford Journal
Craftsman, or Say's Weekly Journal
Daily Advertiser
Edinburgh Advertiser
Gazetteer and New Daily Advertiser
General Advertiser and Morning Intelligencer
General Evening Post
London Chronicle
London Evening Post
London Gazette
Lloyd's Evening Post and British Chronicle.
Morning Chronicle
Morning Post
Norfolk Chronicle
Public Advertiser
Shrewsbury Chronicle
Virginia Gazette
Westminster Journal and London Political Miscellany

Published Primary Sources

Anon., 'Record of the Services of the 33rd (The Duke of Wellington's) Regiment of Foot,' *Colburn's United Service Magazine, and Naval and Military Journal*, 1869, Part III, pp.233–245

André, John, *André's Journal: An Authentic Record of the Movements and Engagements of the British Army in America* (Boston: Bibliophile Society, 1903)

Anon., 'For the Political Magazine' in *The Political Magazine and Parliamentary, Naval, Military, and Literary Journal*, 1781, vol.II, pp.341–343

Anon., 'Baltimore, Maryland, Aug. 29', *The Scots Magazine, 1780*, vol.XLII, 1780, pp.533–535

Bain, James Jr (ed.), 'The Siege of Charleston: Journal of Captain Peter Russell, December 25, 1779 to May 2, 1780', *The American Historical Review*, April, 1899, vol.4, no.3, pp.478–501

Bell Clark, William (ed.), *Naval Documents of the American Revolution* (Washington DC: U.S. Government Printing Office, 1969)

Caruthers, E.W., *Interesting Revolutionary Incidents and Sketches of Character* (Philadelphia: Hayes and Zell, 1856)

Cuthbertson, Bennett, *Cuthbertson's System for the Complete Interior Management and Œconomy of a Battalion of Infantry* (Bristol: Rouths and Nelson, 1776)

Dansey, Paul (ed.), *Captured Rebel Flag: The Letters of Captain William Dansey, 33rd Regiment of Foot, 1776–1777* (Godmanchester: Ken Trotman Publishing, 2010)

Falconer, William, 'Camp, Long Island, July 13, 1776,' in Anon. (ed.), *Collections of the New-York Historical Society for the Year 1872* (New York: The New-York Historical Society, 1873), pp.194–195

Gatliff, H.E. (ed.), *Stations, Gentlemen! Memoirs of James Gatliff* (London: Faber & Faber, 1938)

Gruber, Ira D. (ed.), *John Peebles' American War: The Diary of a Scottish Grenadier, 1776–1782* (Stroud: Sutton Publishing, 1997)

Hadden, James M. (ed.), *Hadden's Journal and Orderly Books: A Journal Kept in Canada and upon Burgoyne's Campaign in 1776 and 1777* (Albany: Joel Munsell's Sons, 1884)

Hanger, George, *Reflections on the Menaced Invasion and the Means of Protecting the Capital by Preventing the Enemy from Landing in any Part Contiguous to it* (London: John Stockdale, 1804)
Howard Henry Peckham (ed.), *Memoirs of the Life of John Adlum in the Revolutionary War* (Chicago: The Caxton Club, 1968)
Howard, William Jr, 'The Rising Sun Tavern and the Rockaway Pass' in Anon. (ed.), *Manual of the Common Council of the City of Brooklyn* (New York: Arthur Brown, 1868), pp.471–476
Howe, Robert, 'The Lee Papers, Volume 1, 1754–1776' in Anon. (ed.), *Collections of the New-York Historical Society for the Year 1871* (New York: The New-York Historical Society, 1872)
Jackson, Robert, *A Treatise on the Fevers of Jamaica* (Philadelphia: Robert Campbell, 1795)
Kemble, Stephen, 'The Kemble Papers, Volume 1' in Anon. (ed.), *Collections of the New-York Historical Society for the Year 1883* (New York: The New-York Historical Society, 1884)
Kemble, Stephen, *Journals of Lieut. Col. Stephen Kemble, 1773-1789: And British Army Orders* (Boston: Gregg Press, 1972)
Lamb, Roger, *An Original and Authentic Journal of Occurrences During the Late American War From Its Commencement to the Year 1783* (Dublin: Wilkinson and Courtney, 1809)
Lamb, Roger, *Memoir of His Own Life* (Dublin: J. Jones, 1811)
Lee, Henry, *Memoirs of the War in the Southern Department of the United States* (Washington DC: Peter Force, 1827)
Martin, Joseph Plumb, *A Narrative of a Revolutionary War Soldier: Some of the Adventures, Dangers, and Sufferings of Joseph Plumb Martin* (New York: Signet Classics, 2010)
Muenchhausen, Friedrich Ernst Von, *At General Howe's Side, 1776-1778: The Diary of General William Howe's Aide de Camp, Captain Friedrich Von Muenchhausen* (Monmouth Beach: Philip Freneau Press, 1974)
Onderdonk, Henry Jr (ed.), *Documents and Letters Intended to Illustrate the Revolutionary Incidents of Queens County* (New York: Leavitt, Trow and Company, 1846)
Paul L. Pace, *Capt. Eyre Coote's 37th Light Infantry Company Order Book, 1778 – 1781*, RevWar'75, <http://www.revwar75.com/library/pace/37-light-OB.pdf>, accessed January 2023
Rogers, George C. Jr (ed.), 'Letters of Charles O'Hara to the Duke of Grafton,' *South Carolina Historical Magazine*, vol. 65, 1964, pp.158–181
Ross, Charles (ed.), *Correspondence of Charles, First Marquis Cornwallis* (London: Murray, 1859)
Saberton, Ian (ed.), *The Cornwallis Papers: The Campaigns of 1780 and 1781 in the Southern Theatre of the American Revolutionary War* (Uckfield: Naval & Military Press, 2010)
Shaw, John Robert, *A Narrative of the Life & Travels of John Robert Shaw, the Well-Digger, Now Resident in Lexington, Kentucky* (Lexington: Daniel Bradford, 1807)
Simcoe, John Graves, *Simcoe's Military Journal: A History of the Operations of a Partisan Corps Called the Queen's Rangers* (New York: Bartlett & Welford, 1844)
Simes, Thomas, *The Military Medley: Containing the Most Necessary Rules and Directions for Attaining a Competent Knowledge of the Art* (London: published by the author, 1768)
Tarleton, Banastre, *A History of the Campaigns of 1780 and 1781 in the Southern Provinces of North America* (Dublin: Colles et al, 1787)

Townsend, Joseph, 'Narrative' in J. Smith Futhey and Gilbert Cope (eds), *History of Chester County, Pennsylvania, with Genealogical and Biographical Sketches* (Philadelphia: Louis H. Everts, 1881)

Tustin, Joseph P. (ed.), *Diary of the American War: A Hessian Journal* (New Haven: Yale University Press, 1979)

Williamson, John, *The Elements of Military Arrangement; Comprehending, the Tactick, Exercise, Manoevres, and Discipline of the British Infantry* London: published by the author, 1781)

Secondary Sources

Atkinson, Rick, *The British Are Coming: The War for America, Lexington to Princeton, 1775-1777* (New York: William Collins, 2019)

Babits, Lawrence E., and Howard, Joshua B., *Long, Obstinate, and Bloody: The Battle of Guildford Courthouse* (Chapel Hill: University of North Carolina Press, 2009)

Bailey, De Witt, *Small Arms of the British Forces, 1664–1815* (Woonsocket: Andrew Mowbray Publishers, 2009)

Bearss, Edwin C., *The Battle of Sullivan's Island and the Capture of Fort Moultrie* (Washington DC: National Park Service Division of History, 1968)

Bicheno, Hugh, *Rebels & Redcoats: The American Revolutionary War* (London: Harper Collins, 2003)

Brereton, J. M., and Savory, A.C.S., *The History of the Duke of Wellington's Regiment (West Riding) 1702-1992* (Halifax: The Duke of Wellington's Regiment (West Riding), 1933)

Burdick, Kim, 'What they Saw and Did at Yorktown's Redoubts 9 and 10', *Journal of the American Revolution*, <https://allthingsliberty.com/2020/04/what-they-saw-and-did-at-yorktowns-redoubts-9-and-10/>, accessed 31 January 2023

Carpenter, James Linwood, *The Yorktown Prisoners: A Narrative Account of the Disposition of the British Army Which Capitulated at Yorktown, October 19, 1781* (Williamsburg: College of William and Mary, 1950), <https://dx.doi.org/doi:10.21220/m2-0mfs-s403>, accessed January 2023

Carpenter, Stanley D.M., *Southern Gambit: Cornwallis and the British March to Yorktown* (Norman: University of Oklahoma Press, 2019)

Clayton, Anthony, *The British Officer: Leading the Army from 1660 to the Present* (Oxon: Routledge, 2006)

Conway, Stephen, *The British Army, 1714–1783: An Institutional History* (Barnsley: Pen & Sword Military, 2021)

Draper , Lyman Copeland, *Kings Mountain and its Heroes* (Cincinnati: Thomson, 1881)

Dillon, John, *All at Sea: Naval Support for the British Army during the American Revolutionary War* (Warwick: Helion, 2019)

Dunkerly, Robert M., *Decision at Brandywine: The Battle on Birmingham Hill* (Yardley: Westholme Publishing, 2021)

Dunkerly, Robert M., *Redcoats on the Cape Fear: The Revolutionary War in Southeastern North Carolina* (Jefferson: McFarland & Company, 2012)

Fischer, David Hackett, *Paul Revere's Ride* (Oxford: Oxford University Press, 1994)

Fischer, David Hackett, *Washington's Crossing* (Oxford: Oxford University Press, 2004)

Frey, Sylvia R., *The British Soldier in America: A Social History of Military Life in the Revolutionary Period* (Austin: University of Texas Press, 1981)

Guy, Alan J., 'The Army of the Georges 1714–1783' in David Chandler and Ian Beckett (eds), *The Oxford History of the British Army* (Oxford: Oxford University Press, 1994), pp.92–111

Gilbert, Stephen, 'The Long and the Short of It: Military Hairstyles during the American Revolution Part 1 (of 3): British Army Hairstyles', *The Brigade Dispatch*, vol.XXXV, no.1, Spring 2005, pp.10–19

Hagist, Don N., *British Soldiers American War: Voices of the American Revolution* (Yardley: Westholme Publishing, 2012)

Hagist, Don N., *Noble Volunteers: The British Soldiers Who Fought the American Revolution*. Yardley PA: Westholme Publishing, 2020

Hagist, Don N., *These Distinguished Corps: British Grenadier and Light Infantry Battalions in the American Revolution* (Warwick: Helion, 2021)

Hoock, Holger, *Scars of Independence: America's Violent Birth* (New York: Crown, 2017)

Houlding, J.A., *Fit for Service: The Training of the British Army, 1715-1795* (Oxford: Clarendon Press, 1981)

Horn, Jeff, *Economic Development in Early Modern France: The Privilege of Liberty, 1650–1820* (Cambridge: Cambridge University Press, 2015)

Hubner Brian E., *The Formation of the British Light Infantry Companies and their Employment in the Saratoga Campaign of 1777* (Saskatoon: unpublished dissertation, 1986)

Johnston, Henry P., *The Battle of Harlem Heights, September 16, 1776* (New York: The Columbia University Press, 1897)

Kopperman, Paul E., 'The Medical Dimension in Cornwallis's Army, 1780-1781,' *The North Carolina Historical Review*, vol. 89, no. 4, 2012, pp. 367–98

Lee, Albert, *History of the Thirty-third Foot, Duke of Wellington's (West Riding) Regiment*. Norwich: The Empire Press, 1922

Lender, Mark Edward and Stone, Garry Wheeler, *Fatal Sunday: George Washington, the Monmouth Campaign, and the Politics of Battle* (Norman: University of Oklahoma Press, 2016)

Lewis J.D, *NC Patriots 1775–1783: Their Own Words, Volume 2 (Part 1)* (Little River: J. D. Lewis, 2012)

Lodge, Mark Andrew, *To What Extent Can the 33rd Foot be Considered a Model of a Late Eighteenth-Century Infantry Regiment During the Period 1769–1781* (The University of Leeds, School of History, 2005)

Lossing, Benson John, *Our Country: A Household History for all Readers, from the Discovery of America to the Present Time* (New York: The Amies Publishing Company, 1888)

Martin, James Kirby and Lender, Mark Edward, *A Respectable Army: The Military Origins of the Republic, 1763–1789* (Chichester: John Wiley & Sons, 2015)

Mayhew, Athol, 'British Bayonets' in *The Illustrated Naval and Military Magazine, Volume 1* (London: The Illustrated London News, 1884), pp.56–65

McCandless, Peter, *Slavery, Disease, and Suffering in the Southern Lowcountry* (Cambridge: Cambridge University Press, 2011)

McCullough, David, *1776: Britain and America at War* (St Ives: Penguin, 2006)

McGuire, Thomas J., *The Philadelphia Campaign Volume I: Brandywine and the Fall of Philadelphia* (Mechanicsburg: Stackpole Books, 2006)

McNeill, J. R. *Mosquito Empires: Ecology and War in the Greater Caribbean, 1620–1914* (Cambridge: Cambridge University Press, 2010)

Middleton, Richard, *Cornwallis: Soldiers and Statesman in a Revolutionary World* (New Haven: Yale University Press, 2022)

Mills, Walter, *Arms and Men: A Study in American Military History* (New Brunswick: Rutgers University Press, 1981)

Morrill, Dan L., *Southern Campaigns of the American Revolution* (Mount Pleasant: The Nautical & Aviation Publishing Company of America, 1993)

Munn, David C., *Battles and Skirmishes of the American Revolution in New Jersey* (Trenton: Department of Environmental Protection, Bureau of Geology and Topography, 1976)

Odintz, Mark Frederick, *The British Officer Corps, 1754–1783* (Ann Arbor: University of Michigan Dissertation Services, 1988)

O'Shaughnessey, Andrew, *The Men Who Lost America: British Command during the Revolutionary War and the Preservation of the Empire* (London: Oneworld, 2013)

Paterson, James, *History of the County of Ayr, with a Genealogical Account of the Families of Ayrshire* (Edinburgh: Stevenson, 1852)

Piecuch, Jim, *The Battle of Camden: A Documentary History* (Charleston: The History Press, 2006)

Rees, John U., 'Eyewitness to Battle: Alexander Dow's Account of a 1777 Skirmish and the 1778 Battle of Monmouth', *Brigade Dispatch*, vol.XXIX, no.1, Spring 1999, pp.15–16

Smythies, Raymond Henry Raymond, *Historical Records of the 40th (2nd Somersetshire) Regiment* (Devonport: Swiss, 1894)

Sparks, Jared (ed.), *The Writings of George Washington* (Boston: Russel et al, 1834)

Spring, Matthew, *With Zeal and With Bayonets Only: The British Army on Campaign in North America, 1775–1783* (Norman: University of Oklahoma Press, 2008)

Stedman, Charles, *The History of the Origin, Progress, and Termination of the American War* (London: Murray, Debrett, Kerby, 1794)

Sterling, Anthony, *The Story of the Highland Brigade in the Crimea* (London: Remington and Company, 1895)

Stokeley, Jim, *Fort Moultrie: Constant Defender* (Washington DC: US Department of the Interior, 1985)

Strachan, Huw, *British Military Uniforms, 1768–1796: The Dress of the British Army from Official Sources* (London: Arms and Armour Press, 1975)

Urban, Mark, *Fusiliers: Eight Years with the Redcoats in America* (London: Faber and Faber, 2007)

Urwin, Gregory J. W., '"To bring the American Army under strict Discipline": British Army Foraging Policy in the South, 1780–81', *War in History*, 2019, vol.26 (1), pp.4–26

Scotti, Anthony J., *Brutal Virtue: The Myth and Reality of Banastre Tarleton* (Westminster: Heritage Books, 2007)

Stacy, Kim R., 'The Land Battle for Sullivan's Island, Charles Town, South Carolina, June–July 1776', *Journal of the Society for Army Historical Research*, vol.92, no.371. Autumn 2014, pp.189–209

Ward, Christopher, *The War of the Revolution* (New York: The MacMillan Company, 1952)